Economic Transformation, Democratization and Integration into the European Union

Also by Heather D. Gibson

THE EUROCURRENCY MARKETS, DOMESTIC FINANCIAL POLICY AND INTERNATIONAL INSTABILITY

ECONOMIC INTEGRATION AND FINANCIAL LIBERALIZATION: Prospects for Southern Europe (*co-editor*)

INTERNATIONAL FINANCE: Exchange Rates and Financial Flows in the International System

Sponsored by the Subcommittee of the Nature and Consequences of Democracy in the New Southern Europe of the Joint Committee on Western Europe (1975–96) of the American Council of Learned Societies and the Social Science Research Council.

Economic Transformation, Democratization and Integration into the European Union

Southern Europe in Comparative Perspective

Edited by

Heather D. Gibson
Assistant Economic Advisor
Research Department
Bank of Greece
Athens

First published 2001 by
PALGRAVE
Houndmills, Basingstoke, Hampshire RG21 6XS and
175 Fifth Avenue, New York, N. Y. 10010
Companies and representatives throughout the world

PALGRAVE is the new global academic imprint of
St. Martin's Press LLC Scholarly and Reference Division and
Palgrave Publishers Ltd (formerly Macmillan Press Ltd).

ISBN 0–333–80122–9

This book is printed on paper suitable for recycling and
made from fully managed and sustained forest sources.

A catalogue record for this book is available
from the British Library.

Library of Congress Cataloging-in-Publication Data
Economic transformation, democratization and integration into the
European Union : southern Europe in comparative perspective / edited
by Heather D. Gibson.
    p. cm.
Includes bibliographical references and index.
ISBN 0–333–80122–9
    1. Europe, Southern—Economic conditions. 2. Europe, Southern–
–Economic policy. 3. Europe, Southern—Economic integration. 4.
Europe, Southern—Politics and government. 5. European Union–
–Europe, Southern. I. Gibson, Heather D., 1961–

HC244.5 .E523 2000
330.94—dc21

                                              00–055687
10   9   8   7   6   5   4   3   2   1
10   09 08 07 06 05 04 03 02 01

Printed in Great Britain by Antony Rowe Ltd, Chippenham, Wiltshire

In memory of Vincent Wright
Scholar, mentor and Mensch

Contents

List of Tables

List of Figures

Preface

The preface to *The Politics of Democratic Consolidation: Southern Europe in Comparative Perspective*, edited by Richard Gunther, P. Nikiforos Diamandouros and Hans-Jurgen Puhle, the first in a series of volumes, systematically presented the intellectual rationale for, and background to, this project on the 'New Southern Europe', undertaken in the context of the renewed interest in the nature and dynamics of modern democratic regimes prompted by such major contributions as *The Breakdown of Democratic Regimes*, edited by Juan Linz and Alfred Stepan, and *Transitions from Authoritarian Rule*, edited by Guillermo O'Donnell, Philippe C. Schmitter, and Lawrence Whitehead.

The agenda of that first volume was to move the frontier of inquiry beyond transitions to democracy and to engage in a systematic examination of the requisites of democratic consolidation, using insights and lessons derived from the study of Southern Europe, conceptualized, for reasons extensively discussed in Edward Malefakis's contribution to *The Politics of Democratic Consolidation*, as comprising Greece, Italy, Portugal, and Spain. The rationale for such a conceptualization goes well beyond the obvious similarities stemming from socioeconomic modernization in the post-World War II period and democratization since the 1970s. It reflects, rather, deeper structural and historical parallels. The most salient among these are linked to the four countries' similarities in (a) physical characteristics, i.e., a Mediterranean climate, a pronounced mountainous topography, dearth of coal and iron deposits, but relative abundance in nonferrous minerals; (b) agricultural patterns, i.e., prevalence of luxury crops, such as wine, olives, and fruit, that require marketing, preclude subsistence farming, are labour intensive and thus resist modernization and retard the rural exodus to urban centres this implies; (c) the salience of regionalism (itself the byproduct of mountainous topography), the antagonism between highlanders and plains people that this breeds, and the social banditry naturally issuing from such antagonism; (d) a strong maritime tradition resulting from proximity to the sea and the plethora of nearby islands; and (e) the early development and persistence over time of complex urban structures linked to some of the factors just mentioned (crop diversity, maritime tradition) but also to easy access to the complex civilizations of the ancient Middle East.

Put otherwise, the object of inquiry was to establish the long-term and short-term parameters that either promoted or acted as confining or as facilitating conditions for democratic consolidation. In pursuit of this goal, the contributors to that volume systematically examined the impact on consolidation of socioeconomic modernization, the character of the predecessor nondemocratic regime, civil–military relations, international factors, collective actors, institutions, organized interests, and political parties.

The Politics of Democratic Consolidation also sought to place democratic consolidation in the broader context of the overall process of democratization and to point to its links with phases analytically or temporally anterior or posterior to it. In this context, we specifically pointed to the period of 'democratic persistence' as a phase in the democratization process subsequent to consolidation, in which political arrangements, crafted during the transition and institutionalized during consolidation, acquire further roots and contribute to the deepening of democracy and to the improvement of its quality, or, conversely, experience erosion that may lead to deconsolidation and breakdown or reequilibration and renewed persistence.

The major conclusion of Volume 1, which serves as an underpinning for the more specific inquiries undertaken in each subsequent volume, is that, in at least two major areas, those of socioeconomic development and politics, Southern Europe has, over the past few decades, undergone a fundamental structural transformation, as a result of which it irreversibly crossed a critical threshold in its transition to modernity. More specifically, the region's spectacular socioeconomic modernization, initially observed in Italy beginning in the 1950s and amply reproduced in the other three countries since the 1970s, has enabled it effectively to leave behind a legacy of socioeconomic decline and delayed development dating back to the seventeenth and eighteenth centuries. Succinctly put, Southern Europe has, in the course of the past four decades, ceased being part of the semiperiphery of the world system, and has entered its centre.

A similar qualitative change has taken place at the level of politics. The region's successful democratization over the past half century, and the consolidation, since the 1970s, of democratic regimes in the four countries comprising it, has freed it from a legacy of right wing authoritarianism that had plagued it since the Napoleonic period, and had stood at the root of its abortive democratic experiments over the past century-and-a-half. As a result, the region's political fortunes have taken on a distinctly modern quality and have allowed for its incorporation in the universe of democratic regimes heretofore inhabited by advanced industrial democracies. Taken together, these two structural transformations lend substance to the central claim of the intellectual project that gave rise to this series, concerning the emergence, in recent decades, of a 'New Southern Europe', qualitatively different from its 'Old', incarnation, that has successfully leapfrogged into socioeconomic and political modernity.

The aim of this project is to explore various dimensions of democratic persistence by attempting to answer one general question: does democracy make a difference? Put otherwise, our research agenda takes democratic consolidation as its starting point and explores its impact on, or significance for, politics, economics (in the present volume), the state, and the interplay between culture and politics, systematically highlighting the changes that have taken place in Southern Europe over the past 30 years or so, by juxtaposing preauthoritarian with postauthoritarian arrangements and experiences. We also seek to place the experience of democratization in Southern Europe in a broader context by means of comparisons with both advanced industrial democracies in northwestern Europe and, to a lesser extent, democratic experiments in selected countries of Latin America and Eastern Europe.

Whereas the focus of the other volumes in the series is more on democratization, the central aim of this volume is to chart the structural socioeconomic transformation experienced by these countries. In particular, it analyses their move from closed and inward-looking economies to outward-looking economies, largely through active integration into the European Union. These important economic changes occurred within a relatively short space of time and, of course, have taken place against the background of important socio-political developments including the consolidation of democracy. The various contributions in the volume come from authors from a number of social science disciplines and they cover a broad range of economic issues including the process of trade liberalization, labour markets structures, the role of tourism, industrial policy and privatization, financial liberalization and the importance of EU structural funds. The focus of each chapter is on the motivation for economic change and, in particular, the role of integration into the European Union. At the same time the problems encountered and the lessons to be learnt for other countries undergoing a similar process are analysed and expanded.

The intellectual history of this project

The intellectual history of the various initiatives that eventually gave rise to this project are perhaps worth recounting briefly. The initial stimulus for the creation of a committee of social scientists interested in studying the evolution of the Southern European transitions to democracy was provided by the events that toppled the authoritarian regimes of Greece and Portugal in 1974. Following a series of formal and informal meetings over the ensuing two years, a research group was formed, called the Committee on Southern Europe (COSE), whose purpose was to promote the systematic study of the region from the end of the Napoleonic Wars to the present. The eventual product of this initiative was the creation of an informal, interdisciplinary network of scholars interested both in Southern Europe as a region and in the particular historical or political processes it exemplifies best, such as rapid and profound socioeconomic transformation in late-developing societies and successfully, negotiated transitions to democracy. This coordinated research effort helped raise the visibility of the south European region in meetings of professional associations at the national level (in particular, the political science and sociological associations in Europe and the United States, including the Council of European Studies in the latter), the regional level (e.g., the European Consortium for Political Research, where a separate Southern European Study Group was set up in the early 1980s), and the international level (e.g., the International Political Science Association and the International Sociological Association). The result was a significant accumulation of knowledge on various dimensions of the polities, economies, and cultures of Southern European societies, with significant spill-over effects for both area studies and comparative analysis.

This process reached happy fruition in 1987–88. Two informal meetings served as the immediate stimulus for a new round of activity. The first took place in the context of a conference on transition and consolidation in Latin America and Southern Europe, organized at the Kellogg Institute of the University of Notre Dame, in April 1987. This was followed by a second crucial planning session, which brought together a larger number of European and American specialists on Southern Europe in the magnificent setting of the European University Institute, in San Domenico di Fiesole, near Florence, in September 1987. It was in the sedate and austere premises of the Institute that the central themes informing this project were initially articulated, and widespread consensus was reached on the desirability of focusing not on transition but on consolidation, whose qualitatively different attributes and properties had yet to be seriously studied and analysed.

These activities culminated in a decision to approach the Joint Committee on Western Europe of the American Council of Learned Societies (ACLS) and the Social Science Research Council (SSRC) with the idea of sponsoring this activity. The joint committee's prior interest in democratization and regime transition in Southern Europe made it an appropriate vehicle for a larger undertaking centred on democratic consolidation. Endorsing the idea of such an initiative, in December 1987, the joint committee proposal to the boards of ACLS and SSRC, the establishment of the Subcommittee on the Nature and Consequences of Democracy in Southern Europe, which following approval, formally came into being in April 1988, co-chaired by P. Nikiforos Diamandouros (University of Athens) and Richard Gunther (Ohio State University).

The subcommittee's charge was dual: '(1) to engage in a systematic study of the nature of democratic consolidation in Greece, Portugal, Spain, and post-fascist Italy, by exploring its cultural, economic, political, and social dimensions; and (2) to use insights derived from this regional case study to contribute to the emergent, more general theoretical debate concerning the properties of, and processes involved in, the consolidation of democracy.' There were five interrelated dimensions of change in the 'New Southern Europe' that the subcommittee was to explore: processes of democratic consolidation, the nature of democratic politics, economic and social relations in the region, the changing functions of the state in the post-Keynesian era, and the dynamics of cultural change.

The final step towards the realization of what had, for more than a decade, been an elusive goal came in May 1988. At that time, the Stiftung Volkswagenwerk, underscoring its role as a preeminent European institution committed to the fostering of social science across national borders, agreed to provide generous support for a multi-year programme of research, conferences, and publication activities designed to produce five or six collective volumes dealing with the interconnected dimensions of change mentioned above and drawing together the major theoretical findings issuing from the project. With additional support from the Werner-Reimers Stiftung and the German Social Science Study Group on Spain and Portugal, the project was formally launched in Bad Homburg, Germany, in July 1989 where specific conference plans were made. It is hoped that these conferences and resulting published volumes will fulfill the subcommittee's mandate, which was to more fully integrate Southern Europe into the mainstream of comparative social science research, and to derive from the study of its democratization experience insights capable of contributing to the fast-growing body of theoretical literature on democratization.

Acknowledgements

The numerous intellectual debts accumulated over the years in connection with the intellectual, organizational, financial, and administrative aspects of the overall project of which this volume forms a part have already been gratefully recorded in the acknowledgements section of Volume 1. Here, we shall confine ourselves to thanking all those individuals and institutions who contributed to the birth of this volume. We should like to begin by thanking the Levi Foundation in Venice for having hosted the second of the two conferences that gave rise to the volume. Thanks also go to Maria Carrilho and Manuel Villaverde Cabral for facilitating the organization of our first conference in Sintra, Portugal.

We should also like to express our deep appreciation to Dr Helga Junkers, of the Volkswagen Stiftung, for supporting our efforts and for ensuring the continuous flow of the financial support that made both this volume and the larger project of which it is a part possible. Thanks are also due to Dr Kenton Worcester, the programme director at the Social Science Research Council, and Elizabeth O'Brien, the staff assistant, who provided steady and reassuring administrative support and guidance to the subcommittee's activities relating to this volume. Finally, we should like to express our sincere appreciation to Macmillan for having agreed to host this volume of the series.

P. Nikiforos Diamandouros and Richard Gunther
General Series Editors

Acknowledgements

This book grew out of research funded by the Social Science Research Council in the US. A Subcommittee on Southern Europe (chaired by Richard Gunther, Professor of Political Science at Ohio State University and Nikiforos Diamandouros, Professor of Political Science at Athens University) was formed with a grant from the Volkswagen Stiftung to examine the process of change that has been accompanying the consolidation of democracy in Southern European countries. As part of this larger project, two conferences were organized on aspects of economic transformation in Southern Europe since democratization in the mid-1970s and it was decided to write up the various contributions in the form of an edited volume. All the participants acknowledge with thanks the funding that enabled this research project to go ahead and are grateful to Nikiforos Diamandouros and Richard Gunther for their useful comments on various drafts of the book. I would also like to thank Linda Auld for her careful and efficient editing of the manuscript. Finally, I am very grateful to Euclid Tsakalotos who not only made extensive comments on a number of the individual chapters of the book but also provided invaluable support throughout the sometimes trying process that editing a book of this size entailed.

List of Contributors

Heather D. Gibson	Economic Research Department, Bank of Greece, Athens, Greece
Louka T. Katseli	Department of Economics, University of Athens, Greece and Centre for Economic Policy Research, London, UK
Antigone Lyberaki	Department of Economic and Regional Development, Paneion University, Athens, Greece
Enzo Mingione	University of Milano-Bicocca, Italy and Fondazione Felicita ed Enrico Bignaschi e Figli, Milan, Italy
Achilleas Mitsos	Director in EU Commission, Brussels, Belgium
Tommaso Padoa-Schioppa	Member of the Executive Board, European Central Bank, Frankfurt
George Pagoulatos	Department of International and European Economic Studies, Athens University of Economics and Business, Greece
Massimo Roccas	Research Department, Bank of Italy, Rome, Italy
Yiannis Stournaras	Commercial Bank of Greece and Department of Economics, University of Athens, Greece
Euclid Tsakalotos	Department of International and European Economic Studies, Athens University of Economics and Business, Greece
Allan M. Williams	Department of Geography, University of Exeter, UK
Vincent Wright	was a fellow of Nuffield College, Oxford University, UK

1
Economic Change in Southern Europe: Prospects for Convergence

Heather D. Gibson[1]

This book is a study of 'the evolution of specific economies in their particular niche'.[2] The study encompasses three Southern European countries, namely Greece, Portugal and Spain. Italy is also considered, although because of certain differences with the other three, it is sometimes fully integrated into the analysis and elsewhere merely used as a point of reference.

The first question that arises is whether these economies do, in fact, constitute a coherent whole. As in all such groupings, this question cannot be answered in the abstract and its validity forms a central concern of the analysis. But we would argue that these economies share enough common characteristics for this grouping to be a useful and informative first approximation.

First, there is the obvious geographical link of Southern Europe. Greece, Italy and Spain are all countries of the Mediterranean, not only in the narrow geographic sense but also historically and culturally. Portugal is so strongly associated with these other three that it is not too much of an exaggeration to suggest that it is an honorary member of the Mediterranean world. The latter is significant because it reminds us of the importance of, what we can call, 'mental' geography – a process in which countries, and their people, position themselves with respect to other areas. Whatever these economies represent, few would doubt the fact that they are clearly neither central nor northern Europe.

Second, it is the case that the Southern European economies (hereafter, SEEs[3]) share a remarkable similarity in their recent political and economic history. The mid-1970s saw the 'end of dictatorships' in all three countries and thereafter the consolidation of democracy. This political history interacted with economic processes and the goal of economic development and it was most visible in the increasing integration of these economies into the European Union in the 1980s.

A third reason why they are a useful grouping is that they have all experienced fairly swift economic change since the mid-1970s. It is the aim of this book to catalogue that change and to consider the forces that have promoted it. That is not to say that the 'trajectories' followed by individual SEEs have been identical – the extent and deep-seatedness of change, as we shall see, has differed across countries. Moreover, the pace of change has varied not only between countries but also across time – periods of compressed and rapid change ('leapfrogging') are often followed (or preceded) by periods of either consolidation or stagnation. But whatever the differences, a central aim of the book is to consider the extent to which the period of change has resulted in what might be termed a 'New Southern Europe'. In the past, the SEEs have been considered, from an economic point of view, as the underdeveloped or backward countries of Europe,[4] characterized, *inter alia*, by a large and fragmented agricultural sector, poorly developed infrastructure, labour-intensive industries and 'old-fashioned' economic policies.[5] In many ways, the changes that have taken place in recent years can be portrayed as an attempt by the governments of SEEs to place their countries at the heart of the European project. The extent to which they have succeeded will determine whether the term the 'New Southern Europe' can indeed be applied.

Fourth, the SEEs have also faced, to a large degree, a common external environment. Before the mid-1970s, when all three economies were under politically authoritarian regimes of various sorts, the external economic environment was a remarkably favourable one. However, as we shall see, this was to a large extent reversed in the period of the consolidation of democracy. Furthermore this unfavourable world economic environment continued in the 1980s and 1990s. This was bound to influence not only the nature of the SEEs' economic development in this period but also the dominant political strategies adopted to promote economic prosperity and deepen the process of democratic consolidation.

Finally, and in part in response to the above, we have also witnessed a convergence in the dominant politico-economic strategies of the SEEs. By the late 1980s, this strategy conceptualized the future of these economies as part of a more integrated Europe. The promise of a more united Europe was one of greater political stability. It also offered the possibility of greater economic prosperity in an increasingly competitive and unstable world economic environment through the pooling of resources, the strength provided by being part of a larger economic block, and, not least, higher levels of solidarity and cooperation. The adoption of this strategy has been neither linear nor unproblematic, and indeed is being challenged anew at the time of writing as the moves to an even more integrated Europe have faltered following the crises in the European Monetary System in the early 1990s, growing political disagreements about when and how to achieve monetary union and the parallel hesitation about the viability and desirability of greater political union.

Given the importance of the European element in the dominant strategy of the SEEs, an unravelling of the process of European integration could have serious implications for both politics and the economy in these countries. However, our task here is not to speculate about the future but rather to give a broad introduction to some of the common features introduced above as well as outlining the contributions to this volume. The remainder of this opening chapter is divided into two sections. In the first section we examine the niche in which the SEEs were operating. That is, we focus on the world economic environment of the postwar period. In the second, we offer a framework, which can help us understand how SEEs responded to the international context and explain the similarities and differences between them. We also discuss in some detail the remaining chapters.

SEEs and the world economy

At about the time that the SEEs underwent their transition to democracy, the world economy experienced a major shift in economic performance. Whatever the exact timing of this phenomenon, the reversal of fortune, which is to a large extent still with us, was so dramatic that we are entitled to speak in terms of a regime shift. The economic performance in the postwar era before this shift was so impressive that it has been labelled the 'Golden Age' of capitalism (Marglin and Schor, 1990). The remarkable figures for growth, investment growth and productivity growth during the Golden Age can be seen in Table 1.1. Furthermore, we should point out that these figures represent a vast improvement on anything in the period preceding the Golden Age. Growth in the 1950s and 1960s was not only exceptional, but recessions merely represented a slowdown in the rate of growth rather than negative growth. Investment and productivity growth

Table 1.1 The Golden Age and its decline

	Growth		Investment		Productivity	
	pre-1974	post-1973	pre-1974	post-1973	pre-1974	post-1973
OECD	4.76	2.55	6.19	1.74	3.66	1.57
EU (12)	4.75	2.43	6.18	1.40	3.96	1.75
Greece	6.74	2.26	7.90	−0.49	n.a.	1.25
Italy	5.36	2.81	6.69	1.62	4.98	2.18
Portugal	5.80	2.84	7.78	1.93	6.53	1.06
Spain	5.92	2.54	8.36	2.43	5.17	2.66

Notes: Growth is the average percentage rate of growth of GDP across countries and time. Investment is the average percentage rate of growth of real investment again averaged across countries and time. Productivity growth is the rate of growth of real GDP over employment. The EU(12) are the 12 members of the EU prior to the extension in January 1995. Data is generally available from 1950 to 1990. Exceptions include: Greece – productivity figures from 1978 only; Italy – productivity from 1954; Portugal – all data from 1953 except productivity (from 1960); Spain – all data from 1954.

Source: author's calculations from CEP-OECD dataset, see Bagliano *et al.* (1991) and Bell (1993).

Table 1.2 Unemployment and inflation experience in OECD countries

	Inflation		Unemployment	
	pre-1974	post-1973	pre-1974	post-1973
OECD	4.88	9.13	2.38	5.88
EU (12)	4.67	9.21	2.81	7.85
Greece	4.96	15.82	n.a.	5.51
Italy	4.28	12.51	7.44	9.02
Portugal	2.95	17.19	n.a.	6.81
Spain	6.77	11.99	1.58	13.65

Notes: Data is generally available from 1950 to 1990. Exceptions include: Greece – unemployment from 1978 only; Italy – unemployment from 1954; Portugal – all data from 1953; Spain – all data from 1954. The figures are averages across time and (where applicable) countries.

Source: author's calculations from CEP-OECD dataset, see Bagliano *et al.* (1991) and Bell (1993).

both contributed to this growth performance. At the same time, inflation was low and the period was characterized by, more or less, full employment (Table 1.2).

But equally clear from these tables is the reversal of fortune post-1973. The decline in growth, and productivity and investment growth, together with the emergence of stagflation (high inflation and unemployment) are clearly illustrated. A number of explanations have been proffered. These include: supply-side factors such as the exhaustion of cheap and plentiful labour supply or a similar exhaustion of the potential for investments embodying existing technology; demand-side factors such as the decline in the influence of Keynesian economic policies; distributional conflict and a falling profit share with a correspondingly detrimental effect on investment; growing rigidities in the economic system such as trade unions, minimum wages and extensive welfare systems; and economic shocks – notably the oil crises of 1973–4. There is little agreement in the literature about the relative importance of these factors,[6] and clearly a discussion of this is beyond the scope of this introduction. What is important is to re-emphasize that whereas Italy enjoyed a return to democracy during the Golden Age of capitalism, the SEEs experienced this return at a time when conditions in the world economy had significantly worsened (see Chapter 2).

It is also important to discuss briefly how this decline in economic performance was associated in turn with the decline of certain international institutions and politico-economic arrangements that had characterized the Golden Age. Particularly important in this respect was the breakdown of the Bretton Woods system, which was signposted by the movement to floating exchange rates in the early 1970s. The Bretton Woods system, comprising not only a system of fixed exchange rates, but also other institutions such as the World Bank (created to provide finance for development in low-income

Table 1.3 World trade

	Growth of Exports	
	pre-1974	*post-1973*
OECD	7.96	4.70
EU (12)	8.66	4.74
Greece	11.93	6.19
Italy	11.14	4.83
Portugal	8.68	5.14
Spain	13.41	5.16

Source: author's calculations from CEP-OECD dataset, see Bagliano *et al.* (1991) and Bell (1993).

countries), the International Monetary Fund (IMF, designed to provide financing for the functioning of the exchange rate system and to oversee the world economy in general) and the General Agreement on Trade and Tariffs (GATT, concerned with the negotiated lowering of trade impediments), signalled in the postwar era a desire to increase cooperation in international economic affairs thereby avoiding the disastrous consequences of the lack of such cooperation in the inter-war years. This more stable international framework must clearly have contributed to the impressive growth in world trade in the postwar period (Table 1.3).

By the late 1960s, however, strains in this institutional framework were beginning to reveal themselves.[7] In particular, there was great downward pressure on the dollar partly as a result of the increase in the supply of dollars associated with the financing of the Vietnam War. Eventually this speculative pressure became so great that, in 1971, the Americans abandoned the link between the dollar and gold which had been at the heart of the Bretton Woods system. For two years, a modified type of fixed exchange rate mechanism was tried, but failed, and by 1973 most leading currencies were floating.

This breakdown in the exchange rate system had wider implications. It was associated with a general decline in the degree of cooperation between countries. The institutions of Bretton Woods were no longer regarded as a potential forum for cooperation between the major industrial economies. The general view was that, with the adoption of floating exchange rates, countries were now free to pursue whatever economic policies they wished: the exchange rate would equilibrate the balance of payments imbalances which might result. But this sanguine view was not borne out by future events.

The two oil price rises in 1973–4 and 1979–80 were a large shock to oil importers requiring both financing of the resultant current account deficits and adjustment of economies. Exchange rate changes did not eliminate the balance of payments imbalances as expected and countries were forced to undertake deflationary policies. A coordinated response to this shock might have been helpful. However, the climate in the international monetary system did not favour cooperative responses and countries had to try to adjust to the oil shock in their own way.

Moreover, the experience with floating exchange rates quickly revealed their drawbacks. Floating exchange rates are highly volatile and a number of countries have experienced periods of prolonged undervaluation and overvaluation (misalignment, to use Williamson's (1983) phrase). Such conditions are hardly conducive to international trade: while periods of undervaluation over-encourage investment in the tradeables goods sector, periods of overvaluation make it very difficult for industry to compete.[8]

The consequences, therefore, of the breakdown of Bretton Woods were serious: the world economy was left with a system where economies, especially small open ones, did not appear to have much policy autonomy (especially macroeconomic policy autonomy); yet, at the same time, cooperation was absent. The response, in more recent years, has been two-fold. First, there have been certain tentative moves since the mid- to late-1980s towards more cooperation among the Group of Seven industrial countries.[9] Second, there has been a tendency to form regional blocks – the North American Free Trade Agreement, cooperation among Asian-Pacific countries and, of more relevance here, European integration, to which we have already said the SEEs are committed. These blocks help to increase the economic power of their members beyond that which they would have individually. It is for this reason that they are particularly attractive to small countries.

We now turn to the politico-economic arrangements which underpinned the Golden Age era and which were radically challenged in the subsequent period. The Golden Age, and its economic success, was supported by what has been termed a democratic consensus – or, in other words, a truce between labour and capital. This is why this era is also often referred to as one of social democratic consensus (Glyn *et al.*, 1990; Tsakalotos, 1991). Under this arrangement – and simplifying greatly for analytical purposes – workers, and their union and political representatives, agreed to various extents, to abandon their challenge to capitalist property rights and to limit their intervention to indirect means. In return, capitalists, and their political representatives, accepted a commitment to higher wages, full-employment and the welfare state. The commitments in turn implied a certain guarantee by both right and left-leaning parties to use economic policies to support these ends. Therefore, this compromise provided a favourable framework for investment and growth.[10]

As with the international financial institutions, discussed above, these politico-economic arrangements underwent a period of decline, which can be dated somewhere in the late 1960s. For our purpose what is important to stress is that during the 1970s, there was a gradual shift in the economic priorities of developed countries. These changes reached their zenith in the early 1980s with the election of Margaret Thatcher as Prime Minister in the UK and Ronald Reagan as US president. The new policies, which were to become known as Thatcherism or Reaganomics, involved the abandonment of full employment as a policy priority, a decline in Keynesian policies and, more generally, the adoption of a neoliberal approach to economic policy-making. The latter was first signalled at the macroeconomic level – with the introduction of monetary targets and attempts to cut the fiscal deficit; it quickly found expression in more microeconomic areas through privatization, liberalization of financial markets and so on. In short, the 1980s was the period when the former social democratic consensus in many developed countries broke down. That is, the commitment to full employment, a strong welfare state and policies to narrow inequality was continually eroded. By contrast, there was a rise in the importance given to the market in solving economic problems and priorities.

How did these changes affect the SEEs? In a sense this is the subject of much that follows in the book and all we provide here is a brief overview. The worsening world economic environment had two immediate consequences. First, the search for economic prosperity and development could not rely on an external engine of growth as it had in the previous era. Second, it became increasingly clear that small open economies, such as the SEEs, had limited autonomy in economic affairs. In short, there was little room for 'bucking the trend' – something that is apparent from Tables 1.1 and 1.2, which show that SEEs shared fully in the broad, and deteriorating, economic trends.

Clearly a number of possible responses were available. These were often the subject of bitter controversy, especially in the early period of democratization after dictatorship, reflecting differences of priorities and interests within each country. The debate, for instance, between those who favoured inward-looking policies and those who preferred more outward-looking politics was a difficult and often protracted one. Portugal's immediate post-dictatorship experience was that of widespread nationalization and an attempt at an autarkic solution, while the Greek socialists came to power in 1981 on an initially openly hostile, anti-European platform. However, over time, such responses lost ground in favour of a strategy of linking the fate of SEEs with the wider process of European integration.

All three SEEs had some association with Europe even before the restoration of democracy. Spain signed an association agreement with the EU and Portugal joined EFTA (the European Free Trade Area) in 1959; Greece signed an association agreement later, in 1962. Full EU membership did not occur until the 1980s: Greece joined in 1981; Spain and Portugal were admitted as full members in 1986. But by the late 1980s the dominant politico-economic strategy was for even stronger integration with the EU. This approach was thought to have a number of attractions, which would help in particular to consolidate democracy and end the years of relative isolation.

For example, Europe provided a way out of the lack of policy autonomy which, as we noted above, is characteristic of small economies in today's international environment. European integration also created new markets for Mediterranean goods (Chapter 3). Finally, it allowed for structural changes (such as the improvement of infrastructure) to be undertaken with the help of money from the EU (Chapter 9). Overall, the strategy adopted by SEEs reflects the view that the goals of convergence on European standards of living and becoming part of Europe in a broader sense were best achieved through greater integration into the EU.

However, while such a strategy clearly has its benefits, it is not without certain costs. A number of policies adopted by SEEs can be rationalized in terms of their participation in Europe[11] – membership of the EU does not give countries autonomy in policy-making, rather it allows all members some say in the policy-making process. However, this implies that policies often have to be adopted which involve costs. At the macroeconomic level, adjustment in the form of reducing inflation and budget deficits towards the targets set in the Maastricht Treaty has involved large costs, particularly for those on low incomes. At the microeconomic level, SEEs have adopted the policies of privatization of state firms (Chapter 7) and financial liberalization (Chapter 8). In short, the EU and developments in other EU countries have been important in determining the form that economic change in SEEs has been taking. Of course, the desirability of many of these changes is an important and interesting question and is one that recurs throughout this book.

Catch-up and convergence: a framework for understanding the evolution of economies

How have the economies of Southern European countries responded to this international environment and growing integration into Europe? How have SEEs sought to bring about economic change and move towards the goal of convergence on other EU countries? To what extent can we talk of the 'New Southern Europe'? The answers to these questions form the substance of the contributions to this book. In this section, we seek to provide a framework in which the issues facing SEEs can be understood. Such a framework is also useful for bringing out some of the similarities and differences between the countries.

The study of economies such as the SEEs which are evolving in the context of a niche which itself is changing is a difficult one. Surprising as it may seem, economists have often not spent much time understanding economies as systems or how they evolve over time.[12] Indeed the general approach of economics with its emphasis on axiomatic model building and its individualist perspective is not, in general, conducive to the questions raised here. However, in spite of these difficulties, there have been some attempts by economic historians,[13] by growth theorists[14] and by development theorists.[15] But it is unlikely that such a complex issue can be approached from just one academic discipline or one methodological standpoint. It is for this reason that this book brings together social scientists from differing disciplines with very different methodological standpoints to shed light on how these economies have evolved since the restoration of democracy and also what we can expect from them in the future.

Although there are many different possible approaches to studying these economies, in this introduction we want to give a broad framework, taken from the economics literature, on which some of the ideas presented in this book can be hung. In other words, we do not purport to claim that this is *the* model which is crucial to all that follows. Instead, it can be thought more as a starting point without wanting to claim that other starting points might not have proved just as useful. The advantage of the framework we shall propose is that it is flexible enough to allow some modifications (either additions or deletions) or differences in emphasis (some of which might be quite critical of the basic framework).

The framework uses the concept of catch-up or convergence and the factors which determine it.[16] The basic argument is that convergence will occur semi-automatically provided market mechanisms are allowed to operate. Countries with lower per capita income and labour productivity have a greater potential for rapid growth.[17] In other words, growth rates should be inversely related to the initial level of productivity or income relative to that of the 'centre' or 'leader' country. This has been termed β-convergence by Barro and Sala-i-Martin (1992) and they show that it follows naturally from neoclassical growth theory. The reason for this potential is related to the question of technology and its embodiment in a country's capital stock. Lower income/productivity countries tend to have less capital and moreover the capital that they do have tends to embody outmoded technologies. Capital will tend to flow to these low income regions since it is scarce and this aids both capital accumulation and enables more up-to-date technologies to be introduced. By contrast, higher income countries already have capital that embodies the most recent technological developments and hence have less opportunity for growth. The catch-up hypothesis therefore suggests that followers will tend to converge on the leader and indeed the more backward the followers are to begin with, the more quickly they will grow.[18]

Abramovitz (1986) suggests four possible extensions to the simple mechanisms at work in the catch-up process. First, as the capital stock grows and capital becomes less scarce, so its price will fall, encouraging further productivity growth as the capital–labour ratio rises. Second, rising output and demand increase the opportunities for using technologies that embody economies of scale. Third, gains may result from disembodied technological improvements – for example, improved organization of production.

Finally, productivity gains may result from the elimination of disguised unemployment (particularly in the agricultural sector).

Dowrick and Nguyen (1989) provide some comprehensive tests for convergence of purchasing power parity adjusted per capita income measures within OECD countries. Their tests involve running the following regression:

$$q_i = \text{constant} + \alpha(I/Q)_i + \beta \ln Y_{i0} + \gamma l_i + e_i$$

where q_i is the average annual growth rate over the whole period of country i relative to the lead country (the US); $(I/Q)_i$ is a proxy for the rate of growth of the capital stock (investment); l_i is the rate of growth of employment; e_i is the error term; and $\ln Y_{i0}$ is the logarithm of trend real GDP per capita relative to the US in the base year, year 0. This last variable seeks to capture total factor productivity growth and hence catch-up or β-convergence. The intuition is that the lower the level of initial GDP per capita relative to the US, the greater the potential for catch-up and hence the higher the rate of growth of output. Thus if catch-up is a phenomenon with some empirical relevance, then we would anticipate that β will be significant and have a negative sign. This is indeed what Dowrick and Nguyen find.[19]

An interesting question is whether or not catch-up occurs at a steady pace over time and between countries, controlling for their initial levels of development. With respect to the time dimension to catch-up, Dowrick and Nguyen (1989) find strong support for convergence in the period 1950 to 1973 which gets weaker thereafter (although, it should be noted that they do not find the difference between the two sub-periods to be statistically significant). This suggests that catch-up occurs more intensely in periods when the world economy is healthy and growing. Individual country performance is also examined. Using their regression results, they adjust actual growth rates for expected catch-up and then decompose this adjusted growth rate into growth resulting from employment deepening, growth resulting from capital deepening and an unexplained residual. While care needs to be taken in interpreting any residual, it could be argued that it reflects differing realizations of catch-up potential. Some countries, such as Germany and Japan appear to have grown consistently faster than either catch-up, capital or labour deepening can explain. The SEEs, on the other hand, have had a more mixed experience – with the exception of the 1960s, they have grown more slowly than would have been expected given their initial level of per capita income. The reasons behind these different realizations of potential are complex and highlight the point that catch-up is not a uniform process across all countries and nor does it imply that all countries adopt similar economic policies or develop similar economic structures. This is just as true for SEEs as it is for the industrial countries more generally and the following chapters of the book explore this in some detail.

Figures 1.1 to 1.3 graph an index of per capita income for Greece, Portugal and Spain using purchasing power parity (PPP) exchange rates. In Figure 1.1, the US is the lead country and hence takes a value of 100 in every period. Thus the scale on the y-axis can be read as a percentage of US per capita income at any time. Figure 1.2 uses the EU 12 as a comparison where each country's GDP is weighted by its population. Both Figures tell a similar story. Spain has always had a higher per capita income than either Greece or Portugal. They also indicate that the speed of catch-up was rapid in the 1960s but tailed off after 1973 since when the experience of SEEs has

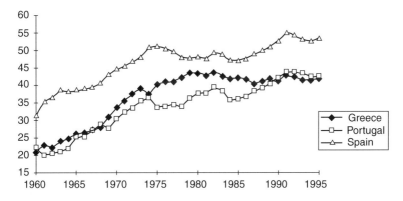

Figure 1.1   Index of per capita income (US = 100)
Source: Own calculations from OECD *National Accounts*, volume 1, various years.

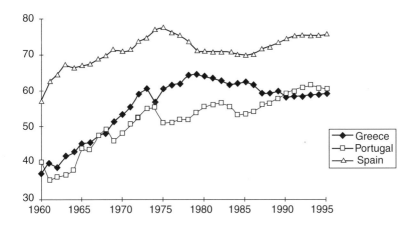

Figure 1.2   Index of per capita income (EU = 100)
Source: Own calculations from OECD *National Accounts*, volume 1, various years.

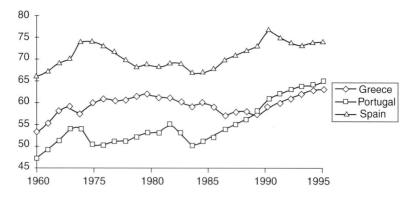

Figure 1.3 Index of per capita income (OECD = 100)
Source: OECD *National Accounts*.

been more mixed. Figure 1.3 uses the OECD as a whole as a comparison. This places the experiences of Greece and Portugal in a better light: Portugal has been converging on the OECD average since 1985; Greece, since 1990. Aside from this general picture, there are also some differences between the countries. The post-1973 experience has not been uniform. Greece does worse than both Portugal or Spain in a large part of the post-1973 period, with the result that Portugal's per capita GDP had passed that of Greece by the late 1980s. Indeed, Greece has shown a tendency towards divergence from the EU average especially since the late 1970s. This suggests that factors internal to countries are also important in determining the speed of catch-up and not just the external environment (see also Alogoskoufis, 1995). In other words, the speed of catch-up, as we discuss in some detail below and which forms an important theme of the book, may depend on the economic environment created by domestic policy. This includes not only macroeconomic policy, but also industrial policy, attitudes towards the state *versus* markets, regional policy and labour market conditions to name but a few.

Larre and Torres (1991) argue that the differing experiences of Greece, Portugal and Spain in the mid- to late-1980s can be explained in terms of the extent to which they introduced reforms that enhanced the role of the market in their economies. In particular, they argue that whereas Portugal and Spain actively promoted an extension of the market mechanism – through the introduction of lower tariffs, enhanced labour market flexibility, financial deregulation and so on – Greece did not. As a result, the Greek economy continued to suffer from major supply-side rigidities which kept the rate of return on capital low. By contrast, Spain and Portugal enjoyed a rapid increase in foreign direct investment in the late 1980s, something which, Larre and Torres argue, is indicative of these structural changes. It also helped to boost growth significantly, restoring the process of convergence. Policy developments within the EU are therefore seen by Larre and Torres in a positive light – by encouraging SEEs to extend the scope of the market, they enhance the catch-up process. Barros and Garoupa (1996) conclude similarly for Portugal and Spain.

However, this is perhaps too optimistic a reading of the late 1980s' experience of Portugal and Spain. As the figures indicate, the quicker convergence of the late 1980s was not continued into the 1990s. This more circumspect reading of the SEE's recent experience with convergence is supported by other researchers who focus on *regions* within the EU (Armstrong, 1995; Button and Pentecost, 1995; De La Fuente, 1998; Neven and Gouyette, 1995). Barro and Sala-i-Martin (1992) who, on a data sample for EU regions in the core northern economies, found a rate of β-convergence around 2 per cent both over the whole sample period (1950–85) and across subperiods. Armstrong (1995), Button and Pentecost (1995) and Neven and Gouyette (1995) extend the analsyis to include the SEEs. Their results suggest that the inclusion of Greece, Portugal and Spain reduces the rate of convergence for the post-1970 period, indicating that regions in the SEEs have been catching up at a slower rate than their northern counterparts.

Thus convergence does not seem to occur as smoothly or perhaps as automatically as the simple theory predicts and it is not clear that a mere extension of the market mechanism is enough. It is thus necessary to look at some modifications and extensions to the simple theory. In doing so, we move some way from the basic story and enrich it substantially. We consider here three possible extensions: the question of path dependence; the role of capabilities and institutions; and, finally, some political economy considerations.

Economists are increasingly recognizing that the future performance of any economy is likely to be highly dependent on where it has come from and where it is now. This is known as path dependence and it can imply that it is very difficult to alter some aspect of the economy, even if ultimately it would be in the economy's interests. This is often referred to as the economics of 'qwerty' – typewriter keyboards are a good example of path dependence and the costs of alterations. It has been recognized for some time now that the layout of a typewriter keyboard is not optimal for the user. Users would benefit if the letters were differently placed. However, the cost of changing is so enormous – typists would have to relearn the layout of the keyboard – that it is not likely ever to be undertaken. Yet if it were, we know that the benefits (faster and more accurate typing) would in the long run outweigh the costs.

Krugman (1994) discusses the issue of path dependence and its implications for growth and development. In particular, he notes that path dependence is very useful in explaining the location of economic activity (either between countries or within countries). In a world of increasing returns to scale and external economies, industry may begin to locate in clusters. Path dependence arises here because once a few firms locate in a particular region, it becomes worthwhile for other firms in the same area of business to do likewise. The example of Silicon Valley is illustrative. A few high-tech firms were established with support from Stanford University. Their presence attracted other high-tech firms and growing development of the area. Krugman (1994) argues that industrial location and consequent growth can therefore be explained by a combination of historical accident and path dependence.

The point of this analysis for our purposes should be clear. Catch-up may not be as simple as the theory suggests. If a country has benefited from industrial development in fast growing areas, this can help to promote a virtuous circle of development and hence convergence. By contrast, countries could get locked into a vicious cycle where catch-up is thwarted. Catch-up, therefore, is no longer divorced from the historical path which an economy has followed. The implications are two-fold. First, policies that encourage the development of certain industries can help to encourage further development. Japan and the south-east Asian newly industrializing countries (NICs) are often used as examples where industrial development has been promoted in areas which are fast-growing with consequent benefits for the rest of the economy. The second implication is that concentration in location of economic activity as a result of such development may lead to large regional inequalities within countries. In this case, regional policies become important. As we shall see later in the book (Chapter 9), the EU has been important in directing funds towards SEEs and to particular regions within them in an attempt to raise their level of development. Funds for infrastructural projects and investment in the development of human capital skills can provide a basis from which catch-up processes can be enhanced.

Such an extension and implicit critique of the *simple* convergence story is in fact one aspect of a more general critique which can be made. The convergence story is highly teleological in nature. In reality, we cannot always assume that all economies are heading in the same direction or towards the same model of economic development. Mingione, in his chapter on the structuration of labour markets in SEEs (Chapter 5), illustrates this point perfectly. He argues that there is a specific Southern European model of development (as distinct, say, from the northern European model) which is at its most successful in northern Italy and we should be careful not to assume that Southern European economies could ever become like their northern neighbours. Instead, their path of convergence may take a rather different character, reflecting the countries' economic, social and cultural histories.

The second modification/extension is that offered by Abramovitz (1986). He argues that the potential for catch-up is dependent on what he terms 'social capability'. This is defined in terms of 'political, commercial, industrial and financial institutions' (p. 388). He suggests that it is a dynamic concept, which depends not so much on existing institutional structure but rather on the ability of that structure to change and thereby promote the adoption of new technologies. It is also dependent on the extent to which 'vested interests and customary relations' operate to prevent change (something which we discuss in more detail below). Recognition of 'social capability' or the 'capacity for development' is clearly important in explaining why different countries catch up at different rates.

What exactly does this entail? Abramovitz himself is rather agnostic about the role of the state, for example, in promoting 'social capability'. And of course, there are economists such as Larre and Torres (1991) who believe that catch-up requires merely an extension and a freeing-up of markets. It can be argued, however, that catch-up is likely to depend crucially on the development of appropriate institutions. Markets can often signal what may be wrong with an economy (declining market shares etc), but this does not imply that economies necessarily have the capacity to respond – the quality of an economy's institutions may be crucial here.

The role of institutions as both vehicles for changes and as constraints on change and hence their impact on the economic performance of differing economies has not often been central to many economic analyses (Henley and Tsakalotos, 1993). In most cases they are seen in a negative light and often charged with distorting the market mechanism. A first step to acknowledging the importance of institutions is realizing the extent to which both companies and nations compete not only on price but on a whole set of non-price factors such as quality, design and research and development (R&D).[20] There is a growing sensitivity amongst economists on the extent to which institutions can influence these issues and the extent to which this determines the ability of regions or nations to improve their real economy and thus compete successfully at the international level. One area that has been given much attention is the labour market and the question of what types of labour market best promote good economic performance. Social scientists have examined a number of issues here: whether centralized or decentralized institutions are more conducive to better economic performance; the extent to which employers organizations should coordinate their actions; and whether mature corporatist economies, that have a good employment record compared to more pluralist economies also rely on a level of consensus on both the means and ends of economic policy between the major economic actors (that is, the unions, employers and the state).[21] There is a similar literature on financial institutions.[22]

There are a number of common themes in this literature that are worth pointing out. Soskice (1991) has argued that those economies best able to compete have what he has termed 'flexibly co-ordinated systems', which he defines as those 'characterised by relatively long-term and high trust relations with and between institutions, and at micro as well as macro levels'. This seems an interesting attempt to bring together the economics of markets and institutional analysis. Market analysis often suggests a world of isolated atomized individuals who only relate socially to each other through the market.[23] This seems to be severely out of step with how markets are experienced in a real economy where they operate through a web of institutions: the state, employers and workers organizations, banks, multinational companies, and so on. Furthermore the latter are not merely 'imperfections' to the working of the market as they are often seen in the orthodox economics literature. Indeed most of the time markets work because of the existence of such institutions. In other words, institutions have an important role in making market exchanges possible – through providing information, reducing uncertainty and in Soskice's schema allowing long-term trust relationships, which are important to competitiveness, to develop. However, as Soskice is keen to point out these institutions do not replace the market and are indeed reliant on it to a large extent to ensure that economic agents accept 'that they are engaged in competitive markets' (Soskice, 1991, p. 51).

Such an approach has much to say on why certain economies outperform others. But, more importantly, it suggests that it is of paramount importance to get not only 'markets right' but also 'institutions right' if nations or regions are to perform well and converge. The experience of SEEs with the convergence process post-1973 can perhaps be better understood by examining whether these economies have developed a flexible thinking capacity, which could have allowed them to respond to the changing external conditions after 1973 more satisfactorily. On the face of it, it appears that they have not and that there is still much work to be done. What exactly has been done and what still remains to be done is a theme that recurs throughout this book.

The final modification/extension, which we can add to the basic convergence story, is to introduce some political economy considerations. In particular, in view of one of the main themes of this book, there is the question of the relationship between catch-up and the political regime. The literature examining the effect of democratization on economic performance comes to no firm conclusions as we shall see below. But this does not imply that political economy considerations are not important. Any strategy of convergence and the changes in economic policy associated with it will inevitably have winners and losers. As Dearlove and White (1987, p. 2) have argued it is important to analyse:

> the political nature of *economic reform coalitions* and the relation between economic reform 'from above' (state sponsored) and 'from below' (socially demanded). One may well doubt the capacity of state

elites to transform themselves and undermine the basis of their own power and privilege (unless in unavoidably dire straits). The political basis of economic restructuring will be stronger if there is the possibility of alliances between reform-minded elements of the established regime and those social interests from below that are dissatisfied with the *status quo* and set to benefit from reform.

The role of organized interests and their consequences for economic performance is something that was first recognized and analysed in some depth by Olson (1965, 1982). He argued that interest groups in society may decide to oppose certain proposed policy changes if they are perceived as damaging their interests. In this way, governments can find a brake put on changes that were designed to try, for example, to improve the economic performance of a particular country. By contrast, if interest groups are to help in promoting policy changes then they must be encompassing enough to ensure that any support for a particularly strategy is maintained.

In the context here it is clear that, if policy changes are required to promote convergence, then they may be opposed by groups that believe they benefit more from the present set-up. The SEEs have not escaped this problem and indeed may even have suffered more acutely than other economies. The nature of the reigning dictatorships and undemocratic regimes implied the exclusion of many groups from society, both at the political level and in economic terms. The rapid accumulation of the 1950s and 1960s, for example, had often passed many groups by. In that sense, the restoration of democracy in all three countries posed an important challenge. Previously excluded groups made demands that were difficult for incoming governments not to meet. It is perhaps no coincidence that all three countries experienced a wage explosion after the fall of the dictatorship. This had important consequences for profits, investment and hence ultimately growth, especially since it occurred at the time of large oil price rises and a general deterioration in the world economy. The challenge for democracy was whether these countries could develop a set of political institutions that would allow fair debate on the sharing out of the gains of accumulation without risking economic inefficiency and putting accumulation itself into jeopardy. Ultimately the lesson is that in the absence of some means of solving the distributional conflict (whether democratic or, as before the mid-1970s, authoritarian), economic crisis is likely to result. The success of countries in catching up is thus likely to be dependent on their success in handling these political/economy considerations.

All these factors bring us rather a long way from the simple convergence story outlined above. In the following chapters, as we shall see, there are echoes and development of all three of the themes, which we have included as extensions/modifications. The authors seek to provide a picture of development in SEEs both internally and in their relations with the EU.

After an overview chapter by Roccas and Padoa-Schioppa, the book is organized in two broad sections. Chapters 3 to 5 provide an account of different facets of the Southern European experience – trade and industry, tourism and employment – and the structural adjustment that has occurred. In Chapters 6 to 9, the emphasis shifts more to policies – their source, design and implementation and the extent to which they have contributed to economic change and the creation of a new Southern Europe.

In Chapter 2, Roccas and Padoa-Schioppa essentially set the scene by providing an in-depth treatment of postwar economic and political development in the SEEs and Italy. It is important to note that the chapter does not attempt to provide an up-to-date account – the recent changes in all the areas they discuss are, after all, the focus of the remainder of the book. Instead, they focus on the periods both before and after the restoration of democracy and compare events in Greece, Portugal and Spain both with each other and with Italy's postwar development. Italy experienced rapid industrialization between 1951 and 1963. Roccas and Padoa-Schioppa attribute this not only to economic factors (such as abundant labour supply, an investment boom and the opening up of the economy), but also to political factors and associated government policies, which fostered the development of a mixed economy. These factors, they argue, contributed to a rapid modernization of Italian industry, not only in terms of its productive capacity but also with respect to its ability to develop, market and distribute new products.

Although industrialization in Italy was successfully promoted, success in other areas of economic and social reform was more limited. In the latter half of the 1960s industrial conflict and social unrest resulted from demands by workers to share in the proceeds of success – higher wages and better social welfare provision among others. With the worsening external conditions, it was more difficult for Italy to face these challenges and still continue with rapid economic growth. As a result investment slowed and macroeconomic imbalances worsened.

The story of economic development in Greece, Spain and Portugal is broadly very similar to that of Italy, although the timing of industrialization and internationalization differs. In particular, whereas in Italy industrialization and an opening of the economy occurred after the fall of fascism, in the other three it occurred before the transition to democracy in the early 1970s – in particular, in the 1960s. Again high investment rates and an increase in trade played important roles. But strict control over trade unions meant that labour on the whole benefited little and all three countries lacked even a basic welfare state.

The transition to democracy in Greece, Portugal and Spain, unfortunately coincided, as we noted above, with the end of the 'Golden Age' of postwar development. This implied a reversal of the previous large gains in standards of living observed in the 1960s – catch-up as we observed earlier came to a halt and some of the previous gains were reversed. At the same time democratization led to the unleashing of pent-up demands from previously repressed groups in society. As in Italy, the pressure to meet these demands quickly led to severe macroeconomic imbalances and poor investment performance. Hence the analysis of Roccas and Padoa-Schioppa does lend some support to the view elaborated above that political economy considerations will crucially determine economic performance.

Roccas and Padoa-Schioppa conclude by examining the evidence on the link between democracy and economic performance. As mentioned above, previous research has tended to find little evidence of any statistical connection – the only possible connection running from economic growth to calls for a democratization of political institutions and this comes about because with growth usually comes closer contacts with the outside world. The detailed and careful analysis of the four SEEs undertaken in this chapter seem to bear this conclusion out: Italy initially experienced successful economic growth in the aftermath of the transition to democracy; the other three, by contrast, seem to have faired more poorly.

Chapters 3 to 5 examine the conditions in SEEs more closely, by focusing on different aspects – the internationalization of these economies, the changing structure of industry, the role of tourism and the structure of labour markets and the importance of the informal sector. Katseli's contribution sets the SEEs in the context of the growing internationalization of the world economy. She argues that increased European integration generally can be seen as a strategic trade policy response to growing internationalization – an increased role for transnational corporations (TNCs), the associated growth of foreign direct investment and a growth in capital flows in general. The challenge facing SEEs in such an environment was to engineer structural change in their industrial capacity to enable them to compete in world markets.

A reduction of tariffs and other trade restrictions occurred in Greece, Portugal and Spain following their accession to the EU with the result that trade with the EU increased steadily. Greece and Portugal tend to engage in a lot of inter-industry trade; Spain less so, reflecting its more advanced industrial capacity. Katseli argues, however, that all three countries faced problems of competitiveness throughout the 1980s and into the 1990s. These problems reflect weak industrial structures, which have responded inadequately to the challenges posed by internationalization and growing integration into the EU. To a great extent these weaknesses have been mitigated by the transfer of substantial amounts of EU funds. Crucial, therefore, to the success of these economies is the use to which these funds have been put. Katseli contends that whereas Spain and Portugal have used the funds fairly successfully, Greece has been less successful, lacking a clear strategic plan.

In conclusion, Katseli argues that the differing fortunes of the SEEs in the 1980s can be attributed in general to the quality of adjustment of their political systems. All three have faced common shocks (oil price rises, EU entry and the associated opening and liberalization of their economies). But the variety of outcomes can be attributed to differences in their ability to organize and promote industrial restructuring.

Tourism has played a major role in SEEs since the 1950s, both economically (as an important source of foreign exchange earnings and income more generally) and socially (in terms of opening up these economies to outside influences even when domestic regimes were highly restrictive). Williams provides a comprehensive examination of the economic role for tourism in the transformation of SEEs. There is also a brief discussion of the political and policy implications of the development of tourism.

Much of the tourist industry in southern Europe is characterized by mass tourism – that is the attraction of large numbers at low prices. But even within this paradigm, the income generating potential can vary hugely depending, among other things, on the source of tourists – British tourists, for example, tend to spend much less than do North Americans or Germans; price and exchange rate movements – tourism of this type is very price elastic; and the degree of political uncertainty – tourism declines dramatically in periods of political unrest.

Williams discusses both the advantages and disadvantages of tourism as an important economic sector. Among the advantages are the relatively quick realization of returns on any investment and its contribution to the balance of payments. However, the disadvantages of mass tourism are also becoming evident. In particular, it can lead to large regional disparities, the dependence on foreign tour companies (which often expropriate a large part of the profits), its ability to create only seasonal jobs and, increasingly, its negative environmental impact. Some of these disadvantages lead Williams to suggest that there is a need for greater state control than has been seen in the past. Tourism has been almost exclusively left to market forces in SEEs. But some state intervention seems particularly pressing in view of the fact that consumers of tourism are now becoming rather more discerning about the product on offer – greater quality is being demanded. The ability of SEEs to respond flexibly to these new demands will crucially determine the future role for tourism in raising income levels in SEEs.

Finally, Mingione focuses in Chapter 5 on a highly pertinent aspect of SEEs – the structure of their labour markets. He argues that all four SEEs can be characterized by the same model of capitalist development, with northern Italy merely representing a successful variant of the model in comparison to the other areas. The features of this model include the fact that these countries were late to industrialize, that they are characterized by a disproportionate number of family enterprises and self-employment (in comparison to northern Europe), and that regional inequalities are common. All these features influence the structuration of labour markets and the characteristics of the employment experience in SEEs.

In his chapter, Mingione explores the origins of the Southern European model and its development in recent years. In particular, among the labour market features explored are: the role of informal employment; the importance of kinship and extended family networks in performing social welfare functions usually provided by the state in northern European countries; the multi-activity nature of employment experience for many people; gender distinctions in both employment and unemployment; and the role of migration. Similarities and differences between the four countries are also examined in some depth and they are compared as a group to other European countries.

Overall, therefore, the picture that emerges from these chapters is that SEEs tend to share a number of characteristics that distinguish them from their central and northern European neighbours. Many of these characteristics (their poor and limited industrial structure, their dependence on mass tourism, the role of the informal sector, their lack of welfare provision, etc) may explain to a great extent the differences in the standards of living between the north and south of Europe. Moreover, these characteristics limit the extent to which we can talk of a New Southern Europe. Change has undoubtedly occurred but not to the extent required if convergence is to be fully realized.

However, as Mingione argues, one must be careful not to conclude from this that development along northern European lines should be further encouraged. In this respect the analysis of Chapters 6 to 9 is important – here the focus shifts from the characteristics of these economies more towards the implementation and design of policies: both those which have contributed to economic change in the 1980s and 1990s; and those required to further economic development into the next century. In particular, policies towards industry and finance are examined along with the role of the EU in transferring funds to these countries as part of its attempts at regional development.

The relatively underdeveloped nature of industry in Southern European economies – something which clearly comes out of Katseli's contribution – makes industrial policy an important area for promoting economic change. Lyberaki takes this topic up in her contribution and focuses in particular on future prospects for change in Southern Europe as a result of the various industrial policy initiatives emanating in recent years from the EU. The aim of this chapter is to examine how industrial policy can be tailored to the challenges that the SEEs face in the next century.

She argues (developing some of the points made by Katseli) that the changing international environment has warranted a change in the direction of industrial policy. It is no longer desirable (and indeed perhaps not possible) to intervene solely in a direct manner in industry or, at the other extreme, to leave industrial development simply to the market. Instead, intervention requires to be more regulatory-intensive, aimed at developing mechanisms whereby both private and public interests can be combined and fostered. Such an approach, it is argued, can better promote success in today's more complex post-Fordist (post mass production) industrial structure. Moreover, it is more suited to dealing with small- and medium-sized enterprises, which are so prevalent in SEEs. The aim of such intervention is the promotion of greater cooperation between small- and medium-sized firms to aid greater networking and the encouragement of resource pooling (especially in the areas of marketing, design and innovation).

Within this context, European initiatives on industrial policy are examined in some depth. The EU White Paper on Growth, Competition and Employment published in 1994 stresses the need to move away from traditional industrial policies (for example protectionism, increased government spending) towards some of the concerns noted above. Lyberaki, in particular, focuses in some depth on an important area for SEEs – policies for small- and medium-sized enterprises. She concludes that EU industrial policy is showing some signs of meeting the challenge posed by new industrial structures in the global economy. However, the ability of SEEs to benefit fully depends also on their capacity to take advantage of EU-funded initiatives. In this respect the relative underdevelopment of national, regional and local administrative and institutional structures to facilitate policy implementation remains a problem.

In the later 1980s and into the 1990s, SEEs adopted a new policy towards industrial companies in state hands – that of privatization. This has formed an additional policy in the attempts to transform the industrial structures of SEEs. Pagoulatos and Wright focus on the experience of privatization in Greece, Portugal and Spain. They compare these experiences both between the three countries themselves and with the experience in northern Europe, especially in France and the UK. They begin their chapter with a discussion of the scope and condition of state-owned industries in the three SEEs as it existed prior to privatization. They also discuss the conditions which promoted calls for privatization programmes. These included: the desire to meet targets set by the EU for budget deficits; the changing character of many industries; the globalization of both product and financial markets; and, finally, the ideological rise of the right and the decline of the social democratic consensus. The comparison with Britain and France makes it easier to understand the degree of success of individual country programmes. For example, in France and Britain most public sector industries were profitable, thus facilitating their successful sale and financial markets were developed enough to handle large share issues. Such conditions did not exist in the SEEs and this has tended to slow the privatization process. However, in addition to noting these economic barriers to privatization, they also explore a number of political barriers, in particular related to the degree of support for the privatizing government both from within its own ranks and outside.

Not all three countries have gone down the same routes towards privatization, nor have they faced identical constraints. One factor, for example, is the extent to which they have been willing to allow sales to foreign concerns. Portugal and Spain have been much less reluctant than Greece to sell state industries to foreigners and this has made the process of privatization easier.

They conclude on an optimistic note arguing that the move towards a mixed economy, with significant introduction of the market can be seen to represent a move away from the transitional period following democratization to a greater emphasis on competing in world markets and dealing with European integration. Such a conclusion contrasts somewhat with the views expressed by Katseli and Lyberaki.

An important area of reform in many countries, both developed and underdeveloped, has, in recent years, been the financial sector. SEEs have been no exception. Gibson, Stournaras and Tsakalotos examine the scope of financial reform and consider whether the reforms are likely to aid the convergence process. They argue that reform of SEEs' financial sectors was well overdue. For too long, the operational efficiency of financial intermediaries has been poor and consumer choice extremely limited. Moreover, the government exercised a large degree of control over all aspects of finance. Throughout the 1980s the project has been one of liberalization, the encouragement of financial markets, and an opening up of the economies to external financial flows.

Much of the impetus for these changes came from the association of SEEs with the EU – the desire and often the obligation to increase financial integration with other European countries. The rationale for the programmes is put forward and critically appraised, in particular in terms of their likely effect on economic convergence. They conclude that although liberalization is important, it is crucial that future developments involve more emphasis on promoting more effective financial institutions and the construction of longer-term trust relationships between finance and industry. The development of financial markets alone is unlikely to provide these economies with the 'social capability' (Abramovitz, 1986) to catch up with their European partners. Indeed, it may even hinder it by promoting short-termism in financial relations.

As already noted, SEEs receive large transfers from the EU. Mitsos, in Chapter 9, examines the rationale and contribution of EU regional/cohesion policy to SEEs and, more generally, the development of EU policy in this area. This is clearly an important topic – the funds devoted by the EU to cohesion could enable SEEs to alter the structure of their economies in a radical and positive direction, as many of the authors in this volume have indicated. He argues that there are three possible grounds for supporting cohesion policies. First, equity considerations may dictate that regional inequality has a negative effect on the social welfare function of both donor regions and recipient regions. Second, regional transfers may be desirable in order to aid the development of backward areas. In this case, regional aid should be invested in sectors that will help promote development. Finally, one might give a purely compensatory argument for regional transfers. In other words, since some areas lose from increased integration, they should be compensated by those areas which gain. While these arguments are not contradictory, they clearly have different implications for the transfer of funds – both in terms of amount and the use to which it might be put.

EU policy in the area of income redistribution was first explicitly stated in the Single Act of 1986 (which set out the 1992 programme). The aim of reducing disparities between the regions of the Union became explicitly recognized and structural funds were made available. This move was further strengthened in the Maastricht Treaty which set up a Cohesion Fund, which directs money at the four cohesion countries (Greece, Ireland, Portugal and Spain) rather than to regions within these countries.[24] In terms of the structural funds, Greece and Portugal are entirely Objective 1 regions, that is they are entitled to funds as lagging regions. Much of Spain and the Italian Mezzogiorno also qualify. Mitsos notes that for Greece and Portugal EU funds now contribute to around 2 to 4 per cent of GDP per annum, a not insubstantial amount.

Mitsos further analyses the use to which structural funds are put in SEEs. In Greece and Spain infrastructural development is the most common use. In Portugal the largest proportion goes to human resource development. Other uses in all countries include industry and service development and agriculture. Cohesion funds are, by and large used for infrastructure projects where large externalities are present. But critical to SEEs is the real impact of projects funded by EU transfers. Studies conducted by the EU on the use of structural funds indicate that the rate of growth is permanently raised by the transfers by some 0.5 per cent per annum (although not surprisingly there are difficulties in measuring this effect).

Mitsos concludes on an optimistic note. While problems may exist with respect to the design and implementation of policies for the promotion of convergence, convergence or cohesion is finally a major issue on the EU agenda and the funds provided can help with the development of fairly backward areas in SEEs.

What therefore can we conclude from the analyses conducted here for the future of development in SEEs? We argue in the concluding chapter that what is clear is that SEEs have experienced many difficulties since democratization. Transformation of their economies has been a slow and often painful process. Moreover, although there a signs of a new Southern

Europe emerging, the process can hardly be said to have been completed. Per capita income levels in Greece and Portugal, for example, are still only just over half of the EU average.

It seems likely that SEEs' fortunes will continue to be bound up with those of the EU and its other member states. In this respect the existence of tensions in the EU are a worrying development. Integration is not costless and this is particularly true for the SEEs, which began the process of integration at a lower level of development and still remain relatively underdeveloped. As a result, Greece, Portugal and Spain will continue to require transfers from richer EU member states.

But the transfer of funds is, of course, not enough. It is the use to which these funds are put that might crucially determine the success of these economies in converging on EU standards of living. What is needed is a sustained transformation of the deeper structures of SEEs. It is not enough to control macroeconomic imbalances, extend the scope of the market and assume that convergence will follow. What this book illustrates is the importance of the institutional structure of these economies if the goal of convergence is to be achieved.

Notes

1. I would like to express my thanks to Euclid Tsakalotos who made extensive comments on this chapter and took time to discuss it with me.
2. This is borrowed from Goldin (1995).
3. When referring to the Southern European economies (SEEs) here we mean Greece, Portugal and Spain. Where Italy is also included this is made explicit.
4. It is interesting to note that with the adoption of the capitalist economic system by Eastern European countries, the SEEs no longer appear as the economically weakest countries of Europe (in its wide sense). They remain, however, among the weaker countries of the European Union.
5. We use the term 'old-fashioned' here to refer to policies that, for better or worse, are no longer on the agenda of European governments. They include policies such as trade protection and a high degree of regulation of most sectors of the economy (industry, services, finance, etc).
6. For accounts of the causal factors listed above, see Glyn *et al.* (1990), Boltho (1982), Krugman (1987) and Lindbeck (1985).
7. Again, a detailed account of the reason for this decline in postwar international financial institutions is beyond the scope of this introduction. For a detailed account of the history of the international financial system in the postwar period, see Gibson (1996).
8. The extent to which exchange rate volatility adversely affects trade is a controversial issue and it has been difficult to find evidence supporting the view that volatility *per se* is harmful. The evidence that long periods of under or overvaluation can be harmful, causing resources to be reallocated between tradeables and nontradeables, is stronger, as Williamson (1983) argues.
9. In the later 1980s, specific agreements were reached about intervention to manage the major international currencies and, in particular, in the Plaza and

Louvre agreements to manage the dollar. More recently, the Group of Seven meetings at the IMF have provided a forum for policy discussion among the major industrialized countries.

10. The SEEs, of course, had not shared in this social democratic consensus in the pre-1974 period – their political systems precluded it. However, it can be argued that they had their own equivalent – state corporatism (Alogoskoufis, 1995; Katseli, 1990). In other words, the state directed the economy to a large extent: through intervention in the financial system to allocate and price credit; through the control of trade unions in order to make for peaceful industrial relations; and, while the state did not direct the amount of goods to be produced and their prices, market signals were nonetheless rather ineffective.

11. Of course, it could be argued that dominant groups in these societies would have wanted to undertake policies of this type in any case but this is a moot point here.

12. See, for example, Henley and Tsakalotos (1993).

13. See Goldin (1995).

14. The *Journal of Economic Perspectives* provides a good account of endogenous growth theories in its 'Symposium on "New Growth Theory"', vol. 8, no. 1, Winter 1994, pp. 3–72. See also the policy forum on growth in the *Economic Journal*, vol. 102, pp. 598–632.

15. Gerschrenkon (1962).

16. One could distinguish between catch-up and convergence in the following way. Catch-up implies that countries all aspire to sharing certain characteristics (in this case usually per capita income) of some lead country (usually taken to be the US). Convergence on the other hand could be taken to imply that all countries move towards each other in terms of whichever characteristic is chosen. Moreover, this could involve per capita income in the US, for example, falling towards some norm, while other countries experience a rise. In the literature we discuss here, catch-up and convergence are generally used interchangeably. In other words, the idea of convergence is that all countries converge on the lead country.

17. It should be pointed out that this idea of catch-up or convergence should not be taken to imply that countries have necessarily adopted similar policies of have similar economic structures. Instead it is a concept that describes outcomes in the narrow sense of some measure of living standards. As we shall see, in many areas SEEs still have different economic structures both between themselves and when contrasted with the rest of Europe.

18. There is now a huge literature on this topic and it is not the place to cover it all here. For good reviews of the literature, see De La Fuente (1997) and Rassekh (1998).

19. It is also what numerous subsequent researchers have found. One of the major debates, however, concerns what other factors should be included in the regression. Neoclassical growth theory suggests savings (or investment) and labour force growth (as Dowrick and Nguyen include). Others include human capital accumulation (Mankiw *et al.*, 1992), macroeconomic factors (Andres *et al.*, 1996), financial development (Berthelemy and Varoudakis, 1996), etc. In the case where other variables are included, we are testing for conditional (β-convergence. This is a much weaker hypothesis since it states that countries converge on their own steady states, which because of different human capital, savings behaviour etc may be rather different. Thus the extent to which

countries converge on each other and per capita inequalities decline may be limited. For these reasons and others, Quah is critical of the concept of (β-convergence (Quah, 1996; see also Cho, 1996).

20. Lyberaki in Chapter 6 provides a more in-depth account of such issues.
21. See, for example, Bruno and Sachs (1985), Calmfors and Driffill (1988) and Henley and Tsakalotos (1991; 1992; 1993).
22. See Chapter 8, this volume.
23. For example, in the pure Walrasian system, agents meet only briefly to conduct trades, which are organized by the auctioneer. Trades only occur when equilibrium prices are reached. There is therefore no incentive to develop long-term relationships.
24. The differences between these funds and their goals, means of operation, etc are explained in some detail in Chapter 9. What is important here is not so much the details of these funds but the fact that they exist and continue to be created.

Bibliography

Abramovitz, M. (1986) 'Catching up, forging ahead and falling behind', *Journal of Economic History*, vol. XLVI, no. 2, pp. 385–406.

Alogoskoufis, G. (1995) 'The two faces of Janus: institutions, policy regimes and macroeconomic performance in Greece', *Economic Policy*, no. 20, April, pp. 147–92.

Andres, J., Domenech, R. and Molinas, C. (1996) 'Macroeconomic performance and convergence in OECD countries', *European Economic Review*, vol. 40, pp. 1683–704.

Armstrong, H. W. (1995) 'Convergence among regions of the EU, 1950–90', *Papers in Regional Science*, vol. 74, no. 2, pp. 143–52.

Bagliano, F.-C., Brandolini, A. and Dalmazzo, A. (1991) 'The CEP-OECD Data Set', Centre for Economic Performance, London School of Economics, Discussion paper, no. 118.

Barro, R. J. and Sala-i-Martin, X. (1992) 'Convergence', *Journal of Political Economy*, vol. 100, no. 2, pp. 223–51.

Barros, P. P. and Garoupa, N. (1996) 'Portugal-European Union convergence: some evidence', *European Journal of Political Economy*, vol. 12, pp. 545–53.

Bell, B. (1993) 'The CEP-OECD Data Set', Institute of Economics and Statistics, University of Oxford.

Berthelemy, J. C. and Varoudakis, A. (1996) 'Economic growth, convergence clubs, and the role of financial development', *Oxford Economic Papers*, vol. 48, pp. 300–28.

Boltho, A. (ed.) (1982) *The European Economy: growth and crisis*, Oxford University Press, Oxford.

Bruno, M. and Sachs, J. (1985) *Economics of Worldwide Stagflation*, Harvard University Press, Cambridge, MA.

Button, K. J. and Pentecost, E. J. (1995) 'Testing for convergence of the EU regional economies', *Economic Inquiry*, vol. XXXIII, pp. 664–71.

Calmfors, L. and Driffill, J. (1988) 'Bargaining structure, corporatism and macroeconomic performance', *Economic Policy*, no. 6, April.

Cho, D. (1996) 'An alternative interpretation of conditional convergence results', *Journal of Money Credit and Banking*, vol. 28, no. 4, pp. 669–81.

Dearlove, J. and White, G. (1987) 'Editorial introduction to: The Retreat of the State?', *IDS Bulletin*, vol. 18, no. 3 (Institute of Development Studies, University of Sussex).

De La Fuente, A. (1997) 'The empirics of growth and convergence: a selected review', *Journal of Economic Dynamics and Control*, vol. 21, pp. 23–73.

De La Fuente, A. (1998) 'What kind of regional convergence?', paper presented to Royal Economics Society Conference, Warwick, March.

Dowrick, S. and Nguyen, D. (1989) 'OECD comparative economic growth, 1950–85: catch-up and convergence', *American Economic Review*, vol. 79, no. 5, pp. 1010–30.

Economic Journal (1992) 'Policy Forum: The determinants of economic growth', vol. 102, no. 412, May, pp. 598–632.

Gerschrenkon, A. (1962) *Economic Backwardness in Historical Perspective*, Harvard University Press, Cambridge, MA.

Gibson, H. D. (1996) *International Finance*, Longman, UK.

Goldin, C. (1995) 'Cliometrics and the Nobel', *Journal of Economic Perspectives*, vol. 9, no. 2, Spring, pp. 191–208.

Glyn, A., Hughes, A., Lipietz, A. and Singh, A. (1990) 'The rise and fall of the Golden Age', in Marglin and Schor (eds).

Henley, A. and Tsakalotos, E. (1991) 'Corporatism, profit squeeze and investment', *Cambridge Journal of Economics*, vol. 15, no. 4, December, pp. 425–50.

Henley, A. and Tsakalotos, E. (1992) 'Corporatism and the European Labour Market after 1992', *British Journal of Industrial Relations*, vol. 30, no. 4, December, pp. 567–86.

Henley, A. and Tsakalotos, E. (1993) *Corporatism and Economic Performance*, Edward Elgar, Aldershot, UK.

Journal of Economic Perspectives (1994) Symposium on 'New Growth Theory', vol. 8, no. 1, Winter, pp. 3–72.

Katseli, L. T. (1990) 'Economic integration in the enlarged European Community: structural adjustment of the Greek economy', in Bliss, C. and Braga de Macedo, J. (eds), *Unity with Diversity in the European Economy*, Centre for Economic Policy Research, Cambridge University Press, Cambridge, UK.

Krugman, P. (1987) 'Slow growth in Europe', in Lawrence, R. and Schultze, C. (eds), *Barriers to European Growth*, Washington DC, Brooking Institution, pp. 48–76.

Krugman, P. (1994) *Peddling Prosperity*, Norton, New York.

Larre, B. and Torres, R. (1991) 'Is convergence a spontaneous process? The experience of Spain, Portugal and Greece', *OECD Economic Studies*, no. 16, Spring, pp. 169–98.

Lindbeck, A. (1985) 'What is wrong with the west European economies?', *World Economy*, vol. 8, June, pp. 153–70.

Mankiw, G. N., Romer, D. and Weil, D. N. (1992) 'A contribution to the empirics of economic growth', *Quarterly Journal of Economics*, vol. CVII, no. 2, pp. 407–37.

Marglin, S. and Schor, J. (eds) (1990) *The Golden Age of Capitalism*, Oxford University Press, Oxford.

Mihail, D. (1995) 'The productivity slowdown in Greece', *Labour*, vol. 9, no. 2, pp. 189–205.

Neven, D. and Gouyette, C. (1995) 'Regional convergence in the European Community', *Journal of Common Market Studies*, vol. 33, no. 1, pp. 47–65.

Olson, M. (1965) *The Logic of Collective Action*, Harvard University Press, Cambridge, MA.

Olson, M. (1982) *The Rise and Decline of Nations*, Yale University Press, New Haven, CT.

Quah, D. (1996) 'Empirics for growth and convergence', *European Economic Review*, vol. 40, pp. 1353–75.

Rassekh, F. (1998) 'The convergence hypothesis: history, theory and evidence', *Open Economies Review*, vol. 9, pp. 85–105.

Soskice, D. (1991) 'The institutional infrastructure for international competitiveness: a comparative analysis of the UK and Germany', in Atkinson, A. B. and Brunetta, R. (eds), *Economics for the New Europe*, Macmillan, London.

Tsakalotos, E. (1991) *Alternative Economic Strategies: the case of Greece*, Avebury, Aldershot, UK.

Williamson, J. (1983) *The Exchange Rate System*, Institute for International Economics, Washington, DC.

2
Economic Change and the Process of Democratization in Southern Europe

Massimo Roccas and Tommaso Padoa-Schioppa

This chapter provides an overview of the process of economic change and democratization in Italy, Spain, Portugal and Greece. There are important points in common in the experience of these four countries: they began industrialization later than the countries of Northern Europe; they were subjected to fascist or right-wing authoritarian dictatorships; and their economic transformation and democratization interacted with a process of international opening and integration in the European Community (EC).[1]

The analysis focuses on developments following democratization in Italy (in the 1940s) and both before and after the end of dictatorship in the 1970s in Spain, Portugal and Greece. The two cases are discussed separately because of the decades dividing them, but also because of the authors' personal experience of the evolution of Italy in the period under review.

The first part of this chapter examines some general problems involved in treating cases that refer to different periods and shows important disparities, under the common heading of 'economic change and the process of democratization'.

The second part reviews the Italian experience from 1951 to 1979, concentrating on the developments that are most relevant for the purposes of comparison with the other three countries.

Developments in Spain, Portugal and Greece from 1960 to 1992 are analysed in a third part, which is divided into three periods: the years of dictatorship, those immediately following it and the more recent period of democratic normality and active participation in the EC's initiatives. A last part concludes.[2]

Comparing Italy with Spain, Portugal and Greece

Democracy was restored in Italy in 1946 and in the following year, with the signing of the Peace Treaty, Italy was accepted into the community of

Western, market-oriented democracies after years of isolation. The first two decades of postwar democracy coincided with the transformation of Italy from a semi-agricultural country into a modern industrial economy. Democracy and economic change unfolded within the framework of Western trade and economic liberalization, with Italy participating first in the new international organizations built after the war and then in the EC.

When this process began in the late 1940s, many of the basic features of Italy's economic structure were not unlike those of Spain, Portugal and Greece some 10 or 15 years later: low productivity in agriculture, which accounted for the largest share of total employment; technological backwardness and dualism in the structure of industry; exports consisting mainly of agricultural products and 'traditional' manufactures; a high ratio of expenditure on food to total private consumption; a chronic trade deficit; the critical importance of emigration as both a social stabilizer and a source of foreign exchange; and, finally, public sector inefficiency. The similarity is closest with Spain, whose size and population are comparable to Italy's. However, conditions in Italy, as later in Spain, Portugal and Greece, differed from those typical of underdevelopment, since the country had an industrial base and did not have to contend with widespread malnutrition, endemic diseases, illiteracy and, above all, a population explosion.[3]

To assess the performance of the four economies in catching up, it is important to measure the per capita GDP gap between them and the advanced European countries on the eve of their economic take-off. Unfortunately we lack reliable data for such comparisons. As estimated by Fuà (1980), in 1950 Italy's real per capita GDP was around 54 per cent of that of the advanced European countries, compared with 41 per cent for Spain, 35 per cent for Greece and 30 per cent for Portugal; in 1960 the corresponding figures were 61, 42, 37 and 28 per cent.[4]

Geographically, Italy and the other three countries share a number of characteristics, including climate, which makes them competitors in agriculture (for example, fruit, olive oil and wine) and tourism, and a tradition of close contacts with other Mediterranean countries. Historically, they are the only countries of Western Europe not reached by the Protestant Reformation; the attitudes, habits and character of their peoples exhibit a number of typically 'southern' traits. Politically, all four countries developed parliamentary systems before the onset of dictatorship; the size and organizational strength of left-wing parties following democratization was also a common trait and distinguished them from many other semi-industrial countries.

Against these similarities, there are several important features that set the Italian experience apart from that of the other three countries. Four differences stand out:

1. *Periodization and the temporal relationship between economic transformation and democratization.* Democracy was restored in Italy three decades before

it was re-established in Spain, Portugal and Greece, although the latter had a quasi-parliamentary regime at the time of the 1967 military coup. The rapid growth that transformed the structure of Italy's economy occurred after the fall of fascism (between 1951 and 1963), whereas the corresponding developments in the other countries largely coincided with the final period of dictatorship. A comparative analysis of 'economic change and the process of democratization' in Italy on the one hand and Spain, Portugal and Greece on the other must, therefore, refer to different periods marked not only by different political and economic conditions at the international level, but also and especially by quite different domestic political regimes in the initial phases of economic transformation.

2. *The reasons for the fall of dictatorship.* The end of dictatorship in Spain, Portugal and Greece was not accompanied by a collapse of the countries' administrative, social and economic structures. In Spain and Greece the main features and trends of the economy were not significantly altered as a direct result of the change of regime. Though influenced by international events, and precipitated in Greece and Portugal by military setbacks, the end of dictatorship in all three countries also reflected internal developments. Economic changes were particularly important in creating the conditions for restoring democracy. In Italy, by contrast, the fall of fascism, with the attendant social and economic breakdown, was the consequence of a disastrous war. That economic transformation was not the primary cause of Italy's political transformation is even clearer when one considers that Italy had been a parliamentary state for 60 years before Mussolini's March on Rome and that the Allied occupying powers were determined to impose parliamentary democracy in any event. Thus, in the case of Italy an investigation of the interrelationships between democratization and economic transformation can be confined to postwar developments. A related feature of the Italian experience was the need to rebuild the country after the war.

3. *The international environment.* The international environment in which democratization took place was very different in Italy compared with the other three countries. In 1945–8 the attitude of the Western powers to a country like Italy, situated on the frontier between the communist and capitalist blocs, was determined almost exclusively by the aim of preventing Soviet expansion and the establishment of a communist government. The United States held undisputed leadership in the West; and although Italy regained the status of a nation enjoying full economic and political independence, the American military presence, the 'Soviet threat' and the pressing need for US material assistance for reconstruction inevitably conditioned the choices of the Italian electorate and the Italian government.

When dictatorship came to an end in Spain, Portugal and Greece, cold war confrontation had largely given way to coexistence. The European 'core' was now a strong, wealthy and politically stable area and US supremacy was no longer absolute. Spain, Portugal and Greece were peripheral countries of minor importance in a continent dominated by the EC. In particular, Spain's peaceful and smooth transition to democracy seemed to present no important political dangers.

In two further, important respects the international economic context in which Spain, Portugal and Greece achieved rapid industrial transformation differed from that in which Italy had done so. First, giant multinational corporations had emerged as worldwide economic agents capable of influencing the course of development, and particularly the structure of foreign trade, in host countries (see Katseli in this volume). Foreign investment played a more important role in the economic transformation of Spain, Portugal and Greece than in Italy's postwar development. Second, third world countries had emerged as important exporters of manufactures, whereas Italy, earlier, had not had to face fierce competition from much-lower-wage NICs in its efforts to penetrate the markets of advanced Western countries.

4. *Economic liberalization and EC membership.* In postwar Italy the choice between an inward and an outward-looking economic strategy was for some years a subject of debate, although the majority of the country's political forces supported the latter alternative. By contrast, when democracy was restored in Spain, Portugal and Greece this was no longer an issue: imports and exports of goods and services were already a significant share of GDP in all three countries; Portugal had joined EFTA (European Free Trade Association) in 1959; Greece had signed an association agreement with the EC in 1962; and Spain had put an end to autarky in 1959 and concluded a preferential trade agreement with the EC in 1970 (though it remained a relatively protected economy). The main obstacle to their full membership of the EC before democratization had been the negative attitude of European countries towards their political regimes.

Italy's relationship with the process of European integration differed markedly from that of the other three countries. In the first place, from the very beginning Italy had been an active participant in postwar European cooperation projects and as a founding member of the European Economic Community in 1957 had been able to ensure that its interests were taken into account. By the time the others applied for membership (Greece in 1975, Portugal and Spain in 1977), there was limited scope for new members to change EC structures, rules and policies in ways that were consonant with their specific conditions and interests. Moreover, in the early 1950s a realistic case could have been made (and indeed was made by many) for Italy not to join the Community, whereas in the late 1970s participation in an EC that already included most of Western Europe was perhaps Hobson's choice for Spain, Portugal and Greece.

Second, Italy had faced adapting to EC discipline when the other founding members were similarly engaged and EC rules mainly involved trade and agriculture. This facilitated the task, although Italy had also to meet the challenge of catching up with its more developed partners. By contrast, the efforts of Spain, Portugal and Greece to catch up with the rest of the Community and adapt to EC trade and agricultural rules came at a time when the other countries had accomplished the necessary adjustment and all members of the Community, new and old alike, were called on to introduce basic reforms in their monetary, financial and services sectors in view of the establishment of the single European market.

One final distinction is worth mentioning and it concerns *internal development gaps*. At the beginning of their rapid economic transformation, all four countries faced large regional disparities and, more generally, serious imbalances between urban or coastal areas and inland rural areas.[5] In Italy the problem was (and still is) particularly severe because the imbalances had sharper geographical contours and stronger historical determinants. While it is difficult to say whether regional disparities were larger in Italy in 1951 than in the other countries in the early 1960s, only in Italy did they involve a sharp division of the country into two halves. The North–South divide already existed when Italy was unified in 1861, but was subsequently accentuated until the 1950s by a series of developments. The failure to close the North–South gap during the following decades was perhaps the most negative aspect of Italy's postwar economic performance.[6]

Differences between Spain, Portugal and Greece

In grouping Spain, Portugal and Greece for the methodological reasons mentioned earlier, it is nonetheless necessary not to lose sight of the very important differences that exist between the three. Briefly these are:

1. *Geography.* Spain is distinguished by an area and population, as well as by the prospective size of its domestic market, which are roughly comparable to those of France, Italy or the United Kingdom. Like Italy, Spain borders directly on the European 'core', a fact that facilitates transport and communications with the industrial centre of Europe. Portugal and Greece are on the other hand truly 'peripheral'. As for Greece, the Balkans cut the country off from industrial Europe and a mountainous mainland and innumerable islands make transport and communications difficult.

2. *History.* Although Greece won independence from the Ottoman Empire in 1832 with the help of the great powers of Europe, it has only existed within its present borders since 1922, when it gave up the territory it had won in Asia Minor and added 1.3 million refugees to its population

of around 5 million. For centuries the nation's history had mainly reflected its relationship with Constantinople and the Ottoman Empire, the role of the Orthodox Church and recurrent rivalries and wars in the Balkans. Outside of Greece proper, Greek trading communities had prospered throughout the Eastern Mediterranean. All these factors, together with the geographical configuration of the country, help to explain certain basic features of the Greek economy after World War II: its 'external' orientation; the importance of shipping and insurance interests; and an agricultural sector where productivity was low and the average size of farms very small as a result of the land reform implemented to assimilate the inflow of Greeks from Asia Minor.

By contrast, both Iberian countries have been unified nation-states with stable borders for centuries (although Portugal was incorporated into Spain from 1580 to 1640). They shared the experience of the Christian Reconquest and overseas imperial expansion and an attachment to the Catholic faith. Until recent times, agriculture in important parts of both countries was dominated by big landed estates. Unlike Spain, however, Portugal never truly attained the status of a great power in Europe; its long-standing alliance with Great Britain gave the latter an important influence on Portuguese political and economic developments.

3. *Politics in the twentieth century.* The background against which democratization in the mid-1970s has to be set varies markedly between the three countries. Portugal had enjoyed democracy and parliamentary order in only a limited sense before 1926. The dictatorship established in that year lasted 48 years, during which the country's cultural isolation from democratic Europe was almost total. The end of the dictatorship was precipitated by the unsuccessful wars to retain the African empire and involved a military coup, followed by a 'revolutionary' period of radical politics and upheaval in which the hard-line Portuguese Communist Party figured prominently.

As in Portugal, dictatorship in Spain lasted for decades. It had been preceded by a long period of parliamentary rule, including the Republican–Socialist government of 1931–6, and the rebellion that marked its birth in 1936 was followed by three years of civil war. From the late 1950s onwards Spain's cultural isolation from Europe was less pronounced than Portugal's. Unlike Portugal, but like Greece, Spain managed to make a fairly smooth transition to parliamentary rule.

The contemporary history of Greece is set apart from that of the Iberian countries by its involvement in the World War II, including Axis (Germany, Italy and Bulgaria) occupation and the development of a popular resistance movement. The end of the civil war of 1945–9 saw the restoration of a quasi-parliamentary regime in which the Communist Party was outlawed and the army never came under parliamentary control. The country gradually opened to external relations and its political and cultural life became more dynamic in the early 1960s. To an extent, the 1967 military coup and the comparatively short dictatorship, which never enjoyed mass support and left no strong imprint on Greek society, can be viewed as a parenthesis in modern Greek history, a last-ditch attempt to halt the country's progress towards political and social liberalization.

4. *Economic conditions.* At the beginning of the 1960s Spain was more highly developed than Portugal and Greece thanks chiefly to the initial lead it had built up before World War I, with the creation of infrastructure (railways in particular), the growth and mechanization of mining, the establishment of two important regional poles of manufacturing (iron and steel, chemicals and textiles) and the founding of major banking institutions. Foreign capital played a large role in this economic modernization and industrialization, which resembled the process that unfolded in Northern Italy during the same period and had no parallel in either Portugal or Greece. From 1913 to 1930 Spain's industrial lead over the other two countries widened further.

Economic change in Italy, 1951 to 1979

By 1951 Italy had surpassed its pre-war levels of production and income and completed postwar reconstruction. From then until 1963 the Italian economy expanded continously, growing by almost 6 per cent a year and outpacing every other Western country except Japan. This period, later called the 'economic miracle', saw Italy transformed from a semi-agricultural country into a modern, industrial nation.[7]

From the end of the war to 1950, not only had Italy accomplished reconstruction, but fundamental political, institutional and economic choices had been made that created the framework in which the economy would develop in the years to come.[8] The first free elections, held in 1946 in conjunction with the referendum that determined the transformation of Italy from a monarchy into a republic, led to the formation of a coalition government of all the parties that had emerged from the anti-fascist movement. In June 1947, at the very time when the United States launched the Marshall Plan, Prime Minister Alcide De Gasperi, a Christian Democrat, felt strong enough to form a new government that excluded the Communists and Socialists. This prepared the ground for vigorous measures of economic stabilization, which put an end to spiralling inflation and restored confidence in the lira, whose parity remained unchanged until 1971.

In December 1948 the republican Constitution was approved and entered into force. An important factor in creating a climate favourable to saving, investment and private enterprise was the Christian Democrats' landslide victory (48 per cent of the vote) in the first general elections held under the new Constitution. A short time later a split in the powerful, leftist-dominated General Confederation of Labour spawned two smaller confederations linked to government parties. In the meanwhile, the Italian government, overcoming criticism from industrial interests, made the basic decision to proceed rapidly with trade liberalization. In April 1948 Italy participated in founding the Organization for European Economic Cooperation, which fostered the gradual elimination of trade quotas. In July 1950 it joined the European Payments Union. The following year it became a founding member of the European Coal and Steel Community, the nucleus from which the EC would develop. The decision to take part in Western economic liberalization and cooperation, as noted by Carli (1993, posthumous memoirs), stemmed essentially from political motives, but economic considerations also contributed. First of all, there was the distasteful memory of fascist autarky. Second, the option in favour of rapid industrialization required access to the large and fast-growing markets of the West for Italian producers, given the poor conditions of the domestic market and the need to obtain foreign exchange with which to pay for imports of raw materials and intermediate goods. A final incentive was the large flow of American aid to countries participating in the liberalization process (from 1948 to 1952 Marshall Plan aid to Italy amounted to around 28 per cent of the value of Italian imports). It is interesting to note that while the government trusted in the ability of Italian industry to cope with foreign competition, the left-wing opposition was less optimistic about the prospects of industrial development (a view shared by a large part of industry itself) and concentrated in the late 1940s on organizing agricultural workers and campaigning for land reform.

Table 2.1 shows the evolution of the Italian economy from 1951 to 1963. The 12 years can be divided into two periods, 1951–8 and 1958–63, basically before and after Italy's membership of the EC. The economy's outstanding growth cannot be explained by any single factor but rather by a combination of interrelated factors whose relative importance changed over time. Four of these need to mentioned:

1. *The abundant supply of labour released from agriculture.* Manufacturing output grew at an annual rate of 6.7 per cent in 1951–8 and 10.3 per cent in 1958–63, while industrial wages, initially much lower than in other European industrial countries, did not outpace productivity. Wage moderation was favoured by the lack of trade-union militancy, reflecting the responsible attitude of union leadership, the political weakness of organized labour and the retaliatory measures deployed by firms to ensure discipline on the shop floor.
2. *The investment boom and the consequent rise in productivity.* Fixed capital investment grew by around 11 per cent a year throughout the period. Its growth was strong in both industry and agriculture and even stronger in residential construction. Investment rose from 18 to 25 per cent of GDP,

Table 2.1 Italian economic indicators (average annual compounded rates)

	1951–63	1951–58	1958–63	1963–79	1963–69	1969–73	1973–79
GDP per capita	5.1	4.8	5.6	3.8	4.6	3.6	3.2
Industrial value added	8.5	8.2	9.0	4.5	5.6	4.6	3.3
Manufacturing value added	8.2	6.7	10.3	6.4	6.7	7.0	5.6
Industry productivity (value added per person employed)	5.6	5.2	6.1	4.1	5.4	4.0	2.9
Manufacturing industry productivity (value added per person employed)	6.0	4.5	8.2	5.4	6.0	5.8	4.5
Gross fixed investment	10.7	10.7	10.7	2.6	4.8	2.8	0.3
Export volume	11.3	8.2	15.9	10.3	14.5	6.9	8.5
Consumer prices	2.9*	2.2**	3.2	8.8	3.4	6.5	16.1

Sources: ISTAT.
*1953–63
**1953–58

and the average ratio of 21.5 per cent for the period was one of the highest in Europe. For the economy as a whole, productivity rose at an annual rate of 4.6 per cent in 1951–8 and 7.0 per cent in 1958–63, with even faster gains in agriculture than in industry. The prolonged investment boom was made possible by a number of factors, including: Italian households' high propensity to save; the large profits and high rates of self-financing that firms achieved thanks to wage moderation; orthodox monetary and fiscal policies, which kept average consumer price inflation to 2.9 per cent a year and government deficits to below 2 per cent of GDP; and the fact that Italy's defeat in the war and its postwar inflation freed resources by eliminating colonial expenditure and drastically reducing the burden of military spending and public debt servicing. However, a major thrust for the growth in investment and productivity was provided by the large-scale reallocation of resources, modernization of agricultural techniques and, above all, widespread technical innovation in industry, which was able to introduce methods developed abroad after years of isolation.

3. *The opening of the economy through trade liberalization and the decision to take part in the Common Market.* The issue of European Economic Community membership was much debated before 1957, with opposition voiced not only by the Left (although the Socialists abstained in the final vote in Parliament) but also by some spokesmen for industry, who feared that certain branches of Italian industry would not be able to stand the test of competition. Time proved these apprehensions to be unwarranted.[9]

Italy's impressive export performance in the period under review is shown in Table 2.1. Even before the 1957 Treaty of Rome total exports, consisting largely of manufactures, grew by over 8 per cent a year. In the years immediately following EC membership total export growth accelerated to about 16 per cent a year, but exports to the EC shot up to annual growth of 26 per cent (and to 31 per cent for manufactures). Tariff reductions probably had a larger impact on Italian exports than on those of other EC countries, as a larger proportion of the former consisted of traditional, highly price-elastic products. However, the trade-creation effect of tariff reduction, as normally evaluated, does not entirely account for Italy's export boom. Indeed, it is probable that a much more important factor was the drive by Italian manufacturers, anticipating rather than responding to the elimination of trade barriers and consequent increase in competition, to modernize, rationalize and expand plant, achieve economies of scale, improve the quality of output, analyse foreign markets, develop better distribution networks and gain a deeper understanding of the institutional, social and cultural characteristics of Italy's partners. The environment of restored freedom and democracy was crucial in unleashing the 'animal spirits' of a new generation of entrepreneurs. In the light of this dynamism and change of perspective, the period from 1951 to 1963 can be characterized as one of 'export-led growth', though not in the strict Keynesian sense; after all, fixed investment grew faster than merchandise exports in 1951–8 and domestic consumption of durables almost as fast in 1958–63. During these years, moreover, and up to 1973, Italy enjoyed favourable terms of trade *vis-à-vis* the raw material and oil producing countries, while the balance of payments was kept in equilibrium, despite a chronic trade deficit, thanks to emigrants' remittances, receipts from tourism and foreign investment.

4. *Growth-oriented government policies.* Government policies favoured private property and fostered economic expansion, saving and enterprise. The authorities rapidly dismantled most of the pervasive system of economic regulation erected by the fascist 'corporative state' and constantly promoted international liberalization and cooperation. Nonetheless, government policies did not completely abandon state intervention: albeit on a limited scale, land reform was implemented and agriculture continued to be protected; the prices of certain goods and services continued to be regulated; exchange controls remained in effect and were not phased out until the late 1980s and abolished in 1992 as part of EC financial liberalization; the banking and financial systems were subject to a host of regulations; and special measures were developed to assist specific sectors (housing, agriculture and, above all, the South). The system of state-owned enterprises in industry, communications and banking, largely a legacy of state-sponsored rescue operations in the 1930s, was retained and expanded. During postwar reconstruction and the 'economic miracle' these state enterprises played a very important role in promoting growth and supporting private industry by developing basic sectors such as iron and steel, energy and motorways, which would not have attracted private capital on account of their uncertain or less-than-immediate profitability. The Southern Italy Development Fund, established in 1950, initially provided a significant boost to economic development in the Mezzogiorno.

A second phase in Italian postwar economic change took place between 1964 and 1979, and was characterized by rapid social change and associated problems. By 1963 Italy had largely achieved its industrial transformation and enjoyed almost full employment, the latter due partly to a fall in labour force participation rates and an acceleration in emigration to a rate of some 280,000 people a year. However, certain distortions produced by the process of economic development that were to become increasingly serious had begun to emerge. First and foremost among these were the acute urban and social problems created by the mass exodus from the countryside and especially the migration from the South to the industrial cities of the North, where housing and social services were stretched beyond the limit.

With the boom in demand and the first large wage increases, inflation began to pick up and the trade and payments balances deteriorated. In 1963 prices rose by 7.5 per cent and the current account balance swung into deficit (1.4 per cent of GDP). These conditions prompted a tightening of monetary and fiscal policy in 1964–5, which led to slower growth, the elimination of labour bottlenecks, lower inflation and large balance-of-payments surpluses in the second half of the 1960s. The cost of this stabilization was a drastic slowdown in investment, which only grew by 3.8 per cent a year in 1963–71, as against 10.7 per cent in 1958–63. Investment was also adversely affected by the fear with which middle-class Italians and businessmen viewed the Socialist Party's entry into the government coalition in 1963. Industrial productivity nevertheless continued to rise rapidly (5.4 per cent a year) until 1969 thanks to a thoroughgoing rationalization of factory work, which allowed previously installed capital to be exploited in full. At the same time, rising unemployment and the consequent curbing of wage increases enabled firms to recoup profitability. Although consumption continued to increase, exports were the chief component of demand and made it possible for the economy as a whole to continue to grow and the balance of payments to remain in equilibrium despite large illegal exports of capital.

The hopes that the new centre-left coalition would help Italy eliminate the remaining social and economic gap separating it from the most advanced European countries were not fulfilled, however. The completion of this process would have required new policies to improve housing, health and education, to eliminate administrative inefficiencies, widespread tax evasion and building speculation, and to promote competition in the non-tradables sector. These problems were not adequately addressed. Policies to promote the development of the South failed to create the environment needed for economic take-off. The quality of life deteriorated in Italy's overcrowded cities. Social frustration and resentment began to grow and working class militancy increased. This protest erupted in the student revolt of 1968 and the labour movement's 'hot autumn' of 1969, which initiated a long period of industrial conflict.

The contract settlements to the industrial disputes of 1969–70 involved a large increase in labour costs and a marked decrease in labour mobility and flexibility. This reduced firms' profitability and capital expenditure, which in turn curtailed their productivity growth and international competitiveness. A process of decentralization in the industrial sector emerged in response to this situation: to avoid the wage schedules and labour rigidity imposed by the increasingly militant trade unions, large and medium-sized industrial concerns increasingly outsourced to smaller firms, where some of the new provisions of contract and labour regulation did not apply, industrial relations were less tense and labour, fiscal and other regulations could often be evaded.

These changes did not affect certain specialized manufacturing districts in northern and central Italy, where small, independent producers continued to flourish and became more competitive. Industrial decentralization broadened small firms' product base and enhanced their importance in Italian industry. In the years that followed 1969–70 manufacturing districts of this kind developed rapidly, representing a growing share of the industrial sector and spreading a new model of industrialization.[10]

In 1966–70 per capita GDP had grown at an average rate of 5.5 per cent. In 1971 and 1972 growth slowed down to around 1 and 2 per cent respectively. The inflationary impact of the new wage settlements was initially checked by a restrictive monetary policy, but the 1973 oil shock, which originated massive balance-of-payments deficits, and the rapid devaluation of the lira in the wake of the breakup of the international system of fixed exchange rates in 1971–3, soon added inflationary fuel. Consumer prices accelerated from 2.7 per cent in 1969 to 4.8 per cent in 1971 and 10.8 per cent in 1973, to peak at 19.1 per cent in 1974. They then decelerated slowly to 14.8 per cent in 1979, only to bounce back to 21.2 per cent in 1980 as a result of the second oil shock. The 1973 oil shock and the consequent slowdown in economic expansion in the West caused Italy's growth rate to remain at 3.2 per cent between 1973 and 1979. Domestic demand only grew at about half that rate in this period: in fact, following the sharp deterioration in the terms of trade and balance of payments after 1973, an aggressive export strategy was pursued and successfully carried out by Italian firms despite the unfavourable situation of world trade.

Having failed to take advantage of the boom of the 1960s to modernize its infrastructure and administration and adopt social welfare measures commensurate with its level of development, Italy now faced popular demand for such changes in the adverse domestic and international setting of the 1970s. Important progress was achieved in social legislation and political reform. The Labour Rights Act was enacted in 1970. The passage of the divorce law in 1970 and legalization of abortion in 1975 changed profoundly traditional patterns of family life. The 1975 law on sexual equality ended the lesser status of Italian women before the law, gave them one of the most advanced legal positions in Europe and helped to boost female participation in the labour force. Though its results proved somewhat disappointing in later years, the regional reform promulgated in 1970 and fully introduced in 1976 was another significant accomplishment. The reform, envisaged in the Constitution of 1948 but never implemented, devolved on regional government councils several important functions that had been performed by central government.[11]

The 1970s also saw the creation or strengthening of the modern welfare state in such areas as health care and pension provision, the enactment of educational reform, the elimination of geographical wage differentials and the abolition of outdated forms of landholding (eg, sharecropping). The importance of these strides should not be underestimated, bearing in mind, for example, that a part of the population had previously not been covered by subsidized health care or the pension system.

These reforms greatly increased the state's role in the economy. They did not, however, help to upgrade the quality of state action and of 'public goods' provision. Little was done to rationalize and modernize the machinery of central and local government, which, with significant exceptions, particularly in the north and centre, remained inefficient. Reforms were not part of a comprehensive programme that set clear priorities, ensured consistency between the various measures and, most importantly, provided for financial coverage of the resulting increases in public expenditure. They were introduced piecemeal, largely in response to one group or another and as instruments to achieve wider political consensus. Their implementation led to the creation of new strongholds for the parties in power, reinforcing clientelistic and patronage relations between public authorities and citizens and enlarging the scope for corruption.

As a result of all this, and also because economic growth turned out to be much slower than in earlier years, the social legislation of the 1970s led to a continuous acceleration in public expenditure and ever larger budget deficits, which in turn reinforced the inflation stemming from the rise in wages and the deterioration in the terms of trade. The condition of public finances was also aggravated by growing state intervention in the form of both direct takeovers and injections of public funds in ailing public and private sector companies, often at the behest of coalitions comprising management, trade unions and staff. The structure of public expenditure, which increased from 34.4 per cent of GDP in the two years 1969–70 to 42.0 per cent in 1978–79, was steadily distorted in favour of transfer payments to households and firms and interest on the growing public debt, to the detriment of both public investment and consumption. Despite large increases in direct taxation, the fiscal deficit began to balloon: general government net borrowing rose from around 3 per cent of GDP in the three years 1968–70 to 7.5 per cent in 1971–3 and 10.5 per cent in 1980–2.

In 1979 the European Monetary System (EMS) was launched with Italy as a founding member, though the lira enjoyed a special, wider fluctuation band until January 1990. In 1980 the Italian economy was rocked by the second oil shock. These events largely conditioned the economy's evolution in the 1980s, introducing specific features different from those that had prevailed in the preceding 20 years. This, together with the fact that events that occurred 35 years and more after the fall of fascism cannot reasonably be included in a discussion of 'economic change and democratization', make it advisable not to go beyond 1979 in this review of the Italian experience. Nevertheless, recent data on the Italian economy are presented as necessary terms of comparison with those of Spain, Portugal and Greece in the rest of this chapter and passing mention is made here of Italian economic trends in the eighties.

The further deterioration in Italy's terms of trade as a result of the second oil shock and the ensuing general stagnation of economic activity in Europe caused Italy's rate of economic growth to fall from an average of 4.4 per cent in 1975–80 to 1.2 per cent in 1980–5. Growth later picked up, but not enough to allow Italy again to outpace other European countries by a wide margin. Whereas the Italian economy had grown by 3.8 per cent a year in the 1970s, compared with the EC12 average of 3.0 per cent, from 1980 to 1991 its growth rate of 2.3 per cent was exactly the same as that of Italy's EC partners. Industrial output expanded at a slightly slower rate in Italy than in the EC on average. It should be noted that in 1980 Italian per capita GDP had finally caught up with, and indeed surpassed, the average level in the EC12: it was 102.5 per cent of the Community average, compared with 86.6 per cent in 1960 (Figure 2.1); over the same period the

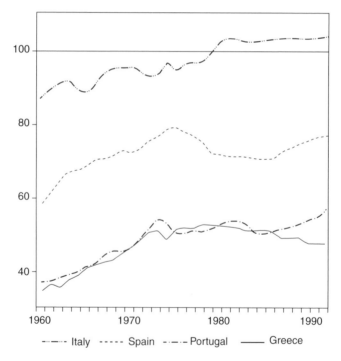

Figure 2.1   Gross Domestic Product at current market prices per head of population*
(EC12 = 100)
* Purchasing Parity Standard
Source: Commission of the European Communities, *European Economy*, n. 54, 1993.

proportions *vis-à-vis* France and Germany had risen from respectively 73 and 80 per cent to around 90 per cent.

The sharp slowdown in Italian growth after 1980 reflected not only the unfavourable international environment and other structural factors, but also the need to attack the twin problems of inflation and public finances. In 1980 inflation rose to 21.2 per cent, compared with an average of 13.7 per cent in the EC12, and the budget deficit grew in 1981 to 11.6 per cent of GDP, compared with 5.5 per cent in the EC12. Since membership of the EMS limited recourse to currency depreciation as a means of compensating for the inflation differential, monetary policy had to be more restrictive and, what is more important, management and labour gradually came to recognize that rises in wages and prices would now have a direct impact on external competitiveness and the level of economic activity. Thanks in part to this disciplinary factor, trade unions took an increasingly responsible attitude in industrial relations and matters concerning the labour market. The final step in this long evolution was the abolition, in 1992, of the indexation of wages to inflation and the signing, in 1993, of a tripartite agreement between employers, unions and the government on the method and content of labour contract renewals. Inflation was brought down from 21.2 per cent in 1980 to 10.8 per cent in 1984 and, with the assistance of the 1986 oil countershock, 5.0 per cent in 1988 (compared with 3.6 per cent for the EC12).

Adjusting public finances proved much more difficult, however. The stock of public sector debt rose from 40.9 per cent of GDP in 1970 to 59.0 per cent in 1980, and reached 100.9 per cent in 1990 and 111.0 in 1992. Unlike many European countries, Italy did not implement a plan of fiscal adjustment in the 1980s. Such a step would have required, on the supply side, the introduction of measures to rationalize the public sector and closely monitor its efficiency and, on the demand side, stringent control of actual requirements and of the entitlements of individuals and firms to free public services, subsidies and transfers. Nonetheless, more limited corrective action was taken with the realistic aim of keeping the overall deficit from growing and reducing the deficit net of interest payments. The latter – the so-called primary deficit – rose from 4.4 per cent of GDP in 1980 to 6.5 per cent in 1985 and came down to 3.2 per cent in 1988; in 1992 it gave way to a primary surplus of 0.4 per cent of GDP. The correction was thus too little and too late to prevent a gradual rise in the debt/GDP ratio.

Economic change in Spain, Portugal and Greece, 1960 to 1992

A comparative treatment of economic change in Spain, Portugal and Greece involves considerable difficulties of periodization. The basic phases of economic development and such central events as the transition to democracy and entry to the EC did not proceed side by side. Reference will therefore be made to national developments, within a framework that identifies three broad periods: 1960 to 1973, 1974 to 1985 and 1986 to 1992. The first period was ushered in by important changes in economic policy and saw the three countries gradually increase their external openness and record rapid economic growth in connection with the long expansion throughout the Western world. The end of that expansion was followed by democratization in the three countries. The second period was mainly one of low growth, high inflation and rising unemployment in the world economy. For the three countries its beginning coincided roughly with the establishment of democratic institutions and application for EC membership; its second part saw the consolidation of democracy; it closed with Spain and Portugal entering the EC at a time when they – but not Greece – were experiencing renewed economic expansion after years of slow growth. The third period was characterized by the three countries' active participation in the EC and its launching of new common policies.

The years before democratization: 1960 to 1973

In 1960 Spain had a population of 30.6 million, Portugal one of 8.4 million and Greece one of 8.3 million, while Italy's population was 50.2 million. Based on purchasing power parities, Italy's per capita GDP was 86.5 per cent of the EC12 average. By contrast, Spain, Portugal and Greece lagged far behind: 58.3, 37.2 and 34.4 per cent respectively (Figure 2.1).

The sectoral distribution of the labour force and output in the three countries at the beginning of the period under review is shown in Table 2.2, which reveals two general features. First, the basic structure of the three economies recalls that of Italy a decade earlier. Second, the structure of the Greek economy was weaker than that of the two others despite the equivalence of per capita GDP with Portugal: although a larger proportion of the labour force was employed in agriculture, the primary sector's share of total output was similar in Greece to that in the other two countries, while industry accounted for a far smaller share of both the labour force and output than in Spain and Portugal. Greece was thus industrially lagging behind the Iberian countries and the productivity of its agricultural sector was much lower relative to that of industry or services than in Spain and Portugal.

From 1960 to 1973 the three countries recorded very rapid annual GDP per capita growth, averaging 6.1 per cent in Spain, 6.8 per cent in Portugal and 7.1 per cent in Greece, compared with 3.9 per cent in the EC12;[12] as a result, per capita GDP rose from 58.3 to 76.4 per cent of the EC12 average in Spain, from 37.2 to 54.1 per cent in Portugal and from 34.8 to 51.1 per cent in Greece. In all three countries, as in Italy during its 'economic miracle', industry led the way, with impressive growth rates of 10 to 11 per cent. Taking account of the steep decline in the agricultural workforce, the rate of

Table 2.2 Structure of Southern European economies

	1951	1960	1973	1985	1990
Employment distribution of the economy (percentage composition)					
Italy					
agriculture	45.2	32.6	18.3	11.2	9.0
industry	26.4	33.9	39.2	33.6	32.4
of which:					
manufacturing	20.1	24.2	29.6	23.2	22.5
services	28.4	33.5	42.5	55.2	58.6
Spain					
agriculture		38.7	24.1	18.2	11.8
industry		30.3	36.8	31.9	33.4
of which:					
manufacturing		23.0	25.6	22.9	22.3
services		31.0	39.0	49.9	54.8
Portugal					
agriculture		43.9	27.2	23.9	17.8
industry		31.3	34.6	33.9	34.8
of which:					
manufacturing		22.6	24.9	25.8	25.1
services		24.8	38.2	42.9	47.4
Greece					
agriculture		57.1	36.8	28.9	24.5
industry		17.4	27.6	27.4	27.4
of which:					
manufacturing		11.6	18.3	18.9	19.1
services		25.5	35.6	43.7	48.2
Sectorial composition of GDP (at current prices) (percentage composition)					
Italy					
agriculture	19.8	12.3	7.8	4.5	3.1
industry	37.1	41.3	42.2	35.2	33.0
of which:					
manufacturing	28.8	28.6	30.0	24.2	22.2
services	43.1	46.4	50.0	60.4	63.8
Spain					
agriculture		22.0	10.1	5.9	4.5
industry		32.8	37.4	37.3	34.5
of which:					
manufacturing		26.7	26.1	27.7	20.3
services		45.2	52.6	56.8	61.0
Portugal					
agriculture		23.5	14.7	8.0	5.8
industry		34.4	39.5	39.6	34.8
of which:					
manufacturing		27.9	31.3	30.4	27.9
services		42.1	45.8	52.5	59.4
Greece					
agriculture		20.2	18.0	15.5	13.8
industry		22.8	29.3	26.2	24.1
of which:					
manufacturing		14.5	17.8	16.3	14.3
services		56.9	52.6	58.3	62.1

Sources: For Employment distribution, OECD Labour Force Statistics; for Sectorial composition, OECD, Historical Statistics and National Accounts. Data for Italy in 1951 are from Istat.

growth of agricultural output in Spain and Greece (2.3 and 4.2 per cent per year respectively) reflected exceptionally large productivity gains. In Portugal, by contrast, agricultural output only increased by 2.2 per cent a year in 1960–5, by 1.3 per cent in 1965–70 and not at all in 1970–3, owing to the absence or failure of policies to solve the sector's structural problems.

Important changes took place in the manufacturing sector in all three countries. Between 1960 and 1973 the share in the sector's value added of the three traditional categories of consumer goods (food, beverages and tobacco; textiles, clothing and footwear; wood, cork and furniture) fell from 48.7 to 34.7 per cent in Spain, from 45.9 to 40.0 per cent in Portugal and from 60.7 to 48.0 per cent in Greece, reflecting the growth of other manufactures such as intermediate, capital and 'non-traditional' consumer goods.[13] The change in the composition of industry was particularly impressive in Spain and modest in Portugal, while in Greece it was very rapid but insufficient to overcome the initial gap.

Massive investment played a fundamental role in the three countries' economic and industrial growth.[14] In Spain and Portugal particularly, abundant capital spending (and, in some sectors, foreign direct investment) led to the large-scale introduction of up-to-date machinery and foreign know-how in manufacturing, and stimulated competition. Together with the improvement in the sectoral composition of output, these factors contributed to the dramatic rise in productivity shown in Table 2.3.

Growth was also boosted by merchandise exports, which were increasingly directed towards the EFTA and EC countries and expanded at an annual rate of 12.3 per cent in Spain, 12.2 per cent in Greece and 8.5 per cent (to 1972) in Portugal, as against a rate of 9.1 per cent in the EC12. The share of manufactures in total exports rose rapidly to reach around 70 per cent in Spain and Portugal and 48 per cent in Greece.[15] Together with a growing surplus on invisibles, this enabled the three countries – Spain in particular – to step up their merchandise imports, including intermediate and investment goods needed for industrial and technological development.

As a result of the countries' opening to foreign trade, exports and imports of goods rose from 35.1 to 39.8 per cent of GDP in Portugal, from 25.8 per cent to 30.2 per cent in Greece and from 12.3 per cent (1961) to 20.3 per cent in Spain (Table 2.4). It is to be noted that Portugal's foreign trade included large flows with its African colonies, whereas Spain's had been checked during the 1940s and 1950s by political isolation and inward-looking economic policies. Including trade in services, the index of external openness rose from 41.2 to 60.4 per cent in Portugal, from 25.8 to 39.4 per cent in Greece and from 17.1 to 29.9 per cent in Spain (while in Italy it rose from 26.5 to 39.7 per cent).

The development effort led to large trade deficits, but overall balance-of-payments problems were overcome thanks to inflows from tourism,

Table 2.3 Evolution of economic indicators (average annual compounded rates)

	1960–73	1973–80	1980–85	1985–92[1]
(A) Real GDP per capita				
EC12	3.9	2.0	1.2	2.4
Italy	3.8	2.9	1.1	2.6
Spain	6.1	1.1	0.8	3.9
Portugal	6.8	1.4	0.1	3.8
Greece	7.1	2.3	0.7	1.1
(B) Industrial production (excl. construction)				
EC12	5.7	1.7	0.6	2.0
Italy	6.5	2.8	−0.7	2.1
Spain	11.3[2]	2.4	0.7	2.1
Portugal	10.1	4.7	3.4	4.4
Greece	11.0[3]	4.1	1.4	0.0
(C) Export volume				
EC12	9.1	4.6	4.1	4.1
Italy	11.5	5.7	4.4	3.6
Spain	12.3	9.4	9.3	6.4
Portugal	8.5[4]	n.a.	n.a.	9.6
Greece	12.2	9.0	3.2	4.6
(D) Gross fixed capital formation				
EC12	5.6	0.4	−0.8	4.2
Italy	4.7	1.5	−0.9	3.2
Spain	10.4	−1.0	−1.5	8.1
Portugal	7.9	1.1	−4.4	8.3
Greece	10.0	−1.1	−2.3	1.5
(E) Total productivity (real value added per person employed)				
EC12	4.4	2.2	1.8	1.6
Italy	5.7	2.8	1.1	2.5
Spain	6.3	3.4	3.1	1.3
Portugal	6.5	3.2	1.5	2.6
Greece	8.1	2.7	0.0	1.2
(F) Manufacturing ind. productivity (real value added per person employed)				
EC12	5.3	2.5	3.1	2.1
Italy	4.3	5.1	3.8	3.6
Spain	7.7[5]	3.1	4.5	0.6[5]
Portugal	8.6	n.a.	n.a.	n.a.
Greece	7.4	1.9	−0.5	−0.4
(G) Inflation (consumer prices)				
EC12	4.6	12.3	8.9	4.6
Italy	4.7	16.8	13.8	5.7
Spain	6.8	17.9	12.2	6.3
Portugal	5.2	22.7	23.2	11.0
Greece	3.3	17.3	20.7	17.4

Sources: (A) OECD, Historical Statistics and national Accounts. (B) and (D) EC, European Economy n. 54, 1993. (C) OECD, Historical Statistics and Economic Outlook; IMP, International Financial Statistics. (E) and (F) OECD, Historical Statistics. (G) OECD, Historical Statistics and Main Economic Indicators.
[1] 1985–91 for Real GDP per capita; 1985–90 for total productivity and industrial productivity.
[2] 1961–73. [3] 1962–73. [4] 1960–72, as reported in Baklanoff (1978). [5] Total industry.

emigrants' remittances, shipping services (in Greece) and, to a smaller extent, foreign investment. All these receipts reflected the phase of strong growth in the industrial economies of the West. Until the general international exchange rate realignment of 1971 and the free fluctuation of 1973, the external parities of the escudo and the drachma were fixed and the peseta was only devalued once (in 1967, by 16.7 per cent).

Improving terms of trade in all three countries and rising labour productivity allowed inflation to be kept at 5.2 per cent in Portugal and 3.3 per cent in Greece. In Spain inflation was higher throughout the period: 6.8 per cent on average, compared with 4.7 per cent in Italy. The 1973 oil crisis caused a leap in inflation in the three countries and Italy, reflecting their heavy dependence on energy imports: in 1974 the inflation rate rose to between 27 and 29 per cent in Portugal and Greece, to 19 per cent in Italy, and to almost 16 per cent in Spain.

It is not easy to assess the effect on wages of the repression of working class movements in the three countries before the restoration of democracy. The problem is complicated further by the fact that wage statistics for these countries are very unreliable and by the need to consider productivity trends and emigration flows. According to EC data, in Greece real unit labour costs for the economy as a whole fell markedly both in 1960 to 1965, before the coup, and in 1968 to 1973; in Portugal they fell until 1969, then edged upwards to regain their 1960 level by the end of the period. In Spain, after rising rapidly between 1960 and 1967, they remained broadly unchanged to 1974. In Italy, as in the EC12, real unit labour costs for the economy as a whole were only marginally higher in 1973 than in 1960 (Table 2.4). It is equally difficult to analyse the trend of unemployment in the three countries, since all had a large underground economy and widespread hidden unemployment. According to official data, from 1960 to 1973 unemployment remained constant at, or fluctuated around levels of 2.5 to 3.0 per cent in Spain and Portugal and declined from 6.1 to 2.0 per cent in Greece (while it rose from 5.5 to 6.2 per cent in Italy). However, these positive results were due to massive emigration; despite their rapid growth, the three economies were unable to create new jobs for the millions of workers released from their rural areas.

In contrast with the years following the transition to democracy, when the basic institutions of the modern welfare state were introduced, budgets did not present significant disequilibria in this period. Portugal, however, was burdened with the increasing costs of supplying economic assistance to the African colonies and fighting colonial wars: military spending accounted for some 40 to 45 per cent of total government expenditure in Portugal in 1973. Defence spending was also substantial in Greece. In this respect, Spain, like Italy before, enjoyed the advantage of being able to concentrate public resources on civilian expenditure. The ratio of general government expenditure to GDP rose in all three countries between 1960

Table 2.4 Evolution of economic indicators

	1960	1973	1980	1985	1992
(A) Exports/GDP					
EC12	14.8	18.4	22.1	25.5	21.9*
Italy	9.2	13.4	17.2	18.5	14.6
Spain	6.2	7.1	9.7	14.6	11.2
Portugal	13.3	15.1	18.5	29.3	21.6
Greece	5.8	8.9	12.9	13.6	12.3*
(B) Imports/GDP					
EC12	16.0	19.4	24.8	26.2	23.3*
Italy	11.9	16.8	22.0	21.3	15.4
Spain	6.1	13.2	15.9	18.0	17.4
Portugal	21.8	24.7	37.1	39.4	35.6
Greece	20.0	21.3	26.5	30.6	30.5*
(C) Exports + Imports of goods and services/GDP					
EC12	38.2	47.0	54.4	60.3	54.4
Italy	26.5	39.7	46.5	46.0	36.5
Spain	17.1	29.9	33.2	43.5	38.0
Portugal	41.2	60.4	69.4	78.7	62.1
Greece	25.8	39.4	47.1	54.0	55.7*
(D) Real unit labour costs (index 1980 = 100)					
EC12	96.4	97.5	100.0	95.9	93.1
Italy	98.5	100.3	100.0	99.6	96.3
Spain	91.4	98.4	100.0	90.6	84.5
Portugal	89.5	89.3	100.0	91.4	84.5
Greece	119.0	88.9	100.0	110.7	93.9
(E) Unemployment rates					
EC12	2.4	2.7	6.2	11.0	10.1
Italy	5.5	6.2	7.5	10.1	11.5[†]
Spain	2.4	2.5	11.1	21.1	18.4
Portugal	1.9	2.5	7.7	8.5	4.0
Greece	6.1	2.0	2.8	7.8	9.2
(F) General Govt. expend./GDP					
EC12	31.8	38.9	45.2	49.6	50.7
Italy	30.1	37.8	41.9	50.9	53.2
Spain	13.7	23.0	32.0	41.2	45.1
Portugal	17.0	21.3	25.9	43.4	46.1
Greece	17.4	21.1	33.2	48.8	48.3
(G) Net Govt. balance/GDP					
EC12	0.7	−0.7	−3.6	−5.0	−5.2
Italy	−0.9	−7.9	−8.6	−12.6	−9.5
Spain	n.a.	0.8	−2.6	−6.9	−4.8
Portugal	0.6	1.4	−3.8°	−7.4	−5.1
Greece	n.a.	−1.4	−2.9	−14.5	−10.6

Sources: (A) and (B) OECD, National Accounts and Monthly Statistics of Foreign Trade.
(C) OECD, Historical Statistics and Quarterly National Accounts.
(D) EC, European Economy n. 54, 1993.
(E), (F) and (G) OECD, Historical Statistics and Economic Outlook.
*1991, [†] From national data, ° Average for 1979, 1980 and 1981.

and 1973, but only in Spain did it rise significantly faster than in the rest of Europe (see Table 2.4). At the end of the period, general government spending as a share of GDP was therefore still far lower than in the advanced European countries. Public expenditures were financed mainly through taxation: in 1973 Spain (like Portugal) ran a budget surplus while Greece had a budget deficit of only 1.4 per cent of GDP (that year the Italian deficit had reached 7.9 per cent of GDP). In all three countries the role of the state in the economy was very important. At the beginning of the period under review, despite the low incidence of government expenditure, particularly in Spain, where it was reflected in glaring infrastructure deficiencies, and the fact that public industrial enterprises only played a significant role in Spain (somewhat on the pattern of IRI in Italy), the state largely determined the allocation of resources throughout the economy. In Spain and Portugal this was a legacy of the autarkic corporative state of the 1940s and 1950s. The means of production were privately owned, but firms were subject to strict control by a large bureaucracy through the administrative approval of investment decisions, credit and foreign exchange allocation, differential interest rates, tax rates and subsidies, and the regulation of foreign transactions. The guidelines of national economic strategy were determined by an elite of government officials connected with a narrow (especially in Portugal) oligarchy of large private industrial and banking groups (and big landowners), which were granted monopolistic privileges in return for their renouncement of economic freedom. During the period under review, state control of private activity gradually diminished and the government elite came to include more and more European-oriented technocrats. This liberalization was most pronounced and began earliest in Spain, where the basic decision to terminate autarky had been made in 1959 and licensing of domestic firms' industrial investment was abolished in 1963. In Portugal it began in 1963 and was given further impetus when Caetano succeeded Salazar in 1968. The state, however, continued to play a central role in the economy. In Spain a policy of industrial development was successfully pursued, though opinions differ on the contribution of the direct entrepreneurial function that state enterprises, in contrast with Portugal and Greece, filled in this period (see Martin Aceña, 1991); from 1964 formal 'indicative' planning was adopted (it existed in Portugal too).

The situation in Greece at the outset of the period was different in that a semi-parliamentary regime, not a dictatorial corporative state, had been in existence since the early 1950s and the industrial sector was much smaller than in either Spain or Portugal. Nonetheless, the intervention of the state in resource allocation through a panoply of regulations distorted the economy, particularly in the banking and financial sectors, creating favourable conditions for widespread political patronage and corruption. Like Spain and Portugal, Greece had basically followed an import-substitution strategy until 1960.

Table 2.2 shows that by the end of the 1960 to 1973 period the share of agriculture in total employment had fallen by some 15 percentage points in Spain, by 17 points in Portugal and by 20 in Greece, while the share of manufacturing industry had risen to about 25 per cent in Spain and Portugal and to more than 18 per cent in Greece. Agriculture's contribution to GDP fell by 10 to 12 percentage points in Spain and Portugal but only by about 2 points in Greece.

In summary, the strong growth of the three economies between 1960 and 1973 stemmed from a variety of factors. As in Italy between 1951 and 1963, economic and industrial growth was made possible by abundant capital spending and the plentiful supply of cheap labour, which helped wages, very low at the beginning of the period, to grow more or less in line with the rise in productivity. Political repression of the labour movement also served to keep labour costs in check, but the specific contribution of the political regime to wage moderation is hard to pin down: in all likelihood, the strongly repressive environment favoured strict labour discipline and flexibility in the use of labour rather than low wages *per se*.

The role of the state in the economy was very important in all three countries. Economic activity was subject to a host of regulations, which were only partly dismantled or simplified during the period. The impression is that only in Spain (and not without serious limitations) were the various instruments of state control actually designed and used to launch and support accelerated industrialization and not just to sustain the economy in general and ensure political and social control. In Portugal, the state's efforts were increasingly absorbed by colonial problems and by the financial and military effort of preserving the African empire.

As in Italy in the late 1940s and the 1950s, rapid and largely export-oriented growth was also made possible by the gradual liberalization of private industrial activity, which was opened to foreign firms, and especially by the liberalization of foreign trade. Spain first applied for EC membership in 1962 and signed a preferential trade agreement with the EC in 1970; Greece signed an association agreement in 1961; Portugal, a member of EFTA since 1959, began negotiations with the EC in 1972. External liberalization enabled the three countries (Spain in particular) to introduce modern industrial techniques on a large scale. It lowered the barriers to access of their products to the rapidly growing markets of the advanced European countries and forced domestic enterprises to face foreign competition. At the same time, millions of Spanish, Portuguese and Greek workers were allowed to emigrate to those countries, while the massive inflow of European tourists boosted the development of the tourist industry. All these elements of closer contact with Europe were also important in promoting cultural change and making an otherwise isolated population keen to establish a liberal political regime.

Spain, Greece and Portugal, like Italy, rode the long wave of postwar economic expansion that lasted in the West until the 1973 oil crisis and indeed made their rapid economic development possible. However, Italy enjoyed a very considerable head start, having launched its major industrial transformation more than a decade earlier, and was thus able to profit from about 25 rather than only 13 years of uninterrupted Western growth.

Transition to and consolidation of democracy: 1974 to 1985

While democratization in Italy went together with the beginning of the protracted postwar economic boom throughout the West, in Spain, Portugal and Greece the transition to democracy coincided with a severe world economic crisis that forced all the Western countries to make sweeping changes in their economic structures and policies. In both cases it is difficult to distinguish between economic changes that were associated with the return to democracy and those that represented responses to external developments.

The fall of the dictatorships occurred almost simultaneously in the three countries (1974–5), but the re-establishment of normal democratic life proceeded with notable differences from country to country (see Diamandouros (1986)). In Greece, where the military junta had only been in power for seven years, parliamentary democracy was immediately restored and the first free elections were held in 1974. In Spain, where the regime's end had already been in sight and its repressiveness had weakened in the last years before Franco's death (November 1975), the normal workings of democracy and trade-union freedom were restored in 1977 and the new constitution approved in 1978; despite (or perhaps thanks to) this interregnum, the transition to democracy took place in a smooth and peaceful way, favoured by a corporatist system of agreements among the social partners ('pactismo'). The great economic improvements recorded in the 1960 to 1974 period certainly contributed to this peaceful transition. In Portugal, by contrast, the sudden fall of the dictatorship in the April 1974 officers' revolution, which was a direct consequence of the war in Africa, was followed by political strife verging on civil war. Parliamentary democracy was restored in 1976, but the sweeping nationalizations that were carried out during the preceding two years produced major disruptions in the economy. These were later remedied only gradually, and then only in part (see Chapter 7, this volume).

In all three countries – just as in Italy – heavy dependence on energy imports made the 1973 oil shock create serious balance-of-payments and inflation problems. Inflation was also fuelled by the large wage increases that accompanied the return to democracy. The difficulty of financing external current account deficits led all four countries to increase their foreign indebtedness and resort to currency depreciation, which reinforced the wage–price spiral. In all four, investment slowed down drastically or contracted.

In general, however, compared with the years from 1960 to 1973, the period under review saw a pronounced weakening in both the stability of the economic trends in each of the three countries and the similiarity between them. It is thus necessary to offer a brief account of economic developments country by country.

The first ten years of democracy in *Spain* (where political uncertainty prevailed until the early 1980s) were marked by unfavourable external developments and difficulties of economic policy management,[16] coupled with structural rigidities and inefficiencies in the goods, labour and financial markets. This resulted in: uninterruptedly negative net fixed capital formation after 1974 (see Table 2.3; gross fixed capital formation declined from 28.3 per cent of GDP in 1974 to 19.2 per cent in 1985); a slowdown in growth from an average annual rate of 2.1 per cent in the years 1974–7 to one of 0.4 per cent in 1978–85; a severe and protracted banking crisis; and, finally, high inflation, which accelerated from 11.4 per cent in 1973 to 24.5 per cent in 1977 and then gradually slowed to 15.5 per cent in 1980 and 8.8 per cent in 1985.

Spain's response to the 1973 oil shock was slow and calculated to avoid political and social tensions during the difficult transition to democracy. As a result economic adjustment had still to be completed when the second oil shock hit the country.[17]

Minimal growth in domestic demand, rigidities in real wages and the labour market and the drying up of outlets for Spanish labour in Western Europe (in fact there was a massive return of Spanish workers from abroad) caused the unemployment rate to rise steadily from 2.5 per cent in 1973 to 21.1 per cent in 1985, a level almost twice that of any other OECD country (while industrial employment fell from 3.4 to 2.6 million between 1977 and 1985). The increase in public transfer payments and subsidies due to economic stagnation, the need to satisify long pent-up social demands and a fiscal reform that provided for devolution, causing the central government to lose control over expenditure, pushed up public expenditure from 23.0 per cent of GDP in 1973 to 41.2 per cent in 1985. Despite the introduction of a modern system of progressive taxation, the growth in public expenditure, together with persistent widespread tax evasion, caused a swing from a budget surplus of 0.8 per cent of GDP to a deficit of 6.9 per cent over the same period.

The stagnation of domestic demand and the growth of exports (favoured by a continuous fall in the effective exchange rate of the peseta) helped to bring the external current account back into balance in 1984–5. The 1982 devaluation had been accompanied by monetary stringency and structural reforms in industry, energy and the labour market. Long-term capital movements had been substantially liberalized by 1985 and wage competitiveness *vis-à-vis* other industrial countries, which had deteriorated until 1979, recovered impressively up to 1985 (unit labour costs relative to those in Spain's industrial competitors were 22 per cent lower in 1985 than in 1980). As a result of these developments, when economic activity picked up in 1985 Spain had corrected some of its most worrying macroeconomic imbalances and despite the relative weakness of its industrial sector and the persistence of structural problems (distortions in the labour market, lack of competition, inefficiency of public sector), was in a better position to face the challenge of entry into the EC on 1 January 1986.

Between 1974 and 1985 *Portugal* experienced severe economic disruptions. The nationalization of domestic banks and insurance companies, which controlled most of the country's large industrial firms, and of such basic industries as steel and shipbuilding in 1975 caused the public sector's share of national value added to rise to around 25 per cent in 1976, undermining private sector confidence and making the state responsible for almost half of total capital formation and for 27 per cent of manufacturing investment. However, the bulk of this investment was in uncompetitive industries, most of them in the very branches that other European countries had slated for drastic reduction. At the same time, Portugal's most serious structural problem, the near stagnation of agricultural production, instead of being resolved, was probably made worse by the collectivization of agriculture in the South.

In 1976 the first parliamentary elections were followed by the adoption of the new constitution, which provided for the irreversibility of preceding nationalizations. Although democracy was established, political instability continued to characterize Portugal until 1985. Strong domestic demand enabled the economy to grow at an annual rate of more than 4 per cent in the five years from 1976 to 1980, although a first stabilization package had been agreed with the International Monetary Fund (IMF) in 1977–8, and even in 1981–2, after the second oil shock, the growth rate was over 1 per cent, compared with an average of zero in the EC12. Despite the inflow of some 800,000 refugees from Africa, the official unemployment rate only increased from 2.5 per cent in 1973 to 7.3 per cent in 1982; it peaked at 8.5 per cent in 1985, when the average for the EC12 was 11.0 per cent. However, these positive results were achieved at the price of massive current account deficits (13.4 per cent of GDP in 1982), spiraling external and domestic indebtedness (government expenditure grew from 21.3 per cent of GDP in 1973 to 47.9 per cent in 1983) and high inflation (about 23 per cent a year in the period, with a peak of 28.8 per cent in 1984). A drastic change in the course of economic policy became unavoidable in 1983 to 1985 and was also a condition for IMF assistance. It led to negative growth and a collapse of investment, but also reduced inflation to 19.6 per cent in 1985 and to 11.8 per cent in 1986, and caused public expenditure to come down from the peak of 47.9 per cent of GDP in 1983 to 43.4 per cent in 1985.

At the end of the period under review, when the treaty of accession to the EC was signed (June 1985), Portugal still suffered from political and economic uncertainty, distortions in its productive and financial structures, an oversized public sector, swollen by the post-1974 nationalizations, and administrative regulation of its goods, labour and credit markets. Nonetheless, the country seemed to be emerging from a decade of upheaval and finally heading towards macroeconomic stabilization.

The division of the post-dictatorship era that we have applied to the other two countries does not fit the *Greek* experience, which can be best understood by breaking it down into 1974 to 1980 and 1981 to 1992 subperiods. This is because the most important change in democratic Greece occurred in 1981, when the Socialist party come to power after the Karamanlis years and Greece became a full member of the EC on 1 January.

From 1974 to 1980 per capita GDP grew at comparatively high rates, averaging 2.3 per cent despite a fall of 4.0 per cent in the first year as a direct consequence of the oil shock. Total gross fixed capital formation grew by 7.3 per cent a year from 1976 to 1979. However, private investment in manufacturing declined over the same period, perhaps as a result of the uncertainty in the political situation following the restoration of democracy. The economy's sustained growth reflected the social and political constraints, also at work in Spain and Portugal, which precluded adopting the necessary adjustments to the 1973 oil shock. Domestic demand was buoyed by rapid wage growth, which pushed up real unit labour costs by some 10 per cent between 1974 and 1978, and by expansionary demand management policies, while official unemployment remained below 2 per cent until 1979. The price of this performance was a postponement of necessary structural adjustments, insufficient modernization of private industry (where troubled firms took on even more debt), persistence of both large current account deficits (from around 6.1 per cent of GDP in 1974 to 5.5 per cent in 1980) and high inflation (rising to 24.9 per cent in 1980) and the continuous expansion of government expenditure (from 21.1 per cent of GDP in 1973 to 33.2 per cent in 1980, causing the budget deficit to grow from 1.4 to 2.9 per cent of GDP).

During this period the high level of state intervention in the economy did not diminish. The traditional links between state-owned financial institutions and large family-based private industrial groups continued to hinder development of entrepreneurship, access of new firms to the market, and industry's flexibility and capacity for adjustment in general. The traditional division of the economy into official and informal markets for goods, labour and credit was reinforced, the former basically being regulated from above, with a lack of clear market signals capable of activating appropriate reactions on the part of economic agents, and the latter mainly comprising the small business sector, where competitive conditions and behaviour prevailed.

The 1981 elections brought the Socialist Party to power. The new government launched an ambitious programme of social change, economic modernization and industrialization aimed at giving a new content to the newly established democracy. The experiment was carried out over two terms of office, 1981–5 and 1985–9. The first basically coincided with the initial phase of Greek membership of the EC, during which tariff barriers – but not other trade barriers – were rapidly dismantled; by the end of the second term Greece's trade with the EC had been almost completely liberalized.

While the opening of the economy was taking place, 'democratic planning' was launched (more in theory than in fact), with the aim of increasing investment, improving the structure of industry and promoting technological innovation so as to boost labour productivity and enhance industry's competitiveness. At the same time, the government intended to improve the conditions of workers, correct the balance of power in the economy and foster participation while restoring macroeconomic equilibrium. The results of the combination of contradictory elements in the first phase of the experiment proved disappointing. From 1985 onwards the government concentrated its effort on stabilizing the economy but only achieved modest progress even in this more limited field.[18] The post-1985 policies did little to remedy, and indeed may have, especially after 1987, accentuated, the most serious, long-standing problems of the Greek economy – above all, rigidities, lack of competition and a dearth of modern entrepreneurship (especially in industry).

From 1981 to 1990 per capita GDP grew by only 1.0 per cent a year, compared with average annual growth of 2.5 per cent in Spain, 2.1 per cent in Portugal and 2.2 per cent in Italy. This long period of relative stagnation was unprecedented in postwar Greek history and, moreover, was followed by another two years of less than 1 per cent growth, owing to the world economic downturn. Industrial production grew by just 1.0 per cent a year from 1981 to 1990 and decreased by 1.5 per cent in 1991–2. These results stemmed from lack of investment: the volume of total capital formation declined so strongly until 1987 that despite the subsequent turnaround its average annual growth for the decade was still zero, compared with 4.9 per cent in Spain and 2.7 per cent in Portugal. This lack of investment cannot be attributed primarily to excessive wage growth, as real unit labour costs, after jumping by 10 per cent in the first three years of Socialist government, fluctuated downwards and by 1990 were back to their 1981 level. A more important cause was probably the lack of confidence among domestic and especially foreign investors faced with what they could only consider adverse conditions: a government officially committed to a programme of socialist transformation; the increasing role of the state in production; an industrial policy focused on supporting traditional manufacturing branches that were obsolete by international standards; little progress in reducing structural rigidities in industry and scaling down administrative regulation of the goods, labour and financial markets; and the government's record of failure in seeking to eliminate the most glaring macroeconomic imbalances.

While official unemployment remained comparatively low (not more than 2.8 per cent up to 1980, rising to 7.9 per cent in 1983 and fluctuating around that level until 1990), the protracted stagnation did not even serve to bring down inflation. In sharp contrast with all the other European countries, prices rose in Greece by 24.9 per cent in 1980 and by an average of 19.0 per cent during the 1980s (18.6 per cent in the three years 1990–2). Over the same period inflation was gradually reduced in Spain from 15.6 per cent in 1980 to 4.8 per cent in 1988 (6.2 per cent a year in 1990–2) and in Portugal it fell from 19.8 per cent in 1980–2 to 9.7 per cent in 1988 (11.2 per cent in 1990–2). Despite weak domestic demand, the unfavourable export performance of an increasingly uncompetitive industrial sector, now operating in a liberalized EC trade framework, and the negative impact of slow European growth on foreign receipts from services led to large current account deficits throughout the 1980s, which caused the country's foreign indebtedness to increase. Government expenditure went out of control, rising from 33.2 per cent of GDP in 1980 to 48.8 per cent in 1985 and 52.5 per cent in 1990, with the budget deficit growing from 2.9 per cent of GDP in 1980 to 14.5 per cent in 1985 and 18.6 per cent in 1990. Subsequent improvement reduced the deficit to 10.6 per cent of GDP in 1992.

Despite differences in the policies pursued in the three countries, certain similarities can be identified in the pattern of economic developments in the first decade after the transition to democracy. In all three countries the fall of dictatorship was immediately followed by large increases in real wages and the political and social climate made it impossible for the authorities to impose the adjustments required by the first oil shock. In all three, the initial albeit inevitable institutional uncertainty, the depressive effect of political confusion on private investment, the jump in wages and the impossibility of denying long pent-up demands for better working conditions and social services combined with the negative factors at work in all the industrial countries after 1973 to make the rise in inflation, the deterioration in the current account, the growth in public spending and budget deficits, and the slowdown in industrial activity more severe than elsewhere. It is worth noting that, for the reasons mentioned above, Italy's performance in these fields was not much better.

The three countries' economic performance in this period had the additional, more serious, consequence of widening the gap with the advanced European countries, which had narrowed thanks to the enormous progress they had achieved in the preceding period. In Spain, per capita GDP had risen from 58.3 to 76.4 per cent of the average for the EC12 in 1960 to 1973; after peaking at 79.2 per cent in 1975, it decreased to 71.7 per cent in 1980 and 70.4 per cent in 1985. In Portugal, after rising from 37.2 to 54.1 per cent between 1960 and 1973, the ratio was back to 50.1 per cent in 1985. In Greece, after increasing from 34.8 to 51.1 per cent, it remained at roughly that level throughout the second period (51.2 per cent in 1985). By comparison, the Italian ratio, which had risen from 86.6 to 93.4 per cent in the earlier period, rose further to 102.5 per cent in 1980, and the same figure was recorded in 1985.

However, this sobering assessment of the three countries' performance needs to be qualified in three ways. First, it has generally been observed that industrial latecomers tend to catch up during periods of general international expansion and lose ground during periods of world recession. Second, in historical perspective, the economic cost that by any reasonable calculation can be specifically attributed to the process of democratization in the three countries appears to have been relatively small and well worth the result – a peaceful, comparatively rapid and successful resumption of democratic life. By contrast, one has only to think of the price being paid by the former socialist countries of Eastern Europe in terms of GDP collapse and economic and social disruption, let alone the dramatic economic and human cost of defeating dictatorship and establishing democracy in Germany, Italy and Japan.

Third, the exceptional per capita GDP growth achieved by the three countries in 1960 to 1973, particularly Portugal and Greece, was largely made possible by the emigration of millions of people abroad, at no small human cost. In 1973 to 1985 this outflow was stemmed by the drastic decline in the demand for foreign labour in the countries to which Spanish, Portuguese and Greek workers had traditionally emigrated. Moreover, Portugal had to accommodate 800,000 refugees from its colonies. Thus, whereas total population had increased by around 14 per cent in Spain and 7 per cent in Greece and had decreased by 1 per cent in Portugal in the earlier period, between 1973 and 1985 it rose by respectively 11, 11 and 15 per cent.

During this period agriculture's share in total employment continued to decline, but mainly to the benefit of the services sector. A similar shift occurred in the sectoral composition of GDP, although the reduction in agriculture's share was very small in Greece. The external opening of the three countries continued to increase. Productivity advanced at a much slower rate than in 1960 to 1973, reflecting the slackness of investment; only Spain recorded significant progress in 1980 to 1985 (Table 2.3).

From 1986 to 1992

After the consolidation of democracy in the first half of the 1980s, political life developed normally in the three countries during this period, which began with Spain and Portugal's full membership of the EC in 1986 and Greece's transition to full trade liberalization within the Community. The problems that loomed largest for the three countries were not those of integration into the EC open trade arrangements or participation in the common agricultural policy – trade integration had begun even before they became full members of the Community and only in Greece was the agricultural sector important enough to employ more than one fifth of the labour force – but rather the implications for their relatively weak economies of the Community's decision to establish a single market by 1993.[19]

As noted in the previous section, during the 1980s the Greek economy did not undergo fundamental changes in its basically negative performance. By contrast, Spain and Portugal recorded significant improvements in the second half of the decade, with notable similarities between the two countries, which also showed steadily growing integration with one another.

Between 1985 and 1991 the average annual growth of per capita GDP picked up considerably in the Iberian countries: compared with the first half of the 1980s, it rose from 0.8 to 3.9 per cent per year in Spain and from 0.1 to 3.8 per cent in Portugal. Industrial production between 1985 and 1992 grew by 2.1 per cent a year in Spain and by 4.4 per cent in Portugal where it was assisted by a surge in foreign direct investment (which had already accelerated in Spain in the first half of the 1980s). Unemployment fell from 21.1 to 18.4 per cent in Spain and from 8.5 to 4.0 per cent in Portugal, while the average rate for the EC12 only declined from 11.0 to 10.1 per cent. A crucial factor in GDP growth was the revival of investment activity. In the seven years the annual increase in gross fixed capital formation was 8.1 per cent in Spain and 8.3 per cent in Portugal, as against 1.5 per cent in Greece. Buoyed by the prospect of the single market, foreign direct investment is estimated by Larre and Torres (1991) to have risen from roughly 5 to 11 per cent of total investment in Spain between 1985 and 1989 (as against 2 per cent in 1980) and from 4 to 10 per cent in Portugal (2 per cent in 1980), while only increasing from 4 to 6 per cent in Greece (5 per cent in 1980).

Iberian investment and economic growth reflected the upturn in investor confidence as a result of some improvements in macroeconomic performance and structural and market reforms enacted in Spain beginning in the early 1980s and in Portugal from 1985 onwards. Inflation fell from 12.2 to 6.3 per cent a year in the former and from 23.2 to 11.0 per cent in the latter between 1980 to 1985 and 1985 to 1992. Real unit labour costs declined between 1985 and 1992 from 90.6 to 84.5 per cent of their 1980 level in Spain and from 91.4 to 84.5 per cent in Portugal; in Greece the ratio only declined from 110.7 in 1985 to 106.4 per cent in 1990, though it later fell to 93.9 per cent in 1992; it declined from 99.6 to 96.3 per cent in Italy. Whereas public finances were out of control in Greece throughout the 1980s, with an improvement only in 1991–2, in Spain and Portugal public expenditure in relation to GDP was stabilized between 1985 and 1990, only to increase again in 1991–2. The budget deficit diminished from 6.9 to 4.8 per cent of GDP in Spain and from 7.4 to 5.1 per cent in Portugal between 1985 and 1992, while in Greece it grew from 14.5 per cent in 1985 to 18.6 per cent in 1990 before diminishing to 10.6 per cent in 1992.

After losing ground *vis-à-vis* the advanced countries for about a decade after 1973, Spain and Portugal began to catch up again from 1985 and in 1992 recorded per capita GDP levels amounting to around 76 and 60 per cent, respectively, of the EC12 average. Over the same period Greece's ratio continued to deteriorate, to around 49 per cent.

The progress in implementing structural reform and reducing market rigidities, more pronounced in Spain than in Portugal, contributed to improved macroeconomic performance and enabled Spain to join the EMS, with the wider 6 per cent fluctuation band, in June 1989 (Portugal adopted a less binding 'shadow exchange arrangement' from October 1990, but was able to join ERM in April 1992). In both countries trade liberalization was accompanied by improvements to industrial structure consistent with comparative advantage, allowing them to secure larger export market shares, although Spain alone would appear to have achieved a significant increase in intra-industry trade as a proportion of total trade with the EC.[20] In both countries some of the labour market rigidities were eliminated and the industrial presence of the state was reduced. In this regard, Portugal took a major step in 1989 by amending the article of the Constitution that had made previous nationalizations irreversible.

Spain began financial liberalization in the mid 1970s, in contrast with the general pattern whereby trade is liberalized before the financial sector. Portugal's liberalization only started in 1984, but the country was able to proceed rapidly on that road, abolishing its monetary policy based on credit ceilings in 1991, allowing competition of foreign with domestic banks, and eliminating capital controls in 1992. In Greece, the new conservative government in charge from 1990 introduced macroeconomic stabilization measures to correct major financial imbalances, and policies aimed at deregulation and privatization. These policies continued with the re-election of the socialists (PASOK) in 1993.

Despite important advances in all three countries, the distance between their banking systems, stock markets and mechanisms of credit allocation and those of other EC countries remains considerable. Whereas Spain has made good headway towards a strong financial sector, the financial structures of Portugal, and especially of Greece, are still fragile, casting some doubt on their ability to cope with EC financial competition in the years ahead.

Conclusions

In the light of the foregoing review, we turn now to a number of basic issues on which the experience of South European countries can offer invaluable insights. The most fundamental is the interrelationship between democracy and economic development: do growing levels of income and economic modernization favour the adoption of democratic forms of government? Does the establishment of democracy foster accelerated growth?

On the first question, econometric studies of the empirical linkages between economic growth and democracy across many countries do not seem to show any automatic causal relationship running from economic development to democratic institutions and political and civil rights. This comes as no surprise, considering the many different reasons why people may value freedom and democracy and the many possible reasons for the collapse of a dictatorship: in Italy and Germany, for example, as well as in Portugal, Greece and Argentina in the 1970s, the collapse was due to, or at least triggered by, defeat in war or simply an unsuccessful military adventure. However, some empirical studies (see for example Helliwell (1992)) do show that higher levels of economic development generally tend to be associated with democratic forms of government and the establishment of political rights and liberties; in such studies the effect appears to flow from economic growth to democracy and not *vice versa*. This too is hardly surprising, as income growth is usually accompanied by improvements in education, migration from the countryside to the more dynamic towns and cities, shifts from farming to industrial activities and the external opening of a country: all such factors are likely to increase the population's quest for an 'open society', where civil rights, democratic procedures in choosing governments and social mobility are well established. Moreover, the complexity that an economy attains as it reaches higher levels of development makes further economic growth dependent on, and thus tends to create demands for, greater economic freedom, in the form of wider scope for initiative-taking, creativity, participation and decision-making capacity on the part of managers, workers and the population in general: these demands are likely to be associated with, or to generate demands for political liberties.[21] Of course, in such cases satisfaction of these demands will in its turn lead to further economic growth.

Although economic success in Spain provided the Franco regime with a precious asset in support of political immobility (as pointed out by Merigo (1982)), it seems that more than in Portugal or Greece the increasing economic and social complexities consequent to rapid growth created strong pressures for political change and democratization. At the same time, this rapid growth and the accompanying economic and social transformation made it possible to eliminate or reduce the major cleavages between the main sections of the nation that had long impeded social reconciliation and to marginalize extremist political forces (see Diamandouros (1986)). One way in which economic transformation unquestionably fostered democratization was the association of growth with closer contacts with the advanced, democratic countries through the development of the tourist industry, mass emigration and foreign direct investment. This is true not only for Spain, but also for Portugal and Greece. Moreover, in all three countries middle- and working-class incomes rose, even under dictatorship, enough to increase the consumption of radio, television, foreign travel and other items that spread awareness of political and social conditions abroad, thus producing an international 'political demonstration effect'. Likewise, in Italy the economic and social changes and income gains of the years of the 'economic miracle' of the 1950s helped prompt popular demands in the 1960s and 1970s for the transformation of institutions, regulations and practices that were perceived as outdated and related to an 'incomplete' democracy.

On the other hand, in a weak or shallow democracy a surge in popular demands for fuller democracy and civil rights, fuelled by intense economic growth and social transformation, may induce a dictatorial response as a way to deny those demands, which may be regarded by segments of the political and economic establishment as a threat to its power and the existing order. This seems to be what happened in Greece in the 1960s and, looking beyond Southern Europe, in Chile in 1973 and China in 1989. Such experiences illustrate that there is no mechanical link between economic growth and democracy, although the social and cultural changes associated with economic development will tend to engender demands for more democracy and freedom.

Concerning the converse question – the influence of democratization on economic growth – surveys of recent research work have led to the conclusion that 'the aggregate evidence does not support any significant linkage between the level of democracy and subsequent economic growth' (Helliwell, 1992) and that 'we do not know whether democracy fosters or hinders economic growth' (Przeworski and Limongi, 1993). This accords with common sense: the essence of democracy is free choice and majority rule, and faster growth is only one of the possible priorities of citizens, who may well prefer other goals (such as greater equality in income distribution or more extensive labour legislation and social security) whose implications for economic growth depend on the specific situation. And even where programmes to promote rapid economic growth are established as the priority, democracy is no guarantee that they will be formulated and implemented more efficiently than under a less democratic regime. Indeed, the opposite may occur, as in a democracy any major programme can only be implemented if a broad social consensus is created around it. Since this often involves accommodating divergent interests, in democratic countries where procedures to reach efficient social agreement have not been adopted the programme is more likely to lack consistency in its formulation and be subject to *ad hoc* modification in the course of its implementation.

In the case of Italy the transition to democracy after the war is commonly held to have been a decisive factor in the subsequent 'economic miracle' by reopening Italy to economic and cultural contacts with more advanced countries. For Spain, Portugal and Greece, whose economies had been opening up and growing rapidly since the early 1960s, the answer is less straightforward. The uncertainty connected with the transition to democracy probably impeded investment and growth in the years immediately after the end of dictatorship, but this is more a problem of *political stability*, which tends to favour growth, other things being equal, than of *democracy*. Moreover, the fall of dictatorship in these three countries set off claims for higher wages, better working conditions and social legislation, while the initially unsettled political situation and the need to appeal to voters in the first general elections made it harder for government authorities to impose the necessary adjustments to the 1973 and (with some qualification as regards Spain) the 1980 oil shocks. These factors aggravated a fall in investment, surge in inflation and swelling of public expenditure and budget deficits that probably would have taken place in any case, as occurred in Italy and other countries. But in historical perspective, all these adverse developments, like the upheaval in Portugal in 1974–6, can be viewed as the unavoidable short-run costs of transition to democracy.

In the long run, the establishment of genuine democracy, providing for citizens' active participation in all aspects of a country's life and channels for free and open public debate, would seem to be more propitious to economic growth than the fettering of freedom and creativity and the suppression of workers' claims. Here again the Italian experience is instructive. In the 1950s and 1960s organized labour was relatively weak and the essence of democracy, the possibility of replacing the party in power, was undermined by the widespread conviction that the chief opposition party, the Communists, who rejected the market economy outright, were hostile to democracy and would never be brought into government. This 'immobile democracy', which would remain until the 1980s, and the weakness of organized labour probably contributed to the 'economic miracle', curbing workers' demands and allowing firms to achieve high profitability and investment. It also had negative consequences, however.

First, when the trade unions eventually gathered strength at the end of the 1960s, they successfully pressed large wage claims and the adoption of social legislation all at once. The resulting pressure on corporate profits and public finances proved unsustainable and generated serious economic disequilibria, which were compounded by the difficult state of the world economy after 1973.

Second, due to the lack, even as a long term prospect, of alternation in government, a large segment of the population and especially of the working class, supporting opposition parties, felt excluded from public life, believed it had no stake in the solution of the nation's economic problems and was systematically hostile to any policy the government proposed, irrespective of its merits. This encouraged radical positions and demands that the system could not possibly satisfy. At the same time, it deprived

Italy of the constructive contribution of many public-spirited and civic-minded citizens.

Third, the fact that the opposition was unlikely to come to power also allowed the parties in power to flout the elementary principles of good government. Corruption and political patronage increasingly permeated public life. The shocking extent and gravity of such practices, which also contaminated parts of the opposition, would only become apparent in the early 1990s.

Another basic issue in judging the experience of Southern European countries is the role played by external influences, and in particular by the EC, in the process of economic development and democratization. There is little doubt that the paramount factor in the large economic gains of all four countries was the impetus imparted by rapid growth throughout the West. The gap with the more advanced countries was significantly narrowed during periods of international cyclical expansion.

Membership of the EC and participation in its liberalization polices was another important stimulus to economic transformation. In all four countries the prospect of EC membership and then the actual abolition of barriers to the circulation of goods and factors of production triggered improvements in domestic firms' competitiveness in order to ensure their survival and growth in this new setting. Such efforts included restructuring and modernization of industrial firms and, later, of financial intermediaries and financial systems; the elimination of administrative obstacles to the flexibility and adaptability of firms and of goods, labour, credit and foreign exchange markets; wider use of market signals as guides to the action of economic agents; and attempts to create a more stable general economic framework through the reduction or elimination of macroeconomic disequilibria. The impact of EC membership was perhaps even stronger for Spain, Portugal and Greece in recent years than it had been for Italy in the 1950s and 1960s, when the scope of EC policies had been confined to trade and agriculture.

Yet EC membership does not guarantee economic progress but only offers opportunities. Whether these are seized or not is up to the individual member state. In this respect, the latest opportunity and challenge, that of the single European market, is certainly not without risk. Indeed, if not properly faced, it could involve large economic costs for the member countries, especially the weaker ones. Spain, like Italy, appears to be better equipped to contend with the prospective difficulties. For Greece, which showed worrying signs of economic weakness throughout the 1980s and is now faced with disorder in its Balkan neighbours, complicating communications with its EC partners, the task is more demanding. Portugal seems to occupy an intermediate position in this respect.

While in all four countries EC participation seems to have provided a strong stimulus to economic transformation, in Spain, Portugal and Greece it played another fundamental role, which was absent in postwar Italy: it contributed to the process that led to the fall of dictatorship and to the stabilization of the democratic regime that followed it. In the three countries, as in the EC6 in the 1950s and in the UK before 1973, EC membership was a widely debated issue in many respects. It was opposed in Portugal, and more strongly in Greece, by a large part of the Left. But it was increasingly identified by important sections of the population with the goals of overcoming the political and cultural isolation imposed by dictatorship and of sharing the freedoms and democratic institutions characterizing EC members. In Spain it represented an important point of reference and an element of unification of democratic forces. Since the three countries had been refused membership as long as dictatorships were in power, the desire to join Europe was an important element reinforcing opposition to those regimes. At the same time, the presence of pro-EC sentiment in the movement opposing dictatorship helped reassure some Western powers and some internal forces, favorable to the establishment of democracy but fearful of its possible political consequences, that the end of existing regimes was likely to be followed by insertion of the countries into the stable political and economic framework of EC.

A final issue regards the role of the state in the economy. Some studies (for example, Larre and Torres (1991)) attribute the better macroeconomic and structural performance of Spain and Portugal compared with Greece after 1985 and their better position for meeting the challenge of the single European market to their faster progress in dismantling obstacles to market forces and reducing the state's role in the economy. Admittedly, this progress began earlier and has been greater in Spain than in Portugal, where the welfare state measures that characterized the fall of dictatorship in all three countries were accompanied by large-scale nationalizations in 1975–6. Experience suggests that in many countries the abolition of pervasive administrative controls and artifical props to obsolete, inefficient industries has simplified economic activity, reduced distortions in resource allocation, and promoted entrepreneurship, innovation and managerial responsibility. The cases of Greece and Southern Italy, on the other hand, contain evidence of the stultifying effect of an environment where the success of enterprises depends on political favours and subsidies rather than on competitiveness, efficiency and innovation.

While further action to give greater scope to market forces should be pursued, it should also be recognized that the recipe of reducing the state's role in the economy to the bare minimum and giving free rein to the operation of markets fails to address one of the most urgent tasks confronting the four countries, and perhaps the key problem for Italy at present. This is the task of instilling more economic efficiency and public accountability in the action of the state sector, and at the same time fostering a more responsible and respectful attitude on the part of economic agents and citizens towards public institutions, public property and public money. There is no alternative to progress on this front. The proper functioning of an economy, no matter how market-oriented, inevitably requires some state intervention, especially where industrialization is recent. Even leaving aside such obvious public responsibilities as defence and diplomacy, some public provision of services is absolutely essential. The broadening of free markets and the enhancement of competition themselves require the state to be strong and efficient in establishing and enforcing the 'rules of the game' in each market. The state must also perform, particularly in late-comer economies, many useful tasks in such fields as infrastructure, education and training, research and development, data collection and distribution, and enterprise coordination, especially in the case of industrial restructuring plans. However, as noted by Shapiro and Taylor (1990), in the less advanced countries there is a marked shortage of managerial capacity on the part of the state and a clear tendency to overlook the technical limitations of state intervention. Further progress therefore requires initiatives to upgrade the managerial capacity of the state and ensure greater efficiency in the public sector, together with a realistic restriction of public intervention to programmes that the state can be expected to carry out efficiently.

Let us remind ourselves, in conclusion, that in Italy, Spain, Portugal and Greece, the process of democratization unfolded along different paths and was shaped by each country's specific historical experience and political, social and economic circumstances. The economic transformation that preceded and accompanied the establishment of democracy also varied from country to country, with many differences but also with a number of similarities reflecting both the influence of the same set of external political, economic and technological developments and the existence of some characteristics common to all four countries. In a final assessment we should only like again to stress the particular role played by the strong drive for international opening and economic integration that stemmed from their participation in the EC.

In the years to come the new challenge facing the four countries will be to take part as full actors in the life and future progress of the EC, avoiding the risk of marginalization. The Community, for its part, will have to develop new initiatives in its relations with other Mediterranean countries, where the population explosion is a very real problem, and with the former socialist European countries now engaged in a dramatic struggle to create a market economy. In all likelihood the greatest impact of these initiatives will fall on the Southern members of the EC.

The interrelationships between democracy and economic transformation will certainly remain an essential issue at the world level. Let us hope that the studies of the experience of the Southern European countries make an important contribution to its investigation. Future case studies, however, will now have to embrace new countries: those of Eastern Europe, first and foremost, as well as some in Latin America and, we hope, China.

Notes

1. We adopt the term EC rather than the current title EU (European Union) to emphasize that our analysis is intended to be historical and does not extend to the time when the title EU was adopted by European countries. It should be noted that the majority of the work on this chapter was completed in 1994.
2. The authors are aware of the economic developments in the four countries that are treated at length elsewhere in this book. In this chapter such aspects are only mentioned in passing. The authors wish to thank Daniel Dichter for the editing of this chapter and Stefania Matteucci for assistance in the preparation of statistical tables.
3. It is important to recall that between 1881 and 1914 Italy underwent a first phase of industrialization, which reached exceptionally high rates in the take-off years 1896–1908 and covered a wide spectrum of sectors. There was no parallel to this in either Portugal or Greece and only a limited one, in the decades before 1930, in Spain.
4. See Fuà (1980). The advanced European countries are defined as comprising the European members of the OECD excluding Italy, Spain, Portugal, Greece, Ireland and Turkey. Fuà's study, commissioned by the OECD, is probably the best available analysis of the characteristics of middle-income countries that were late to industrialize and of the specific problems they faced in the 1970s in their efforts to catch up.
5. See Wolleb and Wolleb (1993) on Spain, Portugal and Greece.
6. On the causes of this failure and the present situation of the South see Trigilia (1992) and Sales (1993). Many of the indicators of economic and social development of Southern Italy were similar in the early 1960s to those of Spain, Portugal and Greece. In 1963, for example, while Italian per capita GDP was about 92 per cent of the EC12 average (and the figure for North-Central Italy was 109 per cent, exactly the same level as France), the figure for Southern Italy was 61 per cent: lower than Spain's 67 per cent and higher than Portugal's 39 per cent and Greece's 37.5 per cent. It might therefore seem productive to compare the experience of Southern Italy, rather than that of Italy as a whole, with those of the other three countries. However, such an exercise would be not only statistically difficult but fundamentally misconceived. For 130 years the Mezzogiorno has been an integral part of a unified state which traditionally concentrated the tools of economy policy at the centre – regional reform and decentralization were only introduced in the 1970s – and saw the Southern elite always play a prominent role in national politics. Southern Italy has never been a separate jurisdiction. Transfers of funds from the rest of Italy to the South have been massive. Thus, it would be misleading to examine political and economic developments in the South outside of the national context. On the other hand, it is important to keep in mind the limited value of many average national indicators used in this chapter for Italy, as they hide large disparities between the two parts of the country.
7. Between 1951 and 1963 the share of agriculture in total employment fell from 45.2 to 26.8 per cent, while that of industry rose from 26.4 to 36.1 per cent and that of services from 28.4 to 37.1 per cent. In terms of contribution to GDP (at

current prices) the share of agriculture fell from 19.8 to 11.9 per cent, while that of industry rose from 37.1 to 39.1 per cent and that of services from 43.1 to 49.0 per cent. On Italy's postwar economic development, see Ciocca *et al.*, (1975), Rey (1982) and Ricossa (1976).

8. As will be shown, these changes went far beyond the shattering of long-established vested interests on which Olson (1982) based his explanation of the divergent postwar economic performance of the victorious nations (Britain, in particular) on the one hand and Germany and Japan on the other. Although the type of organizational changes that Olson discussed were a factor creating the general setting in which the Italian 'miracle' took place, it is worth stressing that it was precisely in the institutional and organizational field that renewal in Italy showed major limitations, with serious negative effects on the country's development in subsequent years. In government departments and agencies, professional, trade and employers' associations, the legal and judicial system, the armed forces and the police, all too often the pre-war structures, procedures and high-level personnel remained largely unchanged.

9. On the process leading to Italy's decision to participate in the European Economic Community, see Willis (1971). On the effects of membership on the Italian economy's performance, see Roccas (1980).

10. Despite local differences, these manufacturing districts have a number of features in common. They consist of networks of closely knit, highly flexible, technologically advanced companies located in areas that specialize in specific branches of production. The companies, small and usually family-owned and managed, compete vigorously with one another but also cooperate in services, purchases and R&D. Industrial associations and local authorities play an active role in providing infrastructure, meeting local problems and maintaining contacts at higher levels. On this phenomenon, from which many important lessons can be drawn for industrial development in Spain, Portugal and Greece, see Pyke *et al.* (1990) and Scott and Storper (1992).

11. Putnam (1993) offers an interesting discussion of regional devolution in Italy, highlighting the importance of the historical differences between Northern and Southern Italy in terms of social development, political egalitarianism and the ability of citizens and entrepreneurs to associate and cooperate in the pursuit of common goals. These factors are cited to account for the fact that the regional reform produced widely divergent results in the two areas even though it had established an identical institutional framework throughout Italy.

12. In the ten years from 1950 to 1960, Greece and Spain had achieved average annual growth of respectively 6.0 and 5.1 per cent (while the Portuguese economy had only grown by 3.6 per cent a year). However, this rapid growth was largely a rebound from wartime and postwar economic contraction.

13. See Tsoukalis (1981), pp. 23–5.

14. Between 1960 and 1973 gross fixed capital formation rose from 20.4 to 26.8 per cent of GDP in Spain, from 23.2 to 26.8 per cent in Portugal and from 19.0 to 28.0 per cent in Greece. Over the same period it rose from 21.4 to 23.9 per cent of GDP in the EC12 and decreased from 26.0 to 24.9 per cent in Italy. Its average annual growth was 10.4 per cent in Spain, 7.9 per cent in Portugal and 10.0 per cent in Greece, as against 5.6 per cent in the EC12 and 4.7 per cent in Italy. In Greece, however, construction accounted for the lion's share of fixed capital investment (more than 70 per cent in the early 1960s, 65 per cent in 1973). For data on foreign direct investment in the three countries in 1966–76 and an analysis of its effect on production and trade, see Vaitsos (1982).

15. These data refer to 1975 and are reported in Bienefeld (1982, p. 110).
16. For 1974 to 1979, see Merigo (1982); for subsequent years, see Vinals (1990 and 1992). See, also, OECD yearly reports on Spain.
17. Some industrial restructuring took place in the late 1970s and early 1980s (according to The Economist Intelligence Unit (1989, p. 179), the contribution to manufacturing value added of the four traditional branches – steel, shipbuilding, clothing and leather – declined from around 28 per cent in the early 1970s to just 16 per cent in 1982). Nonetheless, in 1985, after a decade of stagnant investment, Spain's industrial structure still showed serious deficiencies compared with that of the main industrial countries, notably its inability to move into the fastest-growing sectors of world demand, generally sub-optimal size of firms and marked inferiority in the production of industrial technology (see Martin (1992)). An extensive programme of industrial reconversion was launched in 1984.
18. The Socialist experiment is analysed in detail in Tsakalotos (1991). See, also, Katseli (1990).
19. See Katseli (1989) for a discussion of the risks arising for the weaker and more vulnerable EC countries from the Community's new industrial policy, and Gibson and Tsakalotos (1992) for an analysis of the prospects of Spain, Portugal and Greece in relation to the EC's move towards full financial integration.
20. Despite the marked improvements in the industrial structure and export performance of the two countries, an EC study of developments in the member countries between 1985 and 1989 in 40 'sensitive' industries, ie, those that would be most affected by the establishment of the single European market, revealed dangerous weaknesses in Spain and especially in Portugal (see Commission of the European Communities (1990)). For other assessments of the future position of Portugal individually and of the three countries in the future division of labour within the EC, see, respectively, Corado (1990) and Neven (1990). For the results of a simulation of the overall effects on Spain of the creation of the single market, see Polo and Sancho (1993).
21. A major factor in the collapse of the communist regimes was the leadership's fear of acceding to democratic demands and its consequent refusal to allow the extensive participation, initiative and freedom of choice in the economic field that the increasing complexity of the economy required.

Bibliography

Alogoskoufis, G. and Christodoulakis, N. (1991) 'Fiscal deficits, seigniorage, and external debt: the case of greece', in Alogoskoufis, G., Papademos, L. and Portes, R. (eds), *External Constraints on Macroeconomic Policy: the European Experience*, Cambridge, Cambridge University Press.

Baklanoff, E. N. (1978) *The Economic Transformation of Spain and Portugal*, Praeger, New York.

Bienefeld, M. (1982) 'Impact on Industry', in Seers, D. and Vaitsos, C. (eds), *The Second Enlargement of the EEC. The Integration of Unequal Partners*, Macmillan, London.

Bliss, C. and Braga de Macedo, J. (eds) (1990) *Unity with Diversity in the European Economy: the Community's Southern Frontier*, Cambridge University Press, Cambridge.

Braga de Macedo, J. (1987) 'Portugal and Europe: the longest transition', Centre for Economic Policy Research (CEPR) Discussion Paper No. 163, London.

Braga de Macedo, J. (1990) 'External liberalization with ambiguous public response: the experience of Portugal', in Bliss, C. and Braga de Macedo, J. (eds).

Carli, G. (1993) *Cinquant'anni di vita italiana*, Laterza, Roma-Bari.

Ciocca, P., Filosa, R. and Rey, G. M. (1975) 'Integration and development of the Italian economy, 1951–1971', *Banca Nazionale del Lavoro Quarterly Review*, September, pp. 284–320.

Commission of the European Communities (1990) 'The impact of the internal market by industrial sector: the challenge for the member states', *European Economy*, Special Edition.

Corado, C. (1990) 'Portuguese industry and the effects of EEC membership', CEPR, Discussion Paper No. 428, July.

Dorwick, S. and Nguyen, D. (1989) 'OECD comparative economic growth 1950–85: catch-up and convergence', *American Economic Review*, vol. 79, no. 5, pp. 1010–30, December.

Diamandouros, P. N. (1986) 'The Southern European NICs', *International Organization*, Spring, vol. 40, no. 2, pp. 547–56.

Dolado, J. J. and Vinals, J. (1991) 'Macroeconomic policy, external targets, and Constraints: the case of Spain', in Alogoskoufis, G., Papademos, L. and Portes, R. (eds), *External Constraints on Macroeconomic Policy: the European Experience*, Cambridge University Press, Cambridge.

Ferreira do Amaral, J., Lucena, D. and Mello, A. S. (eds) (1992) *The Portuguese Economy Towards 1992, Kluwer Academic Publishers*, Boston.

Freris, A. F. (1986) *The Greek Economy in the Twentieth Century*, Croom Helm, London.

Fuà, G. (1980) *Problemi dello sviluppo tardivo in Europa*, Il Mulino, Bologna.

Gibson, H. D. and Tsakalotos, E. (eds) (1992) *Economic Integration and Financial Liberalization*, Macmillan, London.

Gibson, H. D., Stournaras, Y. and Tsakalotos, E. (1992) 'The real and financial sectors in Southern Europe: catch-up, convergence and financial institutions', University of Kent, Studies in Economics, No. 92/10, August.

Gorman, G. and Kiljunen, M. L. (eds) (1983) *The Enlargment of the European Community*, Macmillan, London.

Harrison, J. (1993) *The Spanish Economy. From Civil War to the European Community*, Macmillan, London.

Helliwell, J. F. (1992) 'Empirical linkages between democracy and economic growth', National Bureau of Economic Research, Working Paper No. 4066, May, Washington.

Katseli, L. (1981) 'Macroeconomic adjustment and exchange-rate policy in middle-income countries: Greece, Portugal and Spain in the 1970s', Economic Growth Center, Yale University, Discussion Paper No. 374.

Katseli, L. (1989) 'The political economy of European integration: from Euro-sclerosis to Euro-corporatism', CEPR Discussion Paper No. 317, October.

Katseli, L. (1990) 'Economic integration in the enlarged European Community: structural adjustment of the Greek economy', in Bliss, C. and Braga de Macedo, J. (eds).

Jacquemin, A. and Wright, D. (eds) (1993) *The European Challenges post-1992*, Edward Elgar, Aldershot.

Larre, B. and Torres, R. (1991) 'Is convergence a spontaneous process? The Experience of Spain, Portugal and Greece', *OECD Economic Studies*, No. 16, Spring.

Martin, C. (1992) 'El comercio industrial espanol ante el Mercado Unico europeo', in Vinals, J. (ed.).

Martin Aceña, P. (1991) *Ini: 50 anos de industrialization en Espana*, Espasa-Calpe, Madrid.

Merigo, E. (1982) 'Spain', in Boltho, A. (ed.), *The European Economy. Growth and Crisis*, Oxford University Press, Oxford.

Mouzelis, N. P. (1978) *Modern Greece. Facets of Underdevelopment*, Macmillan, London.

Neven, D. J. (1990) 'Gains and losses from 1992' (with discussion), *Economic Policy*, April.

Olson, M. (1982) *The Rise and Decline of Nations*, Yale University Press, New Haven.

Oughton, C. (1993) 'Growth, structural change and real convergence in the EC', in Hughes, K. S. (ed.), *European Competitiveness*, Cambridge University Press, Cambridge.

Padoa-Schioppa, T. (1987) *Efficiency, Stability, and Equity*, Oxford University Press, Oxford.

Papantoniou, J. (1979) 'Foreign trade and industrial development: Greece and the EEC', *Cambridge Journal of Economics*, vol. 3, no. 1, pp. 33–48, March.

Polo, C. and Sancho, F. (1993) 'An analysis of Spain's integration in the EEC', *Journal of Policy Modeling*, vol. 15, no. 2, pp. 157–78, April.

Portuguese Ministry of Finance (1992) 'From P1 to Q2: Portugal's strategy of sustained regime change 1986–1995', Paper presented to the Conference 'The Transition to Economic and Monetary Union in Europe' held in Estoril, 16–18 January 1992.

Preston, P. (1990) 'Spain', in Graham, A. and Seldon, A. (eds), *Government and Economies in the Postwar World*, Routledge, London.

Przeworski, A. and Limongi, F. (1993) 'Political regimes and economic growth', *Journal of Economic Perspectives*, vol. 7, no. 3, pp. 51–69, Summer.

Putnam, R. D. (1993) *Making Democracy Work. Civic Traditions in Modern Italy*, Princeton University Press, Princeton.

Pyke, F., Becattini, G. and Sengenberger, W. (eds) (1990) *Industrial Districts and Inter-firm Cooperation in Italy*, International Institute for Labour Studies, International Labour Organization, Geneva.

Rey, G. M. (1982). 'Italy', in Boltho, A. (ed.), *The European Economy. Growth and Crisis*, Oxford University Press, Oxford.

Ricossa, S. (1976) 'Italy 1920–1970', in Cipolla, C. M. (ed.), *The Fontana Economic History of Europe. Contemporary Economies*. Part I, Collins/Fontana, Glasgow.

Roccas, M. (1980) 'Italy', in Seers, D. and Vaitsos, C. (eds), *Integration and Unequal Development. The Experience of the EEC*, Macmillan, London.

Sales, I. (1993) *Leghisti e sudisti*, Laterza, Roma-Bari.

Sassoon, D. (1990) 'Italy', in Graham, A. and Seldon, A. (eds), *Government and Economies in the Postwar World*, Routledge, London.

Scott, A. J. and Storper, M. (eds) (1992) *Pathways to Industrialization and Regional Development*, Routledge, London.

Shapiro, H. and Taylor, L. (1990) 'The state and industrial strategy', *World Development*, vol. 18, no. 6, pp. 861–78.

Sirowy, L. and Inkeles, A. (1990) 'The effects of democracy on economic growth and inequality: a review', *Studies in Comparative International Development*, vol. 25, pp. 126–57.

Skouras, T. S. (ed.) (1992) *The Greek Economy: Economic Policy for the 1990s, Issues in Contemporary Economics*, vol. 5, Macmillan, London.

The Economist Intelligence Unit (1989) *European Community. Economic Structure and Analysis*, vol. II, London.

Trigilia, C. (1992) *Sviluppo senza autonomia. Effetti perversi delle politiche nel Mezzogiorno*, Il Mulino, Bologna.

Tsakalotos, E. (1991) *Alternative Economic Strategies. The Case of Greece*, Avebury, Aldershot.

Tsoucalas, C. (1969) *The Greek Tragedy*, Penguin Books, Harmondsworth.

Tsoukalis, L. (ed.) (1979) *Greece and the European Community*, Saxon House, Westmead.

Tsoukalis, L. (1981) *The European Community and its Mediterranean Enlargement*, Allen & Unwin, London.

Tullio-Altan, C. (1986) *La nostra Italia*, Feltrinelli, Milano.

Vaitsos, C. (1982) 'Transnational corporate behaviour and the enlargement', in Seers, D. and Vaitsos, C. (eds), *The Second Enlargment of the EEC. The Integration of Unequal Partners*, Macmillan, London.

Vinals, J. et al. (1990) 'Spain and "EC cum 1992" Shock', in Bliss, C. and Braga de Macedo, J. (eds).

Vinals, J. (ed.) (1992) *La economia espanola ante el Mercado Unico Europeo. Las claves del proceso de integraciòn*, Alianza Editorial, Madrid.

Williams A. (ed.) (1984) *Southern Europe Transformed. Political and Economic Change in Greece, Italy, Portugal and Spain*, Harper & Row, London.

Willis, F. R. (1971) *Italy Chooses Europe*, Oxford University Press, New York.

Wolleb, E. and Wolleb, G. (1993) *Sviluppo economico e squilibri territoriali nel Sud Europa*, Il Mulino, Bologna.

Yannopoulos, G. N. (ed.) (1989) *European Integration and the Iberian Economies*, Macmillan, London.

3
The Internationalization of Southern European Economies

Louka T. Katseli

Introduction: The Southern European model in perspective*

The purpose of this chapter is to evaluate the significance of internationalization for the consolidation of democracy in Southern Europe and to highlight those common features and processes that make up what can be called the 'Southern European model' of political and economic development. The study of political and economic transformation in Greece, Portugal and Spain is of heightened interest at a time when Central and Eastern European countries (CEE) struggle to deepen their democracies, and build market economies with a view towards integration into Europe. Despite differences in the order of magnitude regarding transformation requirements, what links the CEE experiment with the Southern European experience is the common challenge to combine democratic consolidation with substantial structural adjustment in the context of a global economy, which is characterized by rapid technological innovation, by trade and financial-market liberalization and by massive deregulation. During the last two decades, Southern European societies and economies had to meet this dual challenge, and, despite substantial difficulties and differences in national strategies, successfully did so.

At the start of the twenty-first century, all three countries have consolidated their democratic regimes and have managed to mitigate internal and external macroeconomic imbalances, by lowering their inflation rates to single digit levels, by stabilizing or lowering their debt/GNP ratios and by improving their current account and basic balance positions.[1] In all three cases there has been a resurgence of growth spurred by a sizeable increase in gross fixed capital formation (Table 3.1). Despite these favourable developments, the costs of adjustment, as measured by high rates of unemployment and growing disparities in income distribution (Table 3.2), make this process at best vulnerable to external shocks and to internal political and economic conditions.

Table 3.1   Macroeconomic developments

	1980–85	1986–95	1994	1995
Real GDP per capita[1]				
(growth rate-av. annual)				
Greece	0.7	0.7	1.5	2.0
Spain	1.0	2.7	2.1	3.0
Portugal	0.9	3.2	0.8	2.5
EU15	1.3	2.0	2.8	2.5
Gross fixed capital formation[2]				
(growth rate-av. annual)				
Greece	−2.3	0.7	0.5	5.8
Spain	−1.5	5.5	1.4	8.4
Portugal	−4.4	6.8	3.9	5.4
EU15	−0.8	3.1	2.2	3.5
Inflation[3] *(av. annual)*				
Greece	21.4	15.7	10.9	9.3
Spain	12.8	5.7	4.7	4.7
Portugal	22.2	9.4	5.2	4.1
EU15	9.8	4.0	3.1	3.1
Net government balance/GDP[4]				
(av. annual)				
Greece	−7.4	−12.8	−12.1	−9.2
Spain	−4.6	−4.8	−6.9	−6.2
Portugal	−6.3	−5.7	−5.6	−5.1
EU15	−4.8	−4.5	−5.8	−5.3

Source: [1,3] OECD (1996), Historical Statistics; [2] OECD (1996), *Economic Outlook*, no. 59; [4] Commission of the European Community, *European Economy*, no. 51 (1992), no. 59 (1995).

The sustainability of nominal convergence achieved so far will critically depend, *inter alia*, on the ability of these societies to enhance human development and to promote social cohesion. As Anand and Sen (1996) insightfully note, growth is a necessary but not sufficient condition for human development, which is defined as the enhancement of a society's capacity to improve present and future standards of living. What is required beyond growth for human development, is the empowerment of society to undertake public action so that unemployment and poverty are reduced, access to high-quality public services, most notably to health, education and training is available to all citizens, and broad participation in decision making is safeguarded. Failure to meet these requirements could easily slow growth, endanger economic stabilization, and downgrade the quality of the democratic process.

The central hypothesis of this chapter is that the Southern European process of political and economic adjustment has been intimately tied to the exigencies or requirements imposed by these countries' international-ization and more specifically by the process of European integration. These

Table 3.2 Economic adjustment

	1980–85	1986–95	1994	1995
Unemployment (%)[1]				
Greece	6.0	8.2	9.6	10.0
Spain	17.0	19.9	24.2	22.9
Portugal	8.0	5.9	6.9	7.2
Employment growth (%)[2]				
Greece	1.4	0.7	1.9	0.9
Spain	−1.8	1.0	−0.9	2.7
Portugal	1.0	0.4	−0.1	−0.6
Trade deficit (as a % of GDP)[3]				
Greece	−8.7	−13.6	−13.8	−15.0
Spain	−0.4	−5.2	−3.8	−4.1
Portugal	−12.0	−11.8	−11.1	−9.8
Capital income shares in the business sector (%)[4]				
Greece	43.4	47.8	50.5	49.4
Spain	33.8	40.5	42.5	43.4
Portugal	28.4	30.5	31.2	32.7
Adjusted wage share: total economy (as % of GDP)[5]				
Greece	75.8	71.9	67.7	67.8
Spain	74.6	67.8	65.7	64.9
Portugal	78.7	71.9	68.9	67.6

Source: [1,2,4] OECD (1996), *Economic Outlook*, no. 59; [3] OECD (1996), Historical Statistics; and Commission of the European Community, Eurostat DGII (1996), no. 8/9; [5] Commission of the European Community, *European Economy* (1996), no. 59.

went far beyond the usual 'consumption' or 'political demonstration'[2] effects that are associated with the convergence of tastes, with free mobility of capital or labour, with the development of the tourist industry, or even with increased awareness of political and social conditions abroad. On the economic front, they include the substantial structural adjustment of these economies to trade and to financial-market liberalization, and the pursuit of disinflationary macroeconomic policies that included the maintenance of an overvalued exchange rate. This policy mix, largely dictated by the requirements of nominal convergence imposed by the Maastricht Treaty, had negative effects on growth and employment, which were, however, cushioned by sizeable transfers provided through the Community's Structural Funds. On the political front, European integration has brought about substantial changes in the role and scope of national governments and in the incentive structure of national political activity. State authorities, in these countries, lost, in a relatively short period of time, their capacity to influence economic activity, through such traditional policy instruments as subsidies, tariffs, quotas, interest rates and exchange rates.

In doing so, they saw their political legitimacy as effective arbitrators of conflicting demands eroded and their capacity to safeguard social cohesion diminished. As a consequence, not only have their economies had to adjust quickly but the 'state-corporatist regimes'[3] of the past (Katseli, 1990) were weakened, bringing about significant changes in the content of political activity, in the role of political parties and in the conduct of policy.

Even though it is premature to detect the full effects of these changes on the evolution of the national political systems, there is no doubt that the integration of the SEEs into European and global markets has already had major distributional effects, with positive and negative repercussions. On the one hand, the process of internationalization has brought about the liberalization of markets, increased competition, greater transparency in policy decisions and enhanced efficiency of administrative and regulatory regimes. On the other hand, it has probably contributed to an increase in unemployment, the worsening of income distribution and the weakening of political participation. If further integration into European and global markets continues to be associated with higher unemployment, increased marginalization and greater vulnerability, then not only will growth prospects be negatively affected, but the political support for deeper European integration will be stalled. Furthermore, if the essence of democracy is 'free choice and majority rule' (Roccas and Padoa Schioppa, this volume), such an outcome will weaken democratic procedures and distort political outcomes. The major challenge for European and national policy making, therefore, at the start of the twenty-first century, is to strengthen further the democratic processes within a unified Europe by closing up the 'institutional or policy deficits' where these arise and by preventing social fragmentation through appropriate growth and redistributive policies. The challenges and the bottlenecks facing Southern European countries in the pursuit of these objectives can serve as a guideline for future developments in Central and Eastern Europe, where these tasks are infinitely greater.

The remainder of the chapter is structured as follows. The second section focuses on the characteristics of the internationalization process of Southern European Economies (SEEs) and its links to European integration. The third section analyses the structural adjustment of these economies necessitated by their entry into the European Union (EU) and more specifically by trade and financial market liberalization. The fourth section highlights the importance of foreign investment and Community Structural funds in that process as well as the role and effects of macroeconomic policy in the post-Maastricht era. Finally, the last section discusses some of the effects of European integration on the functioning of domestic political systems and on the role of national governments and draws implications for the policy mix requirements necessary to underpin structural adjustment with growth at the European and national levels.

The internationalization of Southern European economies: globalization, regionalization and European integration

The internationalization of SEEs over the last two decades is closely linked to the process of European integration, which is taking place in the context of rapid globalization of economic activity. The 'global order' of the 1980s and 1990s bears little resemblance to that of the 1960s and 1970s. The internationalization of product, financial and capital markets and more recently of labour markets via migration flows, is proceeding fast in the context of an increasingly multipolar world-economic structure. World trade grew apace outstripping output by a considerable margin throughout most of the 1980s. At the same time, foreign direct investment (FDI) outflows increased at the unprecedented annual average rate of growth of 34 per cent between 1985 and 1990, approximately three times faster than the growth of merchandise exports which was limited to 13 per cent and the growth of world output which hovered around 12 per cent (Katseli, 1993a; UN, 1992, p. 1).

Since the beginning of the 1990s, the US has no longer held an overwhelmingly dominant position in economic affairs. It has fallen behind the UK as a capital exporting country, while it has become the largest host country in international capital markets. Japan has emerged as a major industrial and financial power and a major home country of FDI outflows. Europe has proceeded fast to integrate and expand its own market in an attempt to regain lost market shares in world markets. A host of new important players – not least the dynamic East Asian economies – have increasingly made their mark on the world scene. Finally, Eastern and Central European countries are undergoing radical economic reform and are raising their claims in world capital markets.

New actors besides governments have been playing the leading role in the internationalization process. While, as recently as the 1970s, leading scholars predicted that, over the following 20 years, about 300 firms would become truly multinational, according to UN estimates (UN, 1992, p. 11f), the total number of Transnational Corporations (TNCs) in 1990 exceeded 35,000, with more than 150,000 foreign affiliates.

The process of internationalization has been underpinned by the explosion of technological innovation, which, has, in turn, affected corporate strategies. The rapid introduction and diffusion of new technologies has led to the creation of new products, has transformed production processes and has lowered barriers to entry in existing markets (Stevens and Andrieu, 1991). Moreover, in the fast growing, technologically advanced sectors, the growing fixed capital cost of R&D and of capital equipment, as well as accelerating technological obsolescence, have increased both the cost of entry and business risks and have intensified the need to increase productivity, through restructuring, to stay competitive.

Corporate strategies have adjusted accordingly. TNCs have taken actions to cut costs through technological upgrading or through reorganizing production at the global level, in a way that exploits local comparative advantages such as lower labour costs, specialized skills or geographical proximity to markets. In their effort to entrench home market positions, to reap economies of scale or to penetrate new markets, many companies have chosen to enhance their global competitive position through mergers, joint ventures, minority stakes in either companies or through non-equity collaborative arrangements. Thus, in the late 1980s (Figure 3.1), the number of mergers rose rapidly both at the national, Community and international levels (Figure 3.2).

The growing complementarity between commodities and services, itself a by-product of technological developments, has created incentives for the deregulation and liberalization of major services such as banking, insurance and communications. This process has, in turn, allowed the increased tradeability of services. Thus, by the late 1980s, the share of services in the world stock of FDI reached 50 per cent and services accounted for some 55 to 60 per cent of annual capital flows (UN, 1991, p. 15).

The world economic order of the 1990s therefore, had little in common with a world of 'post-industrial societies'; it could better be characterized as a 'knowledge-based global order', where TNCs emerged as principal actors, controlling not only an increasing portion of world trade in goods and services, but, more importantly, the pace and direction of international transfers of technology (Katseli, 1993a).

The peak of this international activity coincided with the post-1985 acceleration of European integration. The deepening and enlargement of the

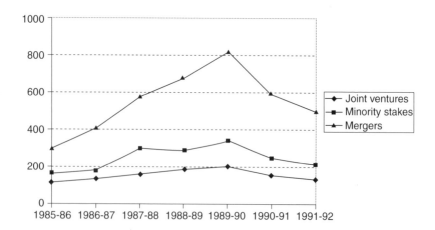

Figure 3.1   Number of mergers, minority stakes and joint ventures with an effect in the Community

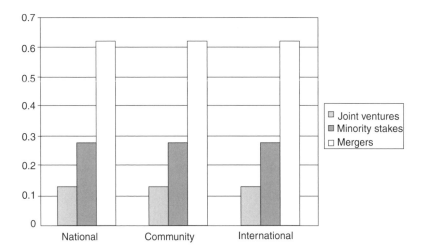

Figure 3.2 Distribution of national, Community and international deals (1986–92)

European Community, during that period, was, intimately tied to the change in corporate strategies spurred by technological innovation, by globalization and by the liberalization of capital flows in both commodity and service markets. Confronted with steadily declining market shares in third markets, especially in the fast-growing, technologically advanced industrial sectors, European firms sought to reap strategic advantages from the potential of a European Internal Market. As evidenced by official statements of the Commission of the European Communities (1989), the creation of the Internal Market was supposed to lead to four principal types of effect:

- a significant reduction in costs due to a better exploitation of economies of scale associated with the size of production units;
- an improved efficiency in enterprises, a rationalization of industrial structures and a setting of prices closer to costs, all resulting from more competitive markets;
- an increased flow of innovations in processes and products stimulated by the dynamics of the Internal Market; and, finally,
- adjustments between industries, due to a fuller play of comparative advantages in an integrated market.

Thus, the creation of a European Internal Market was expected to enhance the competitive position of European firms, through the provision of incentives for the development of 'regional core-network strategies', that is, regional internal networks that would exploit the comparative advantages of member-states and of European regions through trade–investment interlinkages. This expectation was largely shared by firms themselves, which proceeded to take investment positions throughout Europe and to expand intra-Community trade and business arrangements (Table 3.3). As a consequence, industrial concentration, measured by the share of top-five EC firms in total value-added increased in almost all industrial sectors, with the exception of construction materials, electronics and computers (Table 3.4).

In the light of these developments, both the deepening and enlargement of the European Community can be considered as institutional changes that were complementary to the trade and investment policies of European firms, which sought to enlarge and integrate their home base in order to protect their own markets and to enhance their productivity and competitiveness.

The second enlargement of the Community, in the mid 1980s, which brought Spain and Portugal into the European Union, can thus be viewed as a move consistent with the regionalization strategies of European corporations and compatible with the objectives of both national and European policy makers that gave new impetus and depth to the European internal market. Spain with its population of 39 million inhabitants, and its common borders with France, offered not only an enlarged market for European firms but also significant labour-cost advantages for production, relative to the European core regions. Portugal, a much smaller but very open economy, with common borders and significant trade with Spain, was a natural extension of the Spanish and European markets. From a domestic point of view, European integration brought about not only the effective enlargement of markets, but more importantly, the final act legitimizing the democratization process that started in the mid-1970s with the fall of Franco in Spain and Salazar in Portugal.[4]

In Greece, the integration process had started in the early 1960s with an Association Agreement. It was interrupted, abruptly, during the period of dictatorial rule between 1967 and 1974. The return of democracy, in 1974, spurred the resumption of negotiations, which were concluded by the end of the decade. The entry of Greece into the European Community in 1981 signalled, as in the case of the other two countries, the final acceptance of Greece into a democratic Europe. Unlike the case of Spain and Portugal however, Greece's entry into the Community was promoted mostly on political and geo-strategic grounds as opposed to economic ones. Domestic political parties were, in fact, deeply divided on the issue of the potential economic benefits from integration due to fears about the sizeable costs of trade diversion.

In all three countries, the process of European integration was two-pronged. On the one hand, it proceeded through the rapid liberalization of commodity markets, largely brought about through the dismantling of tariff and non-tariff barriers to trade and through a gradual deregulation and liberalization of their respective service sectors. After the implementation of the Single Act in 1987, this process was complemented by the

Table 3.3 Intra-Community trade and business arrangements (Breakdown of M&A operations by country, 1990–92)

Bidder/Target	B	DK	D	GR	E	F	IRL	I	L	NL	P	UK	Multinational	Total	Cross-border	% C.border/total
B	184	1	31	1	4	39		4	10	16		10	1	301	117	38.87
DK	3	522	28	1	7	13	1	2		14	4	47	1	643	121	18.82
D	16	23	2897	2	26	92	1	39	5	47	8	77	12	3245	348	10.72
GR				7		1		1						9	2	22.22
E	2		6		299	14		5			18	10	3	357	58	16.25
F	74	9	190	4	132	1884	6	100	4	39	19	118	16	2595	711	27.40
IRL			10		4	6	72	2		11		72	1	178	106	59.55
I	6		32	1	41	60		775	2	6		20	2	947	172	18.16
L	6	4	11			13		5	1	3		2	1	46	45	97.83
NL	49	11	101	2	24	31		10		646		40	2	916	270	29.48
P											7					
UK	43	14	193	3	59	135	18	35	3	90	5	3190	28	3816	626	16.40
Multinational	5	5	40	3	15	29	1	16		16	4	12		146	146	100.00
Total	388	589	3539	28	611	2317	99	994	25	888	68	3598	67	13211		
Cross-border	204	67	642	21	312	433	27	219	24	242	61	408	67		2727	
Austria	2		48		4	1		6		2		2				
Finland	4	13	40		9	13		4		10	3	22				
Japan	6	3	38		10	20		8		17		56				
Norway	1	13	5		6	3	1			3		15				
Sweden	16	64	69		21	25	2	21		28	1	40				
Switzerland	8	5	192		12	50	2	22		17	2	23				
USA	13	17	226	4	30	86	4	34		42	2	158				
Total	50	115	618	4	92	198	9	95		119	8	316				
Grand total	438	704	4157	32	703	2515	108	1089	25	1007	76	3914	67			

Source: Commission of the European Community, *European Economy* (1994), no. 57; Community Merger Control Policy, own calculations.

Table 3.4   Share of top five firms in total value added of each

Sector	1986	1991	Change (%)
Tobacco	58.39	59.16	0.76
Textiles	7.71	8.24	0.54
Chemicals	42.25	41.48	−0.77
Rubber and plastic products	14.78	21.71	6.93
Construction materials	28.39	24.29	−4.11
Iron and steel	47.21	82.31	35.1
Metal goods	9.79	11.69	1.9
Electronics	33.92	31.48	−2.44
Motor vehicles and parts	55.45	56.49	1.05
Aerospace	51.24	71.97	20.72
Pharmaceuticals	19.28	27.66	8.38
Computers	34.08	33.17	−0.91
Industrial machinery	20.07	20.1	0.03
Drink	39.73	43.24	3.5
Food	16.92	20.37	3.45
Printing and publishing	19.2	19.34	0.14

Source: Commission of the European Community, *European Economy*, no. 57, 1994.

harmonization of policies regarding taxation, public procurement, custom formalities, etc.

The integration of the SEEs into the European market and the deregulation rush it entailed altered the sources of competitiveness for their firms and the sources of comparative advantage for the national economies alike. Firm level competitiveness became increasingly determined by firms' 'technological capabilities', defined to refer to the 'entire complex of human skills – entrepreneurial, managerial and technical – needed to set up and operate efficiently industries over time' (Lall, 1987, 1989, 1990). National or regional competitiveness was, similarly, affected by each country's ability to mobilize domestic human resources, to increase local absorptive capacity relative to new products and services, and to enhance collective technological capabilities.

On the other hand, European integration has also been associated with the steady opening of these countries' capital account, due to the adoption of Community directives for a freer regulatory framework on both inflows and outflows. After the widening of the exchange rate band of the European Exchange Rate Mechanism (ERM) that took place in September 1993, short-term capital controls have also been lifted in all three countries. In the presence of free capital mobility, discretionary regulations, diverging business investment incentives or differential environmental rules can be easily bypassed, through appropriate pricing of international transactions in the 'internal market networks' of transnational companies or through appropriate relocation of selected business activities within the world marketplace. Furthermore, attempts by policy makers to spur growth or employment through the reduction of domestic interest rates can be thwarted by ensuing capital outflows, which deplete foreign exchange reserves and indirectly domestic liquidity. Fiscal and incomes policies are similarly constrained: even the expectation of future 'excessive' budget deficits or of high debt to GNP ratios can trigger offsetting capital outflows in anticipation of future monetization, of higher inflationary pressures and/or of exchange rate devaluation.

The move to wider exchange rate bands within the ERM and towards more flexible exchange rates did not succeed in reinstating the policy autonomy of national policy makers. As governments, private enterprises and even consumers became increasingly more integrated in world capital markets and became net borrowers in foreign exchange markets, the traditional advantages of exchange rate adjustment were eroded. Both entrepreneurs and national governments acquired substantial foreign exchange exposures. Under such conditions, any devaluation of the national currency implies a higher debt burden in home currency units, reducing the incentives for governments to deflate the real value of their debt through devaluation. Furthermore, in integrated markets, domestic variables such as wages, prices or profits are increasingly indexed to the exchange rate, thus, placing an effective constraint on governments' ability to adjust the real exchange rate.

All three countries thus had to face the same policy challenge: namely, to foster the necessary rapid structural change in their productive and technological capabilities without recourse to traditional policy tools, aimed at protecting domestic production and employment. In doing so, they had to operate under the constraints derived from their Community standing. These included, *inter alia*, first, the inability to use freely, protectionist trade or finance-related measures such as tariffs, quotas, subsidized interest rates or preferential tax treatment that could be used to provide incentives for the reallocation of resources. Second, there was the loss of autonomy in monetary and exchange rate policy, that was largely dictated by Germany's interest rate policy, by the anti-inflationary bias of European and national policies and by the functioning of the ERM. The final constraint was the commitment to curtail drastically the government deficit and the indebtedness of the public sector in light of the Maastricht criteria and the negotiated timetable for the creation of an Economic and Monetary Union (EMU) by the end of the decade.

Despite the common application of these constraints across the SEEs, there seem to be some important differences across them that can explain, to a large extent, the differential path of adjustment of these countries to liberalization and integration. Five characteristics stand out as the most important differences between them: size; distance from the industrial centre of

Europe; industrial tradition; speed and sequencing of policy reforms in relation to the time of entry into the Community; and the quality of their
administrative and political system, following the return to democratic rule.

As will be shown in the following sections of the chapter, Spain's large
size, its long industrial tradition[5] and its proximity to the European core
market have made it a profitable location for FDI. The relative stability of
its political system and the relatively superior quality of its administrative
apparatus have provided an environment more conducive to growth and
to structural change, than is the case in the other two countries. Spain also
completed its financial reform in the early 1980s, prior to its accession to
the Community, so that trade liberalization and the internationalization of
capital markets took place in the context of a financially sound system[6]
(Vinals *et al.*, 1990). Despite Portugal's small size, its common borders with
Spain, its significant industrial tradition[7] and its successful stabilization
programmes prior to accession make it a case comparable to that of Spain's,
with which it forms an almost integrated market.

Greece, on the other hand, did not share any of these characteristics at the
time of integration. Its market was historically both small and relatively isolated. Its industrial base was limited. Its administrative system was inefficient
and its institutional system was still highly centralized and fragile. The internationalization and the liberalization of its economy, which accelerated in
the mid-1980s, coincided with a period of major political and financial
reforms. On the political side, the 1980s saw the consolidation of a two-party
system, the decentralization of central government authority towards the
regions and the introduction of major legislative reforms in all areas of social
life. On the economic side, trade liberalization promoted through the gradual reduction of trade barriers coincided with financial liberalization which
was manifested by the dissolution of the Monetary Committee in 1983 and
by the subsequent rationalization of the country's interest rate structure[8]
(Katseli, 1990). The concurrent liberalization of commodity markets and the
reform of the banking system made the burden of adjustment for Greece's
industrial sector more severe than was the case in the other two SEEs.

In conclusion, the effects of internationalization and of European integration on the SEEs have to be analysed in the context not only of the new
global and European market realities, but also in the context of initial conditions and policy choices of the SEEs themselves. It is this which is
attempted in the next section.

Trade and financial market liberalization

The liberalization of commodity markets, through the dismantling of trade
barriers, accelerated in all three countries after 1986. In view of Greece's
earlier accession into the Community, the liberalization spanned a longer
period of time. By 1989, Greek trade *vis-à-vis* Community countries was
almost completely liberalized. Three phases can be distinguished in the

process of integration of the Greek economy: the first, which coincides with the period of Association (1962–81), was characterized by the gradual elimination of tariff barriers coupled with the active use of domestic policy instruments (for example, differential indirect tax rates on imports) for the selective protection of industrial activity.

The second period (1981–6) was characterized by a faster dismantling of existing trade barriers, especially of tariffs and quotas and initial steps towards the liberalization of capital markets. These measures were, however, supplemented by a series of measures aimed at the restructuring of industrial activity and at prolonging the real protection afforded to selected industrial sectors, mainly through the use of non-tariff barriers.[9]

Nominal trade liberalization did not take place with equal force across all sectors. Whereas, throughout the decade, nominal protection rates declined continuously for imports in traditional sectors and for consumer goods, between 1980 and 1985 nominal protection increased in the case of import-competing, capital-good sectors. If domestic production taxes and subsidies are also taken into account, it appears that, in the first part of the 1980s, effective protection in fact increased for intermediate goods and manufacturing equipment and declined only slightly for manufactured consumer goods (Katseli, 1990). Thus, at least until 1987, the decline of nominal tariff protection for imports from the EU countries was largely offset by domestic subsidies and the imposition of domestic taxation.

The third period, 1987–9, was characterized by the gradual elimination of export subsidies and by the dismantling of import credit restrictions. On 1 January 1989, the regulatory tax on imports was abolished. By that time, export subsidies accounted for less than 10 per cent of their corresponding level at the end of 1986. They were completely abolished at the beginning of 1990. Since that time, there has been considerable progress towards public procurement liberalization. Furthermore, important steps have been taken towards the liberalization of the domestic financial system as well as of international transactions in services and of international short-term capital flows (see Chapter 8 in this volume).

In the case of Spain, the magnitude and sequence of its trade liberalization are derived from the clauses of its Treaty of Accession signed with the EU. While Spain got rid of most of its quantitative restrictions in 1986, the timetable for tariff reduction on all other goods spanned the period 1986 to 1993, with an annual decline ranging from 10 per cent to 15 per cent (Vinals *et al.*, 1990, p. 201). For example, while tariff reductions for agricultural goods were to be completed by 1 January 1993, the timetable for fruits, vegetables and vegetable fats was extended to 1 January 1996. As in the case of Spain, Portugal joined the Community in 1986. Its period of transition towards full integration extended to 1996.

The trade liberalization process in both Spain and Portugal, that started in 1986, coincided with a substantial drop in world energy prices as well as with an upturn in economic activity in the major economies (Vinals *et al.*,

1990, p. 195). This relatively favourable external environment eased the burden of trade adjustment in these two economies and contributed to a more favourable economic outcome than was the case in Greece, which had initiated its liberalization process under adverse external conditions.

As trade barriers were progressively lowered in all three countries, relatively high-cost domestic suppliers, especially those that were more heavily protected, were expected to be displaced by lower-cost production from the EU. On the other hand, export growth was also expected to pick up, especially as a consequence of greater specialization towards activities in which each country possessed a comparative advantage relative to its European partners. The actual trade adjustment of the SEEs however, revealed that the elimination of tariffs and quantitative restrictions had negative repercussions for competitiveness which were reflected in substantial import penetration and in the gradual worsening of the trade balance.

Trade-creation effects were small. The evolution of each economy's openness – a good indicator of 'trade-creation' effects – measured by the ratio of total foreign trade to GDP, is presented in Figure 3.3. At current prices, Portugal, the most open economy of all, exhibited a steady increase in the trade/GDP ratio between 1985 and 1990, but experienced a significant decline after that time. Greece's openness, increased between 1980 and 1985, but remained relatively stable in the late 1980s. The same picture emerges for Spain whose trade openness increases, immediately following accession, but is subsequently reduced. Thus, 'trade-creation' effects due to structural trade adjustment were probably small in the case of all three SEEs.

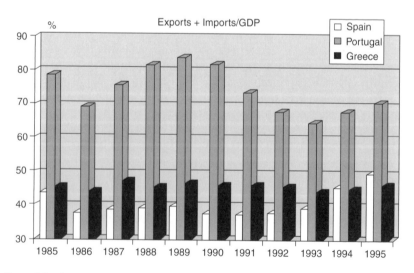

Figure 3.3   Openness indices
Source: *European Economy,* 1995 No 59.

Preferential regional trading with the EU due to integration were also expected to gave rise to 'trade-diversion' effects, as low-cost, third-country producers were squeezed out either by higher cost EU exporters due to the application of the Common European external tariff or by domestic producers. The share of total imports coming from other Community trading partners at the expense of non-members rose dramatically after accession. As can be seen in Tables 3.5a to 3.5c, within a year of their respective accession to the European Union, the SEE's trade balance with the other EU member states deteriorated sharply and the trend continued for the following years. In the case of Spain and Portugal the value of imports from the other Community members more than tripled in three years.

While import penetration from Community countries was especially severe in the case of the Iberian countries, trade reallocation effects, as such, were more pronounced in Greece. Its trade with third countries shrunk considerably and its agricultural trade was redirected towards its European partners. Between 1980 and 1982, agricultural imports from the Community increased by 55 per cent, while imports from third countries declined sharply. Between 1985 and 1989, that is, during the period when all protective trade taxes and subsidies were eliminated, the share of Greece's exports directed to the EU rose from 54 per cent of total exports to 66 per cent and the share of its imports from the EU rose from 48 per cent to 63 per cent (Figure 3.4). It was, probably, the fear of significant trade diversion that prompted Spain to negotiate the postponement of tariff reduction for agricultural goods till 1996, even though on the eve of EU membership, foodstuffs were just about 11 per cent of its total exports of goods and 3 per cent of total imports (Vinals *et al.*, 1990, p. 15).

The presence of trade-reallocation effects, a proxy for trade-diversion effects, was also manifested in the cases of Spain and Portugal. While in 1986, only 50 per cent of Spanish imports came from the EU, by 1990, this ratio increased to 63 per cent (Figure 3.5). Similarly, while in 1986, 60 per cent of Spanish exports were directed to the EU market, the corresponding ratio in 1990 was 72 per cent. In Portugal, both the share of its imports from the EU as well as the share of its exports directed to the EU rose dramatically following accession at the expense of the rest of the world (Figure 3.6). For both countries, Germany and France have been the largest trading partners.

According to all empirical studies, both Portugal's and Greece's trade pattern deviates from the rest of the Community. In both cases intra-industry trade[10] was small relative to the structure of trade in the other European countries. While the share of intra-industry trade in intra-EC trade was only 31 per cent in Greece and 37 per cent in Portugal, the corresponding ratio for Spain was 64 per cent and for France 83 per cent (Table 3.6). The large share of inter-industry trade in the cases of Greece and Portugal suggests that the pattern of specialization was still dictated, at least till the early 1990s, by

Table 3.5 Trade balances (million $)

a Greece

	1980				1981				1982				1983			
	Export	Import	Balance (X−M)	Δ% Improvement	Export	Import	Balance (X−M)	Δ% Improvement	Export	Import	Balance (X−M)	Δ% Improvement	Export	Import	Balance (X−M)	Δ% Improvement
Greece – EC	2534	4340	−1806		1870	4494	−2624	−45.29	2038	4739	−2701	−2.93	2340	4709	−2369	12.29
Greece – Third countries	2619	6208	−3589		2376	4316	−1940	45.95	2260	5287	−3027	−56.03	2073	4791	−2718	10.21
Total	5153	10548	−5395		4246	8810	−4564	15.40	4298	10026	−5728	−25.50	4413	9500	−5087	11.19

Source: IMF: Direction of Trade and Investment Statistics 1987, 1992.

b Spain

	1985				1986				1987				1988			
	Export	Import	Balance (X−M)	Δ% Improvement	Export	Import	Balance (X−M)	Δ% Improvement	Export	Import	Balance (X−M)	Δ% Improvement	Export	Import	Balance (X−M)	Δ% Improvement
Spain – EC	12645	11041	1604		16417	17665	−1248	−177.81	21823	26818	−4995	−300.24	26497	34430	−7933	−58.82
Spain – Third	9602	18922	−9320		10789	17392	−6603	29.15	12369	22295	−9926	−5900.33	13844	25213	−11369	−14.54
Total	22247	29963	−7716		27206	35057	−7851	−1.75	34192	49113	−14921	−90.05	40341	59643	−19302	−29.36

Source: IMF: Direction of Trade and Investment Statistics 1987, 1992.

c Portugal

	1985				1986				1987				1988			
	Export	Import	Balance (X−M)	Δ% Improvement	Export	Import	Balance (X−M)	Δ% Improvement	Export	Import	Balance (X−M)	Δ% Improvement	Export	Import	Balance (X−M)	Δ% Improvement
Portugal – EC	3536	3510.4	25.6		4944	5692	−748	−3021.88	6693	9289.7	−2596.7	−247.15	7827.1	11539.5	−3712.4	−42.97
Portugal – Third countries	2149.1	3542	−1392.9		2297.6	3957.4	−1659.8	−19.16	2627.4	4676.9	−2049.5	−23.48	3162.2	6326.3	−3164.1	−54.38
Total	5685.1	7052.4	−1367.3		7241.6	9649.4	−2407.8	−76.10	9320.4	13966.6	−4646.2	−92.96	10989.3	17865.8	−6876.5	−48.00

Source: IMF: Direction of Trade and Investment Statistics 1987, 1992.

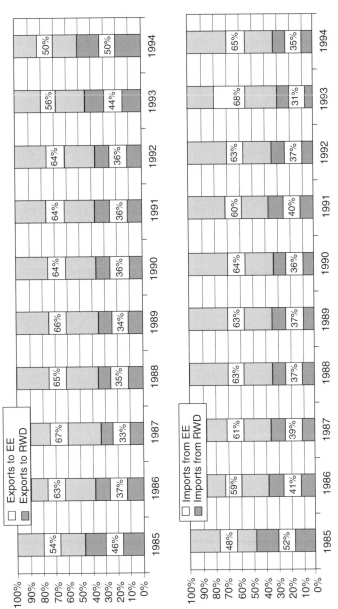

Figure 3.4 Geographic concentration of Greek trade
Source: OECD, 1996 Country Report: Greece.

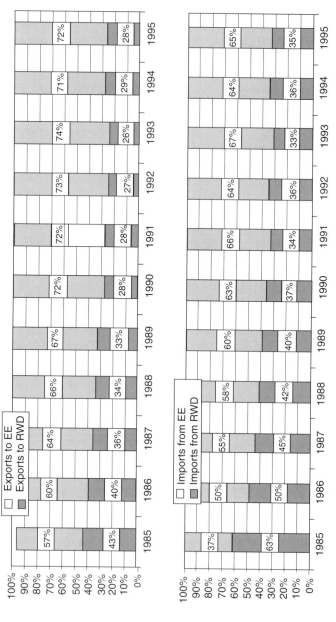

Figure 3.5 Geographic concentration of Spanish trade
Source: OECD, 1996 Country Report: Spain.

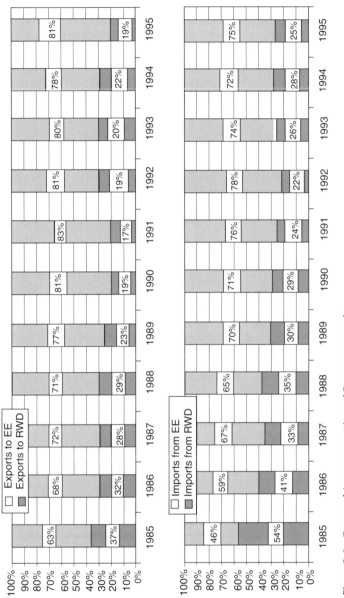

Figure 3.6 Geographic concentration of Portuguese trade
Source: OECD, 1996 Country Report: Portugal.

Table 3.6   Share of intra-industry trade in intra-EC trade

	1970	*1980*	*1987*	*Δ% 1980–87*
Belgium – Luxembourg	0.69	0.76	0.77	0.01
Denmark	0.41	0.52	0.57	0.05
Germany	0.73	0.78	0.76	−0.02
Greece	0.22	0.24	0.31	0.07
Spain	0.35	0.57	0.64	0.07
France	0.76	0.83	0.83	0.00
Ireland	0.36	0.61	0.62	0.01
Italy	0.63	0.55	0.57	0.02
Netherlands	0.67	0.73	0.76	0.03
Portugal	0.23	0.32	0.37	0.05
UK	0.74	0.81	0.77	−0.04

Source: Commission of the European Community, *European Economy* (1995).

relative factor endowments and by traditional comparative advantage considerations. According to the theory, liberalization is expected, in such cases, to favour the expansion of the more traditional, resource-based or unskilled labour-intensive sectors, which use extensively the abundant factors of production at the expense of the more modern, capital intensive sectors.

From a political point of view, the distributional implications of this hypothesis would amount to potential gains from integration for unskilled labour, mostly in the export-oriented industrial sectors, and for those agricultural producers who could expand agricultural production in the enlarged and unified European market. It should be realized, however, that the effective protection offered to northern European producers, through the workings of the Common Agricultural Policy (CAP), in conjunction with trade preferential agreements for Mediterranean products signed by the Community under the Lomé Convention, minimized the expected income gains from trade for southern agricultural producers.

In the case of Spain, on the other hand, the presence of a large share of intra-industry trade in intra-Community trade suggests that comparative advantage was based more on economies of scale or economies of scope and that liberalization would tend to favour the expansion of differentiated products across sectoral categories. From a distributional point of view, this would imply more diffused income gains from trade for Spanish industrial producers and workers, as opposed to the more sector-specific gains expected for Portuguese and Greek labour.

Despite these differences, all three Southern European countries experienced a rapid and generalized deterioration in almost all sectors of economic activity as measured by their revealed comparative advantage.[11] This suggests that their productive industrial structures, heavily protected for a long period of time, had been severely distorted and were largely inefficient, compared to the European core countries. As analysed in the case of Greece and of Spain (Katseli, 1990; Vinals *et al.*, 1990), this was due largely to the workings of the financial system, which, for a long period of time, during the 1960s and 1970s, subsidized, through preferential access and negative interest rates, export-orientated industries. The result of such policies was to overcapitalize those industries that enjoyed access to the financial system and undercapitalize those that did not. This tendency was exacerbated by the widespread holdings of industrial enterprises through majority or minority stakes by banks and by public-sector financial institutions. As a result, when financial liberalization and deregulation raised interest rates to positive levels during the early 1980s, those firms, which were not financially sound enough to compete effectively in world markets, became rapidly overindebted. The industrial crisis that erupted was immediately translated into a banking crisis as debts accumulated and bank portfolios depreciated in real terms. Trade and financial liberalization were thus associated with the decline in industrial activity, the worsening of competitiveness, the rise of unemployment and the aggravation of regional inequalities.

Figure 3.7 presents the evolution of Portugal's revealed comparative advantage measured by the ratio of exports to imports in each sector divided by the overall export/import ratio for manufacturing (OECD, Country Report, p. 24). What is striking is Portugal's post-1986 sharp deterioration of competitiveness especially in its labour-intensive industries, which comprise the larger part of its export base. A similar picture emerges

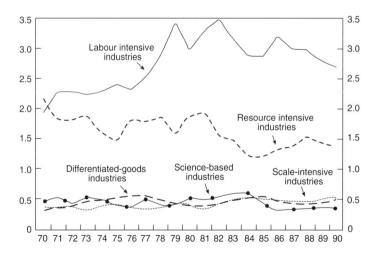

Figure 3.7 Evolution of Portugal's revealed comparative advantage
(As measured by the ratio of exports to imports in the sector divided by the overall export/import ratio for manufacturing)
Source: OECD. *Foreign Trade Statistics. Series C.*

for Greece. Sectoral trade competitiveness deteriorated in all sectors except in basic materials and tobacco, paper and printing (Katseli, 1990, p. 288). Among manufactures, the evidence reveals a slight shift in favour of resource-intensive industries, while the picture for differentiated-good or scale-intensive industries remains largely unchanged.

Before entry, Spain's merchandise trade exhibited a continuous but shrinking revealed comparative disadvantage in the more science-based, strong-demand products, a stable comparative disadvantage in moderate-demand products and an increasing comparative advantage in weak-demand or more traditional products (Vinals *et al.*, 1990, p. 152). Despite its high degree of intra-industry trade, Spain's revealed comparative advantage position also experienced a rapid and generalized deterioration in almost all sectors (Vinals *et al.*, 1990, p. 207). As expected, the deterioration was higher in those sectors and industries which, prior to accession, were more heavily protected, and which, therefore, experienced a larger reduction in protection.

Different indices which measure structural competitiveness confirm the sharp deterioration in post-entry competitiveness. Thus the trade accounts exhibited rising deficits. The trade deficit to GDP ratio increased in Spain from less than one per cent over the period 1980–85 to over 5 per cent in the post-accession period. The trade deficit rose rapidly in Greece during the 1980s and stabilized around 15 per cent of GDP in the early 1990s. Finally, in Portugal, the trade deficit hovered between 9 and 12 per cent throughout the post-accession period (Table 3.2).

Table 3.7 presents Balassa index calculations all three SEEs.[12] The results confirm the deterioration of structural competitiveness immediately after entry, especially in Spain and Greece, with a more mixed picture in the case of Portugal. Additional evidence is presented in a recent study (*European Economy*, Special Edition, 1990), where it is shown that all the stronger sectors declined throughout the 1980s. The expected decline in industrial activity and the downturn of the domestic economies in the second half of the 1980s would have been much worse had it not have been for the upturn in total world trade volumes and the improvement in the countries' terms of trade.

To summarize, European integration, in the case of the SEEs, became identified with economic liberalization which brought about a significant loss of structural competitiveness due to the structural inefficiencies that characterized these countries' productive systems. These included, *inter alia*, the small size of firms, the lack of flexibility in labour markets, the duality of their industrial sector, the absence of modern infrastructure, the presence of organizational inefficiencies in both public and private sectors, and the low level of technical efficiency in production and distribution systems. The presence of these structural rigidities and the ensuing segmentation of financial and labour markets made domestic industrial structures in

Table 3.7 Sectoral evolution of competitiveness (Balassa index)

	Spain				Portugal				Greece			
	1980	1985	1990	1994	1980	1985	1990	1993	1980	1985	1990	1993
Food, beverages etc.	-8.2	15	-14.4	-24.5	-36.2	-31	-38.8	-47.8	20.3	-2.9	-15.5	8.7
Basic metal and semi-finished products	-88.2	-45.8	-32.7	-20.9	-60.6	-45.8	-34.2	-37.6	-45.7	-57.3	-31.2	-49.1
Manufactures	-0.7	7.6	-20.3	-3.9	-20.1	-37.9	-16.9	-16.3	-41.6	-37.9	-66.2	-74.0
– Unspecified	-12.9	66.3	0.0	0.0	52.1	20.5	45.8	0.0	22	20.5	0.0	0.0
Total	-24.3	-10.9	-22.5	-11.5	-33.4	-38.2	-21.4	-22.0	-34.4	-38.2	-42.1	-44.3

Source: OECD, 1996: Greece, Spain and Portugal Country Reports; own calculations.

the SEEs vulnerable to external competitive pressures, and gave rise to severe distortions and to a lack of flexibility, following the post 1985 liberalization of commodity markets (Vinals *et al.*, 1990).

Even though the evidence on the speed and pattern of structural adjustment in these countries is still scant and largely undocumented, a systemic pattern of adjustment appears to emerge. First, large traditional industrial firms which, in a heavily protected environment used to have preferential access to financial markets and operated on 'soft-budget constraints' through direct or indirect subsidies (Kornai, 1986) have closed. Second, this has led to deindustrialization of those regions, where the above-mentioned firms were located, with adverse effects on employment and on relative incomes of these areas. Third, there has been a sharp drop of sales and profitability not only for those small-scale firms that were vertically or horizontally integrated with the large, industrial firms that terminated operations, but also for those that served the local markets that were adversely affected. Fourth, new firms have emerged, more especially in the liberalized service sector but also in industry, that exploited niches of local comparative advantage. Finally, there has been a rapid development of local stock markets, as more firms sought equity financing under more profitable terms than those provided by banks at liberalized high rates of interest.

The restructuring of industrial activity which began in the SEEs following their accession into the European Union and the liberalization of their commodity and service markets is still continuing today, at different speeds, and with various degrees of success. This is evident in the evolution of the Balassa indices, where the negative effects on structural competitiveness have persisted throughout the early 1990s (Table 3.7).

The economic implications of these developments for domestic incomes and well-being were fortunately cushioned by favourable world economic conditions as well as by Community funds and foreign investment that facilitated the adjustment process. It is these factors that probably also help to explain, as will be demonstrated in the following section, the differential path of adjustment between Portugal and Spain, on the one hand, and Greece, on the other. The endogenous capacity of each country to channel domestic savings, foreign capital and Community transfers to productive investment proved to be the determining factor behind the speed of adjustment and overall economic performance. It is this capacity which is also affected by and affects not only economic developments but also the political system and the quality of the democratic process.

The importance of Community funds and foreign investment in structural adjustment and the role of macroeconomic policy

The enlargement of the Community and the adoption of the Single Act in 1986–7 were accompanied, a year later (1988), by the reform of the

Community's Structural Funds (SF). In that context, and with the purpose of reducing the costs of adjustment incurred by integration, the resources of the SFs were doubled from 7.8 billion ECU in 1988 to 14.8 billion ECU in 1992 (1988 prices).

The Community pursued five distinct objectives via that reform, including the pursuit of structural adjustment and development in the least developed regions (Objective 1), industrial restructuring (Objective 2), the reduction of long-term unemployment (Objective 3), the facilitation of youth entry into labour markets through training (Objective 4) and the modernization and adjustment of agricultural structures (Objective 5). Since the purpose of the reforms was the promotion of sustainable convergence and cohesion across member states, the Community chose to develop the synergy of its three Funds – the Regional Fund, the Social Fund, and the Agricultural Guaranty/Orientation Fund (Feoga-Orient) – to upgrade the infrastructure of its member states and to provide incentives for the expansion of productive investment in the Community. Greece, Ireland and Portugal and a few regions in Spain, France, Italy and the UK became eligible for withdrawals under Objective 1.

Based on the initial proposals by the eligible member states, the Community approved the first Community Support Framework (CSF) for each country under Objective 1. The funds committed to Objective 1 for the period 1989 to 1993 amounted to 38.3 billion ECU (1989 prices) – 63.5 per cent of the total structural funds. For measures targeted to Objective 1 countries, Community support could reach 75 per cent of total expenditure. Within the context of the CSF for Objective 1, Spain was expected to receive 9.7 billion ECU (27 per cent of the total from the various funds), Portugal 16.6 per cent and Greece 18.5 per cent (Table 3.8). In per capita terms, these transfers amounted to 1,049 ECU for Ireland, 676 ECU for Portugal, 667 ECU for Greece and 252 ECU for Spain (Katseli and Sapountzoglou, 1992, p. 59).

The distribution of the SFs presented in Tables 3.8 and 3.9 shows that Community funding in Spain was channelled primarily through the Regional Fund, and was used to finance infrastructural investment. Spain chose to direct a large share of Community funds (43 per cent) to modernize its infrastructure and most notably its transportation networks. Portugal chose, instead, to distribute funds more evenly across objectives and gave emphasis to infrastructural development and training, in conjunction with the promotion of firms' competitiveness. In its first CFS, it included programmes aimed at modernizing agriculture and industry such as the PEDAP of 1985 and the PEDIP of 1989. In the PEDIP programme, specific measures were included for the modernization of Portugal's traditional industries. Around a quarter of total funding was directed to training, retraining and active labour-market policies via the Social Fund. Agricultural restructuring absorbed between 10 and 12 per cent of total funding. Greece and Ireland, on the other hand, pursued different investment

Table 3.8 Distribution of structural funds: initiatives in favour of Objective 1 countries (Community support framework 1989–93, million ECU, 1989 prices)

	EC12	%	GR	%	SP	%	PO	%	FR	%	IR	%	IT	%	UK	%
Total	36.2	100	6.7	100	9.7	100	6	100	0.9	100	3.7	100	7.4	100	0.7	100
%	100		18.5		26.8		16.6		2.5		10.2		20.4		1.9	
Regional Fund	21	58	3.7	55.2	6.2	63.9	3.8	66.2	0.4	44.4	1.6	43.2	4.9	66.2	0.3	63.3
%	100		17.6		29.5		18.1		1.9		7.6		23.3		1.4	
Social Fund	9.8	27.1	1.7	25.4	2.3	23.7	2	23	0.3	33.3	1.4	37.8	1.7	23	0.3	33.3
%	100		17.3		23.5		20.4		3.1		14.3		17.3		3.1	
Feoga-Orient	5.4	14.9	1.3	19.4	1.2	12.4	0.2	10.8	0.2	22.2	0.7	18.9	0.8		0.1	3.3
%	100		24.1		22.2		3.7		3.7		13		14.8		1.9	

Source: Commission Report for the Implementation of the Reform of Structural Funds, 1995.

Table 3.9 Percentage distribution of Objective 1 funds by initiative under the first Community support framework (1989–93)

Initiative	EUR.7	GR	E	P	F	IRL	I	UK
1. Modernization of basic infrastructure	30.7	23.8	42.9	21.2	30.7	25.1	33.2	24.5
2. Development of human resources	21.5	14	23	27.8	36.6	22.3	16.9	33.9
3. Utilization of local resources	17.6	16.1	16	18.4	20.5	24.7	16.1	23.8
4. Support of productive activities	6.3	–	7.1	5.9	5.1	–	14.2	–
5. Improvement of enterprise competitiveness	15	10.9	11	13.7	7.1	27.9	19.6	17.8
6. Other	8.9	35.2	–	13	–	–	–	–
Total	100	100	100	100	100	100	100	100

Source: Commission of the European Community, Report for the Implementation of the Reform of Structural Funds, 1991.

strategies, with a larger share of resources going either to agriculture in Greece or to enterprise competitiveness in Ireland.

Greece and Portugal were net beneficiaries of Community resources, while Spain paid to the Community more than it received (Table 3.10). This was largely due to its relatively high contribution to VAT (Katseli and Sapountzoglou, 1992, p. 32), something which was reversed in the 1990s. In 1993, the net fiscal transfers to each country through the Community budget reached 6.5 per cent of GDP in the case of Greece, 0.7 per cent of GDP in Spain and 3.9 per cent in Portugal.[13]

Thus, Community transfers rose to be an important source of foreign exchange and revenues for all SEEs. In Greece, Community transfers financed 15 per cent of total imports in 1990 and 24 per cent of the trade deficit. In 1991, they contributed 20 per cent of the non-tax receipts of the current budget. In Portugal, net transfers financed 33 per cent of total imports in 1986 and 24 per cent of imports in 1990. They covered 83 per cent of Portugal's trade deficit in 1990. In Spain, the corresponding ratios have been much smaller, namely 3.4 per cent of total imports in 1986 and 5.1 per cent in 1990. Net transfers amounting to 4.2 million ECU in 1990, covered 14 per cent of Spain's trade deficit.

Community transfers stimulated total investment demand and expanded incomes that would otherwise have shrunk in view of the overall recessionary effects of liberalization, aggravated by the restrictive fiscal and incomes policies pursued. Thus, Community funding cushioned the adjustment process in the SEEs and eased the burden of adjustment, brought about by trade liberalization and by the ensuing loss of structural competitiveness.

Table 3.10   Net fiscal transfers between member-
states and the Community (million ECUs)

Member-states	1990	1992	1993
Belgium	−774	166	60
Denmark	423	277	377
Germany	−5551	9698	−11830
Greece	2470	3604	4137
France	−1805	−1444	−1020
Ireland	1893	2140	2372
Italy	−417	−504	−1525
Luxembourg	−60	164	190
Netherlands	368	−829	−1327
UK	−3417	−2388	−3126
Spain	−1712	2740	3090
Portugal	601	2140	2508

Source: Commission of the European Community.

These effects were especially pronounced in Portugal and Greece, which received the lion's share of net fiscal transfers relative to their GDP.

At Edinburgh on 11–12 December 1992, Objective 1 regions received an additional 109 billion ECUs from the SFs and 15 billion ECUs from the Cohesion Fund, under a Second Community Support Framework that spanned the period 1993 to 1999. This amount did not include the transfers extended to the recipient countries under other objectives, for example, due to the operations of the Common Agricultural Policy, which were even more significant. Table 3.11 presents the distribution of SFs across the Cohesion countries for the period 1994 to 1999. By the end of the period, Greece and Portugal are expected to have received from all sources,[14] around 17 billion ECUs each, Spain 35 billion ECUs and Ireland around 7 billion ECUs in 1992 prices.

Once again the distribution of funds across initiatives reflects the policy priorities of each country. While Greece allocated substantial resources to the regions and a large share of funds towards the implementation of important infrastructural projects (around 20 per cent of the total), Spain and, even more so, Portugal directed funding to the modernization of their productive systems and to the promotion of industrial restructuring.

The chosen allocation of SFs across different initiatives was not only dictated by economic objectives but can also be understood as rational responses to political pressures. Spain's and Portugal's relatively important industrial enterprises sectors faced increased competition from abroad due to trade liberalization, at the same time that the financial reforms at home and the restrictive macroeconomic policy pursued lowered industrial profitability. The SFs were thus used by the respective governments as a 'hidden subsidy' to industry for retraining activities, for infrastructural investment that would reduce operational costs or for direct support for

Table 3.11 Percentage distribution of Objective 1 funds by initiative under the second Community support framework (1994–99)

Initiative	Greece (%)	Spain (%)	Portugal (%)
1. Infrastructure	20	7	–
2. Standard of living	10	–	9
3. Competitiveness/Productive systems	19	35	46
4. Human resources and employment	18	33	22
5. Reduction of regional disparities	32	25	22
6. Technical assistance	1	–	1
Total	100	100	100

Source: Commission of the European Community, 1995, '7eme Rapport Annuel sur les Fonds Structurels'.

restructuring. The 1989 PEDIP programme in Portugal that underpinned the restructuring of Portugal's traditional industries, most notable the clothing industry, is a good example of direct transfers to specific industries. Benefits were extended to both entrepreneurs and labour and helped mitigate the potential opposition to liberalization and integration.

Similarly, the Greek government's decision to allocate funds more evenly across regions is consistent with the government's preoccupation to support agricultural incomes in what was still a country with an important agricultural sector and to cater to the small-scale, regionally dispersed, economic interests that make up Greece's productive structure.

Thus, Community transfers have not only had a budgetary or macroeconomic impact on the domestic economies, but, most importantly, a developmental one. The magnitude of the developmental impact was intimately tied to the use of resources. Short-run, and long-run effects need to be distinguished in that process. In the short run, transfers increased liquidity as well as domestic income and overall demand in the host economies, boosting the demand for imports and contributing to a deterioration of the trade deficit. At the same time, as demand for domestic services and home goods was raised, the price of non-tradables such as domestic services or housing rose relative to tradables, worsening, in the process, price competitiveness, with further negative effects on the tradable sector.

These 'transfer effects' had differential long-run effects, depending on the use of these resources. In the case where grants succeeded in improving economic productivity because of sizeable investment in physical and/or human capital, the enhancement of the economy's productive capacity in the end led to an expanded production of exportables and a correction of the incurred imbalances. In such circumstances, the deterioration of price competitiveness (that is, the real appreciation of the currency) was sustained without a policy problem.

From a development perspective, SFs were not used as effectively in Greece, as in the other two SEEs, especially during the First Community

Support Framework. As a result, the negative transfer effects on competitiveness that were described above, applied with greater force, than was the case in the other two countries. Policy choices, can be explained in terms of a number of political factors, the more important of which is the lack of politically strong, organized groups that would support industrial restructuring. The large number of small, family owned entrepreneurs that make up the bulk of Greece's industrial enterprises, never coordinated their demands or actions to claim an important share of Community funds. Similarly, since union activity has always been weak in the Greek private sector – contrary to the public one – low political priority was attached to training or to productive restructuring. These factors, in conjunction with the inability of the political system to resist pressures to distribute favours regionally, coupled with the absence of decentralized, intermediate institutions that could manage effectively the allocation of global grants, reduced the developmental impact of the SFs in Greece.

Despite a coordinated effort on the part of the Government to enhance the developmental impact of the Second Community Support Framework with top-down interventions, the results have not been dramatically different. The absorption of funds during the first three years was low (around 50 per cent), in contrast to the high rates achieved in the other two countries (over 100 per cent). With politically strong pressure groups favouring industrial restructuring, both Spain and Portugal, completed infrastructural development in the late 1980s, and succeeded to upgrade their national competitive base via the modernization of their respective industrial sectors. In so doing, productivity was raised and growth accelerated. Industrial restructuring in the Iberian Peninsula was facilitated further by substantial capital inflows that peaked in 1992 (Table 3.12).

The role of foreign direct investment in the integration process

One of the striking characteristics of the internationalization process of the 1980s was the sharp upturn in FDI activity that started around 1985. Total world flows quadrupled from around $50 billion in 1985 to almost $200 billion in 1989, increasing the total world stock of FDI to $1.5 billion. After a short cyclical downturn FDI inflows surpassed $225 million in 1994 (Table 3.12). These flows, which have grown much faster than world exports,[15] have tended to concentrate within the 'Triad', that is, the three large regional markets of OECD countries that include the USA, Japan and the EU. The Triad accounts today for over 80 per cent of the total outward stock and for about 55 per cent of the total inward stock of FDI.

The prospects of a united European market created incentives for investment activity within Europe. Especially after 1985, Europe experienced sizeable increases in both inflows and outflows of capital. While in 1985,

Table 3.12 Distribution of FDI inflows across Southern European countries

	1980–84	1985	1986	1987	1988	1989	1990	1991	1992	1993	1994	1995
All countries (mill. of US $)	49931	49814	78267	132937	158274	195141	183746	157773	168122	207937	225660	314933
EU countries (mill. of US $)	14782	14690	20013	36406	54278	75492	88871	77715	79812	74467	64017	111920
EU over all countries (% share)	29.60	29.49	25.57	27.39	34.29	38.69	48.37	49.26	47.47	35.81	28.37	35.54
Southern EU Members over total EU (% share)												
Greece	3.7	3.6	2.4	1.9	1.7	1.0	1.1	1.5	1.4	1.3	1.5	0.8
Spain	12.5	12.7	17.2	12.6	12.9	11.2	15.6	16.1	16.6	10.9	14.6	7.4
Portugal	1.2	1.3	1.2	1.3	1.7	2.3	2.4	3.1	2.3	2.0	2.0	1.2

Source: United Nations, World Investment Report, various issues; own calculations.

the Community received only $15 billion worth of FDI inflows, by 1990, total inflows exceeded $88 billion (Table 3.12). During the same period, outflows increased from $22 billion to $88 billion (Katseli, 1993a, p. 7). At the turn of the decade, Europe attracted about half of total world FDI, as TNCs took investment positions within an enlarged and integrated European market either as a pre-emptive move against fears of a 'fortress' Europe or as a response to the expected increase in demand and lower costs of doing business within the region.

As noted earlier, there is in fact evidence that in the early 1990s both US and Japanese TNCs followed European 'core-network strategies', that is chose to create a core facility in Europe through FDI exposure and developed a trade-network among their European affiliates. As a result, about a quarter of Japanese affiliates' sales in the EU was being exported, with 92 per cent of those exports destined for other EU countries (UN, 1991, p. 41).

The prospects of an Internal Market by 1992 signalled a regime switch that was accompanied not only by increased capital flows into Europe but also by intra-EC investment activity. According to estimates provided by the UN (1991, p. 27), intra-EC FDI increased from one-quarter of the total inward stock of the EC in 1980, to 40 per cent in 1988. Thus, whereas, in 1980, European TNCs were present only in France (UN, 1991, p. 28), they have accounted, in recent years, for over 50 per cent of the FDI inward stock in France, Belgium, Italy, Portugal and Spain. These developments, in connection with the growing number of mergers and acquisitions presented in Figure 3.1, imply that production relocated within the region during the period 1985 to 1990 and that a growing fraction of intra-regional trade was based on intra-firm sales.

Spain and Portugal became major beneficiaries of this investment activity and became integrated into the regional 'core-network' strategies pursued by international firms. This was to be expected in view of their strong industrial bases and the active restructuring policies that were pursued domestically. In that context, both American and European TNCs increased their presence in Spain even before enlargement. Between 1986 and 1990-1, FDI grew rapidly, rising from less than 1 per cent of GDP in 1986 to 2.5 per cent in 1990 (Gual and Martin, 1995). By 1991, Spain occupied the second position within Europe as a host country for FDI inflows (Table 3.12). FDI into strong demand and technologically-advanced sectors amounted to 88 per cent of total investment, while the corresponding ratios for the moderate and weak-demand sectors were 52 per cent and 11 per cent respectively. Despite the downturn of FDI flows after 1990, Spain's share continued to be considerable (Table 3.12). By the late 1980s, Portugal also started receiving FDI inflows and raised its share to 3.1 per cent of European inflows in 1991. In Greece, net inflows in fact declined during the second half of the 1980s.

The share of average annual inflows in gross domestic capital formation increased in Spain from 9 per cent in 1981 to 1985 to 15.6 per cent in 1986 to 1988 (Vinals *et al.*, 1990, p. 198). The corresponding shares for Portugal during the 1980–2 and 1985–7 periods were 2.1 and 4.1 per cent and for Greece 6.3 and 7.4 per cent (UN, 1991, Table 2). The high share for Greece reflected, however, not so much sizeable increases in inflows of FDI, but rather the relative stagnation of domestic investment.

The deregulation and liberalization of capital markets, as well as the increased complementarity between commodity trade and services, created incentives for the growing tertiarization of FDI inflows in the SEEs. In Spain, the service sector's share in total FDI inflows increased from 36 per cent in 1986 to 55 per cent in 1988. Inflows were directed mainly into finance, insurance, commerce and real estate. The corresponding service share reached 73 per cent in Portugal and 51 per cent in Greece. Thus in all SEEs, foreign capital inflows in services which, up to that time, had remained heavily protected and undercapitalized became sizeable.

Regardless of its direction, FDI contributed significantly to the investment boom experienced by Spain and Portugal in the latter part of the 1980s. It is noteworthy, that while Community gross manufacturing investment has been growing at an average annual rate of 5.7 per cent during 1986–8, the corresponding growth rate for Spain was 26.8 per cent (Vinals *et al.*, 1990, p. 196). Largely as a result of FDI inflows, the share of gross fixed capital formation in total GDP increased from 19 per cent in 1985 to 25 per cent in Spain in 1990 and from 22 per cent in 1985 to 28 per cent in Portugal. In Greece, the investment/GDP ratio has in fact declined from 19 per cent in 1985 to 18 per cent in 1990.

FDI also played an important role in the restructuring of Spanish manufacturing. Attracted by its large market size and its proximity to the European market, foreign capital was directed mainly to the chemical and metal industries, largely for import substitution purposes. Spain, thus, became the only SEE among the three, to attract substantial 'greenfield' investment flows in the early 1990s.[16]

The size of the Spanish market (39 million inhabitants) was one of the most important determining factors behind FDI inflows into that country, especially in services. The combination of size, of a developed industrial base, of relatively low wages and of a liberal trading and investment regime made Spain a primary location for FDI in both goods and services. Spain's policies to use the first CSF to improve infrastructure and to develop its transportation and telecommunication networks contributed to an increase in the absolute productivity of capital and created added incentives for foreign capital, that sought the highest return possible (Katseli, 1993a, p. 24).

Portugal which proceeded fast to integrate its economy into the European market, provided a profitable export base for TNCs. Its relatively low labour and transportation costs as well as its quite developed technical and administrative capabilities, largely due to its industrial tradition, also created advantages for investment attraction.

Both Spain and Portugal, effectively channelling Community funds to productive restructuring, offered a large and sophisticated market for foreign investors, who took advantage of the available opportunities and the expected high rates of return. The productivity of capital was also raised by the countries' active policies to invest in human capital and to retrain workers who were employed in both large and small enterprises. Finally, the timing of their accession and the sequencing of their reforms played a crucial role in creating positive expectations and a virtuous spiral of investment and growth.

Greece was not in a competitive position, at that time, to capitalize on the externalities created by the combination of Community funding and FDI inflows. The small size of its market, in conjunction with high transportation costs to the main European markets created disincentives for capital inflows. These were aggravated by relative policy instability such as the frequent changes in the country's regulatory framework, in tax schedules as well as by the unpredictable delays and cumbersome procedures related to the issuance of permits and licences. Stop-go policies in the early 1990s and the high administrative costs of doing business have also been quoted as major impediments to sustainable capital flows.

It was only after the dramatic developments in Central and Eastern Europe that Greece emerged as a dynamic European country in southeastern Europe. The extension of its effective market resulted in a significant upgrading of its comparative advantage as a host country for FDI, as an export base for the new emerging markets of the area and as an important partner in the rapidly developing energy and transportation networks that link Europe with the Balkans, the Black Sea countries and the Middle East.

The role of macroeconomic policies in restructuring

Last but not least, one should not underestimate the role of macroeconomic policies in the process of structural adjustment of the SEEs. Portugal and Spain had faced severe industrial and financial crises prior to their entry to the Community. Between 1977 and 1984, the increase in the world energy prices coupled with the severe world recession had induced an industrial crisis that had in turn provoked a deep banking crisis. As a policy response, both Spain and Portugal introduced major stabilization packages in the early 1980s in consultation with the IMF and pursued significant tax and financial market reforms.

As a consequence, unemployment in Spain rose from 2.9 per cent in 1974 to 21.4 per cent in 1985. Between 1988 and 1990, that is, following their entry into the Community, wages were adjusted downwards and real unit labour costs reduced. The burden of adjustment fell disproportionately on wage and salary earners, relative to other groups in society. Simultaneously, indirect taxes were increased, prices charged by public sector utilities were adjusted upwards and sizeable increases in interest rates took place. Thus, in both Portugal and Spain, when trade was liberalized, many segments of the capital account had already been opened up and the financial system had become solvent.

In Greece, on the other hand, trade liberalization and financial market reforms were introduced in the early 1980s in parallel with the process of European integration. The rationalization of the interest rate structure in 1983–4 raised interest rates and hit hard those industries which had had traditional access to the banking system at subsidized rates. As many of these 'overcapitalized' companies were export-oriented, they not only became overindebted but their trade competitiveness was severely damaged in the process. Thus, the burden of adjustment from trade liberalization was aggravated by the consequences of concurrent domestic financial liberalization. The annual growth rate of investment hovered around 3 per cent and the growth rate did not exceed 1 per cent until 1995.

These developments help explain the different convergence paths of the SEEs to the Community's average performance. The net FDI inflows of capital attracted to Spain and Portugal in combination with the use of Community transfers towards productive restructuring created favourable expectations and underpinned an investment-led growth process. Growth exceeded 10 per cent in Spain and 8 per cent in Portugal, raising real per capita GDP by 6.2 per cent and 3.8 per cent respectively between 1986 and 1991 (Table 3.13). Productivity growth was relatively fast, contributing to a reduction of inflation to around 5 per cent by 1995 (Table 3.1).

Despite, these developments, the burden of adjustment was far from equitable. The unemployment rate in Spain reached almost 20 per cent in 1990 and rose even further in the 1990s (Table 3.2). At the same time, the adjusted wage share fell by about 10 percentage points between 1980 and 1995 (Table 3.2). The same can be said for Portugal, even though the labour

Table 3.13 The catching-up process in the Community (GDP at current market prices and PPS per head of population; EC = 100)

	Spain	Greece	Ireland	Portugal
1975	81.9	57.3	62.7	52.2
1980	74.2	58.1	64.0	55.0
1986	72.8	55.9	63.4	52.5
1991*	79.0	52.5	68.9	56.3
1992*	79.9	52.1	68.9	56.3
Differences				
1986–80	− 1.4	− 2.2	− 0.6	− 2.5
1991–86	6.2	− 3.4	5.5	3.8

*Economic forecasts, autumn 1991.
Source: Commission services.

market adjustment was less severe and the unemployment rate remained below 10 per cent of the labour force (Table 3.2). In both cases however, the income distribution worsened and the overall wage share in the economy fell in favour of the capital income share (Table 3.2).

Apart from equity considerations however, the combination of trade and financial-market liberalization in conjunction with the pursuit of restrictive domestic monetary policies produced a sizeable increase in nominal and real interest rates in all three countries. The ensuing attraction of short-term capital inflows enhanced international reserves but also led to an increase in monetary liquidity to the extent that these capital inflows were not adequately sterilized.[17] The increase in domestic monetary liquidity was

Table 3.14 Economic policy indicators

	1986–90	*1991–93*	*1994*	*1995*
Spain				
Money growth (% change)	14.5	7.5	7.6	8.8
Government budget balance (% GDP)	−3.8	−5.5	−6.6	−5.9
Gross government debt (% GDP)	44.1	51.5	63.0	64.8
Nominal wages per head (% change)	7.7	8.2	3.1	3.9
Real wages per head (% change)	1.0	2.0	−1.7	−0.9
Greece				
Money growth (% change)	21.1	13.9	8.9	10.4
Government budget balance (% GDP)	−13.0	−11.7	−11.4	−9.3
Gross government debt (% GDP)	66.6	97.1	113.0	114.4
Nominal wages per head (% change)	16.7	10.7	12.8	9.8
Real wages per head (% change)	−0.3	−4.4	1.8	0.6
Portugal				
Money growth (% change)	17.0	12.5	9.4	
Government budget balance (% GDP)	−4.7	−5.6	−5.7	−5.2
Gross government debt (% GDP)	64.4	66.6	69.4	70.5
Nominal wages per head (% change)	16.4	11.0	4.8	6.0
Real wages per head (% change)	4.2	0.7	−0.7	1.7

Source: Commission of the European Community, *European Economy* (1996), no. 61; Annual Economic Report for 1996.

Table 3.15 Real effective exchange rates

	Real effective exchange rate (1990 = 100)			Real effective exchange rate (% diff.)		
	Spain	*Portugal*	*Greece*	*Spain*	*Portugal*	*Greece*
1980		91.1	101.7			
1981	82.5	96.2	105.3		6	3.54
1982	82.4	95.7	109.3	−0.12	−0.52	3.80
1983	72.2	88.8	101.1	−12.38	−7.21	−7.50
1984	74.3	90.3	98.0	2.91	1.69	−3.07
1985	75.7	91.3	94.8	1.88	1.11	−3.27
1986	80.6	90.5	88.8	6.47	−0.88	−6.33
1987	83.9	89.2	90.9	4.09	−1.44	2.36
1988	87.7	89.8	93.2	4.53	0.67	2.53
1989	93.0	93.8	94.2	6.04	4.45	1.07
1990	100.0	100.0	100.0	7.53	6.61	6.16
1991	101.2	106.8	101.2	1.20	6.80	1.20
1992	102.1	116.6	104.5	0.89	9.18	3.26
1993	89.4	111.7	104.1	−12.44	−4.20	−0.38
1994	84.4	109.3	104.4	−5.59	−2.15	0.29
1995	86.6	112.8	108.2	2.61	3.20	3.64

Source: IMF, International Financial Statistics, Yearbook, 1996.

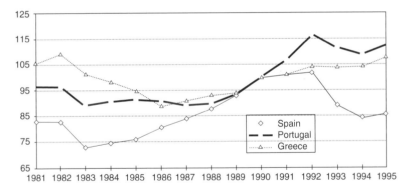

Figure 3.8   Real effective exchange rate (1990 = 100)
Source: IFS, Yearbook, 1996.

further aggravated by Community transfers (to the extent that these were not sterilized either). As a consequence, domestic money growth between 1986 and 1990 rose on average by 21 per cent in the case of Greece, 17 per cent in the case of Portugal and 15 per cent, in the case of Spain (Table 3.14). Thus, between 1986 and 1992, production costs rose faster in the SEEs relative to their main trading partners and the real exchange rate appreciated by 29 per cent in Portugal, 27 per cent in Spain and 18 per cent in Greece (Table 3.15; Figure 3.8).

The cumulative deterioration in structural and cost competitiveness during this period precipitated the first ERM crisis and led to subsequent devaluations of the peseta and the escudo. Between 1992 and 1994, the real effective exchange rates of the peseta and the escudo depreciated by more than 17 per cent and 6 per cent respectively. During that same period, the Greek drachma has continued to appreciate in both nominal and real terms. This process continued until 1998 when the drachma depreciated by around 14 per cent before entry for the first time into the ERM. In summary, all three countries relied on real exchange rate appreciation to disinflate their economies up to the point where this policy option proved unsustainable due to its negative consequences for cost competitiveness in integrated world markets.

The evolution of both price and structural competitiveness in the SEEs is reflected in their balance of payments adjustment. The post-entry deterioration of the trade balance to GDP ratio continued up to 1992 in both Spain and Portugal and was reversed thereafter largely as a consequence of the real exchange rate adjustment. The appearance of a foreign exchange constraint was postponed through the inflow of Community transfers and private capital. Thus, despite their large and increasing trade deficit, the current account deficit to GDP ratio remained small, while large surpluses were recorded in the basic balance, which also takes into consideration the inflow of long-term capital (Figure 3.9). The pursuit of a more flexible exchange rate policy after 1992 improved competitiveness and trade performance in the Iberian peninsula countries and, as expected, reduced the surpluses recorded in the basic balance.

In summary, structural adjustment in all three SEEs was underpinned and facilitated by substantial financing provided by the Community through the latter's Structural Funds and, in the case of the Iberian-peninsula countries, by private foreign capital inflows. These resources eased the burden of adjustment of domestic social groups, even though labour bore the brunt of the adjustment, especially through increased unemployment.

In the case of Spain and Portugal, stabilization measures and reforms of the banking sector preceded the subsequent trade and capital market liberalization associated with their European Integration. The adjustment process proved relatively easier while productive restructuring did not give rise to a prolonged recession as it was the case, in Greece.

From a political point of view, both in Spain and Portugal the available resources were channelled, more effectively, into productive uses, largely because of the pre-existence of a strong industrial base and of organized pressure groups. Thus, capital owners, entrepreneurs and partly labour, in Spanish and Portuguese industries, formed what turned out to be a 'development coalition', favouring European integration and restructuring that was underpinned by substantial claims on financial resources. In the case of Greece, on the other hand, no such coalition could be formed as the few overindebted, problematic industries crumbled once protection was effectively removed.

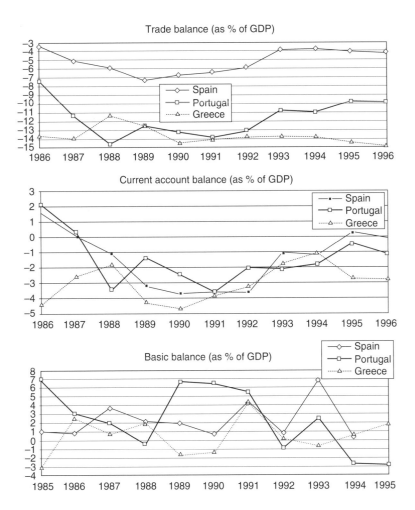

Figure 3.9 Balance of payments
Source: OECD, *Economic Surveys* (Portugal, Spain, Greece), 1996 and OECD, *Main Economic Indicators*, 1996.

Convergence and divergence in the internationalization process of SEEs: a challenge for social cohesion and democratic consolidation

The analysis so far has highlighted the effects of internationalization and of European Integration on the SEEs and has underlined the importance of Community transfers and of FDI inflows in cushioning the recessionary impact of liberalization. The adjustment process was shown to be facilitated in those countries – most notably in Spain and Portugal – by transfers and investment activity, which sustained demand and contributed to productive restructuring through productivity increases in the tradeable sector of the respective economies. In those countries, real convergence proceeded faster and stagflationary outcomes were prevented.

Even in those cases, however, adjustment across markets has not been uniform. While financial markets have tended to respond fairly quickly to favourable changes in the underlying risk-return prospects, labour-market adjustment was costly. The perseverance of high unemployment despite adequate growth performance, the presence of job mismatches, the recorded limited labour mobility to fill job vacancies and the growing gap between existing capabilities and new skill requirements (Katseli and Tsamourgelis, 1993; Vinals *et al.*, 1990) have demonstrated the presence of major structural rigidities in the functioning of labour markets. These have limited employment creation and have contributed to the deterioration of income distribution. These rigidities, which are still prevalent today, cannot be corrected only through natural market adjustment or through appropriate macroeconomic policies but require in addition the pursuit of active labour market policies that aim at employment creation, skills development and effective labour market intermediation. The pursuit of such policies has been inhibited so far by the lack of sufficient instruments, by institutional and/or political constraints and by the inability of administrative and political systems to respond to the new challenges in innovative ways.

Internationalization, and even more so participation in the EU, has limited the ability of national governments to intervene directly in markets. In less than a decade, these governments have transferred major decision-making power over macroeconomic policy both to Brussels and to the German Bundesbank. In the first post-entry period, they gave up the use of traditional economic instruments such as tariffs, quotas, taxes or subsidies, as means to protect domestic industry or special social groups in their respective societies. Traditional 'economic and political rents', associated with these policies, were virtually eliminated by the early 1990s. In the post-Maastricht era, all governments faced the challenge of meeting the criteria, of curtailing government expenditures and of sizing down the government sector itself, often at high political cost. Public sector employment, a favorite form of political patronage in economies where employment and income prospects remain uncertain, was drastically curtailed. Finally, prior to their entry into EMU, the right to seigniorage and the use of the exchange rate have been surrendered. Domestic political systems have thus had to adjust to this substantial transfer of domestic competencies to European institutions and at the same time to streamline their domestic policy agendas in order to converge on the Maastricht criteria and to prepare their domestic economies for joining EMU.

In most cases, governments and political parties have found themselves unprepared to cope with this new political reality. At a time when market liberalization and integration produced recessionary effects and increased uncertainty due to the transitory pains of restructuring, national governments lost much of their political legitimacy as effective arbitrators of conflicting demands and as procurers of an effective 'social safety net' through the provision of public goods.

Not only have governments lost important degrees of freedom in the regulation of the domestic economic activity and in traditional policy instruments to affect employment and incomes, but they have had to cut budget deficits, eliminate subsidies and manage successfully, over a short period of time, the restructuring of a number of key sectors.

Furthermore, as 'rents' associated with the imposition of tariffs, the provision of tax subsidies or of cheap credits were virtually eliminated, the extension of political patronage through such means was removed abruptly. This does not mean that 'rent-seeking' disappeared. It is still prevalent today in various public-sector economic activities such as the procurement of government contracts, the awarding of large-scale projects, the sale of large-scale assets in the process of privatization, the workings of emerging stock markets or the disbursement of Community Structural Funds.

Organized labour and political parties have had to adapt to the new political dynamics brought about by liberalization and European integration, to retain their membership while they revamp their agendas and redefine their role at a time when neither claims for higher wages are compatible with convergence programmes, nor traditional political platforms provide answers that appear to work.

These have proved to be major challenges for the SEEs which not only need to bridge the economic gap that separates them from the rest of Europe but, contrary to all other European member states, have not yet completed their democratic consolidation or upgraded fully their democratic processes. In these countries, the process of adjustment involves much greater risks than is the case in countries with long democratic traditions and strong institutions. Growing unemployment, social fragmentation or unequal distribution pose risks not only for social cohesion but for the smooth functioning of the democratic system as well.

The thrust of the policy challenge, for the SEEs, therefore, at the dawn of the twenty-first century, is to strengthen their democratic institutions and to enhance the credibility and effectiveness of their governments. At the same time, they need to promote structural adjustment and upgrade the competitiveness of their economies. To do so they have to raise productivity, through the expansion and modernization of the productive base of the economy, without further increases in unemployment or the marginalization of social groups. For this to be achieved, investment expansion needs to be complemented with active labour market policies and with income redistribution schemes through the national tax and transfer systems and through the Community budget.

Administrative reform and institution building, together with the active promotion of enterepreneurship, have to be integral components of future policy in the SEEs, that is, in countries where attitudes and modes of behaviour remain wedded to the workings and requirements of traditionally protected environments (Katseli, 1990). In the global order of the 1990s, competitiveness is increasingly determined, on the one hand, by the capacity of firms to use market information and to develop flexible managerial structures and to link themselves to international networks and, on the other, by the capacity of administrative systems to deliver efficiently public services.

Thus, the issue that will prove critical for the process of adjustment will be the capacity of the SEEs to develop entrepreneurial capabilities in both the private and the public sectors. This can be facilitated by the appropriate selection of 'development agents' in an individual or institutional sense. As Hirschman, has pointed out, a major bottleneck for development in most developing countries is not the shortage of capital, skilled labour or foreign exchange, but the capacity of the society to organize itself for development. This is especially true in the SEEs, where the centralization of authority and the workings of a highly interventionist system for a long period of time have contributed to the prevalence of 'endogenous inertia' by weakening incentives for entrepreneurial initiatives, by limiting the expansion of capabilities through learning by doing and by hindering the development of independent and autonomous institutions.

The provision of incentives, the enhancement of domestic capabilities and the strengthening of appropriate institutions can be regarded as the most important policy priorities for the mobilization of resources and for the active support of development initiatives at the national, regional or local levels. These are also preconditions for sustainable democratic consolidation at a time of rapid change.

Notes

* Research assistance by Dr Theodore Pelagidis, Mr Stavros Zografakis and Ms Marianna Paschali are gratefully acknowledged.

1. The current account balance includes the net trade, the net service and the transfer payments of a country, while the basic balance is the current account plus the net private long-term capital balance.

2. See Chapter 2 in this volume.

3. 'State corporatism' has been identified by Katseli (1990) as the voluntary cooperative regulation of conflicts over economic and social issues through a highly structured and interpenetrated set of political relationships by the state, banks and business, augmented at times by unions and political parties. Strong corporatist structures have a pervasive ideology of social partnership shared by the

leaders of government, banks and a small subset of business; they rely on the cooperative efforts of relatively centralized institutions representing those interests and they usually lack in worker militancy.

4. In Spain the first elections took place in June 1977 and its new constitution was adopted in 1978; in Portugal, elections took place in April 1975 and the constitution adopted in April 1976.

5. See Chapter 2 – this volume.

6. Contrary to the usual advice of economists on appropriate sequencing.

7. In 1989, the share of industry in gross value added (market prices) in Portugal was 38 per cent compared to 35 per cent in Spain and 27 per cent in Greece. The corresponding shares for agriculture were 6 per cent in Portugal, 5 per cent in Spain and 17 per cent in Greece.

8. The Monetary Committee, appointed by the Minister of National Economy and dating back to the time of the Greek civil war, dictated, up to 1983, the allocation of credit across various industrial sectors and business enterprises. Up to the early 1980s, interest rates on loans were extensively subsidized and mostly negative real interest rates prevailed.

9. A regulatory tax on imports was established in July 1984 which incorporated the protective elements of the indirect tax system. In addition, export subsidies were maintained intact or even increased in the case of small-scale industry and of some important traditional sectors (Maroulis, 1988). By 1985, the average nominal protection rate for all industrial sectors reached 33.6 per cent, down from 45 per cent ten years earlier (Giannitsis, 1988).

10. Intra-Industry trade refers to the trading of products within the same industrial classification; inter industry trading refers to trade across industrial classifications.

11. A country's revealed comparative advantage is its comparative advantage as shown by the trade statistics themselves.

12. The Balassa index measures the net trade balance per sector as a fraction of total trade, i.e., $(X_i - M_i) / X_i + M_i$.

13. The GDP figures for 1993 amounted to 63.2 billion ECUs in Greece, 410.3 billion ECUs in Spain and to 64.4 billion ECUs in Portugal.

14. These include the Community Support Framework (CSF), the Community Initiatives (CI) and the Cohesion Fund (CF).

15. The average annual growth rate of FDI flows was 34 per cent over the 1985–9 period as against 11 per cent for exports and 12 per cent for world output.

16. That is, investment from scratch which involves the construction of new plant, the purchase of new equipment, etc.

17. Sterilization occurs when the central bank prevents capital inflows from affecting the monetary base and hence broader measures of liquidity in the economy. If the foreign component of the money supply increases because of capital inflows, sterilization involves an equal reduction in the domestic component which can be achieved through the sale of bonds.

Bibliography

Anand, S. and Sen, A. K. (1996) 'Sustainable human development: concepts and priorities', Office of Development Studies, Discussion Paper Series, UNDP.

Centre for European Policy Studies (CEPS, 1996) Economic Policy Group, 'North-South in the EMS: convergence and divergence in inflation and real exchange rates', CEPS Paper No. 50.

Commission of the European Community (1989) *European Economy: The Economics of 1992*, no. 35, March.

Danthine, J. P. (1991) 'Wage subsidies or investment incentives: what are the options for public intervention in the East German Economy', CEPS, Economic Policy Group, unpublished.

Diamond, P. (1982) 'Aggregate demand management in search equilibrium', *Journal of Political Economy*, vol. 90, no. 5, pp. 881–94.

Eurostat (1991) *Basic Statistics of the Community*, Brussels.

Gerschenkron, A. (1962) *Economic Backwardness in Historical Perspective*, Harvard University Press, Cambridge, MA.

Giannitsis, T. (1988) *Entaksi stin Europaiki koinotita kai epiptoseis sti biomixania kai sto eksoteriko emporio*, Centre of Mediterranean Studies, Athens.

Gual, A. and Martin, C. (1995) 'Trade and FDI: its impact on Spain', in Faini, R. and Portes, R. (eds), *European Trade with Eastern Europe: Adjustment and Opportunities*, CEPR, Cambridge University Press, Cambridge.

Katseli, L. (1990) 'Economic integration in the enlarged European Community', in Bliss, C. and Braga De Macedo, J. (eds), *Unity with Diversity in the European Community: The Community's Southern Frontier*, Cambridge University Press, Cambridge.

Katseli, L. (1993a) 'Foreign direct investment and trade interlinkages in the 1990s: experience and prospects of developing countries', United Nations Special Studies Series.

Katseli, L. (1993b) 'The second Delors package and its effects on the Greek economy' (in Greek), *Epilogi*, January.

Katseli, L. and Sapountzoglou, G. (1992) 'Koinonikos proupologismos kai diarthrotika tameia stin prooptiki tis ONE', EKEM Study No. 16, July.

Katseli, L. and Tsamourgelis, G. (1993) 'EMU and labour markets in Southern Europe', unpublished paper.

Kornai, J. (1986) 'The soft budget constraint', *Kyklos* vol. 39, pp. 3–30.

Lall, S. (1987) *Learning to Industrialize: The Acquisitions of Technological Capability by India*, Macmillan, London.

Lall, S. (1989) 'Human Resource Development and Industrialization, with Special Reference to Africa', *Journal of Development Planning*, 19, 129–58, reprinted in Keith Griffin and John Knight (eds), *Human Development and the International Development Strategy for the 1990s*, Macmillan, London.

Lall, S. (1990) *Building Industrial Competitiveness in Developing Countries*, OECD, Paris.

Maroulis, D. K. (1988) *Problimata kai prooptikes ton Ellinikon eksagogon*, EKEM, Athens.

OECD, *Country Reports*, 1991/92, OEC, Paris.

Shapiro, H. and Taylor, L. (1990) 'The state and industrial strategy', *World Development*, vol. 18, no. 6, pp. 861–78.

Stevens, B. and Andrieu, M. (1991) 'Trade, investment and technology in a changing international environment', *Trade, Investment and Technology in the 1990s*, OECD, Paris.

UN (1991) *World Investment Report: The Triad in Foreign Direct Investment*, UN, New York.

UN (1992) *World Investment Report: Transnational Corporations as Engines of Growth*, UN, New York.

Vinals, J. *et al.* (1990) 'Spain and the EC cum 1992 shock', in Bliss, C. and Braga De Macedo, J. (eds), *Unity with Diversity in the European Community: The Community's Southern Frontier*, Cambridge University Press, Cambridge.

4
Tourism as an Agent of Economic Transformation in Southern Europe
Allan M. Williams

Introduction: a neglected economic sector

Tourism has struggled to achieve respectability among academic researchers. Nuñez (1978, p. 207), for example, writes of the scorn and suspicion that results from taking seriously such a 'frivolous' topic. Equally, state interventionism in tourism has been minimalist, being restricted to general land use planning, international marketing, and registration/supervision of the standards of facilities. There are minor exceptions, such as the influential role of state subsidies in the 1960s hotel construction boom in the Algarve, and the devalorization (see Lipietz, 1980) of state capital in the construction of airports, motorways and water treatment. However, these are insignificant compared to the major interventionist role of the Southern European states in manufacturing and agriculture (for example, see Williams, 1989). In general, the economic transformation strategies of these states have been notable for their almost total reliance on manufacturing as 'the motor of development'. The classic case is the strategy for the Mezzogiorno, which largely neglected tourism until the 1970s. Barucci and Becheri (1990, p. 227) note that only 'when industrial economies seemed to be in a crisis ... it was natural to wonder what the touristic destiny of the South might be'. The same comment could be applied almost equally well to the south of Europe as a whole.

Yet, tourism has played a major role in structuring economic (and social) relationships in the Southern European economies since the 1950s. At the international scale, tourism is one of the key dimensions of the core–periphery European model identified by Seers *et al.* (1979). In addition, the direct and multiplier effects of tourism are such that it plays a significant role in the balance of payments and the GDP profiles of the Southern European economies. Indeed, at a disaggregated spatial scale, it is possible to identify tourism-dependent or tourism-dominated economies, as in many Greek islands, the Spanish islands and costas, and Madeira. The precise distribution of economic costs and benefits – both sectorally and spatially – in these and other regions is largely a matter of speculation but it is clearly contingent; that is to say, it is dependent on the ownership and structure of capital, and the nature of labour markets and labour migration systems. Perhaps the key to all such analyses is de Kadt's (1979) dictum that tourism is neither 'a passport to development' nor a 'unique devil'. Its role in economic transformation is conditional on the form of tourism and on the structure of the national and regional economies within which it is inserted.

While tourism in Southern Europe has been the subject of a number of empirical studies – some of which are reported in this chapter – it is surrounded by a theoretical vacuum. It is beyond the scope of this chapter to attempt to provide such a theoretical framework, but it is necessary to consider some of the key theoretical elements in order to guide the following analysis. The first point is that the economic importance of tourist arrivals to the national economies can be conceptualized as a potential income stream. In the case of tourism this can be likened to export base theory with tourism generating income from outside the region or country depending on whether the tourists are nationals or foreigners. The tourists, however, are not a homogeneous source of external demand for the services of a country or region so that their impact is not simply dependent on volume. Instead, the potential income stream is highly dependent on market segmentation (Laws, 1991), in terms of which country of origin and social class are key variables. Tourism is generally considered to be an industry with strong growth prospects, based on its high income elasticity of demand (Truett and Truett, 1987). However, individual countries, experiencing factor cost changes (such as real wage increases or as a result of currency appreciation) are also faced with demand functions which are highly elastic with respect to price (Truett and Truett, 1987); this places constraints on their ability to raise prices without fundamentally affecting tourist numbers and sales.

The conversion of potential into actual income streams is highly conditional. In particular, it is dependent on the extent of income leakage from the regional or national economy, which is usually measured via multiplier-estimates (Archer, 1982). Leakages stem from payments for imports, remittances of profits and dividends to the owners of foreign capital, and payment for a proportion of the holiday to foreign airline, tour and travel agency companies (Sinclair, 1991). The extent of income leakage is itself highly dependent on the structure of ownership and external control in the industry. International tourism is not characterized by a high level of multinationalization of the ownership of hotels, restaurants and other facilities (Ascher, 1985). Dunning and McQueen (1982) provide a theoretical explanation for this surprisingly low level of FDI. They argue that there are three reasons for the emergence of international hotel chains; where there are net ownership advantages for example, via branding; where there are location factor endowments (for example, Hyatt users expect to find Hyatts in all major cities); and to internalize market transactions. In mass tourism – unlike business tourism – the first two conditions clearly do not exist. The tourism product being sold (sun, sea, etc) is largely indifferent to branding and location factor endowment. Instead, the emphasis is on price minimization for the total holiday package.

Despite the lack of multinational hotel chains, international tourism is frequently characterized by the presence of powerful intermediaries (tour companies), which exercise oligopolistic power. Oligopoly in this instance is understood as being the existence of a few large firms in the market leading to reduced competition. This allows for the existence of differential profit rates in the industry. In manufacturing, this tends to be based on the prices charged to different groups of consumers. However, in tourism it is firmly based on the prices that these firms pay to the factors of production (sub-contracting hotels, etc). This is an oligopsonistic relationship (Storper, 1985). In the case of the tour companies, oligopoly is also linked to vertical integration (tour companies owning airlines, travel agents, etc). This strategy offers the advantages of decreasing uncertainty, improved synchronization of operations, and increasing market power (Gomez and Sinclair, 1991). In the long term, large companies cannot maintain their positions for they cannot block market entry indefinitely. In manufacturing, the market positions of such companies are also threatened by the implications of decentralizing technologies; in tourism this may be manifested in terms of second home ownership growth and of individual travel, both of which undermine the market influence of the tour companies.

The stream of tourism income generates or sustains employment in the receiving region or country. One of the attractions of tourism to policy makers is that, because of its relatively low capital–labour ratio, there are relatively high employment levels with respect to a given income stream. In practice, of course the capital–labour ratio is contingent. It partly depends on the availability of technology and there is evidence that developments in catering technology (Bagguley, 1990) and in information technology (Bennett and Radburn, 1991) are contributing to an increase in capital to labour ratios; in practice, of course, this is another contingent relationship, as is demonstrated later in this chapter with respect to different forms of tourism and regions.

The capital–labour ratio is also dependent on factor prices, and in this respect the tourist industry has some distinctive features. Tourism labour markets can be characterized as informalized and open (Simms *et al.*, 1988), and, following Atkinson's (1984) terminology, they have well-developed systems of numerical (changes in numbers of workers) and functional (in terms of tasks) flexibility. This is discussed further in Shaw and Williams (1994). In effect, it means that the prevalence of seasonal, part-time, and casual workers, and a lack of internal divisions of labour, are critical to reducing costs; consequentially, this sustains high labour to capital ratios.

Unstable production and uncertain market conditions serve to reinforce the need for numerical flexibility. These labour market conditions are influenced by and influence the gender division of labour and the involvement of migrant workers. Labour markets are socially constructed so that the numbers of female and migrant tourism workers are more than just passive responses to the jobs available. Instead, the presence and degree of assimilation of migrants, as well as wider gender relationships, influence the structure of tourism employment.

One of the key questions in relation to the economic role of tourism is whether and how the expansion of mass tourism has contributed to the emergence of a 'new' Southern Europe. This is a difficult question the response to which depends on both the definition of 'new' and the aspects of tourism expansion that we choose to emphasize. What can be said with some degree of certainty is that the re-creation of Southern Europe as an object of the mass tourist gaze (Urry, 1990) has helped to reconstruct popular northern images of the south of Europe. Southern Europe has now become, in terms of popular consciousness, a locus of consumption and leisure, and this has partly replaced or, at least, supplemented some of the images of underdevelopment. The relationship between such images and the realities of economic processes is a moot point. On the one hand, there are undeniable benefits in terms of the contribution of tourism to the current accounts, GDPs and employment structures of the Southern European countries. There are also important contributions to the reshaping of social relationships, and the creation of entrepreneurial openings which have helped to reshape these economies. Against this, however, mass tourism has created a new set of dependent relationships, while its impacts are massively spatially polarized. The latter point adds weight to the view that the economic transformation linked to tourism development has created not so much a new Southern Europe but a dual or even multiple set of economic spaces, which are highly differentiated in terms of their insertion into the larger European economic space.

These brief conceptual remarks set the scene for the remainder of this chapter, which considers the empirical evidence of the economic role of tourism in the transformation of the economies of Southern Europe. The chapter looks next at demand and the potential income stream from international tourism, then at the total income generated and at leakages from this, followed by a review of the labour market impacts. Finally, the conclusion reviews some of the wider economic, and political and policy implications of the development of tourism in Southern Europe.

International tourism demand and potential income

The potential income from tourism is dependent on more than the absolute volume of arrivals and departures. It also depends on market segmentation – in terms of interests, activities, features and nationalities. Southern Europe has tended to attract mass tourism, which has particular economic limitations. In addition, changes in the potential flow of income over time are dependent on the elasticity of demand. Each of these dimensions is considered in turn and we begin with a review of tourism growth in Southern Europe.

The origins of modern tourism in Southern Europe can be traced to the mid-nineteenth century. While there was some international tourism, particularly in Italy, the main motor of expansion was the emergence of new forms of consumption among the urban middle classes. Tourist towns, such as San Sebastian or Malaga in Spain, and Figueira de Foz and Foz do Douro in Portugal, expanded as new spatial foci of consumption. A classic example was Alicante which, after the opening of a direct railway link to the capital in 1853, became known as the 'Playa de Madrid'. While growth continued through the late-nineteenth and twentieth centuries, it was only in the late 1950s and especially the 1960s that mass tourism emerged. This was predicated on rising disposable incomes among the working and middle classes of northern Europe, and falling real costs of international holidays due to both scale economies and transport technology changes (Williams and Shaw, 1991). The growth in international tourism was truly impressive. In Greece, for example, there were only 37,000 foreign tourists in 1950, 371,000 in 1960, 1,454,000 by 1970 and 5,271,115 by 1980 (Papadopoulos and Mirza, 1985). There was similar rapid growth in Portugal (Lewis and Williams, 1988) and Italy (King, 1991), but the most dramatic expansion was in Spain. On the eve of the Civil War there were only 200,000 foreign visitors; this had risen to 2.5 million in 1955, 14.3 million in 1965 and 30 million in 1975.

The period 1955 to 1972 was a 'golden age' during which tourism appeared to have become semi-autonomous from world economic developments and to thrive on its own momentum. The 1970s and early-1980s were more difficult years for tourism, being affected by rising fuel costs, economic recession, and the political crises surrounding the regime transitions in Portugal and Greece (Buckley and Papadopoulos, 1986; Lewis and Williams, 1991). By the mid-1980s tourism growth rates were recovering and there was a short boost in international tourist arrivals until the early-1990s, when economic crisis again dampened demand. This was accompanied by changes in the social construction of what constituted desirable or fashionable destinations. As a result, international tourism in Spain stagnated in the early-1990s – albeit after exceptional growth rates 1987–9. In contrast, tourism in Greece and Portugal expanded rapidly. Italy had modest tourism growth in the 1980s and the early-1990s compared to the other countries.

The position in 1991 is summarized in Table 4.1. Italy and Spain are two of the most important destinations for foreign tourism at the global level,

Table 4.1 International tourism arrivals, 1977–91

A: 1991

	No of tourist arrivals at frontiers (millions)	No of tourist nights – all means of accomodation (millions)
Greece	8.0	33.3
Italy	51.3	91.0*
Portugal	8.7	22.0
Spain	53.5	74.0

* 1989 data.

B: 1977–91: Five-year average annual changes

	Average Annual No. (millions)			% change compared to previous 5 years	
	1977–81	1982–86	1987–91	1982–86	1987–91
Greece	4.7	6.0	7.9	+26.7	+31.8
Italy	45.6**	50.2	53.5	+10.1	+6.6
Portugal	2.1	4.3	7.3	+104.8	+69.8
Spain	39.7	43.4	52.8	+9.3	+21.6

** 1978–81 only.

Source: OECD, *Tourism Policy and International Tourism in OECD Member Countries*, Annual Reports, 1977–92.

each having more than 50 million tourist arrivals (of all types) in 1991. Greece and Portugal have smaller volumes of tourists but have had more rapid growth rates during the 1980s. Portugal, in particular, has experienced one of the world's fastest growth rates in tourist arrivals during the decade. The exceptionally high growth rates of the early-1980s, when numbers more than doubled, is partly a reflection of the recovery from the disastrous tourism downturn in the 1970s. The high growth rates in the period 1987 to 1991 reflect the increase in short-term visits from neighbouring Spain, especially in the late-1980s following EC accession, as well as the intensification of mass tourism in the Algarve.

Turning now to market segmentation, it is certainly the case that in Southern Europe tourism – whether domestic or international – is characterized by a high level of market differentiation. Italy, for example, relies on its cultural heritage and its climate as tourist attractions. King (1991, p. 61) writes that: 'With regard to historic sites, Italy is undoubtedly one of *the* richest, if not the richest in the world.' Domestic tourism is dominated by a number of cross movements; 'residents of inland districts travelling to take their holidays by the sea; residents of the east and of lowland districts travelling to the fresher air of the mountains for *villeggiatura* holidays in farmhouses, second homes or holiday villages; residents of the northern industrial belt travelling to the Alps for short-stay winter skiing holidays' (p. 73). In general, domestic tourism is more temporally polarized but less spatially polarized than foreign tourism (Lewis and Williams, 1991). Another feature of diversity is the extensive second home ownership in all the Southern European countries. Owning a house or an apartment in a coastal resort is a widely held aspiration and status in all social classes. It can even be argued that the growth of 'weekend homes' represents part of the mythology of what constitutes progress. In practice, the relatively widespread social and spatial distribution of second homes reflects both the persistence of rural–urban ties, with first generation urban dwellers inheriting family homes in the countryside, and the weakness of planning structures, which have failed to control what are often clandestine construction processes.

However, despite its evident diversity, Southern European tourism is dominated by international mass tourism, which is the object of the remainder of this chapter. Mass tourism is a form of mass consumption, with which it has many features in common. Mass production is required as well as growing expenditure on associated consumer goods. Additionally, the few producers who dominate particular markets have the lead role in developing new attractions. Finally, products are little differentiated. The object of the mass 'tourism gaze' (Urry, 1990) is the beach holiday: the ingredients are both natural (coastal environments and climate) and created (restaurants, hotels, etc). These have been blended together by the image-making industry, to create a standard model of the object of mass summer tourism in Europe. The result is a distinctive form of urbanization along the Mediterranean coasts. Mullins (1991, p. 326) writes that: 'Tourist cities represent a new and extraordinary form of urbanization because they are cities built solely for consumption.' These are enclaves which largely contain mass tourism and limit its cultural impact on the larger region.

Mass tourism has a number of dominant characteristics: spatial polarization, market segmentation (based partly on proximity, and differences in national tourism image construction), temporal polarization and resulting environmental pressures. The degree of spatial polarization is acute and is one of the keys to understanding the impact of mass tourism on Southern Europe. In Spain, for example, there are more than 2 million tourists annually in each of Andalucía, Catalonia, the Balearics, Valencia and the Islas Canarias; Andalucía alone has more than 5 million, divided more or less equally between foreign and domestic visitors (Valenzuela, 1991). In Greece, 22 per cent and 15 per cent, respectively, of foreign tourists are to be found in Crete and the Dodecanese (Leontidou, 1991). Temporal polarization – which is a product of the institutional organization of free time, and of the construction of the object of 'the tourism gaze' – is also marked throughout Southern Europe, with more than 40 per cent of tourists arriving in just three summer months. The two forms of polarization have mutually reinforcing effects, leading to the maximization of pressures on the environment and local culture at a few points in space and time. The classic example is Benidorm which has 125,000 registered bedspaces and receives 3 million tourists annually, while its permanent population is only 34,000 (Valenzuela, 1991).

While there are considerable detailed variations in market segmentation in each of the four Southern European countries, the outstanding feature is the degree of domination by two major markets, the UK and Germany (see Table 4.2). In 1991 Germans accounted for more than one-third of the market in Italy and Spain and for almost one-fifth of the market in Greece and Portugal. British tourists accounted for a further one-fifth to one-quarter of the market in Greece, Spain and Portugal. Together they accounted for more than two-fifths of the market in Greece, Portugal and Italy, and for more than 60 per cent in Spain. This has direct implications in that UK tourists have relatively low levels of spending per capita. For example, in Portugal British tourists account for one-quarter of overnight stays but for a significantly lower proportion of tourism receipts (Lewis and Williams, 1988). In contrast, North American tourists account for only 4 per cent of overnights but for 31 per cent of receipts. There are also indirect implications in terms of dependency and oligopolistic relationships, a point which is discussed further in the following section.

Over time there has been a change in the pattern of market segmentation. The British presence in the Greek market increased sharply after 1976, but then levelled off in the late-1980s (Table 4.2); the German presence in this market increased more steadily throughout. The Portuguese experience is not dissimilar, with the market dominance of both the British and German segments increasing over time. The British share however peaked in the mid-1980s and had fallen back by 1991. In contrast, there were relatively small changes in Italy between 1976 and 1991, although there was

Table 4.2 Market segmentation, 1976–91

| | \% of foreign tourists from*: | | | | | | | |
| | UK | | | | Germany | | | |
	1976	*1980*	*1985*	*1991*	*1976*	*1980*	*1985*	*1991*
Greece	11.8	na	20.2	20.9	14.1	na	16.0	19.5
Italy	7.7	9.5	7.7	7.8	35.9	41.2	39.0	36.2**
Portugal	14.9	22.0	34.1	26.3	19.1	19.2	15.0	18.1
Spain	30.6	30.9	25.6	25.6	29.0	31.0	29.9	34.9

* arrivals in frontiers for Greece; nights spent in registered tourist accomodation for Portugal; and nights in hotel accomodation for Italy and Spain.
** 1990.
Source: see Table 4.1.

an increase in the German share to over 40 per cent in 1980 before this subsided gently to its present level. Finally, in Spain, the British and German markets accounted for remarkably constant shares of around 30 per cent each in 1976, 1980 and 1985. Thereafter, the German share increased by some percentage points while the British share fell by a similar margin. Overall, these trends reflect the changing relative strengths and exchange rates of these two large market segments.

Market segmentation is given an additional twist by regional disaggregation. This operates at both ends of the tourist flows. For example, within Germany Dusseldorf accounts for the largest proportion of non-scheduled flights to Portugal, while Munich accounts for 30 per cent of all German visitors to Greece. This is important in so far as each of these regional market segments has different levels of income and expenditure potential. There is also regional segmentation in the destination countries: in Spain, for example, the Balearics attract relatively large numbers of German tourists, while the British are especially numerous in the Costa del Sol (Pearce, 1987b).

Another market segmentation feature is the recent tendency to self-provisioning (Urry, 1990), which is linked to what Gershuny and Miles (1983) term the self-service economy. This is most notable in the accommodation sector, in the growth of second homes. For example, in Spain there are an estimated 2 million second homes, one million of which are owned by foreigners. This generates a sequence of diverse income effects. The initial property investment leads to an infusion of external capital which is largely distributed among land owners and the construction and development industries. Later, second homes may reduce the income stream from tourism if they are rented out to foreign holiday makers who would otherwise purchase accommodation from indigenous owners of hotels or apartments. Later, second homes may become the principal homes of expatriate settlers, and therefore may generate year-round income streams from these 'permanent' visitors. In practice, the balance of income streams depends on the precise patterns of investment and consumption, taxation and utilization of public services, all of which are little researched areas.

A final point to note with respect to the potential income from tourism is that demand is highly elastic in relation to both incomes and prices. Truett and Truett (1987) have used regression analysis to establish these relationships in the cases of both Spain and Greece; they comment that their empirical findings closely approximate to what both economic theory and real-world experiences had led them to expect. This is illustrated by the way tourist arrivals in Spain have fallen sharply in response to the rise in price levels in the 1990s. In 1991 a 20 per cent appreciation of the peseta against sterling contributed to a 3 per cent fall in tourism numbers. This underlines the competitiveness of international markets and the elasticity of demand

and of supply relative to prices. Italy also appears to have lost some its competitiveness in the 1980s relative to its competitors, due to effective price increases and a negative elasticity of demand (Manente, 1986). The vulnerability of the potential income flow is reinforced by the high degree of substitutability between Mediterranean tourist resorts, given their lack of product differentiation. The social construction of mass tourism resorts as sunshine/sea packages to which to escape from the routines of domestic and work life in northern Europe means that destinations have been constructed – in terms of images, architecture and services on offer – as 'identikit resorts'. They offer similar experiences, are interchangeable and virtually the only point of competition is price. Given the strong negative elasticity of demand relative to prices, there is intense pressure on tour companies and their local suppliers to minimize these. Put crudely, sun-seekers faced with a price rise in one country have the option of seeking similar types of holidays in other, lower-priced, Mediterranean countries.

The high levels of product substitutability also contribute to extreme market sensitivity in tourism. The most obvious manifestation of this is the impact of political uncertainty. For example, the numbers of foreign arrivals in Portugal took 4 years to recover from their sharp drop in 1974 following the 25 April coup (Lewis and Williams, 1991). In Greece, foreign tourism suffered a series of external shocks following political instability in 1964, military coup in 1967, Cyprus crisis in 1974 and the oil crisis in 1980. The most severe of these was the Cyprus crisis and the overthrow of the colonels regime, following which there was a 31 per cent fall in the number of foreign tourists. This leads on to a more general consideration of systemic risk in the tourism industry. In the short term, the tourist industry in any one country or region is subject to considerable variations in demand, as has been noted above. However, tourism in the medium term has exhibited relatively low levels of risk, with fairly constant and strong growth in exports in contrast to most economic sectors. The longer term outlook for tourism, however, is characterized by a potentially high level of systemic risk. Ease of entry into the tourism market means that there is a relatively high elasticity of supply and this may threaten the longer-term competitiveness of the established tourism areas. The extent of risk in each of these three time horizons varies considerably between different sections of the tourist industry, as for example between hotels and private rooms to let.

Tourism and income flows

International tourism is a major component of the non-commodity exports of all the Southern European economies. In 1991, for example, the net balance on the tourism account was at least $1 billion dollars in each of the four countries (Table 4.3). Spain had the largest surplus, for, while Italy had a large inflow of foreign exchange, this was matched by a

Table 4.3 International tourist receipts and expenditure, 1977–91 (million current dollars)

A: 1991

	Receipts	Expenditure	Net Balance
Greece	2637	1017	+1620
Italy	18420	11648	+6772
Portugal	3739	1028	+2711
Spain	19158	4555	+14603

B: 1997–91

	Average Annual receipts (million $)			% change compared to previous 5 years	
	1977–81	1982–86	1987–91	1982–86	1987–91
Greece	1529	1461	2300	−4.4	+57.4
Italy	7140	8915	14943	+24.9	+67.6
Portugal	824	1078	2886	−30.8	+167.8
Spain	5951	8372	17062	+40.7	+103.8

substantial outflow so that the net balance was considerably reduced. Given the low levels of domestic foreign tourism participation in Southern Europe (excepting Italy), this is indicative of future changes: the net balance will probably decline in relative terms as outward foreign tourism from these countries expands. Whether the growth rate of international tourist outflows will exceed that of inflows is far from clear. It depends on conditions in international markets as well as cost competitiveness.

The historical picture is somewhat more complex. As expected, Portugal has a relatively high growth rate for tourism receipts; this is higher in the later 1980s although the growth in arrivals was greater in the early 1990s, which is partly explained by the stabilization of the exchange rate after 1985. In Greece the average annual receipts from international tourism fell in the early 1980s but recovered sharply thereafter. Both Italy and Spain experienced strong growth rates in the two periods in the 1980s compared to the previous five-years. The advance in foreign exchange earnings was especially marked in 1987–91. None of these changes can be predicted simply from the totals of foreign tourist arrivals. To some extent, these earnings reflect currency exchange rate fluctuations in this period, notably the weak Greek drachma in the early-1980s and the strong Spanish peseta in the late-1980s. However, a note of caution is required here, for the data for tourism expenditures, especially in the case of Greece, are flawed by substantial informalization of the sector and under-recording of expenditures. The most obvious example of this is the enormous number of unregistered

Table 4.4   Average tourism expenditure per foreign visitor,
1977–91 (current dollars per visitor)

	1977–81	1982–86	1987–91
Greece	325	244	291
Italy	157	177	279
Portugal	392	251	395
Spain	150	193	323

Source: see Table 4.1.

accommodation units which are let to visitors on almost all the Greek islands. It must be allowed therefore that the true expenditure figures for tourism, especially for Greece, are far higher than these data suggest.

Turning to tourism expenditure per visitor, a different pattern emerges. In 1977–81 Portugal had the most efficient income extracting tourism industry, with an average spend per visitor of $392 (Table 4.4). This reflected the relatively elitist nature of its tourist industry and relatively long stays. Greece had the second highest levels of expenditure per visitor, again reflecting relatively long stays. By 1982–6 convergence was evident. Both Portugal and Greece had experienced sharp decreases in receipts, partly reflecting the growth of mass tourism and, in the case of Portugal, short-term visits from Spain. Exchange rate movements also contributed to these changes. In contrast, Italy, and especially Spain, had experienced marked increases in spending per visitor. By 1987–91 Portugal had recovered its clear lead over the other countries, while the strengthening of the peseta contributed to Spain's improved performance. Greece in contrast was the only country whose performance in this last period was less effective than in the late-1970s. Given variations in the lengths of stay, expenditure per night is a more reliable indicator of the 'efficiencies' of the respective tourist industries. Unfortunately, comparable data is not available for Spain, but these data do indicate that Portugal still has the highest rate of spending.

The actual importance of the tourism and travel account to the four economies is highly variable (Table 4.5). Between the late-1970s and the late-1980s the share of tourism in GDP increased sharply in Portugal and modestly in Greece, again reflecting their different performances. Tourism also increased its share of the GDP of Spain but it declined sharply in Italy. The latter has a relatively mature and diverse economy, so that international tourism (for which statistics are more readily available than domestic tourism) accounted for only a small share of its GDP and of its exports by this stage (see also Yannopoulos, 1988). In contrast, the international travel account surplus was equivalent to more than 15 per cent of all exports of goods and services in Spain, Greece and Portugal. The most

Table 4.5 Travel account receipts and the national economy, 1976–90

	% GDP			% exports of goods and services		
	1976–80	*1981–85*	*1986–90*	*1976–80*	*1981–85*	*1986–90*
Greece	4.1	4.1	4.3	20.0	18.8	20.7
Italy	2.2	2.2	1.6	85.2	8.4	7.4
Portugal	3.5	4.6	5.8	15.9	14.4	15.9
Spain	3.3	4.4	4.6	21.9	20.7	24.1

Source: see Table 4.1.

dramatic change has been in Spain where the share of tourism in all exports and services fell from 46 per cent in 1965 to an average of 24.1 per cent in the late 1980s. However, this is deceptive for the contribution of tourism to exports levelled off in the late 1970s and actually increased in the late 1980s. The critical role of the positive tourism and travel account trade balance is that it helped to finance imports, including intermediate and capital goods for other economic sectors. While this relationship cannot easily be quantified, it has been argued forcefully by a number of commentators (Baklanoff, 1978) that the export-led boom of the 1960s was partly underpinned by the recurrent surpluses on the invisibles account, especially from tourism and emigrant remittances.

Turning from the impact of tourism on the current account to its role in production, it has already been noted that international tourism accounts for between 1.5 per cent and 5.8 per cent of GDP in the Southern European countries. In Italy the relative importance of tourism has declined since 1970 (Table 4.5) but elsewhere in Southern Europe it has increased sharply, especially in Portugal. Indeed, one of the attractions of tourism as a basis for economic development is that there is potentially a relatively short realization period in the circuit of capital. Investment in hotels, restaurants and other facilities can realize profits relatively quickly, especially compared to large scale industry. There are also low levels of capital formation required relative to turnover and employment, compared to the manufacturing sector. This is especially true of the commodification of cultural events, international festivals, etc. where the return of capital can be completed in months rather than the years involved in developing a new manufactured product (Harvey, 1990). This argument, however, has one flaw: substantial amounts of capital may be required if airports, major roads, or landscape rehabilitation are required prior to tourism development. In such cases, it has been normal practice for the state to intervene to support private sector capital formation, via the devalorization (Lipietz, 1980) of public sector capital. Examples include the investment by the Greek government in international airports on the Greek islands, or by the Spanish government in the transport and other infrastructure for the Seville international exhibition.

The calculation of the contribution of tourism to the national economies is problematic, not least because tourism tends to be statistically invisible in terms of official data. The data considered so far are officially recorded or estimated direct expenditures by tourists, but these do not take into account the impact of secondary rounds of expenditure on suppliers of goods and services, etc. Consequently, there is a heavy reliance on the use of multipliers to estimate these wider economic impacts. In the case of Portugal, Cunha (1986) estimates that tourism accounts for 5 to 7 per cent of GDP, if direct and indirect production is taken into account. For Italy, Manente (1986) estimates that tourism contributes 4.8 per cent of GDP, with 40 per cent of this coming from foreign tourism. In Spain, the proportion of GDP attributed to tourism is even higher, being around 10 per cent (Valenzuela, 1991). All these estimates are highly dependent on the definitions used and on the methods for calculation of coefficients. The reliance on multipliers also tends to overestimate the importance of tourism, compared to other economic sectors. Nevertheless, these bare statistics do stand testimony to the major role of tourism in the Southern European economies.

Given the spatial polarization of the mass tourism industry, the impact on particular regional economies can be even more marked. In Spain, there is clear evidence that tourism has led to sharp increases in per capita incomes in some of the poorest regions. Valenzuela (1991, p. 54) writes that: 'Tourism is directly responsible for the Balearics and Gerona occupying, respectively, first and second place amongst the fifty Spanish provinces in the league table of per-capita income ... Traditionally, Malaga and Tenerife were backward regions, but tourism has contributed to an improvement in their positions to 28th and 30th places, respectively.' The impact of tourism depends, of course, on regional economic structures. Tourism in Catalonia is located in a more developed region with its own sources of capital. In contrast, tourism in the Balearic and Canary Islands is located in what were some of Spain's and Europe's poorest regions. Tourism has had a far more profound effect in these regions. While income has risen, they have become highly dependent on a small number of foreign market segments and on foreign investment.

While there are some positive indications in Spain of the contribution of tourism to the poorest regional economies, the evidence in Italy is less encouraging. King (1991) writes that: 'hopes that tourism might function as a "leading sector" in the South's development have largely been misplaced.' There are a number of limitations, including the lack of a coherent development strategy, clientelism and favouritism in the distribution of grants, and the failure to promote endogenous capital. Instead tourism has become polarized between a small number of large hotel complexes owned by capital external to the region, and burgeoning second homes. King is reminded of the classic dualistic development, or 'cathedrals in a desert' which has characterized industrial development in the Mezzogiorno.

External income leakages and dependency

While tourism does generate important streams of income for the Southern European countries, the global statistics presented above overstate its importance. International tourism receipts are matched by related expenditures including the purchases of imported equipment and consumables, foreign workers' remittances (see next section), and dividends and profits remitted by foreign companies. There are also the costs of foreign promotions and extra expenditures on imports by nationals, resulting from earnings in and the demonstration effect of tourism. There are few reliable estimates of such leakage effects but in Italy, for example, in 1975 total foreign receipts of $2,578 million were reduced via leakage effects to net earnings of $1,528 million (Mathieson and Wall, 1982).

One of the key elements in leakage effects is the corporate structure of the tourism industry, and this is linked to the larger question of dependency and external ownership. The extent of foreign ownership clearly has an influence on the level of profit remittances and the leakage of tourism expenditures and income. There is certainly a very high level of foreign ownership in the travel industry for, unlike scheduled services, the charter airline business is not subject to strict bilateral market-sharing regulations. However, with the exception of second homes, there is surprisingly little direct foreign ownership of most tourist facilities *within* Southern Europe (UNTC, 1982). For example, Spain's 65 hotel 'groups' own 31 per cent of hotel capacity. Yet only one-quarter have any foreign capital and this exceeds 50 per cent of the total is only one-eighth of the groups (Estudios Turisticos, 1988a). We have already noted the theoretical reasons for this in the case of hotels; the three conditions for the emergence of international hotel chains, according to Dunning and McQueen's (1982) eclectic theory of multinationals, do not apply to the mass tourism market. However, it could be argued that the third of their conditions – internalization of linkages – do offer advantages to tour companies, airlines and large hotels as a means of securing guaranteed markets. The last part of this section looks at the tour companies, which are often the key agent in international mass tourism. They do have oligopsonistic powers in the Mediterranean mass tourism industry but these are not exercised via direct ownership of facilities in these countries.

In order to understand the roles of the tour companies, it is important to re-emphasize that there are highly segmented tourism markets in Southern Europe (Table 4.2). They are all heavily dominated by two national segments, the UK and Germany. This is most extreme in Spain, where 60 per cent of foreign visitors are from these two sources. In particular Mediterranean regional markets, the level of dependency is even greater with 50 per cent of the Algarve market being provided by British tourists. The UK and Germany are also characterized by high levels of concentration in the all-inclusive air holiday ('package') industry. In Germany three companies control 41 per cent of the market (Drexl and Agel, 1987) while in the UK three tour companies control one-half of the market. Yet, the level of foreign direct ownership of hotels and other forms of accommodation is minimal (Fitch, 1987). The most advanced is Touristik Union which in Spain, for example, owns 60 per cent of Hotel Riu with 3,900 beds (Drexl and Agel, 1987). Neckerman and Reisen own the Royaltur group but only own 3 per cent of their accommodation needs in the Balearics and 10 per cent in the Canarias. In contrast, the largest UK company – Thomson – has no directly owned accommodation in Spain (Estudios Turisticos, 1987b). There is, therefore, virtually no internalization by the tour companies in terms of direct investment in the Mediterranean countries. Cals (1984) makes the interesting point that the lack of internalization is facilitated by the development of particular circuits of capital during the tourism development cycle. The initiation of tourism leads to sharp increases in the price of land which generates capital which may be re-invested in tourism enterprises. This ensures that there is a ready supply of sub-contractors to the tour companies.

However, this is not to say there is no external control, only that this is exercised via more subtle means. Several points can be noted here. First, as mass tourism is based on moving large volumes at low prices, this means there is strong downwards pressure on the prices offered to suppliers of tourism services. This is particularly the case in the UK which has some of the lowest levels of spending per tourist among the major countries of tourism origin. Furthermore, price wars among the major tour companies and the travel agents in countries such as the UK have led to a qualitative deterioration in demand during recent years (Furio Blasco *et al.*, 1992).

Second, there is a high degree of market segmentation among tour companies, driven by the search for scale economies. For example, in 1988 the newly merged Thomson and Horizon groups controlled more than 50 per cent of all the UK package holidays to Spain, more than 40 per cent in Greece, and 35 per cent in Portugal (Monopolies and Mergers Commission, 1989). Combined with national market segmentation this gives oligopolistic powers to the major tour companies in some destination regions. Again this results in downwards pressure on prices, and so reduces the potential income benefits for the host countries and regions.

There is ample anecdotal evidence, but little statistical data, to verify these arguments about the pressures on prices. However, there is fragmentary evidence available. The Economist Intelligence Unit (1988) has stated that in Spain 'Hotel profit margins have been steadily cut as pressure from tour operators has risen'. Urry (1990) has also quoted a survey of 57 hotels in Southern Europe; in 39 of these the lowest prices were secured by UK tour companies, reflecting their strong market positions. In Majorca:

> there is overdependence on the UK inclusive tour market, with high volume/low yield business. British tour operators have been able to

command low rates from the island hotel chains in return for increasing numbers of visitors. The operators have in turn reduced prices to the customer as part of a strategy emphasising market share and competitiveness over short-term profitability. The hotels claim to have had no significant rate increases for four years, leaving them without sufficient capital to refurbish their facilities.

Gomez and Sinclair (1991, p. 84) argue that 'the prices which tour operators negotiate with hoteliers are often between 20 and 50 per cent below those charged to tourists on individually organised holidays'. The tour companies also benefit from the operation of a 'release back' system which means that as long as they give seven days notice to the hoteliers, they can cancel their bookings on some rooms without incurring any penalties. This has the effect of passing on some of the risk to the hoteliers without having to relinquish the cost advantages of large-scale, early bookings.

These dependency relationships are not only evident in price structures. The system of sub-contracting, with only limited fixed capital investment in the destination regions by the tour companies, brings other potential problems. It means that the foreign tour companies have little long-term commitment to any hotel, resort, region or even country. Indeed, most contracts between tour companies and hoteliers are made twelve months in advance of the tourists' arrivals (Gomez and Sinclair, 1991). As new destinations become fashionable, or cheaper, the foreign tour companies are in a position to shift their resources and capital assets (marketing ability, computer reservation systems, air fleets, etc) to these new resorts. It makes the existing mass tourism resorts highly vulnerable, and implies that the downwards pressures of prices are structural to the organization of the mass tourism industry.

The existence of such strong external controls in the tourism industry lead to suggestions that mass tourism development strategies tend to involve dependency relationships (Seers *et al.,* 1979). The fact that markets, costs, and even product innovation are determined outside of the Mediterranean region would tend to verify this argument. However, there are considerable differences between the four countries: Italy, compared to Portugal for example, has greater product diversity and a well developed domestic tourism market, which supplements foreign tourism.

Employment and labour markets

Employment is another widely used indicator of the economic importance of tourism. But it also has wider ramifications as many of the social and cultural impacts of tourism are transmitted via labour markets. In terms of estimating the importance of tourism as a source of jobs, the problem yet again is that of 'statistical invisibility'. Hence there is considerable reliance on the calculation of multipliers. According to Valenzuela (1991, p. 41) tourism in Spain accounts directly for 0.7 million jobs and indirectly for a further 0.5 million. The figures for Italy are comparable, with 0.8 million direct and 0.4 million indirect jobs. However, there is a further problem of clandestine employment, linked in Italy to illegal immigration. Consequently, King (1991) considers that the real employment impact of tourism exceeds 1.5 million and could be as high as 2 million. The employment figures for Portugal are more modest, there being an estimated 145,000 jobs in tourism. Again, the regional impact of tourism is highly differentiated and in Portugal, for example, 68 per cent of all job are to be found in Lisbon, the Algarve and Madeira. Each of these labour markets has its own distinctive features in terms of alternatives to tourism, seasonality and inter-relationships with other sectors of the economy and with household budgets.

Polarization is the key to the labour market impact of mass tourism in Southern Europe. First, employment structures in tourism are highly polarized by size. While there are some large companies (a few hotel chains, air carriers, etc), the vast majority of enterprises are relatively small scale. This contributes to a high degree of informality in tourism labour markets. Second, enterprises also face far more extreme temporal variations in demand – by season, weekend/weekday, during the day – than almost any other economic activity. They tend to respond to this via numerical and, or functional flexibility (Atkinson, 1984). In Spain, for example, Furio Blasco *et al.* (1992) report that 47 per cent of employees in tourism in 1991 were on temporary contracts, while 22 per cent were irregularly employed (whether in relation to social security, or outright clandestinely). Nevertheless, it is important not to exaggerate these 'peculiar' characteristics of tourist labour markets. Lever (1987) argues that for many tourism workers the only alternatives available for them are equally precarious work in agriculture or construction; in contrast, 'their position as wage laborers in tourism is more clearly defined, which means that they have easier access to protection from labor legislation and from trade unions'. The third element of polarization is spatial, for the geographical concentration of tourism demand requires the assemblage of labour at the point of demand. In mass tourism, this essentially means the leisure towns along the coast, with a few important exceptions such as Florence and Madrid.

Two important labour market impacts follow from this polarization. First, there is a socially constructed gender division of labour. Women carry into the workplace their subordinate status in society at large. They are often employed in making beds, serving meals or working in kitchens, in other words a replication of the household division of labour. This applies as much to mass tourism as to farm, or other forms of small-scale locally controlled, tourism. In mass tourism, in particular, there is a highly segmented labour force and a high degree of specialization in the production of tourism services. Women, with monotonous regularity across the Southern European mass coastal tourism resorts, are seen to dominate many

of these less-skilled, and lowest-paid labour market segments. It is important to emphasize that tourism does not just provide low-level jobs for
women. Instead, the very existence of a pool of women in the labour market, and the social possibility of paying them low wages or keeping them
on temporary or part-time contracts, contributes to the construction of the
core–periphery divide in the labour force, and to the existence of particular
forms of labour market segmentation.

Tourism does provide some sources of income and economic independence for women, particularly in regions where there were traditionally
few economic possibilities outside of the household and of farm economy.
However, the point that must be emphasized here is that tourism only
offers very limited opportunities for women to change their status or to
acquire greater independence, as opposed to just acquiring supplementary
household income. This is a point emphasized by Hadjimichalis and Vaiou
(1986, p. 17) writing about tourism on the Greek island of Naxos: 'rooms-
to-let is a household operation run almost entirely by women … Cleaning
rooms and serving guests is regarded as an extension of daily housework,
"naturally" women's work. Negotiating prices and making contracts with
the authorities is usually left to men.' Elsewhere, they have argued that
'the survival of such businesses depends on the ability to exploit family
labour where sexual and age divisions of labour are quite strict'
(Hadjimichalis and Vaiou, 1992, p. 174). Nevertheless, the contribution of
tourism to gender relationships is more complex than has hitherto been
suggested. Tourism does offer some independence and economic opportunities to many women and, however constrained, these should not be
underestimated.

The second labour market impact is that the spatial polarization of
tourism requires the assemblage of labour forces in the new leisure towns,
which exceed the capacity of local labour markets. As a result, a system of
immigration may develop; this may be seasonal or permanent depending
on the nature of the regional economy. Cavaco (1980) has shown that the
Algarve tourism industry is dependent on a daily commuting labour market as well as two main streams of migrant workers. The first is from villages in the hinterland which are beyond daily commuting distance. The
second is drawn from the poorer villages of the other regions of Portugal.
Potentially, the latter may facilitate the transfer of remittances from one of
the more developed to the less developed regions of the country.

Each of these labour market strategies has different economic and cultural impacts, both for the tourism area and for the migrants' home areas
(Table 4.6). In general it can be argued that daily commuters have no significant cultural impact and considerable economic impact on their home
areas. Bennett (1986), for example, notes the inter-sectoral transfers of
incomes from tourism to agriculture in the commuting villages of the
Algarve. The same applies to seasonal labour migrants although they may

Table 4.6   The impacts of different forms of tourism on labour migration

Migration systems	Impacts			
	on the tourism area		on the migrant's home area	
	economic	cultural	economic	cultural
daily commuter	limited	none	major	none
seasonal migrant	limited	limited	major	limited
permanent immigration	major	limited/major	limited	none
international migrant	limited	major	limited	major

have a greater cultural impact on their home areas and the tourist area. For example, Fraser's (1974) study of an Andalucian village shows the inter-generational conflicts between older residents and the seasonal migrants among the younger generation who work during the summer in the Costa del Sol tourism industry. The cultural tensions are sometimes matched by economic difficulties as the younger generation turn their backs on the hardship of agricultural work.

Another group of migrant workers are the permanent immigrants who can have a considerable cultural impact on the tourism areas, but this is a strangely neglected research topic. Valenzuela (1991) reports that 25 to 30 per cent of the populations in the Mediterranean provinces of Spain were immigrants in 1981, with a large part being drawn by the prospects of tourism employment. The actual pattern of migration is complex: it can be inter-regional, as from Andalucía to the Balearics, or intra-regional as from the interior of Andalucía (Granada, Jaén provinces etc) to the Costa del Sol. These involve very different social impacts. In the Costa Brava resort of Lloret del Mar, the migrant workers tend to be from the poorest of Spanish regions – 60 per cent are from Andalucía and 20 per cent are from Extremadura (Lever, 1987). They tend to be young women partly because they accept lower wages than men but partly because they are more flexible workers. A fourth and final stream of immigrant labour are the international migrants. This is a highly polarized group. At one extreme there is a small group of foreign managers who form part of the structures of dependency in tourism (de Kadt, 1979). However, most international migrant workers occupy the bottom rungs of the occupational hierarchy, undertaking some of the least secure and lowest paid jobs. Their insecurity is compounded by the illegal status of many such workers. Illegal immigrants are especially important in the tourist industries of Spain and Italy, and less so in Greece and Portugal. In Italy, particularly in Rome and other major cities, for example, there are large numbers of illegally hired hotel and restaurant workers from Ethiopia, the Philippines and other Third World countries (King, 1991; Montanari and Cortese, 1993). Many jobs are gender and nationality specific, such as Filipino domestic servants, and Senegalese street traders. Even in the Greek island of Naxos, illegal foreign workers are crucial to the survival of one half of the tourism businesses (Hadjimichalis and Vaiou, 1992). It is not simply a case of the tourism sector attracting illegal workers; in Italy, Dell'Aringa and Negri (1987) have argued that the existence of a pool of immigrant labour has contributed to the expansion of the underground economy, attracting capital and labour from the legal economy.

These brief discussions of gender and migration serve to highlight an important point: the impact of tourism must be seen in broader societal context, not as some unique free-standing process. Tourism jobs – whether undertaken by men or women – can provide an important contribution to household economies. King (1991, p. 71) writes of Italy that: 'the solidarity of the family as both a social and an economic unit enables the dovetailing of two or more activities, different members working on a full or part-time basis in different sectors, perhaps from a residential base or a farm in the agricultural hinterland.' The growth of farm and rural tourism provide even greater opportunities for linkages between the tourism and agricultural sectors. In this sense, developing tourism enterprises or working in tourism offers an alternative to emigration among the strategies available for the survival of household economies. These two are not, however, mutually incompatible; both King *et al.* (1984) in Amantea in Calabria, and Mendonsa (1983) in Nazare in Portugal, report on returned migrants investing in tourism enterprises.

Tourism is also an economic sector which appears to offer some possibilities for occupational and social mobility. It has relatively low entry thresholds in terms of the capital and skills required for establishing enterprises, especially in comparison to manufacturing. Therefore, in addition to offering a complementary source of income for some household economies, it can also provide the opportunity for a social and economic break for lower income households. This argument receives some support from Cals' (1984) contention that, in the early stages of tourism development, land price inflation generates a new circuit of indigenous capital. However, this argument has its limitations, for there are minimum capital requirements even if these can appear modest. For example, Mendonsa (1983) in Nazare found that, other than formal tourist businesses, about one half of all households had rooms to let. These provided, on average, $500 income at a time when mean household income was only $3,160. But the letting of rooms depended on home ownership. 'The ownership of housing is therefore a crucial production factor. These members of the community who do not have housing to rent out, and who lack other means of production, cannot share in tourism's benefits' (p. 228). Hence 'tourism tends to support existing class structure in the community' (p. 220). There is unfortunately a fundamental lack of research on the question of tourism asa channel for social mobility for individuals and households. However, sufficient evidence is available to emphasize that the opportunities are at least matched by the constraints.

Conclusion: tourism development, policies and politics

The golden age of tourism growth in Southern Europe was in the period 1955 to 1972. Thereafter, growth has been far more uncertain even if the overall trend has been upwards. In terms of absolute numbers tourism is most important in Spain and Italy which feature among the world's three leading international tourism destinations. However, in terms of growth rates, Portugal has had the most impressive performance in recent years. Although there have been variations in the timing of tourism, and in its exact form within and between the Southern European countries, the dominant trend has been the expansion of mass tourism. This has been characterized by spatial polarization, market segmentation, and especially a high degree of reliance on the UK and Germany, and highly elastic demand conditions in relation to prices and incomes. These have provided the essential ingredients in the creation of a highly dependent form of tourism development.

The positive economic impact of tourism is most clearly evident in the current accounts of these countries. International tourism makes a massive positive contribution to the current account in all four countries, but especially in Spain. As would be expected, however, the rate of growth of the surplus on the tourism account has been greatest in Portugal. Perhaps of greatest interest, however, are the data on per capita tourism expenditures, which represent a crude measure of efficiency of the different tourism industries in their ability to extract income streams from the tourists. Portugal emerges as the clear leader in this respect although there must be some reservations about the reliability of the data on financial flows. Consideration of the relative importance of tourism income in relation to both the current account total and GDP reveals that Spain has been the most tourism-dependent economy but that this is declining as the national economy expands and diversifies. Nevertheless, tourism continues to be one of the most important sectors in the economies of all the Southern European countries.

The general contribution of tourism to the economies of southern Europe is, therefore, abundantly clear, even if the precise economic and social impacts are highly contingent. As such, therefore, it is surprising that tourism has received so little attention from the state. Richter (1983) classifies tourism as a 'chosen' policy: 'it is not a policy foisted or a reluctant regime by political pressure like agrarian reform, language policy, or some industrialization policies. In its initial stages, there is very little conflict apparent over it.' This has certainly been the case with tourism where, until recently, state policy has been minimalist and non-controversial; the principal areas of intervention have been promotion, regulation of hotels and other establishments, and supporting investments in airports and other infrastructure. This is now changing with an environmental backlash among increasingly well organized pressure groups. In Spain, for example, this has led to the Ley de las Costas to prevent further infringement of the coastlines.

Yet there are important implications of tourism which would seem to demand greater state intervention. They can be characterized as distributional questions; who gets what, where from tourism? Mass tourism has developed as a highly polarized form of economic sector. It has created jobs and wealth in the new tourist towns of the Mediterranean regions. Yet, much of the employment has been as 'peripheral workers'. There have also been massive negative externalities in terms of cultural disruption and environmental destruction. This has been dramatically illustrated by the impact of the growth of algae on resorts such as Rimini (Becheri, 1991). But there has also been general despoilation of much of the coastline as a result of intensive over-development. The main beneficiaries have been international tour companies and some small segments of the national bourgeoisie. In contrast, the spatial polarization and the construction of labour markets has meant that the spread of benefits has been constrained and limited.

Second, there are important but rarely discussed long-term implications of changes in the tourism product cycle (Butler, 1980). He argues that in the mature stage of the cycle, resorts will plunge into decline unless they are reinvigorated by significant new investment and by innovation. It can be argued that many of the older, larger Southern European resorts are now at the critical point in the resort cycle. Recent evidence from Spain suggests that some resorts have already started to decline in terms of demand. It is likely that more and more resorts will face the challenge in future of adapting to new forms of demand, and increased competition. It is conceivable that, in coming decades, the mass tourist resorts will undergo restructuring equivalent to that experienced by some of the non-industrial towns in recent years. This argument may be too pessimistic and, for example, Morgan (1991) comments that the tourism product of Mallorca is in fact a series of variable products, each of which has its own life-cycle, not all or even any of which are locked into inevitably declining trajectories. Even so, there are bound to be difficult policy decisions to be taken with respect to the future of these Mediterranean resorts.

Tourism will face new challenges. At the very least most tourism regions will have to face choices about diversifying their markets, imposing stricter development controls, and improving product quality; but there are real constraints on the ability of the state to influence such changes in a sector dominated by foreign tour companies and fragmented indigenous capital.

A more radical objective would be to develop an alternative tourism (de Kadt, 1990). This would not damage the environment, would involve smaller scale developments, would not exploit local people and would be environmentally and culturally sustainable. Alternative tourism could assume one of several forms – green tourism, eco-tourism, etc. In the 1990s the debate has shifted on to the merits of sustainable tourism, conceptualized as a minimum to be a form of activity which does not reduce the tourism resources available for future generations. However, sustainable tourism also involves notions of equity in sharing the benefits of, and access to, tourism, as well as community involvement and control over tourism. As an agenda, therefore, it would seem to demand more effective forms of local democratic participation in shaping the tourism destinations of individual communities.

Irrespective of whether sustainability provides a realistic agenda for tourism development in any region, it poses three particular problems for Southern Europe. First, will sustainable tourism ever replace the mass tourism industry that brings more than 50 million foreigners a year to Spain alone? And what will alternative tourism offer to the owners of capital and the communities living in the traditional mass tourism resorts? Are such centres of consumption to undergo the social and political agonies of economic restructuring that have already been witnessed in the centres of production in Southern Europe (for example, in Setúbal or Bilbao) as well as in northern Europe. Finally, is a policy of more dispersed, small-scale tourism really desirable, or will it merely spread even more widely the negative cultural and environmental impacts of tourism? Perhaps the real issue for Southern Europe is whether the principles of (greater) sustainability can be introduced into the ageing mass tourist resorts. It is a question that they may not be able to avoid as the increased emphasis on quality issues (including the environmental dimension) in consumption also permeates mass tourism markets.

There are also wider questions here of the apportionment of tourism income between different sectors, in particular between the state, indigenous private capital and foreign capital (in the form of airlines and tour companies). There are constraints – particularly within the Single Market of the European Community on the ability of the state to limit foreign investment in and control of the tourism industry. The development of indigenous airlines and tour companies able to compete with the foreign oligopolies would of course increase the national share of the tourism income which would accrue to the Southern European economies. However, there seem to be limited possibilities in this direction at present; indeed there is a real concern that as national tourism grows in these countries, foreign capital will come to dominate their tour company and travel agency structures (Gomez and Sinclair, 1991). One solution would be some form of tourism tax so as to increase state income from tourism; this would also implicitly recognize the role of the state in providing devalorized capital (in airports, roads, etc) to support the tourism industry. There is however a major difficulty in implementing any such tax in the face of the high elasticity of demand relative to prices. It is precisely because of these difficulties that the idea has been mooted that the southern European countries should try and form a cartel so as to give them countervailing power in their dealings with the international tour companies. There would, however, be two difficulties with any such cartel. First, which countries would have to be included to make it effective given that the tourism product on offer is Mediterranean beach holidays? Could it, for example, be effective without the inclusion of Turkey or Tunisia? Second, would such a cartel be compatible with the competition rules of the European Community?

Finally, we turn to the wider political significance of tourism. There is scattered evidence that tourism contributed to the conditions which led to regime transition in Southern Europe in the 1970s. The boom in international mass tourism in the 1960s had demonstrable cultural and social impacts, particularly in Spain, via the demonstration effects of tourist behaviour. The challenge to traditional mores and customs coincided with growing economic and political tensions within the dictatorial regimes. Tourism was important in this if only because it highlighted differences in standards of living and in individual liberties between the tourist masses and the Spanish and Portuguese who lived and worked in the tourist enclaves. Moreover, these cultural impacts were not limited to the tourist enclaves, for the systems of labour migration ensured that they rippled out into other regions as, for example, Lever (1987) reports in the case of Lloret del Mar, and Fraser (1974) in the case of a *pueblo* in the Costa del Sol. It is ironic that tourism had such effects given that the Franco regime perceived tourism as being instrumental in establishing its international legitimacy.

During the process of regime transition, the contribution of tourism was of lesser significance; the main impact seems to have been the decrease in tourist numbers in Greece and especially Portugal in the mid-1970s following the publicity which surrounded the overthrow of the dictatorships. This probably served to underline the limitations of autonomous economic policies in relatively small open economies (Selwyn, 1979). In the 1990s tourism is probably best characterized as simply another sectional interest which has particular concerns about some elements of macroeconomic policy such as wage levels and exchange rates. It is also an industry that is likely to be affected by developments in European integration. Economic convergence as a precondition for economic and monetary union will limit the scope for using devaluations to counter factor cost inflation; this could have significant implications given the elasticity of demand relative to holiday prices. Furthermore, one of the considerations that could lead to a rise in one of the factor costs – of labour – is the Social Agreement appended to the Treaty of Union signed at Maastricht.

This leads to the final question of whether the democratic transition was in effect an essential precondition for the development of tourism. The simple answer is no given the rapid expansion that occurred before 1974–5, and given the growth experienced in non-EU-member Mediterranean states in the 1980s and early-1990s. Democratization was a precondition for EU membership for Portugal, Spain and Greece but, hitherto, there has been little EU intervention in the field of tourism. Freedom of movement provisions, competition law and other EC measures have barely touched the tourism industry. Reform of the Common Agricultural policy, and the emphasis on diversification have provided a boost to rural tourism throughout the Community but, while important in rural areas, the net effect on the tourist industry is minimal. In other ways, EU membership may even have been harmful to tourism. For example, it is arguable that membership of the ERM led to higher interest rates and overvalued currencies, which reduced the competitiveness of the Portuguese and especially the Spanish tourism industries.

If we move away from narrow considerations of economic consequences, then a more positive relationship with the democratic transition may be identified. Democratization did lead to local communities being able to articulate their opposition to the excesses of tourism growth, while the municipalities gained significant increases in their power to intervene and regulate the industry. This has led belatedly – especially in Spain – to some attempt to achieve more balanced and sustainable tourism expansion. Another factor of change is the emergence of significant communities of permanent or semi-permanent foreign residents in many of Southern Europe's coastal tourism resorts. They are likely to demand greater control over further tourism development, and may form strategic alliances with local community groups in order to pursue such goals. This is likely to be even more pronounced given EU initiatives to extend voting rights to member states' citizens wherever they are resident in the Union.

However, even in respect of the exertion of greater control by local communities, the experience of tourism in the democratic era has been equivocal. For example, Kousis (1984) argues that the arbitrary state-influenced bank lending of the dictatorship years produced a greater diffusion of new investments in tourism than was achieved during and after democratic transition. In the latter period, the emphasis on market principles led to the concentration of new hotels in the already most developed tourist areas. Furthermore the demands of the mass tourist industry, and the strong degree of external control exercised by the tour companies, are such that there are serious doubts as to whether intense competition will allow any significant state or local intervention that fundamentally reshapes the tourism product in contradiction to the dictates of the market.

Bibliography

Archer, B. H. (1982) 'The value of multipliers and their policy implications', *Tourism Management*, vol. 3, pp. 236–41.

Ascher, F. (1985) *Tourism: Transnational Corporations and Cultural Identities*, UNESCO, Paris.

Atkinson, J. (1984) *Flexibility, Uncertainty and Manpower Management*, University of Sussex, Institute of Manpower Studies, Report 89, Falmer.

Bagguley, P. (1990) 'Gender and labour flexibility in hotel and catering', *Services Industries Journal*, vol. 10, pp. 105–18.

Baklanoff, E. N. (1978) *The Economic Transformation of Spain and Portugal*, Praeger, New York.

Barucci, P. and Becheri, E. (1990) 'Tourism as a resource for developing southern Italy', *Tourism Management*, vol. 11, pp. 227–39.

Becheri, E. (1991) 'Rimini and Co – the end of a legend? Dealing with the algae effect', *Tourism Management*, vol. 12, pp. 229–35.

Bennett, M. and Radburn, M. (1991) 'Information technology in tourism: the impact on the industry and supply of holidays', in Sinclair, M. T. and Stabler, M. J. (eds), *The tourism industry: An International Analysis,* CAB, International, Wallingford.

Bennett, R. J. (1986) 'Social and economic transition: a case study in Portugal's Western Algarve', *Journal of Rural Studies*, vol. 2, pp. 91–102.

Buckley, P. J. and Papadopoulos, S. I. (1986) 'Marketing Greek tourism – the planning process', *Tourism Management*, vol. 7, pp. 86–100.

Butler, R. W. (1990) 'The concept of a tourist area cycle of evolution: implications for management of resources', *Canadian Geographer*, vol. 24, pp. 5–12.

Cals, J. (1984) 'Turismo y territorio: los terminos de una dialectica', in Pedreno Munoz, A. (ed.), *Ecologia, Economia y Turismo en el Mediterraneo, Ayuntiamento de Benidorm/Universidad de Alicante*, Alacant.

Cavaco, C. (1980) *Turismo e demografia no Algarve*, Editorial Progresso Social e Democracia, Lisbon.

Cunha, L. (1986) 'Turismo', in Silva, M. (ed.), *Portugal Contemporaneo: Problemas e Perspectivas*, Instituto Nacional de Administrasao, Lisbon.

Damette, F. (1980) 'The regional framework of monopoly exploitation: new problems and trends', in Carney, J., Hudson, R. and Lewis, J. (eds), *Regions in Crisis*, Croom Helm, London.

de Kadt, E. (1979) *Tourism Passport to Development*, Oxford University Press, Oxford.

de Kadt, E. (1990) *Making the Alternative Sustainable: Lessons from Development for Tourism*, Discussion Paper 272, Institute of Development Studies, University of Sussex, Brighton.

Dell'aringa, C. and Neri, F. (1987) 'Illegal immigrants and the informal economy', *Labour*, vol. 1, pp. 107–26.

Drexl, C. and Agel, P. (1987) 'Tour operators in West Germany', *Economist Intelligence Unit, Travel and Tourism Analyst*, May, pp. 29–43.

Dunning, J. H. and McQueen, M. (1982) 'The eclectic theory of the multinational enterprise and the international hotel industry', in Rugman, A. M. (ed.), *New Theories of the Multinational Enterprise*, Croom Helm, London.

Economist Intelligence Unit (1988) *Spain and the Balearic Islands*, Economist Intelligence Unit, International Tourism Reports, London.

Estudios Turisticos (1987) 'Estudio sobre los precios de los "packages" ofertados por operadores turisticors europeos en 1987', *Estudios Turisticos*, no. 95, pp. 3–22.

Estudios Turisticos (1988a) 'Inversiones extrajeras en imuebles. Provincias de Malaga y Alicante', *Estudios Turisticos*, no. 99, pp. 45–111.

Estudios Turisticos (1988b) 'Concentracíon y asociacionismo enpresarial en el sector turistico', *Estudios Turisticos*, no. 103, pp. 3–33.

Fitch, A. (1987) 'Tour operators in the UK', *Economist Intelligence Unit, Travel and Tourism Analyst*, March, pp. 29–41.

Fraser, R. (1974) *'The Pueblo: a Mountain Village on the Costa del Sol*, Allen Lane, London.

Furio Blasco, E., La-Roca Cervignon, F. and Sanchez Velasco, A. (1992) 'Turismo, medio ambiente y mercado de trabajo. Algunas consideraciones en torno a la insecion pefierica de la economia valenciana', Paper presente to the Seminario internazionale, 1992 e Periferie d'Europa, Lecce.

Gershuny, J. I. and Miles, I. D. (1983) *The New Service Economy*, Frances Pinter, London.

Gomez, V. B. and Sinclair, M. T. (1991) 'Integration in the tourism industry: a case study approach', in Sinclair, M. T. and Stabler, M. J. (eds), *The Tourism Industry: an International Analysis*, CAB International, Wallingford.

Guitart, C. (1982) 'UK charter flight package holidays to the Mediterranean, 1970–78', *Tourism Management*, vol. 3, pp. 16–39.

Hadjimichalis, C. and Vaiou, D. (1986) 'Changing patterns of uneven regional development and forms of social reproduction', unpublished paper, Athens.

Hadjimichalis, C. and Vaiou, D. (1992) 'Intermediate regions and forms of social reproduction: three Greek case studies', in Garofoli, C. (ed.), *Endogeneous Development and Southern Europe*, Avebury, Aldershot.

Harvey, D. (1990) *Postmodernism*, Blackwell, Oxford.

Hudson, R. and Lewis, J. (1984) 'Capital accumulation: the industrialization of southern Europe', in Williams, A. (ed.), *Southern Europe Transformed*, Harper and Row, London.

King, R. (1991) 'Italy: multi-faceted tourism', in Williams, A. M. and Shaw, G. (eds), *Tourism and Economic Development: Western European Experiences*, Belhaven Press, London.

King, R., Mortimer, J. and Strachan, A. (1984) 'Return migration and tertiary development: a Calabrian case study', *Anthropological Quarterly*, vol. 57, pp. 112–24.

Kousis, M. (1984) *'Tourism as an agent of social change in a rural Cretan community'*, PhD thesis, University of Michigan.

Laws, E. (1991) *Tourism Marketing: Service and Quality Management Perspectives*, Stanley Thornes, Cheltenham.

Leontidou, L. (1991) 'Greece: prospects and contradictions of tourism in the 1980s', in Williams, A. M. and Shaw, G. (eds), *Tourism and Economic Development: Western European Experiences*, Belhaven Press, London.

Lever, A. (1987) 'Spanish tourism migrants: the case of Lloret de Mar', *Annals of Tourism Research*, vol. 14, pp. 449–70.

Lewis, J. R. and Williams, A. M. (1988) 'No longer Europe's best kept secret: the Algarve's tourist boom', *Geography*, vol. 74, pp. 170–2.

Lewis, J. R. and Williams, A. M. (1991) 'Portugal: market segmentation and regional specialization', in Williams, A. M. and Shaw, G. (eds), *Tourism and Economic Development: Western European Experiences*, Belhaven Press, London.

Lipietz, A. (1980) 'The structuration of space, the problem of land, and spatial policy', in Carney, J., Hudson, R. and Lewis, J. (eds), *Regions in Crisis*, Croom Helm, London.

MacCannell, D. (1973) 'Staged authenticity: arrangements of social space in tourist settings', *American Sociological Review*, vol. 79, pp. 589–603.

Manente, M. (1986) 'Il turismo nell economia Italiana' in *Secondo Rapporto sul Turismo Italiano*, Ministero del Turismo e dello Spettacolo, Rome.

Mathieson, A. and Wall, G. (1982) *Tourism: Economic, Physical and Social Impacts*, Longman, London.

Mendonsa, E. L. (1983) 'Tourism and income strategies in Nazare, Portugal', *Annals of Tourism Research*, vol. 10, pp. 213–38.

Monopolies and Mergers Commission (1989) *Thomson Travel Group and Horizon Travel Ltd: A Report on the Merger Situation*, HMSO London.

Montanari, A. and Cortese, A. (1993) 'Third world immigrants in Italy', in King, R. (ed.), *Mass Migrations in Europe*, Belhaven, London.

Morgan, M. (1991) 'Dressing up to survie: marketing Majorca anew', *Tourism Management*, vol. 12, pp. 15–20.

Mullins, P. (1991) 'Tourism urbanization', *International Journal of Urban and Regional Research*, vol. 15, pp. 326–42.

Nuñez, T. (1978) 'Touristic studies in anthropological perspective', in Smith, V. L. (ed.), *Hosts and Guests: the Anthropology of Tourism*, Basil Blackwell, Oxford.

OECD (1971) *Tourism Policy and International Tourism in OECD Member Countries*, OECD, Paris.

OECD (1981) *Tourism Policy and International Tourism in OECD Member Countries*, OECD, Paris.

OECD (1990) *Tourism Policy and International Tourism in OECD Member Countries*, OECD, Paris.

Palomcque, F. L. (1988) 'Geografia del turismo en Espana', *Documents d'Analisi Geografica*, vol. 13, pp. 35–64.

Papadopoulos, S. I. and Mirza, H. (1985) 'Foreign tourism in Greece: an economic analysis', *Tourism Management*, vol. 6, pp. 125–37.

Pearce, D. G. (1987a) 'Spatial patterns of package tourism in Europe', *Annals of Tourism Research*, vol. 14, pp. 183–200.

Pearce, D. G. (1987b) 'Mediterranean charters – a comparative geographic perspective', *Tourism Management*, vol. 8, pp. 291–305.

Pearce, D. G. (1988) 'Tourism and regional development in the European Community', *Tourism Management*, vol. 9, pp. 13–22.

Richter, L. K. (1983) 'Tourist politics and political science: a case of not so benign neglect', *Annals of Tourism Research*, vol. 10, pp. 313–35.

Seers, D., Schaffer, B. and Kiljunan, M. L. (1979) *Underdeveloped Europe: Case Studies in Core Periphery Relations*, Harvester Press, Hassocks.

Selwyn, P. (1979) 'Some thoughts on core and peripheries', in Seers, D., Schaffer, B. and Kiljunen, M. L. (eds), *Underdeveloped Europe*, Harvester Press, Hassocks.

Shaw, G. and Williams, A. M. (1994) *Critical Issues in Tourism: A Geographical Perspective*, Blackwells, Oxford.

Simms, J., Hales, C. and Riley, M. (1988) 'Examination of the concept of internal labour markets in UK hotels', *Tourism Management*, vol. 9, pp. 3–12.

Sinclair, M. T. (1991) 'The tourism industry and foreign exchange leakages in a developing country', in Sinclair, M. T. and Stabler, M. J. (eds), *The Tourism Industry: an International Analysis*, CAB International, Wallingford.

Smith, V. L. (1978) *Hosts and Guests: an Anthropology of Tourism*, University of Philadelphia Press, Philadelphia.

Stock, R. (1977) 'Political and social contributions of international tourism to the development of Israel', *Annals of Tourism Research*, vol. 4, pp. 30–42.

Storper, M. S. (1985) 'Oligopoly and the product cycle: essentialism in economic geography', *Economic Geography*, vol. 61, pp. 260–82.

Truett, D. B. and Truett, L. J. (1987) 'The response of tourism to international economic conditions: Greece, Mexico and Spain', *Journal of Developing Areas*, vol. 21, no. 2, pp. 177–90.

Turner, L. and Ash, J. (1975) *The Golden Hordes: International Tourism and the Pleasure Periphery*, Constable, London.

UNTC (1982) *Transnational Corporations in International Tourism*, United Nations, New York.

Urry, J. (1990) *The Tourist Gaze: Leisure and Travel in Contemporary Societies*, Sage Publications, London.

Valenzuela, M. (1991) 'Spain: the phenomenon of mass tourism', in Williams, A. M. and Shaw, G. (eds), *Tourism and Economic Development: Western European Experiences*, Belhaven Press, London.

Williams, A. M. (1989) 'Socialist economic policies: never off the drawing board?', in Gallagher, T. and Williams, A. M. (eds), *Southern European Socialism: Parties, Elections and the Experiences of Government*, Manchester University Press, Manchester.

Williams, A. M. and Shaw, G. (1991) 'Western European tourism in perspective', in Williams, A. M. and Shaw, G. (eds), *Tourism and Economic Development: Western European Experiences*, Belhaven Press, London.

Yannopoulos, G. N. (1988) 'Tourism, economic convergence and the European South', *Estudios de Economia*, vol. 8, pp. 197–216.

5
Labour Market Segmentation and Informal Work

Enzo Mingione

Structuration of the social division of labour within the Southern European variants of industrial development

The four countries which make up Southern Europe, Italy, Greece, Portugal and Spain, show some similarities and many differences in terms of employment and labour market structuration. In this chapter, starting from the similarities I discuss the hypothesis that these countries constitute variants of the same model of capitalist development, typical of latecomer economies where family enterprises and self-employment are persistently dynamic, the formation of a fully proletarianized manufacturing working class is limited, and non-wage contributions to the livelihood strategies of households and, as a consequence, irregular forms of work are disproportionally diffused. The inclusion of the Italian case represents the major obstacle to the exploration of this hypothesis, not because Italy is industrially more advanced than the other three countries but because it is composed of two extremely different and divergent parts: the centre-north and the south. For this reason, Italy is seen as consisting of two different cases (Garofoli, 1991; Mingione, 1990a). I investigate whether it is possible to consider these two cases as opposite variants of the general model: northern Italy being an example of where family entrepreneurial resources and non-wage contributions to survival have been used to promote industrial development along a successful alternative path to the more proletarianized and capital-concentrated variants; and southern Italy being an example of a late-developing agrarian society that has been de-ruralized and modernized without passing through the stage of acute industrialization and sufficiently extensive diffusion of competitive manufacturing initiatives, either decentralized from outside[1] and/or promoted by the development of local petty commodity production.

The study of the structuration of the labour market poses serious difficulties even in a single case,[2] but is extremely complicated when dealing with complex economies and all the more so in the comparative analysis undertaken here. The complications are mainly of a methodological nature: the interpretation of sources and data and the need to link macroindicators of economic development and different forms of employment, underemployment and unemployment with the micro socio-demographic livelihood arrangements of households. In order to achieve this goal, more importance is attached to the historical patterns in the hypothetical Southern European model than to conventional economic and employment data.

Overall, the hypothesis of the Southern European model of modernization put forward here is critical of any idea of stages of development (Rostow, 1960) and is based on the assumption that patterns of transformation are varied and cannot be repeated. In other words, it is impossible for them to be transferred from the more advanced to the less advanced cases. This is true in general and also in those cases included in the Southern European model: for example, the other Southern European countries cannot follow in the footsteps of northern Italy. A further implication is that the approach, discussed below, of the *Second Industrial Divide* (Piore and Sabel, 1984), the micro paradigm of the Italian industrial districts (Becattini, 1987; Goodman *et al.*, 1989) and the successful experience of the so-called 'Third Italy' (Benko and Dunford, 1991; Benko and Lipietz, 1992; Hilpert, 1991) cannot be generalized and used to understand or forecast the paths of development of other Southern European regions. On the basis of this assumption I look briefly at how some general trends of the last two decades, such as the increase in informal activities, have impacted on Southern European labour markets both within the general model and in particular cases. This is a delicate question because the real meaning of the transformation process has to be grasped in depth, something not immediately manifest from the data on employment and unemployment. For instance, the European country with the highest rate of growth in self-employed jobs is the UK, which does not necessarily mean that this country is becoming more similar to the Southern European cases. Since the rate of proletarianization has been historically high in this country, de-industrialization and de-proletarianization is a particularly acute phenomenon. However, the real terms of this process have to be studied in detail (what kind of new jobs, done by whom, within which household and community structure?). Moreover, such a study would probably show that the convergence with the Southern European model is, at least in the main, only apparent.

It is particularly important when studying the Southern European cases to avoid some generalizations and simplifications that have at times been attractive to those interpreting the recent socio-economic transformations. One stereotype is that the Southern European economics are attracting foreign capital and are successful because they are characterized by a considerable presence of irregular forms of employment, which are confused with flexible forms of employment (see also Curry, 1993; Hadjimichalis and Vaiou, 1990a; Pollert, 1991). It should be clear that irregular employment is neither automatically flexible (on the contrary, it sometimes reflects rigid and backward conditions that are not favourable to successful capitalist ventures) nor particularly competitive (especially since irregular work is increasingly concentrated in the services, as documented in each southern European case) (see Piore, 1986; Sayer, 1989). The other stereotype interpretation is centred on the industrial district and on the so-called 'Third Italy model', mentioned above. The idea is that success in the 1970s and 1980s in the regional economy of central Italy can be fully explained starting from the cases of a few specialized industrial districts (like Carpi in Emilia and Prato in Tuscany), which in reality constitute only a tiny and exceptional part of the larger regional economy. As will be seen later, exactly the reverse is true: that is, we can understand the success and vitality of these industrial districts only when we have a clear picture of the regional socio-economic background. The 'reverse approach' is misleading but particularly attractive as it assumes that it is sufficient to identify a few dynamic industrial districts in order to understand a region or a country and identify its economic and social prospects and the industrial policies favouring further development (see also Amin and Robins, 1990; Amin and Thrift, 1992; Hadjimichalis, 1994; Perulli, 1993).

The historical foundations of the Southern European model of labour market structuration are varied and lie mainly in the fact that they are late-industrializing countries where the state has persistently protected the productive role of small and family enterprises. They may be summarized as: persistence and innovation in traditional and agrarian social arrangements; relatively high rates of family businesses and of informal work; the limited diffusion of a fully proletarianized (highly dependent on wage income) manufacturing working class; persistently low rates of non-agricultural female employment accompanied by limited achievements in direct state provisioning of welfare services; informalization in recent years coinciding with the decline of fordism and de-industrialization in other advanced industrial contexts.[3]

Before analysing specifically the terms of the question of labour market structuration and the presence of informal work, it is worth briefly discussing, from a comparative angle, the two important themes of welfare systems and regional inequalities. According to the comparative framework proposed by Esping-Andersen (1990) for welfare systems in advanced industrial societies, all the Southern European countries fall within the 'conservative' model of welfare capitalism. This author concentrates in particular on the case of Germany as an example of such a model, but he also provides ample evidence to show that the Southern European countries are characterized by similar patterns, often to a greater degree than in Germany. The typical features of this model hinge on the crucial role maintained by family and voluntary agencies in the provision of welfare services. Welfare policies are formulated to complement the essential role of family provision, so that income transfers to families are disproportionally high while the provision of welfare services by the state remains less widespread than in the Scandinavian 'social-democratic' model and market welfare services are less developed than in the Anglo-American 'liberal' model. At the same time, the participation of married women in non-agricultural paid employment is relatively discouraged and, even though substantially on the increase in recent decades, still falls well below the levels reached in other cases. In this respect, the Southern European variants (with the exception of Portugal)[4] are, as we shall see, markedly more radical than the German case, that is, the level of participation of women in formal and recorded paid work outside agriculture is lower than in Germany. This is true also in industrially advanced northern Italy, even when taking into account the reasonable assumption that a part of adult female paid work is not officially recorded.

It is on the basis of the great variability between different cases that, as suggested by some critics of Esping-Andersen (Cochrane and Clarke, 1993; Ferrera, 1993; Leibfried, 1992; Taylor-Gooby, 1991) the 'conservative' model should be divided into two groups of variants. The first is typical of countries, such as Germany and France, where the welfare mix has been shaped by efficient state policies for regulating the labour market, particularly in favour of job insertion for young native workers to be sheltered from competition with large waves of immigrants. This feature is more developed in the German case than in any other variant with the result that unemployment in Germany is now quite different from the rest of Europe in that the number of unemployed young people is very low. The second group typical of the Southern European countries, is more radically familistic, that is, characterized by a larger persistence of family firms also outside agriculture, less dynamic and more delayed industrial development and consequently a long tradition of emigration and extremely weak state policies for regulating the entry of young workers into the labour market, given that they were destined for selection by migration rather than through competition to enter the local labour market. This means that the welfare mix is even more unbalanced towards family (here the term 'familistic' is intended in the sense only of a relatively high rate of responsibility and burden on the family in the provision of welfare and care services) and voluntary forms, inevitably made relatively more particularistic and uneven, of provision of support and welfare services. As we shall see, this then shapes the demographic and householding patterns, favouring a delayed but very marked decline in the birth rate, long cohabitation of adult children with their parents and, in general, a higher probability of cohabitation or, in any event, intense interrelationship and solidarity between relatives of different generational groups.

The radical familistic patterns of the Southern European welfare system affect particularly the structuration of the youth labour market. Unemployment is highly concentrated among young people (under 25), who constitute between 40 and 50 per cent of the unemployed and 80 per cent of the long-term unemployed as against rates in the other European countries that never exceed 33 per cent and 50 per cent respectively (IARD, 1996; Mingione and Pugliese, 1995; Reyneri, 1996). This situation contrasts sharply with that in Germany, where efficient training and work insertion programmes have been developed with the result that young people find good permanent jobs and become independent from their parents soon after leaving school. In the Southern European countries, entry into the labour market by young people is poorly assisted by state-run programmes, which has led to the youth unemployment crisis of recent decades being offset by very long periods of cohabitation with parents.[5] This phenomenon is more accentuated in southern Italy and in Spain where the consumption resources of households and the working expectations of school-leavers have increased considerably while good employment opportunities have fallen. In Portugal and Greece, both consumption resources and expectations have increased less while in northern Italy good employment opportunities have matched the expectations of a demographically decreasing cohort of school-leavers, particularly in the second half of the 1980s.

The Southern European countries are persistently characterized by regional inequalities (Wolleb and Wolleb, 1993) and this fact has important consequences for labour market structuration and the local prevalence of different forms of survival arrangements and of different work cultures. This is true both of Italy considered as two separate cases and for more advanced northern Italy alone. The discussion of whether or not persistent regional diversity constitutes an essential feature of the Southern European model of industrialization is beyond the scope of this chapter. However, it is worth mentioning some of the causes and patterns of regional inequalities as they have important repercussions on labour market structuration. At the root of many regional diversities we find different agrarian regimes in terms of both the geographical and climatic features of local agricultural traditions and, even more, of the historically consolidated system of ownership and land cultivation. The historical division between latifundia and diverse regional peasant and family farming traditions is particularly marked in Spain, Portugal and both southern and northern Italy. In this respect, Greece is the only Southern European case where the agrarian and latifundia question has not constituted a serious problem in recent times as it was resolved following major redistribution in 1871 and 1923 (the latter being associated with the exchange of populations after the Greek defeat in Asia Minor).

Furthermore, industrial development has remained particularly concentrated in certain regions and localities and shown only a relatively limited tendency to spread beyond them, with the exception of northern Italy in the last two decades. Not even the series of regional development policies adopted in the last three decades have been very successful (Wolleb and Wolleb, 1993). In both northern Italy and Spain the core of postfordist industrial restructuring is found in the localities of early industrial concentration: only parts of the traditional advanced development axis have declined, hit by de-industrialization (like Piedmont and Liguria in northern Italy and the North Atlantic belt in Spain), while others (like Lombardy in Italy and Catalonia in Spain) persistently remain the core of industrial development and new regions have been incorporated in the core area of high growth (Madrid in Spain and Emilia Romagna and the North-East – the three Venetian regions in northern Italy). The same is true to a different extent of Greece and Portugal where particularly dynamic industrial development has remained confined to the metropolitan poles of Athens–Piraeus and Salonika and of Lisbon and Oporto, respectively. In fact, none of these countries shows a clear division between 'rust-belt' and 'sun-belt' regions but, rather, the continuing importance of some areas of industrial concentration in contrast with the chronic difficulties of less developed regions.

Origins and causes of the Southern European social division of labour model

The historical roots of the Southern European model

The historical basis of this model consists in a delayed industrial transition in which some specific, but locally varied, agrarian structures and arrangements have maintained and even increased their importance. The regions in the north-west of Italy, in particular Lombardy, represent the only relevant exceptions. Here, starting in the second half of the eighteenth century, important agricultural innovations and large-scale investment in textiles and engineering sparked a feeble process of industrialization, which accelerated in Lombardy when, after the fall of the Napoleonic empire, the region assumed with Bohemia the crucial role of industrial core in the Austro-Hungarian empire. The unification of Italy in 1860 constituted an economic setback for some decades due to the limitations of the internal market, but, by the beginning of the new century (Gerschenkron, 1962), with the rearmament of Italy and the public works connected with the development of the railway network, north-western Italy achieved a definitive take-off. However, even thereafter and up to the end of World War II, Italian industrial development was inhibited by the limited internal consumer market conditioned by backward agrarian settings in the rest of the country (Castronovo, 1975).

The other countries in Southern Europe were only marginally involved in industrial transformation, located around important trade centres like Barcelona, Naples, Lisbon and Athens. The agrarian capitalist transition progressed at a slow pace both in regions characterized by the persistence of latifundia, like southern Italy and southern Spain, and in those characterized by small peasant farming or where commercial family farming was developing, like Greece, central and north-eastern Italy and Catalonia, and also in Portugal, where a conservative mix of latifundia in the south and minifundia in the centre-north prevailed up to the 1974 revolution. The manpower freed by the slow development of capitalist farming was mostly driven to intercontinental migration (and, in the case of Portugal, also to settlements in the African colonies) by the weak immediate prospects of local industrial development. In the case of north-western Italy, the newly formed manufacturing working class was recruited from the countryside surrounding the industrial cities and a considerable part remained worker-peasants for generations (Villa, 1986). The same phenomenon occurred later on in the industrializing regions of Spain (Catalonia, El Pais Valenciano, the Basque Country) at least up to the 1960s when industrial development began to attract migrants from the less developed regions of Spain.[6]

Italy: the 'Southern question' and the 'three Italies'

In 1945 Southern Europe was still characterized by a marked prevalence of agricultural employment and rural settings broken only by concentrated pockets of industrial development, of which the largest and most important was the 'industrial triangle' in the north-west of Italy. It was mostly in the following decades that a significant degree of industrial transformation took place, though with wide regional and national differences, which had a considerable effect on labour market segmentation and work cultures. Italy became clearly divided into three different regions: the so-called 'Three Italies' (Bagnasco, 1977). The north-west developed into the core of the Italian 'industrial miracle', which attracted large waves of migrants to industrial cities and into large manufacturing concerns highly export-oriented and increasingly organized along taylorist lines.[7] The centre and north-east, later called the 'third Italy' (the north-west being the first and the Mezzogiorno the second), was characterized by slow economic growth, relatively high socio-geographical stability and the consolidation of cooperative family farming and of small industrial concerns mainly oriented to local markets. In the south, agrarian reform and the economic policies of the central state dismantled the agrarian regime. A high wave of emigration, chaotic urbanization and the spread of a modern system of monetary consumption[8] increasingly supported by external resources were the main features of social transformation in the south in this period.

In the early-1970s, the first and third Italies appeared quite different from one another. The north-west was characterized by a numerous working class employed in large manufacturing concerns and living either in metropolitan cities or in single-industry towns and districts. The rapid and chaotic economic growth of the previous decades had not been matched by sufficient development of housing and welfare service provision. The average income was more than double that of the rest of the country but the quality of life suffered from poor standards in education, housing, health, local transport and urban infrastructure.

The third Italy had remained less developed and was still characterized by a rate of employment in agriculture more than double that in the industrial triangle (15 per cent as against 7 per cent). The high degree of social stability accompanied by a constant slow growth of local markets favoured the development of cooperative agricultural and food industries and of small industrial ventures both in traditional (shoes, clothing, furniture, etc) and innovative sectors (light machinery and engineering, electrical appliances and durables).[9] Social stratification was centered on family businesses in agriculture, craft activities, manufacturing and local services where the divisions between employers and employees were not very pronounced. The social division of labour was often interlinked with the family and kinship organization where unpaid family help played a highly important role. It is for this very reason that the third Italy model of industrial development has been assumed to be persistently based on extensive use of informal work, even if in the 1970s and 1980s successful manufacturing and service firms almost entirely regularized employment conditions for family helpers and other previously irregular workers in order to avoid excessive taxation (Mingione, 1990b, 1991).

As I have already anticipated, the success of the third Italian economy in the 1970s and 1980s has been partially confused with the success of some industrial districts in the region, particularly the two textile districts of Carpi in Emilia (specialized in garment and advanced light technology for garment production) and Prato in Tuscany (specialized in wool production, above all production of recycled wool instead of raw material) (see particularly Becattini, 1987, 1989). It is not the success of the industrial districts that explains the features of the regional economy but the reverse. Already in the mid-1970s Bagnasco (1977) insisted on the fact that the conditions of social and political stability, based on the absence of waves of immigration and emigration and the traditional distribution of the population in a very articulated system of medium cities and towns and the prevalence of long established network- and cooperative-oriented family farming concerns (Brusco, 1979) are the crucial factors in explaining both the regional success and the extraordinary dynamic nature of the local industrial districts. This has been reflected also in a relatively high standard of life and in the capacity to modernize successfully crucial sectors of public and private welfare services, like education, health, professional, craft and technical training, etc, due both to stronger and more efficient local administrations and to social stability.

In the South, during the same period, a rapid de-ruralization process was set in motion mainly by emigration, the modernization of consumption through high state expenditure in public works and income-support policies, whereas industrialization was only limited and sporadic and led by the location of heavy petrochemical and steel plants in the development poles and by a certain amount of decentralization of fordist durable goods factories to the metropolitan district of Naples and to sites around a few other major cities, like Catania and Bari.[10] The radical decline of employment in agriculture was compensated for, up to the mid-1970s, mainly by emigration and by the growth in the number of construction workers, the great majority precariously employed (Sylos-Labini, 1964), traditional private service workers (also in this case largely irregularly employed) and employees in public administration. Within the manufacturing sector, the relatively slow growth of employment in large modern capital-intensive decentralized concerns barely matched the decline of local traditional industries and crafts, squeezed out of the market by exposure to international competition through the modernization of consumption (Graziani, 1978). The labour processes in both construction and private services remained highly labour-intensive as they were based on irregular employment and low productivity. Most recently, in the wake of the oil shock, the end of emigration and a proportionally large surge of de-industrialization have led to a period of very high and persistent unemployment, reaching levels (a peak of 21 per cent in 1989) even higher than in Spain. In fact, as we will also see below, Spain and southern Italy are in most respects the two cases that appear most alike, even though the former is more dynamic and heterogeneous while the latter is now rigidly structured around patronage-oriented public policies and income-support programmes.

The postfordist adaptation features of the northern Italy variant

The three Italies of the 1970s offer a typological range of labour market segmentation patterns that can be usefully applied to interpret the other southern European countries. However, before doing so it is worthwhile to point out some typical common features of the first and third Italy which throw light on some peculiarities in the Southern European model of labour market structuration, even in the case of fordist industrialization. These features have become crucial factors in recent years in achieving adaptation to the postfordist transition and have marked out convergent paths which are making the two northern Italian regions increasingly homogeneous.

The most important of these common features arises from the fact that household and kinship networks have retained and adapted their crucial strategic economic role. In the cases of families of self-employed and small manufacturing and service workers, largely predominant in the social textures of the third Italy and of the periphery of the industrial triangle, family and community networks have been used to promote economic

innovation and a complex and successful mix of new professions, cooperative ventures, advanced consultancy and community economic infrastructures for R&D, global marketing, advertising and financial assistance.[11] The
familial orientation was of great importance also in the case of working-
class families living in the Milan, Turin and Genoa metropolitan regions
and employed in the large fordist concerns. In fact, the manufacturing
working class, largely composed of recently migrated families from the
south, obtained a relatively comprehensive system of social security, job
stability and family wages during the 1960s and early-1970s. This applied,
however, almost exclusively to adult male breadwinners and was poorly
complemented by the inadequate development of welfare services provision. As a consequence, a system of social relations with the nuclear family
household at its core, supported by kinship, neighbourhood and work-
mates' networks became established and developed a great sense of responsibility for fostering intergenerational social mobility.[12] Formal and
informal resources were maximized towards home-ownership, education of
children and the creation of better employment opportunities for them.
Both the demographic practices of households – increasingly later marriage
age, delayed childbearing, falling birth rate, cohabitation of adult children
with parents – and their economic strategies – income-pooling, informal
support between kinship networks, a marked propensity to save, high
investment in home-ownership, maximization of formal and informal
resources, and a persistent vocation to small entrepreneurship – confirm
this familial physiognomy of the Italian working class.

The second important feature is the diffusion of modernized productive
households ready to adapt to new conditions and able to provide social
integration for the increasingly diversified and complex forms of flexible
employment (Paci, 1978, 1992). Both self-employment and small manufacturing and service units remained relatively widespread even in the large
industrial metropolitan districts of Milan and Turin and even in the period
of maximum success of the vertically integrated and concentrated fordist
organizations during the late-1960s and early-1970s.

The third feature is the informal and decentralized style of relations
between capital and labour (Magatti, 1991, 1993). Even in the north-west,
in the most industrialized and unionized part of the country, during the
1960s and 1970s the problem of transforming the traditional large firms
was solved by decentralizing production, made possible by widespread
paternalism and a high degree of mutual trust in labour relations and by
the presence of a number of small and artisan firms. At the same time, this
condition also made it easier, compared to other industrialized countries,
to re-orient the local economy towards more profitable innovative sectors
instead of just de-industrializing the old districts. This became a crucial
success factor as soon as the fordist conditions of mass standardized production weakened and were substituted by the search for flexibility, vertical

disintegration and subcontracting chains, socio-economic networking and new forms of complex economic organization.

The Spanish case: the impact of de- and re-industrialization

The other Southern European countries have not been able to follow the northern Italian model due to the lack of the socio-economic conditions and features listed above. There is even a widening gap opening up with respect to southern Italy, particularly in terms of income and modernization of consumption patterns, which in the Mezzogiorno have been heavily supported by redistributive income support policies. Deruralization has proceeded at a relatively slower pace and no other country or region has been able to follow the same patterns of 'modernization without industrial development' (Graziani, 1978). The other Southern European economies have remained less open to integration into the international market, so that they have benefited less from the kind of export-led wave of growth that characterized the first Italian economic miracle in the 1960s. At the same time, Spain and Portugal have benefited from the fact that they were not directly involved in World War II. The former fascist regimes compensated for relative economic isolation with strict control on the demands of working class organizations. This was reflected in high rates of economic growth at least up to the first oil shock in the early-1970s. Greece, for its part, in the last 20 years has progressively accentuated its twin specialization in tourism and shipping and shipbuilding.

Spain is more closely comparable with Italy. The northern Mediterranean and the northern Atlantic industrialized regions have attracted working class migrants from the rest of the country and become centres for large and concentrated manufacturing concerns (Giner, 1980). Also, as in northern Italy, working class culture has retained strong familistic features and remained unopposed to petty entrepreneurship, particularly in Catalonia and in El Pais Valenciano, where small-scale manufacturing for the local market has continued to flourish. However, the persistence of traditional agrarian economies together with limited exposure to international competition have made the Spanish economy rather vulnerable and the effects of the oil crisis have been extremely severe (Salmon, 1991). The slow pace of de-ruralization and the long-term persistence of a low-wage industrial setting has favoured the growth of a wide range of irregular forms of employment in building, private services and tourism, agriculture and manufacturing. In the metropolitan districts of Barcelona and Madrid, these arrangements have been complementary within the family system to the continually inadequate regular wage economy while in the industrial peripheries (for example, in the Valencia area) and in the less developed regions (for example, Andalusia) they have become consolidated as one of the essential elements in a persistently low-income mix. Unlike southern Italy, irregular work in Spain is widespread and increased substantially in the 1980s, even in manufacturing, particularly in subcontracting chains and outwork (Miguelez-Lobo, 1990a; Recio, 1986). In contrast with northern Italy, these manufacturing arrangements are neither particularly dynamic nor subject to regularization. On the contrary, one has the impression that economic growth and the expansion of export potential are contributing to the multiplication rather than to the transformation of these arrangements, as happened in the third Italy and in the peripheries of the Italian 'industrial triangle'. There is a clear labour market explanation for this phenomenon. The northern Italian formalization process took place within a labour market that was growing tight as the reserve supply of cheap labour was dwindling, whereas in Spain persistently high levels of unemployment characterize both the more and the less industrialized regions.

Worthy of mention is the fact that the Spanish labour market was thrown into turmoil during two different phases. From 1977 to 1985 employment declined dramatically at an overall rate of nearly 15 per cent. Employment in construction dropped by more than 35 per cent and the decrease in manufacturing reached nearly 25 per cent, higher than the reduction in agriculture and indicating a de-industrialization trend second only to that in Britain. In the same period, employment in the services sector was basically stagnant. In the second phase, from 1985 to 1990, employment rose substantially and by the end of the period had reached the same absolute level as in 1975. After 1990 another recession hit the country, accompanied by a new wave of de-industrialization and a further increase in the level of unemployment, which already in 1992 passed the peak of 1985 (see Figure 5.1). The growth in employment of 1985 to 1990 was led by the services sector but also by construction (which reached the same levels as in the early-1970s) and there was in addition a milder but marked rise in employment in manufacturing. Unemployment levels were not particularly affected by this rise in employment since the labour

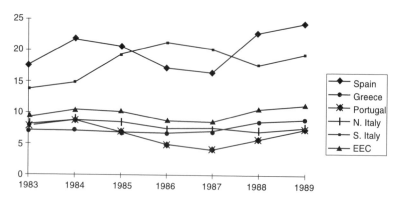

Figure 5.1 Unemployment rate (male and female, 1983–94)

supply, particularly of adult women, expanded in parallel. The rise was also accompanied by a substantial increase in the percentage of temporary fixed-period workers, who passed from 15 per cent of the employed population in 1987 to nearly one-third in 1991.

With regard to the acute decline in employment in the first period mentioned, Jimeno and Toharia advance the following explanation 'the foremost cause of employment losses in the 1975–85 period was the inefficiency and weakness of most Spanish firms, whose viability was based on the existence of cheap labor and lack of competition and on the change in the economic and political environment' (Jimeno and Toharia, 1994, p. 25). The period registered a substantial increase in informal work, particularly in traditional manufacturing and construction, connected also with the first reforms in the social security system, which allowed the adoption of family strategies based on the pooling of various low-income sources (Recio, 1986; Toharia, 1988). These mixes were further developed in the following period with the increasing contribution made by the growth in female and youth temporary fixed-period employment (Cousins, 1994; Hadjimichalis and Vaiou, 1990a). The employment recovery was certainly brought about by the global western recovery of the early-1980s and by the integration of Spain into the EC, which gave a dynamic boost to foreign and joint economic ventures in the export-oriented sectors (Salmon, 1991). Thus, recent Spanish employment history represents a clear instance of a cycle of transformation resulting from the opening up to global market integration, which eliminates a large number of 'inefficient' jobs and creates high levels of unemployment (see Figure 5.1) that cannot be reabsorbed later on even with the return of a favourable economic climate.

Family subsistence mixes in Portugal and Greece

With some variations, we find a similar picture in Portugal and Greece where it is not only a question of the extent or level of industrial development. More important is the persistent, and even growing, complex mix between small family farming, a wide range of regular and irregular activities (in a large part of Greece disproportionally connected with tourism) and the official wage economy. De Sousa Santos (1985) calls these mixes *'a descoincidencia entre producao capitalista e reproducao social'* [a disconnection between capitalist production and social reproduction]. This phenomenon is a particularly clear version of what I have called 'partial proletarization', which may well be one of the crucial characteristics of Southern European societies. In both Portugal and Greece, the features of these mixes are fundamentally based on the persistence and adaptation of micro family farming units, which were originally typical of peasant subsistence economies.[13] Family farming is the central axis around which, on one side, wages are kept low and the conditions of modern industrial employment relatively flexible and, on the other, formal and informal activities by household members in building, crafts, petty commerce and tourism remain viable (Hadjimichalis and Vaiou, 1990a). This is particularly true of villages and towns but also influences to some extent the conditions of life of the working class in the major industrial centres of Lisbon, Oporto, Athens and Salonika. Here, the centrality of family farming clearly no longer applies; but a multi-activity mix nonetheless still characterizes working class family budgets, complementing persistently low wages and the relative inadequacies of welfare state systems. It is evident that these same conditions have a limiting impact on capitalist accumulation and concentration trends, and constantly depress the volume of the official monetary economy, given that they function as a variant of persisting subsistence strategies typical of less developed economies. They are also reflected in a high rate of informal and unaccounted-for activities estimated for both Portugal (Miguelez-Lobo, 1990b; Rodrigues, 1992; Villaverde Cabral, 1984) and Greece (Leontidou, 1993; Mingione, 1990b) at more than 30 per cent of GNP.

Some specific aspects of the Portuguese case can be related to the shock produced by the 1974 revolution and to the exceptional semi-feudal economic regime embroiled in colonial war that characterized the country before the revolution. Not only did the revolution bring about a traumatic change of political regime, it also coincided with the end of the colonial war and empire and with the deep global economic crisis triggered by the oil crisis, leading to a substantial slowing down in emigration after a long period in which large numbers of Portuguese had left the country. At the same time, approximately half a million citizens were repatriated from the former colonies. It was only at this very late stage that a traditional agrarian regime based on a mixture of latifundia and minifundia was radically transformed into cooperative agriculture and into small family farming units, respectively. 'Within the division between wage-workers and the self-employed an acceleration can be observed, starting in 1975, in the decrease of the former balanced by an increase in the latter. ... This phenomenon is probably connected with the worsening of the economic crisis, the increase in unemployment and the growth of the underground economy' (Grosso de Oliveira, 1985, p. 399). A direct longitudinal survey on the conditions of life in three villages around Coimbra (Piselli, 1991) shows clearly that they improved considerably. This was not achieved by following the usual itineraries of economic growth, industrialization, working class mobilization and expansion of welfare services but, rather, through the consolidation of the mix of household strategies centred on family farming and informal activities complemented by some reformist welfare provisions and by a socio-political climate more tolerant towards these very strategies.

In Greece, limited proletarianization and the economic mix based on micro family farming were established much earlier than in Portugal, that is, at the beginning of the century when an independent nation was set up with distribution of the land previously owned by the Turkish landlords. Concentrated capitalist farming has always been a less likely option due to the geographical configuration of the country, so that capitalist control of the productive process has developed instead in the direction of the transformation and commercialization of Mediterranean crops: olives, oil, wine, fruits and vegetables (Mouzelis, 1978). This explains both the capitalist specialization of this country in shipbuilding, shipping and international trade and the persistence of micro-farming even beyond the stage of subsistence agriculture. The great expansion of tourism in the last three decades has also been organized within this typical mix centred on small family farming, at least on the coastal strips and hundreds of more or less small inhabited islands. Thus, the recent development of the tourist industry has further contributed to the consolidation of complex informal strategies (Leontidou, 1993). At the same time, the labour market has remained characterized by the limited presence of workers and families fully dependent on wage income. All this explains why Greece still has today a much higher proportion of self-employed workers (50 per cent) than all the other southern European countries (about 30 per cent) which, in turn, show a much higher rate than the other EU countries where it varies between 10 and 18 per cent (with the exception of Ireland at a constant intermediate level of 25 per cent) (see Figure 5.2).

Postfordist tensions in the Southern European variants of industrialization

When the economic crisis of the mid-1970s and the subsequent postfordist transformations hit Southern European countries, the specific conditions

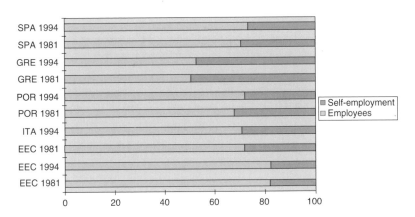

Figure 5.2 Percentage distribution of self-employed and employees (1981–91)

in each case were different but one thing they all had in common was the relatively low level of proletarianization of the labour force. The situation varied from the great importance of small family businesses in manufacturing and advanced services in northern Italy to the micro family farming and informal mixes of Greece and Portugal, the substantial dependence on income-support programmes in southern Italy and the extremely mixed set of arrangements in Spain.

The postfordist transformations helped to reinforce all these types of familistic/semi-proletarianized arrangements, which also included some degree of innovation and successful adaptation. Unemployment and flexible and irregular forms of employment increased a great deal everywhere throughout the 1980s, but to different extents (Pugliese, 1993). Southern Italy and Spain witnessed persistently high levels of unemployment (around 20 per cent) accompanied by an extraordinary diffusion of irregular forms of employment, mostly super-exploited forms of black labour market jobs (see Miguelez-Lobo, 1990a; Pinnarò and Pugliese, 1985) rather than innovative and dynamic flexible arrangements in manufacturing and services. In northern Italy, on the contrary, familistic arrangements have proved particularly favourable to dynamic and innovative postfordist adaptation, which has had the effect of confining unemployment tensions to certain periods only (1979–85 and, probably, resurfacing at the present time) and to the entry phase into the labour market for young workers and adult women. Informal activities have been rather dynamic but increasingly confined to moonlighting and the employment of third world migrants in services. As already seen above, Portugal and Greece have reinforced arrangements centred on micro family farming. In both cases, levels of unemployment have remained lower (climbing slowly from 7 per cent in the 1980s to nearly 9 per cent in 1994 in Greece, and swinging from 8.5 per cent in 1985 down to 4 per cent in 1991 and up again to 7 per cent in 1994 in Portugal) than in southern Italy and Spain (see Figure 5.1), but this is presumably counterbalanced by a higher rate of underemployment, particularly in agriculture, building and tourism. Compared to Greece, Portugal has certainly benefited more from a wave of industrial decentralization and relocation which in the second half of the eighties alleviated the employment and general economic situation without undermining the persistent diffusion of familistic arrangements centered on family farming.

State and family in the structuration of labour markets

There are two further questions I want to consider before making a brief analysis of the labour market structuration in the different branches of the economy. The first is related to the role that nation-states played in promoting the specific features of the Southern European model of labour market structuration. The second concerns the impact of recent transformations on the employment and life conditions of women in Southern Europe.

As already mentioned with regard to the welfare systems, which in all cases are a variant of the German 'conservative/corporative' model, the state plays an important role in the structuration of the specific characteristics of the Southern European variants of industrial society. In the context of diverse political regimes, Southern Europe has been characterized by a consistently favourable attitude towards the family business and distrust of pure free-market arrangements, particularly when they give rise to high capitalist concentration and forms of full-scale proletarization. This has lead to particular fiscal, welfare and economic policies which, in large part as unintended consequences, have contributed to the diffusion of irregular forms of employment and of a relatively high degree of tax evasion.[14]

In the Italian case, lines of continuity can be traced through the pre-fascist, fascist and democratic periods. The pre-fascist regime adopted welfare and economic policies that aimed to wrest control of social security and social services from a working class organization which was growing in strength in the industrializing regions. This approach was to some extent like the one adopted by Bismarck in Germany in the nineteenth century. The policies favoured the formation of a working class 'aristocracy' and were also beneficial to at least some groups among the traditional middle classes, in particular artisans and the independent liberal professions. This approach was made complicated from the very beginning by the dual formation of the nation-state where the 'hegemonic coalition' (Gramsci, 1966, calls it the 'historical bloc') had to bring together an agrarian regime in control of the south and a moderate industrializing elite in the north. Fascism further reinforced this strategy through the setting up of the 'corporative organizations' and the introduction of restrictive conservative measures in favour of the agrarian regime. The postwar moderate government coalitions, centred on the continuity in power of the Christian Democratic Party, had to dismantle the agrarian regime in the south but, essentially, reconstructed a strongly familistic strategy along innovative lines. This was highly protective of small and family businesses and oriented towards preventing diffused and extreme forms of proletarianization, which would have augmented the power of the industrial working class – largely represented by the Communist Party rather than by a social democratic political force. Even more than in the past, economic and welfare strategies had to develop income-support policies in order to bolster through a strongly patronage-based approach the new unstable class of micro family farmers and a very large and increasing semi-proletarian stratum produced by de-ruralization in the south. A high degree of tolerance towards tax evasion by the self-employed had the effect of incorporating into the dominant social coalition a large and composite group from among the middle classes, more entrepreneurial and dynamic in the north and more traditional in the south. This contributed, however, to limiting state resources available for the modernization of public welfare services provision. Thus, when in the 1970s the demand for modern services mainly from the northern working class became irresistible, the necessary reforms were delayed and only partially enacted. Moreover, they had to be financed through a combination of increased taxation of wage work, raising the cost of officially recorded salaried employment, and deficit spending, leading to a skyrocketing national debt. The first part of the combination contributed to the spread of informal employment, particularly moonlighting, which increased considerably throughout the 1980s (Mingione, 1990b; Pedullà *et al.*, 1987). The second part helped to distort further the workings of the market since most of the high-saving propensity of Italians was absorbed by state bonds, giving rise to high interest rates. This combination, in turn, benefited once again family businesses, particularly those which were economically more dynamic and able to withstand the increasing cost of labour through tax evasion and the use of irregular forms of employment and to self-finance innovation through high savings, the high interest from state bonds and good connections with local financial institutions.

Within the role played by the Italian state in structuring the labour market, one aspect has become important since its beginnings in the late-1960s. This is the very high degree of protection of stable employment in large and medium-sized concerns, something conceded to the working class organizations. It applies particularly to adult male breadwinners and accords well with the familistic philosophy of the Italian state. The two crucial institutional forms of this protection are the '*Statuto dei Lavoratori*' [Workers' Statute] and the '*Cassa Integrazione Guadagni*' [CIG, Income-Support Fund], which were the outcome of a long season of radical working class mobilization during the period 1969 to 1971 (centred on the so-called '*Autunno caldo*', the politically hot autumn of 1969). Basically, the Statute limits the right of employers to make workers redundant without providing acceptable and documented justification. The Fund allows workers that would normally be made redundant for economic reasons to be kept on a firm's payroll at approximately 80 per cent of their wages for an agreed period of time, which may even extend over a number of years. In addition, early retirement schemes and mobility lists with high priority for re-employment have also been utilized to ensure the stability of employment for adult males. This has always been reflected in low unemployment rates for adult men, above all in the north where protected concerns are more widespread; leaving aside those drawing on the income-support fund (the *cassaintegrati*), the unemployment rate of males aged 30 to 60 has always been under 2 per cent. This high degree of protection is offset by the scarcity of employment policies in favour of new entrants into the labour market, both young people seeking a first job and women re-entering after a period devoted to family responsibilities. This lack of protection is reflected in the absence of the right to unemployment benefits and of programmes favouring the insertion of the unemployed into stable employment.

This digression on the Italian case will help in providing a brief exposition of the other cases. This is due to the fact that, with some variations, they all followed the Italian model at a much later stage, thereby accentuating some of characteristics of this model, particularly when compared with the achievements and shortcomings in northern Italy.

It was only in the late-1970s, at a time of global economic crises and postfordist transformation, that Spain and Portugal faced the same problem that the new democratic regime in Italy was confronted with in the late-1940s. Greek governments have always had to come to terms with the enduring majority of small family farmers and with an extremely specialized and concentrated form of industrialization (Tsoulouvis, 1987). In all three countries, then, social expenditure by the state remained up to the mid-1970s at very low levels (less than 10 per cent of GNP, at a time when it was already more than double this figure in the advanced industrialized countries) and was largely absorbed by income-support policies (pensions and subsidies). Conversely, public provision of social services were considerably underfinanced. As the market provision of social services also remained relatively undeveloped in social contexts where the majority of the working population had too low incomes to gain access to it, the familial philosophy of governments constituted a cornerstone of social policies.

When, starting from the second half of the 1970s, governments had to face the problem of modernizing the welfare system in countries that were increasingly exposed to international competition, they were confronted with the same high propensity to tax evasion by the self-employed as in the Italian case and with even more diffused underground economies. A considerable expansion in social expenditure, largely financed by increasing the state deficit, and fragmented and often ineffective regulation of the labour market (particularly in Spain where a *Ley del Estatuto de los Trabajadores*, that is a Workers' Statute exactly like the one in Italy ten years earlier, was approved in 1980 and then amended in 1984) have been the most important responses to these problems. Hence, we can say that these countries have reconfirmed the Italian model of state intervention. On the other hand, Spain and Portugal have developed a certain sensitivity to the state deficit, which has helped to keep it at a much lower level than in Italy and Greece. Both the former have invested more than the latter in the modernization of public infrastructures, and in the late-1980s this attracted considerable foreign investment (particularly in Portugal). None of these other countries have attained such a high propensity to protect adult male regular employment in large and medium-sized concerns as in Italy; instead, a kind of dual and familistic philosophy can be traced in all of them, which is also here reflected in persistently high levels of youth and female unemployment (see Figures 5.3, 5.4 and 5.5). Nor have any of them expanded clientelistic income support to the same high level as in southern Italy though similar policies can be identified in each of them, particularly in Greece, rural Spain and, above all, in Andalusía.[15]

As stated above, one of the most important specific features of the Southern European model of labour market structuration concerns the working condition of women: a relatively low participation rate, which is increasing in the face of great difficulties, is reflected in high and growing rates of unemployment. Even in Portugal (Rodrigues, 1992) and northern Italy where, for different reasons, the participation rate of women is higher and unemployment lower, the female unemployment rate is higher or even double that of males. The two extreme cases in this respect are

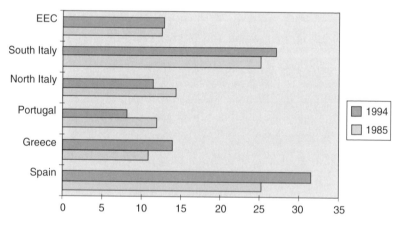

Figure 5.3   Female unemployment rate (1985–94)

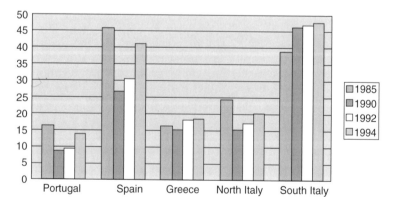

Figure 5.4   Youth unemployment rate (male, 1985–94)

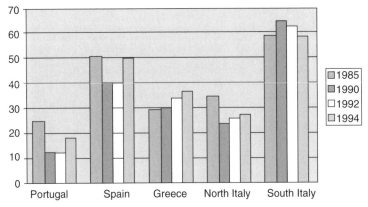

Figure 5.5 Youth unemployment rate (female, 1985–94)

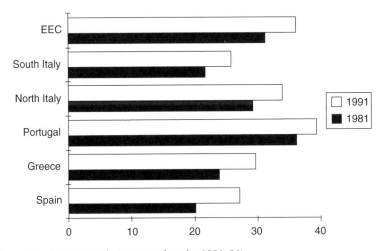

Figure 5.6 Active population rate (female, 1981–91)

represented by Spain and southern Italy, where the percentage of active females in the population of working age is just over 30 per cent and the unemployment rates in 1994 were 31.5 per cent and 27 per cent, respectively (see Figures 5.3 and 5.6). Under these conditions, it is possible to hypothesize that the model as such, probably with the exception of Portugal where also non-agricultural paid female employment constitutes an important element in the particular survival mix discussed above, is persistently based on a high degree of exclusion of adult women from official paid employment, even if demographic and survival conditions are characterized by similar patterns to those in other advanced industrial societies

(Bettio and Villa, 1993): the average ages for marriage and child-bearing have risen, as in central and northern Europe, the average number of children per fertile woman has decreased even more (northern Italy and Spain now have the lowest birth rates in the world) and the average number of members per household is not low only because adult children continue to live with their parents, but has in reality shrunk considerably. These conditions and other indicators confirm that this is not so much a cultural characteristic often imputed to Mediterranean societies (more male chauvinistic and more prejudiced against women in employment) but, rather, a serious limit to labour market structuration which, in turn, has a cultural impact on women's identity. Bettio and Villa (1993) hypothesize that in the Southern European model instead of women achieving emancipation *from* the family through paid work, there is a trend towards women's emancipation *within* the family. Women who achieve higher levels of education and are available for full-time paid work, even if often they become part of the long-term unemployed due to lack of jobs, gain greater opportunities to negotiate crucial decisions in the family, which remains a central economic institution, particularly as within the changes in employment the conditions of life and work chances of adult children greatly depend on their parents and the kinship system.

Similar conditions apply to adult children who are more likely to remain unemployed for long periods, consequently delay marriage and economic autonomy from the family, but negotiate a certain degree of cultural independence inside it, also fostered by higher educational levels than those of their parents.

Features of segmentation and the social division of labour

Agriculture and agrarian aspects

With the exception of northern Italy, the Southern European cases are still characterized by much higher rates of employment in agriculture than the EU average, ranging in 1994 from the 10 per cent of Spain to the nearly 21 per cent of Greece (see Table 5.1 and Figure 5.7). Northern Italy also differs greatly from the rest of Southern Europe in terms of land tenure and use, since the wide river Po valley forming the backbone of the region's agrarian system contains the typical environment suitable for the growing of continental rather than Mediterranean crops. This explains why it is the only large agrarian region in Southern Europe where forms of intensive capitalist farming have become widespread and highly developed. Nevertheless, northern Italian agriculture is not in sharp contradiction with the familistic character of the Southern European model: family farming, increasingly done by part-timers with complementary jobs who are either associated in cooperatives (more widespread in the centre and north-east) or independent farmers (more widespread in the peripheral mountain regions of the north-west) is the most diffused form of organizing production. But it has a radically different role in the structuration of the labour market from that assumed in the rest of Southern Europe, because not only is the rate of agricultural employment rather low (5.5 per cent) but also agriculture does not generate a large number of informal jobs. Part-timers are usually involved in official multiple employment (Brusco, 1979). The number of family helpers has decreased substantially and their position is most of the time correctly recorded and remunerated in order to avoid excessive taxation. Even foreign workers are for the most part in regular employment (Mottura, 1991).

In the rest of Southern Europe, the agrarian process remains persistently labour-intensive and highly seasonal and large capitalist concerns have

Table 5.1 Principal indicators of employment in Southern Europe, 1994

	S	GR	P	*North I	*South I	EEC
Males + Females						
Unemployment rate	24.3	8.9	7	7.6	19.2	11.2
Youth unemployment rate	45.3	27.7	15.1	22.8	51	22.7
Percentage of employed in agriculture	10.2	21.3	11.6	5.5	13.6	5.7
Male						
Unemployment rate	19.9	6	6.1	4.7	15.4	10
Youth unemployment rate	41.2	19.7	13.5	19.2	46.4	22
Percentage of employed in agriculture	11.1	19.1	10.4	5.7	11.9	6.2
Percentage of employed in industry	38.8	29.2	40.2	42.4	29.8	41
Percentage of employed in other activities	50.1	51.7	49.4	51.9	56.8	52.7
Female						
Unemployment rate	31.5	13.7	8	11.2	27	12.6
Youth unemployment rate	50.4	36.9	17	27.3	58.8	23.5
Percentage of employed in agriculture	8.5	25.3	13	5.1	17.6	4.9
Percentage of employed in industry	15	14.9	23.6	25.8	10.7	18.1
Percentage of employed in other activities	76.5	59.8	63.4	69.1	71.6	77
Ratio of employment to working age population 1991 per cent						
M + F	49.8	54.7	71	56.3	52.6	61.1
M	68.6	74.7	84.3	70	71.2	n.a.
F	31.6	35.9	58.7	43	34.7	n.a.

Source: Eurostat Aggregates data, 1980–94; *our elaboration on ISTAT quarterly data of Labour Force.

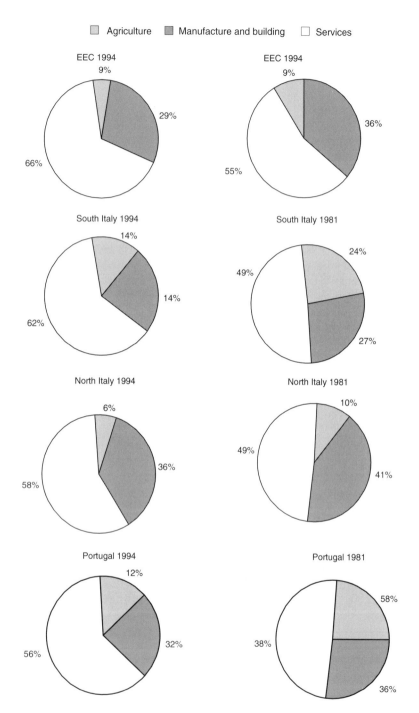

Figure 5.7 Share of employment in the three economic sectors, in Spain, Greece, Portugal, Italy (North and South) and EEC

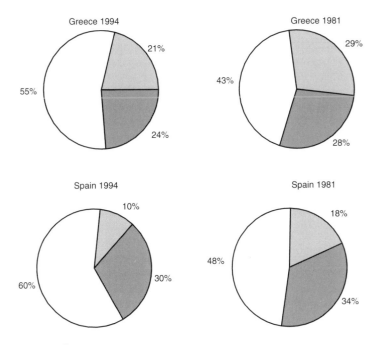

Figure 5.7   (contd)

become established only in limited areas. This is important from the point of view of the structuration of the labour market and for explaining the diffusion of informal activities. In fact, relatively independent of the wide-ranging forms of land tenure (from large estates to small peasant propri-etors and tenants), the history of agrarian regions has everywhere been characterized by the long-term persistence of under-employment and the variety of solutions adopted by the rural classes to deal with this chronic condition. An agricultural working class employed round the year with contractual stability is practically non-existent. Moreover, an upper stra-tum of family farmers competitive on the market and able to finance pro-ductive innovation and sufficient control over the commercialization and transformation of crops is very thin on the ground. Under these conditions the crucial factor in the life strategies of the largest part of the agricultural population, both micro-farmers and agricultural day labourers, are the complementary activities and forms of income necessary to compensate for under-employment. The outcome is various combinations of agricultural work and, on the one hand, of other often informal activities (mostly in building, outwork manufacturing, petty trade and tourism), and, on the other external income support where the decreasing contribution in the form of remittances from emigrated relatives has been, at least in part, offset by state pensions and subsidies to individuals, particularly in southern Italy and Spain.

For various different reasons these livelihood arrangements are extremely vulnerable, which is still reflected today in the decline of the active agricultural population; but their instability is not bringing about, as it has done in other agrarian regions in Europe, the development of advanced capitalist farming. It is leading instead to the systematic abandonment of the least productive land, the ageing and feminization of the workforce and the search for ways to compress the cost of seasonal work in relative terms without radical innovation in the productive process. This last factor is behind the waves of immigrants attracted from underdeveloped countries to southern Italy (Calvanese and Pugliese, 1991), Spain and Greece (Mingione, 1990c) to work as day-labourers during the picking season.

A crucial aspect of the process of de-ruralization in Southern Europe is the fact that survival mixes tend to deteriorate and become totally unappealing to the younger generations, particularly if they have had access to higher education. This provides a further explanation for the relative scarcity of capitalist investment and agrarian innovation, in contrast to what happened during the 1960s and 1970s in northern Italy, and particularly in Emilia Romagna and the Veneto, where the transition to part-time farming and wealthy forms of multi-activity had a highly innovative content and was managed by a generation that had received an education (Brusco, 1979; Mottura and Mingione, 1989).

Even though agricultural forms of employment are declining fast, they still exert a considerable structuring effect on the labour markets due to their special features. They remain a crucial part of the semi-proletarianized livelihood arrangements typical of villages and small towns, but often also transferred to the cities, and they make it highly likely that informal and black labour market working strategies will be adopted, which are most of the time the only available way to obtain income in order to preserve, but not to innovate, uncompetitive agrarian economies. This is largely the case of Greece, southern Italy and Spain. The situation is perhaps different and more dynamic, even though overall poorer, in Portugal where social expectations are lower and there still exists the counterweight of a sizable flow of emigration. In northern Italy, by contrast, these features have disappeared altogether.

Emigration and urbanization

Once again with the important exception of northern Italy, the labour markets in Southern Europe have been characterized by the impact of a long-term wave of mass emigration continuing up to the mid-1970s. As mentioned above, Portugal represents the only case where, though decreasing, emigration is still an important phenomenon. Both emigration and its decline brought about dramatic socio-economic transformations while, at the same time, a chaotic process of urban growth and urbanization was taking place, which in many cases is still continuing today when in other industrially advanced regions trends towards de-urbanization have been noted. Let us look briefly at the most important effects on the labour market arising out of these processes.

It has already been mentioned that an important consequence of the emigration tradition in the Southern European countries is the lack of strong policies to help young people to become more qualified and to enter the labour market. In this respect northern Italy, which has been a region of immigration for over half a century, has also suffered from the emigration vocation of the country as a whole. Here too, young entrants into the labour market face serious difficulties and make up a large share of the unemployed and the near totality of the long-term unemployed (IARD, 1996) while public investment in education and particularly in professional training has remained at low levels compared to that of other industrially advanced countries. In addition to this, the two most important labour market consequences of emigration are the impoverishment of the labour supply, abandoned by the more skillful and entrepreneurial cohorts among the younger generations, and the passive consumptionist role played by the monetary remittances from emigrated relatives. In particular the inter-European migrations, which were predominant in the postwar period, involved in the main a socially and demographically selected group: young adult males, followed later, to only a minor extent, by young adult females, coming originally from not too isolated agrarian regions and frequently after intermediate stopovers in local cities. The process radically modified the structure of the working population both in the migrants' places of origin and in the transit cities. In the former, the distortion in the demographic structure (a relatively older and more feminized population) made innovative economic strategies less likely and reinforced the underemployment arrangements rather than favouring development as many neo-classical economists expected (Lutz, 1962). In the latter, the sizable transit labour force of cheap unskilled young adult males greatly conditioned the productive processes, particularly in the construction industry, which remained highly labour-intensive and characterized by precarious irregular employment.

The financial contribution from the remittances of emigrated relatives, as well as the impact of return migrants later on, had a considerable influence in terms of changing consumption habits rather than fostering productive innovations. It helped to finance home-ownership, the development of self-building and home improvements and an increasing dependence on goods produced outside the local market. Local agriculture and craft and manufacturing production were penalized instead of advantaged by the specific changes in consumption habits. In the meanwhile, state intervention through income-support and public works programmes, above all in southern Italy and Spain, provided a flow of finance, which had similar effects in terms of consumption patterns and further transformed the local labour market. This flow of funds increased the likelihood of urbanization, particularly when it created new jobs in the state sector mostly concentrated in the urban areas. Furthermore, in the cities consumption of standardized food produce is higher and self-provisioning strategies are less viable. These features promoted an itinerary of modernization without acute industrial development, which is most clearly visible in southern Italy where policies based on state patronage made a substantial contribution to its reinforcement, which was also useful to expansion in the northern Italian economy. However, they are found to some extent in the other cases as well, obviously with the exception of northern Italy which, conversely, is characterized by immigration and considerable industrial growth and economic innovation.[16] Overall, emigration contributed at best to the dismantlement of poor rural subsistence economies but at the same time favoured the constitution of semi-proletarianized social arrangements centred on the economic role of family and kinship and having as their basis the diffusion of irregular forms of work discussed in the previous section. This occurred in both the countryside and the cities, where a crucially important role was played by the formation of a disproportionately large group of precariously employed workers in the construction industry.

In order to understand the importance of precarious construction workers in the structuration of Southern European labour markets, it is useful to compare briefly Southern Italy, which roughly represents the rest of Southern Europe in this respect, with northern Italy, which, conversely, is much more similar to other industrial societies. Construction expanded considerably in the postwar period in both parts of the country as an effect of postwar reconstruction, urbanization, the modernization of infrastructures, and economic growth in general. Throughout the 1950s, this sector was much larger in the north where war damage had been more serious and industrial reconstruction was highly concentrated. Work processes remained everywhere labour-intensive and characterized by the use of poorly skilled and low trade-unionized workers on temporary irregular contracts. In the north, this situation remained possible due to the first influx of large numbers of workers from the south. But, starting from the mid-1960s, the patterns of structuration of the two labour markets and productive processes began to diverge substantially. In the north, the progressive decline of an open-ended supply of cheap unorganized labour imposed a reorganization of the sector towards more capital-intensive production and a general regularization of employment conditions (Villa, 1986). In the south, the labour-intensive and precarious features of the sector persisted and, in addition, a long wave of self-building and small-scale restructuring work led to the further development of these patterns in the direction of a marked dualization between a group of more skilled and regularly employed workers and a group of unskilled precarious and temporarily employed workers (Ginatempo and Fera, 1985). Today, in the north construction workers account for less than 10 per cent of industrial employment and are practically all employed with regular contracts. In the south, by contrast, they make up more than 25 per cent of the industrial labour force, outnumbering manufacturing workers in many cities, and the majority of them are still precariously employed (Mingione, 1991). Construction has been the crucial sector for the formation of an urban black labour market, which is now progressively expanding into services. Temporary irregular employment in building still constitutes a crucial factor in the survival mixes of the low-income urban population in the south, most of whom are in a semi-proletarianized condition. Although there is no precise documentation at hand on the other cases, reliable indicators suggest that, with some national and local variations, they lie closer to the southern Italian than to the northern Italian situation. Precarious building employment remains an important constitutive part of the irregular activities which in Southern Europe, with the exception of northern Italy, account for approximately one-third of industrial employment.

The structuration of manufacturing employment

The rate of employment in manufacturing in Southern Europe ranges from the high level of northern Italy (above 30 per cent and accompanied by relatively low employment in agriculture and construction), though now declining rather sharply, to the only slightly lower, but up to 1991 stable, levels of Portugal and Spain (about 25 per cent) and the much lower levels of Greece and southern Italy (below 20 per cent). The last case is the one in the most critical condition since there is a combination of a low employment level and severe de-industrialization, which appears to be inexorable notwithstanding regional development policies and some industrial relocation, like the new FIAT plants at Cassino, Termoli and Melfi. The industrial structure of Greece is also fragile with the older more developed branches vulnerable to processes of decline, which are not sufficiently counterbalanced by relocation and innovative development (Chronaki *et al.*, 1993).

I have already mentioned some of the common features in the manufacturing labour markets and some of the differences between them. The most important among the first are a relatively high degree of concentration in only a few industrial regions, the polarization between medium-large and very small firms and a certain incomplete familistic proletarianization of the working class. In the case of northern Italy industrial concentration which was extremely pronounced in the past, is now less so following 20 years of considerable restructuring, decentralization and diffusion of productive activities from large fordist concerns towards medium and small industries located outside the traditional metropolitan districts of 'the industrial triangle'. Another common factor, where northern Italy again constitutes an exception, is the great and growing importance of industrial investments and reallocations controlled by 'foreign' (including also northern investments in the Mezzogiorno) or joint ventures.[17]

As to the differences, the industrial histories in question are largely diversified in their timing, organization and specialization. Since a detailed analysis is impossible here, I shall limit myself to a few remarks on the industrial division of labour and on different typologies of employment.

The Southern European manufacturing labour markets clearly show that the question of employment flexibility is an ambiguous and complicated one, at least in the current phase of international economic competition.[18] With the exception of northern Italy, where irregular forms of work have been reduced to a minimum through successful 'diffused' industrialization in the 1970s and 1980s, manufacturing employment in Southern Europe ranges from relatively highly protected 'family wage' jobs in large concerns, with some differences between independent firms and joint and foreign ventures, to less protected regular contract jobs in medium-sized, small and micro or handicraft firms and various forms of irregular employment. Both the second and, in particular, the third categories are highly diversified internally in terms of the characteristics of the enterprise, the work agreement and the worker. Among the less protected but regular forms of employment there is a wide range of self-employment and an increasing share of temporary arrangements, while regular part-time jobs are less widespread than in other industrialized societies.[19] A good example is Spain, where the proportion of temporary fixed-term workers in the manufacturing workforce has increased substantially, rising to almost one-quarter in 1990 (Jimeno and Toharia, 1994). The temporary workers, mainly young and female employees, were the first to be made redundant during the negative conjuncture of the early-1990s. This example further confirms the familistic vocation of the employment system centred on high protection of adult male employment at the expense of young and female workers.

The degree of variation is much higher as far as irregular forms of employment are concerned. Even taking into account only the final outwork arrangements of subcontracting chains, different situations exist in the domestic workshops in downtown Naples producing gloves for shops and trade-mark exporters, among the shoemakers working at home for medium-sized and large firms in small towns around Valencia, and in the dressmaking subcontracted by trade-mark firms in Sicilian villages or the home production of toys on a Greek island subcontracted by an export firm.[20] It is certainly true that the near totality of the workers involved are female and that they usually work hard for a low remuneration, which is only viable if pooled with other incomes and contributions; however, it is also true that the internal organization of the labour process varies and that the prospects for such forms of industrial organization are particularly unstable. The Neapolitan underground glove industry has been in existence for a long time, but it is now under threat from the urban reconstruction programmes following the earthquake of the early-1980s. Although other arrangements have arisen more recently, their prospects appear equally uncertain. They are clearly not forms of flexible employment on which to base a new wave of industrialization like the one that took place in Carpi or Prato, in central Italy, in the 1970s. The same can be said of the underground industries producing forged high-fashion garments in southern Italy. Informal arrangements have more solid prospects when they develop strong networking capacities, as in the case of the fur industry in Kastoria in northern Greece (Hadjimichalis and Vaiou, 1990b); but this happens only in a limited number of cases. What we learn from this is that there is a reverse side to the picture of informal flexible employment arrangements in manufacturing (Pollert, 1991). In general, they are a rather unstable part of the survival mix of a semi-proletarianized population in a context where opportunities for regular employment are chronically scarce but there are no alternative paths to industrial development. Only under special conditions can they give rise to prospects for development and, in such cases, we would expect the regularization of informal employment to be undertaken quite soon, as happened in northern Italy in the 1970s.

The cases of Portugal and, in particular, of Spain plainly reveal the limits to waves of re-industrialization during the present phase of global competition and under the social and economic conditions found in Southern Europe. Either, as in Spain (Jimeno and Toharia, 1994), a greater supply of labour is mobilized than can be realistically utilized or, as in Portugal (Rodrigues, 1992), a survival mix is consolidated in a situation where the standard of life remains rather low and the social conditions for economic growth are squeezed by the persistence of under-employment, self-provisioning and emigration. It is, in general, true that the current free-market economic cycle is producing a widening reduction in acceptable employment opportunities (Hadjimichalis, 1994). In some parts of Southern Europe, for instance Portugal, this effect is blocked by the persistence of familistic survival mixes but in others, like southern Italy, Greece and a large part of Spain, there is the risk that the unemployment will become totally unmanageable.

As has emerged several times in this chapter, the case of northern Italy forms an exception. Up until the late-1960s industrialization was concentrated above all in the north-west. The organization of work and production was highly taylorist inside the factory but maintained important familistic features in society, made possible among other things by the flourishing of a large number of small and medium-to-small concerns in the regions surrounding the industrial centres. The birth rate of new industrial firms remained high throughout the 1960s and rose even higher in the 1970s. This situation was not confined to mono-industrial districts and was based on a strong autonomous networking capacity, which explains the diffusion of industrialization in the 1970s and early-1980s. Yet, the fact that the potential for diffusion did not spread from north to south is clearly a sign of the extent to which this kind of development is rooted in local social conditions. De-industrialization – large concerns lost more than half a million jobs in the 1980s – and industrial restructuring were accompanied by diffused industrialization and plant reallocations, but mainly within the region (from Milan and Turin, for example, to smaller cities and new industrial areas within the northern Italian regions) rather than in newly industrializing countries. The manufacturing labour market was radically altered without producing severe social shocks, that is until very recently. This was also due to other factors besides that of diffused industrialization: the highly protected stability of employment for adult male breadwinners; the impact of the demographic decline on the labour supply; the socially compressed number of married women entering the labour market compared to other industrial regions; the growth of good employment opportunities in the advanced services subsector. However two critical difficulties began to develop, mainly due to the mismatch in the labour market. On one side, an increasing undersupply of labour to fill regular semiskilled jobs without career prospects attracted a wave of foreign workers from underdeveloped countries, the only ones able to match the income earned with their conditions of settlement and life strategies (Mottura, 1992). On the other side, young would-be workers with relatively high expectations in an increasingly wealthy and costly social environment are finding good permanent jobs increasingly difficult to come by. The potential aggravation of these processes summed with the prospects for a stronger and less protected wave of de-industrialization throws up critical questions also as to the future of the northern Italian case.[21]

Service industries and informalization in the Southern European variants

The rates of employment in services range from the high level of southern Italy (62.2 per cent) to the relatively low level of Portugal and Greece at 55 per cent (see Table 5.1). But in this case the rates are not particularly significant because they represent very diversified sectors and typologies of employment, from petty trade to advanced economic or welfare services, from highly tenured civil service jobs to a vast array of irregular forms of employment, which include highly paid consultancy, moonlighting and extremely precarious jobs in traditional personal and customer services.

A comparison between northern and southern Italy helps to throw light on the importance of qualitative differences in two cases where the institutional welfare system is the same and, moreover, markedly centralized. In the south, the official ISTAT estimates[22] show that the share of irregular employment in services is nearly double that in the north (over 35 per cent against about 20 per cent). A large number of irregular jobs in the north, however, involve multi-consultancy and professional moon-lighting, which go unrecorded simply in order to evade taxation rather than because they are precarious, unstable and super-exploited forms of employment. In the south this is much less the case. Southern regular employment is particularly concentrated in traditional services, like small unspecialized retail outlets, cafeterias and restaurants, and in public admin-istration where overstaffed and patronage-oriented bureaucracies are quite unable to run the services efficiently. Hospitals, schools and local services, particularly in the large cities, still live up to their notorious reputation for poor efficiency and particularistic strategies.[23] In the north, on the con-trary, advanced private economic services, like banking, insurance, innova-tive research and high technology services, are greatly concentrated. Furthermore public services, which come under the same ministries in Rome as their southern equivalents, are subject to the same institutional rules and are frequently understaffed, manage to keep inefficiency to a much lower level.

I will not go deeper into this aspect or try to explain the reasons for it. What is important to underline here is that service employment can be extremely varied and similar indicators may mean different things. This is especially significant in Southern European labour markets at a time when the majority of the working population is employed in services and it is the sector where there is still a possibility of employment rising to offset job losses in agriculture and industry.

However, the view that it is in the very area of service employment and related social division of labour that the Southern European cases are mov-ing towards increasing homogeneity is equally valid. In other words, if there is a Southern European model of post-industrial labour market orga-nization then it is to be found mainly in the services sector. In this respect, northern Italy also appears to be more or less following the patterns indi-cated by this model while only Portugal stands out as an exception, at least for the present. The patterns in question are: a relatively high and increas-ing level of informalization of employment; a rather modest expansion of both state and market provision of welfare services, compensated for by the persisting crucial role of family and voluntary support; and a cycle of expansion in service employment that is conditioned more by purely polit-ical imperatives than by market economic factors. This state of affairs is reflected, on one side, by the high degree of adaptation of traditional organizations and, on the other, by the relatively low levels of economic efficiency found in both private and public modern services, which are not at all counterbalanced by their high quality; rather the opposite is the case. The ambiguity of the data on service employment is due to the fact that if the level of employment is estimated from a mechanical 'developmental-ist' point of view, that is without taking into consideration the empirical division of service tasks disproportionately occupied by full-time adult housewives, most of the cases appear under-tertiarized. If, on the other hand, the real situation and quality of the services provided is taken into account, most of the cases appear over-tertiarized, that is there is too much employment with respect to the quality and quantity of services the workers are effectively able to produce. It is mostly the persistent importance of family and voluntary responsibility in the provision of services that creates balances between state, market and family provision which are largely different, though equally unstable, from those that are maturing in other industrialized cases.

In employment and labour market terms, the Southern European balance is reflected in the persistently lower official participation rate of adult married women, who are obviously responsible for the most important familial duties, but under changing conditions in respect of the traditional housewife roles, within a modernized, consumptionist and bureaucratized context (in this regard, it is clear that Portugal constitutes an exception for reasons that we have already mentioned). The Southern European syndrome is also reflected in the increasing difficulty for young would-be workers to find acceptable long-lasting jobs. This becomes translated into both high levels of long-term youth unemployment (Figures 5.4 and 5.5) and the diffusion of temporary, unstable and irregular forms of employment in services. The informalization of service employment is connected with the youth unemployment crisis mainly because it encourages availability for this form of work in different ways. Fathers enter into moonlighting activities so as to raise more resources in order to support unemployed adult children; mothers with temporary or part-time irregular jobs do likewise, and the children themselves are available for temporary and casual forms of employment provided that their chances of finding a permanent job are not seriously hampered.[24] But the informalization cycle is also strongly connected with the persistent familistic impact on the labour demand side of services, as it reduces the potential for expansion and rationalization of regular employment in both the private and public spheres of the sector.

The cycle of familistic tertiarization is also contributing to the attraction of migrant workers from the less developed countries, often under irregular conditions everywhere in Southern Europe with the obvious exception of Portugal. The persistence of (in the case of co-resident maids or street vendors) or expansion in (in the case of office messengers or temporary jobs in tourism and trade) the high demand for working profiles consisting in poor pay and low protection does not match with the labour supply mainly for cultural reasons and because of the reluctance to accept working conditions which are so different from life expectations but also because moonlighters or casual temporary workers do not possess the right requisites. Immigrant workers now amount to less than 5 per cent of the labour force (probably more in Greece during the summer) but contribute to the persistence and expansion of the informal and familistic nature of the services sector and dampen further the potential for rationalization of the labour processes.

Conclusion

The hypothesis of a Southern European model of labour market structuration can be a useful tool if it is able to explain a set of specific features and differences in the patterns of socio-economic development which continue over a long period. It has been argued here that the persistence of a strong economic role for the family and a consistently less than fully proletarianized (dependent on wage income) condition of workers should be considered as the core of the model rather than a sign of backwardness. In this respect, the case of northern Italy, even though largely differing from the others, is extremely important for proving the point. In fact, provided that the basic conditions persist and maintain their substantial explanatory force, the model allows for a reasonable degree of variation. Throughout a longer and more successful industrial history, which makes it impossible to view it as an instance of a relatively undeveloped society, northern Italy has persistently maintained the constitutive features of the model. It is, rather, the case of Portugal which raises some questions to which it is at present impossible to give clear-cut answers. The much higher participation of women in paid employment mixes, increasingly outside of traditional roles in agriculture and as family helpers, may well indicate a divergent pattern of development from the Southern European model even if many other features remain the same.

I have already maintained that none of the cases can be considered as *the* model which the others automatically adopt or as pointing to the direction that their development must necessarily take. This needs to be said because the diffused form of industrialization found in the third Italy has often been seen as a model of development in itself (Piore and Sabel, 1984). However, some of the cases may serve as examples showing the range and limits of the model. The two cases at opposite poles which appear most suitable in this respect are northern and southern Italy. In the former, we can appreciate the maximum impact of successful industrialization in a social context which remains permeated by innovative small and family businesses. In the latter, a pattern of modernization is apparently accompanied by considerable expansion of income support and by a very vulnerable process of industrialization. Neither of them represents the future dimension of the model, but they do contribute to spelling out more clearly the range of conditions and problems characterizing these variants of industrial development.

The hypothesis of the Southern European model shows us that the familistic, less welfaristic and less proletarianized features are long-lasting and that the development paths do not take either the Anglo-American or the Scandinavian direction. They also suffer the effects of and respond in a different way to the transformation impact of the postfordist labour market. Long-term youth unemployment is the most relevant symptom of this process. As its social impact is mostly absorbed by the family, under the socio-welfare conditions typical of the model, the phenomenon has probably contributed to a more radical transformation of the demographic and social strategies of families. Long-term low birth rates, rapid ageing of the population, declining geographical mobility together with delayed and less stable marriages are bringing about a marked change in household structure. This transformation will shortly impact with labour market strategies and we do not know how the familistic features will react to such radically changed conditions. Nevertheless, an easy assumption to make is that this prospect will, at least for the next two decades, be to some extent different from that of other societies in spite of the unified European market and the project of European political union.

Notes

1. Decentralization from outside refers to firms or units which are owned by a foreign corporation but which are localized in the area for reasons of expansion or convenience.
2. The labour markets are growing complex and articulated in terms of socio-cultural divisions among various typologies of labour supply (by age, gender, education and training, urban or rural background, previous working experience, socio-cultural expectations and behaviour, etc) ending up in different kinds of jobs (more or less paid and tenured, with or without career prospects, in large or small units, etc). The process of complex articulation of the labour markets (this is what is meant here by structuration), is reflected by the theory of labour market segmentation in rather abstract and relatively simplistic terms. The concept of labour market segmentation was introduced in the USA in the 1950s mainly by Kerr (1950; 1954) and then developed by various authors; important contributions have been made by Doeringer and Piore (1971); Edwards (1979); Edwards *et al.* (1975); Gordon (1972); Gordon *et al.* (1982); Piore (1979); Sabel (1982); Wilkinson (1981); Wood (1982). This theory is based on the assumption that everywhere the most important form of structuration is a dual division between a 'primary labour market' characterized by relatively high income and stability as protected by increasing 'internalization' of the competition (affecting the career of the workers rather than the fact that they are hired and fired many times in their working life), and a 'secondary labour market' highly conditioned by general competition and consequently instability of employment and lower wages. Among the few examples of socio-historical studies of labour market structuration, the work by Paola Villa (1986) on two sectorial cases of adult male employment in northern Italy (steel and building) confirms the relatively low level of full proletarianization even in advanced capital intensive sectors. See also Brusco and Villa (1987).
3. In this chapter I use the estimates of and references to irregular forms of employment and underground economies reported in the EU Report on *Underground*

Economy and Irregular Forms of Employment (Travail au Noir) (1990), particularly the single reports on Spain (Miguelez-Lobo, 1990a), Portugal (Miguelez-Lobo, 1990b), Italy (Mingione, 1990b) and Greece (Mingione, 1990c). To the best of my knowledge, no important research or studies have been carried out updating the interpretation and data of the EEC report, with the exception of the Italian case. Here, the task force constituted within the Central Statistical Office of the Government (ISTAT), led by Professor Pedullà (see Pedullà *et al.*, 1987), has updated the data to the early-1990s and produced an unofficial disaggregation of the estimates by region. Thanks to the work of this team and to the kind contribution of Dott. Simone Ghezzi, who has further elaborated the data, I use in this chapter both the more recent estimates and the disaggregation of the data between centre-north and south.

4. As a Southern European country, Portugal has a relatively high rate of female participation in paid employment. This is not only due to the impact of agriculture and backwardness, but it is also a leftover from the colonial war economy of the 1960s when a great number of males were in the army or colonial workers or migrants.

5. However, it would be wrong to assume that young people cohabit with their parents because they are unemployed. As confirmed by data and surveys (Mingione and Pugliese, 1995), the 'long family' is due rather to cultural practice, reinforced by recent events, whereby children leave their parents only when they marry.

6. In the Spanish case, the waves of industrial growth, de-industrialization and re-industrialization were highly compressed within a short period of about 20 years from the early-1970s to the early-1990s. See, among others: Balfour, 1989; Bosch and Saez, 1991; Jimeno and Toharia, 1994; Salmon, 1991; Toharia, 1988.

7. Standardized production in large factories where the cost efficiency goals of the working process are achieved through production chains, a high degree of specialization of tasks, strict managerial control of production processes and the development of 'scientific' hierarchical organization of management.

8. The modernization of consumption refers to the transformation of the consumption strategies of the low-income groups from the prevalence of rural self-provisioning and subsistence strategies in combination with limited monetary consumption addressed to craft and petty production of the local market to the prevalence of monetary consumption of standardized goods produced by large corporations.

9. For the main socio-economic features of the third Italy see, among others, Bagnasco, 1977; Bagnasco and Trigilia, 1984a,b; Becattini, 1987 and 1989; Capecchi, 1989; Paci, 1980, 1992; Trigilia, 1986.

10. For the development crisis in the Mezzogiorno in the 1970s and 1980s see, among others, Cerase, 1992; Giannola, 1986; Graziani, 1978; Graziani and Pugliese, 1979; Silva and Viesti, 1989; Trigilia, 1992.

11. For the importance of small manufacturing firms and their innovative capacity and dynamism in the Italian case see, in particular, Goodman *et al.*, 1989 and Becattini, 1989.

12. The familistic and intergenerational vocation of the Italian fordist working class has been studied in the metropolitan areas of Milan and Turin. See Bagnasco, 1986; Martinotti, 1982; Mingione, 1994; Negri, 1982; Perulli, 1992.

13. De Sousa Santos, 1985 p. 877, argues with regard to Portugal – but the argument can easily apply to Greece also – that: 'The first, and without any doubt, original factor in explaining the phenomenon is constituted by the wide diffusion of

small family farming in the Portuguese social formation.' Regarding the recent importance of local economic initiatives in Portugal see Syrett, 1993.

14. Apropos of state intervention in regulating the labour market, see Rosenberg 1989, which includes two important essays on Italy (Brusco and Villa, 1989) and Spain (Fina *et al.*, 1989). The comparative analysis of 'families' of welfare states (Esping-Andersen, 1990; Flora and Heidenheimer, 1981; Flora, 1986, vol. 2; Castles, 1993) does not devote particular attention to the Southern European 'family'. Among the four cases, only the Italian has attracted much attention in recent decades, see, among others, Ascoli, 1984; Brunetta and Tronti, 1991; Dente, 1990; Ferrera, 1984; Ferrera, 1993; Paci, 1990. Concerning the income-support system in Italy, particularly in the Mezzogiorno region, see also Boccella, 1982. As for the recent transformations of welfare systems in the 12 countries of the European Union Maurizio Ferrera (1991) has edited a collection which includes short chapters on each case.

15. Clientelistic income support programmes are now increasingly problematic mainly for the financial difficulties of the state, particularly in Italy and in Greece. This, on one side, contributes to destabilize politically the regions with high unemployment and, on the other side, puts great pressures on families supporting long-term young unemployed.

16. As anticipated, however, also northern Italy and the highly industrialized immigration regions, like Catalonia, have suffered some of the consequences of the national outmigration experience, in particular the relatively slow pace of public investments in education, training and labour market policies in favour of young entrants.

17. Increasing dependence on foreign capital and ventures is particularly evident in the second most important industrial area of Southern Europe, that is Catalonia. See, among others, Parellada, 1990; Bosch and Saez, 1991.

18. Through a comparison of the histories of two textile industrial districts in England and northern Italy, Magatti (1991 and 1993) shows that the question of profitably exploiting flexible employment in a successful path of industrial development is an extremely complicated one. Neither the low cost of labour nor its complete subjugation to the requirements of capital are crucial factors. Most of the irregular forms of employment are far from flexible in the above meaning of the term. The northern Italian experience (not only in the third Italy but also in the metropolitan peripheries of the 'industrial triangle' that have played a very important role in the industrial restructuring phase of the last two decades) shows that it is rather a combination of high productivity, voluntary adaptation to flexible working arrangements (convenient also for the workers) and the presence of complementary opportunities that have favoured the Italian version of flexibility, accompanied by the high cost of labour, very rigid legal regulation of the labour market, a rapidly decreasing rate of irregular employment in dynamic branches of manufacturing (the passage from off-the-books family help to contractually hired workers), and low unemployment and persistently high rates of unionization among workers (particularly in the most successful small-to-medium firms in Emilia Romagna, which contradicts the stereotype of a reverse interrelation between rampant postfordist enterprise and unionization).

19. The diffusion of legal and regular forms of part-time work has been opposed by both the workers' and the industrialists' organizations in practically every Southern European country. On the trade unions side, the opposition to a strong

and favourable legalization of part-time employment is easy to understand. This event would have underminded the strong protection in favour of the 'normal' fordist employment conditions of male breadwinner workers. It is more difficult to explain the disfavour of the entrepreneurs and self-employed organizations. Probably, the most reasonable explanation lies in the strongly dual structure of the economic units in these countries. The large units are not particularly interested in these forms of employment and are certainly not willing to enter into a very difficult conflict with the unions on this terrain. At the same time, it is easier for the micro units to continue to use semi-legal or illegal forms of part-time employment rather than to promote a very problematic mobilization in favour of a new legislative solution.

20. See Cotugno *et al.*, 1990 on Naples; Sanchèz, 1986, on the Valencia case; Hadjimichalis and Vaiou, 1990, on the Greek case.
21. In fact the northern Italian situation is made worse by the fact that unemployment is now affecting a crucial stratum of adult male semi-skilled workers, extremely difficult to be reemployed at acceptable conditions in service jobs. This situation may further contribute to the concentration of employment policy resources in favour of this group and to the disadvantage of employment programmes for school-leavers, which, in turn, may further aggravate the sense of exclusion and marginality felt by a generation of young people.
22. As already stated the possibility to disaggregate by regions ISTAT official estimates of the breakdown between regular and irregular forms of employment offers a unique opportunity to understand the different trends of service employment in diverse contexts.
23. That is, a kind of clientelistic climate of welfare provision characterized by interventions in favour of specific groups of individuals and, usually, accompanied by corruption.
24. In the Italian case, these conditions are confirmed by surveys on young generations (Cavalli and De Lillo, 1993) and on youth unemployment (IARD, 1996; IRES, 1992; Mingione and Pugliese, 1993, 1995; Reyneri, 1996).

Bibliography

Amin, A. and Robins, K. (1990) 'Environment and planning', *Society and Space*, vol. 8, no. 1.

Amin, A. and Thrift, N. (1992) 'Neo-Marshallian nodes in global networks', *International Journal of Urban and Regional Research*, vol. 16, no. 4, pp. 571–87.

Ascoli, U. (ed.) (1984) *Welfare state all'taliana*, Laterza, Bari.

Bagnasco, A. (1977) *Tre Italie: la problematica territoriale dello sviluppo italiano*, Il Mulino, Bologna.

Bagnasco, A. (1986) *Torino: un profilo sociologico*, Einaudi, Torino.

Bagnasco, A. and Trigilia, C. (eds) (1984a) *Società e politica nelle aree di piccola impresa; il Caso di Bassano*, Arsenale,Venezia.

Bagnasco, A. and Trigilia, C. (eds) (1984b) *Società e politica nelle aree di piccola impresa; il Caso della Valdelsa*, Angeli, Milano.

Balfour, S. (1989) *Dictatorship, Workers and the City: Labour in Barcelona since 1939*, Clarendon Press, Oxford.

Becattini, G. (ed.) (1987) *Mercato e forze locali: il distretto industriale*, Il Mulino, Bologna.

Becattini, G. (ed.) (1989) *Modelli locali di sviluppo*, Il Mulino, Bologna.
Benko, G. and Dunford, M. (eds) (1991) *Industrial Change & Regional Development*, Belhaven Press, London and New York.
Benko, G. and Lipietz, A. (eds) (1992) *Les régions qui gagnent*, Presses Universitaires de France, Paris.
Bettio, F. and Villa, P. (1993) 'Strutture familiari e mercati del lavoro nei paesi sviluppati. L'emergere di un percorso mediterraneo per l'integrazione delle donne nel mercato del lavoro', *Economia e Lavoro*, vol. XXVII, no. 2, pp. 3–30.
Boccella, N. (1982) *Il Mezzogiorno Sussidiato*, Angeli, Milano.
Bosch, J. and Saez, J. (1991) 'La evolution del sector industrial Catalan 1985–1990', *Economia Industrial*, May/August, pp. 155–69.
Brunetta, R. and Tronti, R. (eds) (1991) *Welfare state e redistribuzione*, Angeli, Milano.
Brusco, S. (1979) *Agricoltura ricca e classi sociali*, Feltrinelli, Milano.
Brusco, S. and Villa, P. (1987) 'Flessibilità del lavoro, segmentazione e livelli di occupazione', *Politica Economica*, no. 2.
Brusco, S. and Villa, P. (1989) 'The state, the unions, and the labor market: the Italian case, 1969–1985', in Rosenberg, S., pp. 127–50.
Calvanese, F. and Pugliese, E. (1991) *La presenza straniera in Italia. Il caso della Campania*, Angeli, Milano.
Capecchi, V. (1989) 'The informal economy and the development of flexible specialization in Emilia-Romagma', Portes, Castells and Benton (eds), *The Informal Economy: Studies in Advanced and Less Developed Countries*, The Johns Hopkins University Press, Baltimore and London.
Castles, F. G. (ed.) (1993) *Families of Nations: Patterns of Public Policy in Western Democracies*, Darthmouth, Aldershot.
Castronovo, V. (1975) 'La storia economica', *Storia d' Italia*, vol. IV, no. I, Einaudi, Torino.
Cavalli, A. and De Lillo, A. (1993) *Giovani anni 90. Terzo rapporto IARD sulla condizione giovanile in Italia*, Il Mulino, Bologna.
Cerase, F. P. (ed.) (1992) *Dopo il familismo, cosa?*, Angeli, Milano.
Chronaki, Z., Hadjimichalis, C., Labrianidis, L. and Vaiou, D. (1993) 'Diffused industrialization in Thessaloniki: from expansion to crisis', in *International Journal of Urban and Regional Research*, vol. 17, no. 2, pp. 178–94.
Cochrane, A. and Clarke, J. (eds) (1993), *Comparing Welfare States*, Sage, London.
Cotugno, P., Pugliese, E. and Rebeggiani, E. (1990) 'Mercato del lavoro e occupazione nel secondo dopoguerra', in *Storia d'Italia. Le Regioni dall'Unità a Oggi: La Campania*, Einaudi, Torino, pp. 1141–85.
Cousins, C. (1994) 'A Comparison of the Labor market position of women in Spain and the UK with reference to the "flexible" labor debate', *Work, Employment and Society*, vol. 8, no. 1, pp. 45–67.
Curry, J. (1993) 'The Flexibility Fetish', *Capital and Class*, Summer, pp. 99–126.
De Sousa Santos, B. (1985) 'Estado e Sociedade na semiperiferia do sistema mundial: o caso portugues', *Analise Social*, no. 87–89, pp. 869–901.
Dente, B. (ed.) (1990) *Le politiche pubbliche in Italia*, Il Mulino, Bologna.
Doeringer, P. and Piore M. J. (1971) *Internal Labour Markets and Manpower Analysis*, D.C. Heath, Lexington, MA.
Edwards, R. C. (1979) *Contested Terrain*, Basic Books, New York.
Edwards, R. C., Reich, M. and Gordon D. M. (eds) (1975) *Labour Market Segmentation*, Lexington, MA: D.C. Heath.
Esping-Andersen, G. (1990) *The Three Worlds of Welfare Capitalism*, Polity Press, Cambridge.

Ferrera, M. (1984) *Il Welfare State in Italia*, Il Mulino, Bologna.
Ferrera, M. (ed.) (1991) *Le Dodici Europe. I paesi della Comunità di fronte ai cambia-menti del 1989–1990*, Il Mulino, Bologna.
Ferrera, M. (1993) *Modelli di solidarietà. Politica e riforme sociali nelle democrazie*, Il Mulino, Bologna.
Fina, L., Meixide, A. and Toharia, L. (1989) 'Reregulating the labor market amid an economic and political crisis: Spain, 1975–1986', in Rosenberg (ed.) pp. 107–25.
Flora, P. (ed.) (1986) *Growth to Limits. The Western European Welfare States Since World War II*, vol. 2, de Gruyter, Berlin-New York.
Flora, P. and Heidenheimer, A. J. (eds) (1981) *The Development of Welfare States in Europe and America*, Transaction Books, New Brunswick, NJ.
Garofoli, G. (1991) 'The Italian model of spatial development in the 1970s and 1980s', in Benko, G. and Dunford, M., pp. 85–101.
Garofoli, G. (1992) 'Les systèmes de petites entreprises: un cas paradigmatique de développement endogène', in Benko and Lipietz, pp. 57–80.
Gerschenkron, A. (1962) *Economic Backwardness in Historical Perspective*, Belknap Press of Harvard University Press, Cambridge, MA.
Giannola, A. (ed.) (1986) *L'economia e il Mezzogiorno. Sviluppo, imprese e territorio*, Angeli, Milano.
Ginatempo, N. and Fera, G. (1985) *L'autocostruzione spontanea nel Mezzogiorno*, Angeli, Milano.
Giner, S. (1980) *The Social Structure of Catalonia*, Anglo-Catalan Society, University of Sheffield Printing Unit.
Goodman, E., Bamford, J. and Saynor, P. (eds) (1989) *Small Firms and Industrial Districts in Italy*, Routledge, London and New York.
Gordon, D. M. (1972) *Theories of Poverty and Underemployment*, Lexington Books, Lexington.
Gordon, D. M., Edwards, R. and Reich, M. (1982) *Segmented Work, Divided Workers*, Cambridge University Press, Cambridge.
Gramsci, A. (1966) *La Questione Meridionale*, Editori Riuniti, Roma.
Graziani, A. (1978) 'The Mezzogiorno in the Italian Economy', *Cambridge Journal of Economics*, vol. 2, no. 2, pp. 355–72.
Graziani, A. and Pugliese, E. (eds) (1979) *Investimenti e Disoccupazione nel Mezzogiorno*, Il Mulino, Bologna.
Grosso de Oliveira, J. G. (1985) 'Mercado de Trabalho, "Dualismo e Accoes Colectivas", in Coloquio Portugal 1974–1984', *Revista critica de ciencias sociais*, vol. I, pp. 397 ff.
Hadjimichalis, C. (1994) 'The fringes of Europe and EU integration: a view from the South', *European Urban and Regional Studies*, no. 1, pp. 19–29.
Hadjimichalis, C. and Vaiou, D. (1990a) 'Whose flexibility? The politics of informal-isation in Southern Europe', *Capital and Class*, no. 42, Winter, pp. 79–106.
Hadjimichalis, C. and Vaiou, D. (1990b) 'Flexible labour markets and regional devel-opment in northern Greece', *International Journal of Urban and Regional Research*, vol. 14, no. 1, pp. 1–24.
Hilpert, U. (ed.) (1991) *Regional Innovation and Decentralization. High Tech Industry and Government Policy*, Routledge, London and New York.
IARD (1996) *Youth Unemployment and Unofficial Economy in Southern Europe*, Milano, Mimeo.
IRES-CGIL (1992) *Caratteristiche e tipologia della disoccupazione in Italia*, Final Report of a Research commissioned by the Ministry of Work.
Jimeno, J. F. and Toharia, L. (1994) *Unemployment and Labour Market Flexibility: Spain*, Geneva, ILO Employment Series.

Kerr, C. (1950) 'Labour markets: their character and consequences', *American Economic Review, Papers and Proceedings*, vol. 40, no. 2 (May), pp. 278–91.

Kerr, C. (1954) 'The balkanization of labor markets' Bakke, E. W. and Hauser, P. M. (eds), *Labor Mobility and Economic Opportunity*, MIT Press, London, pp. 92–110.

Leibfried, S. (1992) 'Towards a European welfare state? On integrating poverty regimes into the European Community', in Ferge, Z. and Eivind Kolberg, J. (eds), *Social Policy in a Changing Europe*, Westview Press, Boulder, CO. pp. 245–79.

Leontiou, L. (1993) 'Informal strategies of unemployment relief in Greek cities: the relevance of family, locality and housing', *European Planning Studies*, vol. 1, no. 1, pp. 43–68.

Lutz, V. (1962) *Italy: A Study in Economic Development*, Oxford.

Magatti, M. (1991) 'Mercato e forze sociali', *Due distretti tessili: Lancashire e Ticino Olona, 1950–1980*, Il Mulino, Bologna.

Magatti, M. (1993) 'The market and social forces: a comparative analysis of industrial change', *International Journal of Urban and Regional Research*, vol. 17, no. 2, pp. 213–31.

Martinotti, G. (ed.) (1982) *La Città Difficile*, Angeli, Milano.

Miguelez-Lobo, F. (1990a) 'Irregular work in Spain', in EEC, *Program for Research and Actions on the Development of the Labour Market. Underground Economy and Irregular Forms of Employment* (Travail au Noir).

Miguelez-Lobo, F. (1990b) 'Irregular work in Portugal', in EEC, *Program for Research and Actions on the Development of the Labour Market. Underground Economy and Irregular Forms of Employment* (Travail au Noir).

Mingione, E. (1990a) 'Il sistema italiano delle divisioni regionali e i processi di informalizzazione', *Inchiesta*, Year XX, no. 88–89, pp. 3–25.

Mingione, E. (1990a) 'Underground economy and irregular forms of employment: the case of Italy', in EEC, *Program for Research and Actions on the Development of the Labour Market. Underground Economy and Irregular Forms of Employment*.

Mingione, E. (1990b) 'Underground economy and irregular forms of employment: the case of Greece', in EEC, *Program for Research and Actions on the Development of the Labour Market. Underground Economy and Irregular Forms of Employment*.

Mingione, E. (1991) *Fragmented Societies*, Blackwell, Oxford.

Mingione, E. (1994) 'Life strategies and social economies in the postfordist age', *International Journal of Urban and Regional Research*, vol. 18, no. 1, pp. 24–45.

Mingione, E. and Pugliese, E. (1993) 'La Disoccupazione', in Paci, M. *Le Dimensioni della Disuguaglianza*, Il Mulino, Bologna, pp. 245–59.

Mingione, E. and Pugliese, E. (1995) 'Modelli occupazionali e disoccupazione giovanile di massa nel Mezzogiorno', in Giullari, B. and La Rosa, M. (eds), *Sociologia del Lavoro*, no. 59–60, pp. 118–44.

Mottura, G. (1991) 'Forme della presenza extracomunitaria nell'agricoltura italiana', in Ceres, *Aspetti economici dell'immigrazione in Italia, Quaderni di Economia del Lavoro*, no. 43.

Mottura, G. (ed.) (1992) *L'arcipelago immigrazione*, Ediesse, Roma.

Mottura, G. and Mingione, E. (1989) 'Agriculture and society: remarks on transformations and new social profiles in the case of Italy', *Agriculture and Human Values*, vol. VI, no. 1–2. pp. 47–58.

Mouzelis, N. (1978) *Modern Greece: Facets of Underdevelopment*, Macmillan, London.

Negri, N. (1982) 'I nuovi torinesi: immigrazione, mobilità e struttura sociale' in Martinotti, (ed.) pp. 53–179.

Paci, M. (ed.) (1978) *Capitalismo e classi sociali in Italia*, Il Mulino, Bologna.
Paci, M. (ed.) (1980) *Famiglia e mercato del lavoro in una economia periferica*, Angeli, Milano.
Paci, M. (1990) *La sfida della cittadinanza sociale*, Edizioni Lavoro, Roma.
Paci, M. (1992) *Il mutamento della struttura sociale in Italia*, Il Mulino, Bologna.
Parellada, M. (ed.) (1990) *Estructura Economica de Cataluna*, Espasa Calpe, Madrid.
Pedullà, G. *et al.* (1987) *Nuove stime della popolazione occupata nella contabilità nazionale*, ISTAT, Roma.
Perulli, P. (1992) *L'Atlante Metropolitano*, Il Mulino, Bologna.
Perulli, P. (1993) 'Towards a regionalization of industrial relations', *International Journal of Urban and Regional Research*, vol. 17, no. 1, pp. 98–113.
Pinnarò, G. and Pugliese, E. (1985) 'Informalization and social resistance: the case of Naples', in Redclift N. and Mingione E. (eds), *Beyond Employment*, Blackwell, Oxford and New York, pp. 228–47.
Piore, M. J. (ed.) (1979) *Inflation and Unemployment: Institutionalist and Structuralist Views*, M. E. Sharpe, White Plains, NY.
Piore, M. J. (1986) 'Perspective on labor market flexibility', in *Industrial Relations*, vol. 25, no. 2.
Piore, M. J. and Sabel, C. F. (1984) *The Second Industrial Divide: Possibilities for Prosperity*, Basic Books, New York.
Piselli, F. (1991) *Medio Occidente. Una periferia d'Europa tra politica e trasformazione*, Marsilio, Venezia.
Pollert, A. (ed.) (1991) *Farewell to Flexibility?*, Blackwell, Oxford.
Pugliese, E. (1993) *Sociologia della disoccupazione*, Il Mulino, Bologna.
Recio, A. (1986) 'Economia sumergida y transformacion de las relaciones laborales en espana', in *'Papers' Revista de Sociologia*, Universitat Autonoma de Barcelona, no. 27, pp. 131–54.
Reyneri, E. (1996) *Sociologia del mercato del lavoro*, Il Mulino, Bologna.
Rodrigues, M. J. (1992) *O Sistema de Emprego en Portugal. Crise e Mutacoes*, Don Quixote, Lisboa.
Rosenberg, S. (ed.) (1989) *The State and the Labor Market*, Plenum Press, New York.
Rostow, W. (1960) *The Stages of Economic Growth*, Cambridge University Press, Cambridge.
Sabel, C. F. (1982) *Work and Politics*, Cambridge University Press, Cambridge.
Salmon, K. G. (1991) *The Modern Spanish Economy: Transformation and Integration into Europe*, Pinter Publishers, London.
Sanchèz, E. (1986) *Traball a domicili*, Institucio Alfons el Magnanim: Institucio Valenciana d'Estudis i Investigacio, Valencia.
Sayer, A. (1989) 'Postfordism in question', *International Journal of Urban and Regional Research*, vol. 13, no. 4, pp. 666–95.
Schmidt, M. G. (1993) 'Gendered labour force participation', in Castles, F. G. (ed.), pp. 179–237.
Silva, F. and Viesti, G. (eds) (1989) *Il difficile sviluppo dell'industria nel Mezzogiorno*, Angeli, Milano.
Sylos-labini, P. (1964) 'Precarious employment in Sicily', *International Labour Review*, March, pp. 268–85.
Syrett, S. (1993) 'Local economic initiatives in Portugal: reality and rhetoric', *International Journal of Urban and Regional Research*, vol. 17, no. 4, pp. 526–46.
Taylor-Gooby, P. (1991) 'Welfare state regimes and welfare citizenship', *Journal of European Social Policy*, vol. 1, no. 2, pp. 93–105.

Toharia, L. (1988) 'Partial fordism: Spain between political transition and economic crisis', in Boyer, R. (ed.), *The Search for Labour Market Flexibility. The European Economies in Transition*, Clarendon Press, Oxford.

Trigilia, C. (1986) *Grandi Partiti e Piccole Imprese*, Il Mulino, Bologna.

Trigilia, C. (1992) *Sviluppo senza Autonomia*, Il Mulino, Bologna.

Tsoulouvis, L. (1987) 'Aspects of statism and planning in Greece', *International Journal of Urban and Regional Research*, vol. 11, pp. 500–21.

Villa, P. (1986) *The Structuring of Labour Markets*, Clarendon Press, Oxford.

Villaverde Cabral (1984) 'A economia subterranea vem ao de Cima: estrategia rurais perante a industrializacao e a urbanizacao', *Analise Social*, vol. XIX, no. 76, Lisboa.

Wilkinson, F. (ed.) (1981) *The Dynamics of Labour Market Segmentation*, Academic Press, London.

Wolleb, E. and Wolleb G. (1993) *Sviluppo economico e squilibri territoriali nel Sud Europa*, Il Mulino, Bologna.

Wood, S. (ed.) (1982) *The Degradation of Work? Skill, Deskilling and the Labour Process*, Hutchinson, London.

6
Industrial Policy for Southern Europe

Antigone Lyberaki

> While industrial policy continues to be controversial, no one is in any doubt as to the responsibility of governments and of the Community to create as favourable an environment as possible for company competitiveness.
>
> White Paper 'Growth, Competitiveness, Employment: the challenges and ways forward into the 21st century', 1994

The debate about industrial policy has always been charged, while the pendulum concerning the desired amount of state intervention and free market forces has been swinging to and fro, reflecting ideological (and balance of power) shifts as much as changing economic circumstances in the world scene. The careful wording chosen in the above European Commission quotation testifies to the charged nature of the debate. This intellectual ambivalence notwithstanding, governments have always intervened (by design or by default) in the shaping of their country's productive structures. Directed public interventions at the sectoral and firm level (often complemented by horizontal actions) seeking to stimulate particular lines of economic activity can be taken as a definition of what constitutes industrial policy in the broad sense (Shapiro and Taylor, 1992, p. 433).

From the point of view of Southern Europe, the relevance of policies stimulating industrial restructuring acquires paramount importance. This is so because the economies broadly referred to as the 'south' tend to share a number of common characteristics, which place them in a disadvantaged, or more vulnerable situation. Indeed, the objective of speeding up economic convergence and catch up between the lagging and the successful economies is explicit in the agenda of the European project. The integration efforts of the European Union (EU) depend crucially on the creation of broadly similar economic conditions, levels of development and social

well-being throughout the European economy. The process of approximation of individual economic performances is usually termed 'economic
convergence'. The issue of catching up or lagging behind is critical not
only from the point of view of the less developed economies but also from
the perspective of the European integration project as well; this is so
because the European economy will be able to reap the benefits of cooperation and specialization only to the extent to which the individual
economies benefit from the integration process. A number of studies
(whose scope has been wider than Europe) have convincingly argued that
there exists a tendency for poorer economies to grow more rapidly than
their richer counterparts, especially after World War II (Abramovitz, 1986;
Baumol, 1986; Dowrick and Nguyen, 1989).

Industrial policy is one of the most powerful vehicles to stimulate catch
up, given the continuing strategic role of industry in the performance of
individual economies. In the contemporary EU jargon, the term 'convergence' has been replaced by 'economic and social cohesion'. In the
Maastricht Treaty, cohesion is mentioned as a central concern in achieving
economic convergence and monetary union among the member states and
regions of the EU. Thus, the objective of cohesion in the context of
European integration implies a commitment on the part of the member
states to the principle of mutual solidarity and the belief that 'collective
action through a partnership between EU and national/regional/local governments can play an important part in improving economic and social
conditions' (Leonardi, 1995, p. 2).

Furthermore, the EU recognizes at an official level, that the process of
economic integration (if left alone) will produce uneven costs and benefits
for the individual economies. So, the 1989 Delors Report on Economic and
Monetary Union (EMU) argued that without a proactive Community policy, the less developed European members may prove to be net losers from
the integration process:

> Historical experience suggests... that in the absence of countervailing
> policies, the overall impact on peripheral regions could be negative.
> Transport costs and economies of scale would tend to favour a shift in
> economic activity away from less developed regions, especially if they
> were at the periphery of the Community, to the highly developed areas
> at its centre. Economic and monetary union would have to encourage
> and guide structural adjustment which would help poorer regions to
> catch up with the wealthier ones.
>
> (CEC, 1989, p. 22)

In this chapter, we consider how industrial policy might be designed to
meet the challenges which the South European economies (SEEs) face in
the EU. Industrial policy here is treated in a rather broad sense, so as to

include a variety of the factors and mechanisms that influence industrial competitiveness. So, alongside the more traditional definitions of competition, R&D and sectoral policies (dealt with in the third section), the discussion also takes into account the terrain of small business development (fourth section) as well as the area of regional policy. Indeed, the latter type of policy appears to be more directly linked to the objective of catching up and convergence. This broader approach offers the advantage of bypassing the sterile debate on the necessity for or redundancy of having industrial policy, while allowing the discussion to concentrate on the real issues involved.

Any discussion of policies does not occur in a vacuum, nor is it possible to imagine ideal policies irrespective of context. Timing is one factor that is largely shaping the context. Inherited structures and institutions is another. Therefore, the discussion on industrial policy in Southern Europe necessarily bears the imprint of both these factors.

First, it is occurring at a time when the prolongation of uncertainty feeds widespread disillusionment with 'magic recipes' (both in their Keynesian and in their liberal variant). Thus, the contemporary approach to industrial policy is firmly situated in a context of uncertainty and pervasive change, under the dual impact of the forces of globalization on the one hand and the rapid diffusion of microelectronics- and communications-related technologies. In other words, industrial policy is forced to abandon the tested recipes for competitive success that had dominated the 'golden age' of the postwar boom, and is currently going through a painful process of experimentation and innovation in order to deal with the new problems of the postfordist times (second section).

The second factor is related to the specificities of the SEEs, which although heterogeneous in most respects, nevertheless share a number of common 'dissimilarities' with their central and northern European partners. The economic structures in the three SEEs and their living standards in the 1970s and early-1980s were comparable. Their recent entrance into the European Union (then European Community) obliged them to cope with an economic shock of significant proportions (see Katseli in this volume). They have traditionally tended to specialize in lower technology manufacturing activities (Caloghirou *et al.*, 1996). All three SEEs have had to cope with the problems associated with the process of consolidation of democracy as late as the 1970s and have experienced various ways in which this process has interfered with the working of their economies. The emergence of strong socialist parties, committed to intervention and to an ideology of 'industrialism' which, despite the virtual absence of deep roots in their respective political systems, have managed to rise to power in a very short period of time, is another common feature (Diamandouros, 1991, p. 15). Furthermore, another common feature shared by the Southern European societies is the populous petty bourgeois strata, composed primarily of artisans, shopkeepers and large numbers of civil servants (and, in the case of Greece, of small land-holders) with considerable social, economic and political significance (Diamandouros, 1991, p. 17). This social configuration gives rise to a very small average size of manufacturing firms and also encourages the family-type of management practices to remain the rule rather than the exception of the industrial structure. Partly due to their political heritage, the economies of South Europe are endowed with different institutional set-ups, different norms and practices underlying the processes of negotiation and conflict resolution, display different dynamics of resistance and accommodation to change, and command different reservoirs of strengths and weaknesses.

At the risk of oversimplification, it could be further argued that the organizational/structural attributes of the business sector are largely different from what constitutes the 'canon' in the more affluent societies of central and northern Europe. Often the size of large firms is too small to realize economies of scale, while the plethora of small enterprises tends to conform more to the 'low road to flexibility' prototype[1] than to any dynamic pattern of localized system of the 'industrial districts' type. What is more, the peripheral European economies tend to be characterized by a lack of supportive infrastructure capable of inducing up-market restructuring, long-term viability and networking among producers (see also Mingione in this volume).[2]

Notwithstanding their common features, variety and heterogeneity among SEEs should be stressed as well. This is evident, when examining economic performance indicators even at the most superficial level; different economies and different regions within the economies display a different potential for adjustment, catch up, convergence and restructuring (Leonardi, 1995; Lyberaki, 1996). This heterogeneous picture can partly be attributed to the different structural and institutional heritage of individual economies and partly to the pursuance of different policy priorities in different areas at different times. And although attributing analytical primacy to structures over policies or *vice versa* is clearly a futile exercise, nevertheless it seems safe to argue that the marriage between policies, institutions and structures has been difficult in most cases, ranging from hopeful to disastrous when examining individual economies.

The above bring us to the question of effectiveness of policies designed and implemented for SEEs. Does the 'rhetoric of convergence and cohesion' coincide with the evidence based on the experience of individual economies of the European south over the past 15 years? Have these countries managed to transform their industrial base in such a way that they can no longer be thought of as the backwater of Europe? In an attempt to unravel the convergence or divergence dynamics of recent years, the final section of the paper examines briefly the comparative performance of SEEs *vis-à-vis* the European average. This exercise produces two distinct scenarios, a successful one concerning Spain and (to a lesser degree) Portugal, and a diverging story referring to Greece. This finding reinforces the original argument of the relevance of the existing institutional set up in determining the limits within which each individual economy has the potential to take advantage of policies designed to speed up restructuring and transformation. It also diverts attention away from abstract discussions on 'best policies *per se*', in the more promising direction of exploring 'national factors' of resistance to adjustment (such as policies, institutions and behavioural patterns, both at the national and the local levels).

New trends in the economies, the societies and the conception of industrial policy

Uncertainty, unpredictability and confusion have marked the economic landscape over the past 20 years. New technologies are changing both markets and techniques of production so radically as to undermine earlier understandings of what is productive and efficient. It seems that we are going through a period of transition to the 'post-industrial' world (Block, 1990). Along this process the basis of competition is changing with the emergence of what came to be called 'the New Competition' (Best, 1990). Price-competitiveness is often overtaken in significance by the non-price factors determining success (the quality of the products, differentiation, reaching the market fast, specialization in products for which there is a rapidly growing demand are some of the crucial non-price factors underlying the changes in trade).

In the 'golden' postwar decades, competitiveness was linked to the capacity of individual economies to replicate the single dominant mode of production which was first developed in the United States and came to be called 'Fordism' (a synonym to the mass production-mass consumption system). In recent years the world has become more complex and uncertain, while competition has become multidimensional and multipolar. The world economy displays a multiplicity of innovation trajectories with rival innovators from all corners of the world. There no longer exists a single dominant best way of doing things. In that sense, industrial success is less a matter of emulation and more a matter of 'inventing' success (Andreasen *et al.*, 1995). Hence, the apparent difficulties with competitiveness have less to do with purely economic variables (such as the wage levels or the amounts of money invested in basic research) and much more to do with the strength or weakness of institutional arrangements for managing innovation, quality and flexibility.

The important discontinuities in economic (and social) development undermine previous ways of thinking. During the postwar period and up till the late-1970s, the hegemonic policy ambience, while emphasizing the optimality of the free market, nevertheless allowed for state intervention on occasions where markets failed to lead to the desired outcomes (absence of markets, presence of externalities, increasing returns to scale, high transaction and information costs etc). Since the beginning of the 1980s, the view that state intervention could successfully remedy market failure came under criticism.[3] A variety of negative arguments have been developed focusing on government failure and the shortcomings of state intervention. Krueger (1990) summarizes government failures, both of omission and commission leading to corruption.[4] Along with these, positive arguments have also been put forward to support the pro-market case.[5] The reflection of the above at the policy level has been crystallized in a new orthodoxy: liberalization. It involves a shift away from state intervention, the dismantling of the various controls on the movement of goods and capital, as well as a political agenda for a generally free-market, non-interventionist approach.

It is against this theoretical and policy background that the new competitive challenges are being dealt with. The intensification of international competition (which is the result of the continuing world economic integration, a process often termed 'globalization') has led to a growing preoccupation with the determinants of competitiveness. As a consequence, academic and policy interest is focusing on issues relating to productivity, technical change and innovation. The orthodox view is that the unfettered market forces are the levers for both static and dynamic efficiency. Therefore, governments and regulators of supranational bodies (such as the European Union) should continue along the path of liberalization and deregulation.

The orthodox views, however, have not gone unchallenged. A host of heterodox approaches argue that market-oriented reforms tend to have some unintended but nonetheless critical implications for economic performance in the longer run. In particular, it has been convincingly argued that market-oriented reforms tend to lead to the neglect or undervaluation of assets and structures that are vital for long-term development. This is so because of the ambivalent effects of competiton and the possibility of conflict between short-run optimization and long-run development.

The role of competition is not always beneficial, because if it comes in large doses then it may discourage long-term firm-specific investment.[6] Essentially, this is a problem of conflict between short-run (static efficiency or order) and long-run (dynamic efficiency or progress) considerations. Recognition that there may be a potential conflict between the needs of progress and order has a long history in economics.[7] Marshall in particular recognized that the struggle for survival might fail to bring into existence firms and institutions that are highly beneficial for long-term development and progress. Thus, in his opinion, progress could be speeded up by judicious intervention that would improve 'people's character and intellect'. What is more, these interventions might add little (if at all) to the immediate efficiency of production, but they would be worth having provided they prepared the way for more effective firms and institutions in the future.

Amsden (1997) provides a more general argument in favour of intervention and against wholesale liberalization as a lever to industrial development. She questions the assumption of the free-market theorists that market failures are more pronounced in more backward economies and that industrialization is a process of moving towards perfect markets. Her main argument is that, although the exchange functions of markets tend to become more perfect as economies mature, 'the production functions deliberately and purposely grow less perfect' (Amsden, 1997, p. 470). Market failures related to production involve distortions in the form of firm-specific technological knowledge, differentiated products, brand names, patents, as well as scale economies and externalities. The technologically advanced economies are endowed with specialized institutions that facilitate the creation of novel products and processes, advantages related to knowledge and high skills, R&D etc. The governments' role in the advanced industrialized countries has been one of joining with the private sector to socially construct competitive assets rather than to create perfect markets. 'In order for postwar latecomers to enter such industries, which constitute the logical second stage of industrial transformation after labour-intensive assembly, their dynamic learning path has had to be one *of creating comparable competitive assets, and not cultivating perfect markets*' (Amsden, 1997, p. 471, emphasis added).

If the case against uninhibited competiton is relatively straightforward (since the poisonous effects of too much or cut-throat competition are easily observable), the debate on the most appropriate ways to encourage innovation and technical change is more complex. With the benefit of hindsight, the process of technical change in capitalist societies appears to involve lots of wasted resources and efforts, and thus, in retrospect, lacks efficiency. Although testifying to the tension between short-term and long-term efficiency considerations, it is argued that it also underlines the difficulties of intervention in this area. The difficulty of intervention is associated with the high degree of uncertainty which is inherently involved in the process of technical change and innovation, and the fact that there is no way of knowing in advance which alternatives are worth pursuing and which are not. Therefore, industrial organization cannot be optimally planned in advance and must involve experimentation through trials and errors rather than through picking winners (Nelson, 1988; Rosenberg, 1992).

The need for variety and experimentation notwithstanding, it has been argued that too much variety and too much experimentation may indeed prove to be harmful for economic progress. Three arguments have been formulated against the unidimensional preoccupation with uncertainty and the resulting impossibility of intervention. The first argument against uninhibited experimentation is that uncertainty is not equally severe in all stages of the life-cycle of a technological paradigm and that it is higher in the initial or 'pre-paradigmatic' phase. Afterwards, the rules of the game become more or less crystallized and there might be space for useful intervention. The second argument is that not all industrial activities and branches exhibit the same degree of uncertainty and thus one should refrain from overgeneralizing. And last, but not least, comes the argument which appears to be directly relevant to policy-making in less developed economies. The main thrust of the argument is that although a business environment that is hostile to experimentation may inhibit indigenous technological development, industrial performance will not necessarily be arrested as long as there is the option of acquiring technology from abroad. A number of highly dynamic formerly less developed countries have based their industrial success on imported technology (Wade, 1990) – the case of Taiwan being most often quoted (Chang, 1994).

The above discussion suggests that there still exist some appropriate forms of state intervention in a dynamic economy (Michie and Prendergast, 1998). While taking into account the deep uncertainties involved in the innovation process and the nature of constraints imposed on the desirable forms that state intervention can take, one has also to recognize the dual role of competition, which can lead to short-term optimization but at the cost of inhibiting longer-run economic development. The market mechanism can be too severe so as to eliminate potential successes or to prevent future successes from ever coming into being at all. In this light, picking winners (in terms of either sectors or firms) may be not only viable but also desirable. Furthermore, allowing for 'too much variety may not only prove wasteful but may also prevent the formation of necessary agglomeration and other external economies of scale and scope which are vital to the development process' (Michie and Prendergast, 1998, p. 403).

Clearly there is no single magical recipe for industrial intervention guaranteeing success. Ultimately, the nature and content of feasible interventions depend on the existing organizational structures. So what has proved to be beneficial for a particular economy may be totally unsuitable for another. But there is scope for devising appropriate industrial policy interventions suited to particular economies. The neoliberal orthodoxy denies it. Nevertheless there are good theoretical and empirical arguments that lend support to this 'interventionist' view. Historical precedents constitute the empirical basis for intervention. Having referred to the theoretical argument above, it is to these historical precedents that the discussion now turns.

In a recent review of the performance of developing economies since 1980, Lall (1998) suggests that received trade theory is incapable of explaining the patterns of industrialization, the successes and the failures. He argues that market failures in the sense of learning, economies of scale, increasing returns and agglomeration externalities constitute the main determinants of comparative advantage. The differences in performance can be attributed to differing initial capabilities ('starting-points characteristics') and more importantly to the learning of new capabilities. If policy intervention can do little to influence the former, there is clearly ample scope to make an impact on the latter, since 'the acquisition of all capabilities requires effort and supportive policies' (Lall, 1998, p. 67). Without denying the real and important danger of government failure (especially if one considers that selective policies are susceptible to hijacking, corruption and agency problems), he argues that development experience provides evidence that government failure is not inevitable. Therefore, the 'economic rationale for selective interventions remains as long as markets fail and governments are capable of improving their capabilities' (p. 69).[8]

The above discussion suggests that the important question is not really about the extent but rather the quality of state intervention (Bardham, 1990, p. 4). The analogy to the new determinants of competitiveness is very clear. As there is increasing concern with the qualitative attributes of goods and services produced and traded (competitiveness being conceived less in terms of quantifiable achievments such as cost reduction), there appears to be developing a parallel concern with the quality of intervening institutions of the public sector bureaucracy. Discussion has been recently focusing on the cultural characteristics of the public sector organizations that have successfully managed to escape the norm of inefficiency and low performance in a large number of developing countries (Grindle, 1997).[9] It follows that encouraging the development of characteristics associated with positive organizational cultures may be an important part of improving not only the performance of the public sector but also of speeding up the industrialization process along viable and strategically dynamic paths.

To conclude the discussion, it is worth pointing out that, without denying the role of competition as the engine of change, it appears that 'paradoxically, an excessive emphasis on market-type flexibility can lock firms and industries into existing products and routines of production. Once lock-in occurs, substantial reforms may be necessary before development once again becomes possible. And it is likely to be only the state that is able both to develop the necessary policy agenda and to force it through' (Michie and Prendergast, 1998, p. 404). To quote Amsden (1997, p. 478) once more,

> as the North Atlantic economies and Japan demonstrate, moving closer to the world technological frontier and becoming internationally competitive have involved a deliberate creation of 'distortions' [rather than] creating perfect markets. The distinction between the two could not be more clear than in the aftermath of restructuring in the last quarter

of the 20th century. In the case of those developing countries that swallowed a neoliberal medicine, many 'market failures' were indeed reduced. But as old social constructions of competitive assets were dismantled, investment and productive capacity fell and has continued to fall for a lengthy time period. ... Despite all the [market-based] reforms, a new social construction of competitive assets will be necessary for a resumption of growth.

This new concern with the qualitative aspects of both production and policy intervention is running contrary to conventional economic wisdom on the possibility of isolating the economic from the social sphere.

The idea that the economy is an analytically separate realm of society that can be understood in terms of its own internal dynamics is gradually losing its credibility. It is being increasingly recognized that social, political and cultural factors constantly shape and influence economic decisions and economic behaviour (be it in the terrain of investment or consumption). It follows that economic performance necessarily depends not only on individual economic choices (producers and consumers) and on state policies that seek to influence the course of economic and industrial development, but also on the vast 'grey area' of social regulation (referring to 'the social arrangements that condition and shape microeconomic choices', encompassing 'all the diverse ways in which individual economic behaviour is embedded in a broader social framework' (Block, 1990, p. 42).

Such an environment of change places emphasis on economic and administrative versatility and requires a new approach to regulation. Industrial policy will need to be sensitive to divergent models of production and changing business profiles (Farrands and Totterdill, 1993). In the pre-crisis era (during what came to be called 'the golden age of capitalism'), the unquestionable premise of industrial policy was the primacy of large corporations in terms of efficiency, innovation, technology dissemination and as levers of modernization. During the 1980s this view came under increasing strain. The break-up, saturation and fragmentation of consumer markets together with the emerging trends favouring customization and specialization have unravelled the advantages of responsiveness, adaptation, flexibility, continuous innovation and quality considerations as safeguarding competitiveness in the long-term. 'New Times'[10] trigger new approaches to industrial regulation in order to promote innovation, ensure the diffusion of innovative practices across the economy and encourage cooperationand networking among smaller firms. Given the accumulated evidence that while large firms remain a very important source of innovation, nevertheless small firms are essential for growth and the diffusion of innovative practices across the economy, the philosophy of industrial policy distances itself both from the idea of direct intervention as a panacea prescription and from the idea that 'non-intervention is the best aid for industrial prosperity'. By doing so, it acquires a regulatory momentum which seeks to develop sophisticated mechanisms of combining public and private interests while keeping a competitive environment.[11]

This regulation-intensive approach to industrial policy appears more appropriate in the face of the increasing complexities of contemporary economies. Furthermore, it can be equally suited to coping with the problems related to different size categories of firms, therefore, in principle, this approach can be fruitful in dealing with the problems of areas hosting large firms as well as areas whose productive structure is primarily made up by small and medium-sized enterprises (or a combination of both).[12] Obviously, a different focus requires different competencies on the part of regulators and policy-makers. And since the incidence of regions densely populated by smaller firms is probably one of the distinguishing characteristics of Southern Europe, it is worth adding a few more ideas on the special 'small-firms-specific' requirements of industrial policy.[13]

Industrial regulation initiatives geared to smaller enterprises need to target two main objectives: First, they need to enable small firms to overcome the disadvantages of small scale production through the provision of sophisticated collective services relating to market intelligence, marketing, design, innovation, production technology and common access to specialized resources (consulting, etc). And second, appropriate mechanisms have to be invented (or supported where they already exist), capable of regulating the organization of joint ventures and subcontracting. In other words, resources and competencies have to be pooled and a competitive profile based on interaction and collaboration rather than on individual performance created, overcoming not 'smallness' but the 'loneliness' which often goes with it. Clearly, these are high targets which can only be pursued with the mobilization and active participation of local entrepreneurs. If, however, participation is a necessary condition, it is not a sufficient one. What is further needed is a web of institutions (small firm oriented agencies, for instance) operating within a broad (but well defined) strategic framework.

The need for a broadly conceived strategic framework takes us to the familiar terrain of the debate on the desirability of industrial intervention. The collapse of the centrally planned economies and the fiscal deadlocks of expansionary policies have reasserted the importance of the market mechanism as a useful instrument regulating economies. It follows that if the market mechanism is expected to operate, it requires a certain degree of macroeconomic stability (hence there is relatively weak opposition to the necessity of accepting stabilization policies wherever the nature of macroeconomic imbalances threatens to destabilize contemporary economies). Having said that, it does not follow that intervention and regulation is less urgent today. Indeed, powerful arguments have been developed stressing old and new forms of market failure. 'Just as there are systemic arguments for relying on market forces to play a centrally important role in modern economies (turbulence and uncertainty rendering central planning virtually impossible), there are parallel arguments for imposing on these market forces a coherent economic strategy within which they are allowed to operate' (Cowling and Sugden, 1990, pp. 11–12).[14]

To wind up the preceding discussion, three issues stand out as crucial for the effectiveness of industrial policy in the contemporary setting. First, there is a need to devise a strategic framework for industrial development in Europe, which should be flexible enough to accommodate the institutional and structural variety of the European economic landscape, and far-sighted enough to encourage long-term competitiveness. An appropriate strategy for industrial intervention attributes a proactive (rather than reactive) role to the supranational authorities. The latter should be expected to play the part of the catalyst on the basis of their strategic oversight of development (not burdened with operational detail) in a limited array of key industries. This role is complementary to the market rather than a substitute to it. The issue then becomes to define (and select) the strategic industries: those that appear to be viable and important in a long-term perspective, but which are vulnerable in the short or medium term without significant intervention. To be effective, this selection process needs to rest on extensive negotiation and consensus building at all levels.

Second comes the issue of decentralization. To be effective, industrial policy 'ought to be conducted at as local a level as possible ... subject to the constraint that it is viable' (Geroski, 1989, p. 25) for a number of reasons: first, because it requires detailed information in order to be appropriately designed; second, because the complexities of policy rise more than proportionately in the number of parties involved; and third, applying policies at the local level ensures their suitability to local preferences and allows choices to be made in a more democratic fashion.

And last, but not least, crucial for the effectiveness of industrial policies is the role of the existing institutions at the domestic and local levels. The role of institutions[15] is becoming increasingly recognized as a crucial determinant of economic and industrial performance by means of influencing the choices or strategies available to individuals and groups. But, acknowledging the importance of institutions in economic performance does not necessarily imply that the existing institutions are *a priori* efficient or optimal. Indeed, the effect of any institutional framework on economic performance cannot be analysed in abstract terms (Henley and Tsakalotos, 1993, p. 43). It follows that the efficiency and the economic potential of any particular economy depends both on policies (designed and implemented at various levels such as the European, the national, the regional and the local) and on the social arrangements that condition and shape microeconomic choices by the economic actors (individuals and collectivities) involved.

Industrial policy in the European Union

Over the past 20 years, the European economy's rate of growth has shrunk from around 4 per cent a year to around 2.5 per cent, while unemployment has been steadily rising. Investment has followed a declining pattern (it has fallen by 5 per cent over the same period). As a corollary to the above trends, the European economy's competitive position *vis-à-vis* its main competitors (USA and Japan) has deteriorated as regards export performance (that is, shares in export markets), research and development (R&D) as well as innovation and the development of new products (Coriat, 1995, pp. 6–15).

Against this background, the European Union has developed a strategy to deal with the 'challenges and ways forward to the 21st century' (White Paper on Growth, Competitiveness and Employment, European Commission, 1994, hereafter White Paper). By doing so, it has distanced itself in a number of ways from the type of 'recipes for industrial success' that have largely characterized the previous era, both in their interventionist-Keynesian and in their laissez-faire/liberal variants. Given the complexity of the current reality and the prolongation of the recessionary phenomena, it comes as no surprise that the new approach sets out to describe what is not an appropriate strategy for Europe, rather than what should be done. Thus, it discards the idea of protectionism, which is seen to be suicidal for the European Union both on the grounds of its own future as well as on the grounds that it contradicts the European objective of encouraging the economies of the poorer countries. Furthermore, it discards the idea of an unlimited increase in government spending, which is seen as feeding inflation and external imbalances and leading to higher unemployment in the long term, without curing any of the causes of the economic malaise. At the same time, it rejects the idea of drastic cuts in wage levels in order to align wage costs on those of Europe's competitors. The latter option is seen as socially unacceptable, politically untenable and economically non-viable, as it deepens further the crisis by depressing domestic demand and undercutting jobs. And last, but not least, the White Paper criticizes the views favouring a generalized reduction in working hours and the introduction of job-sharing as a means of promoting employment, on the grounds that such solutions tend to slow down production.

The scepticism expressed by the European Commission *vis-à-vis* the old recipes for dealing with industrial decline are based on the recognition that the world is changing fast in a number of ways. In geopolitical terms, two developments are stressed. On the one hand, the emergence of new competitors, capable of rapid incorporation of the latest technical progress, has led to an intensification of competition world-wide. On the other, the end of communism has opened up new markets (120 million people in Europe's 'backyard'), which offer a new potential for growth. In demographic terms, of paramount importance appears to be the ageing of the population and the transformation of family structures. In technological terms, the new industrial revolution is causing rapid and all-embracing changes in technologies, production processes, jobs and skills. The economy is becoming increasingly knowledge-based and information-intensive, with far reaching implications undercutting traditional manufacturing activity and boosting services. And last, but not least, the unprecedented interdependence of financial markets following the liberalization of capital movements has ruled out the possibility of insulating individual economies from the hazards of world market trends.

In the light of what is called 'the new decor', the European Commission sets out a number of broad guidelines for the desired shape of a future Europe, whose economy has to be healthy, open, decentralized, competitive and based on solidarity. More specifically, a healthy economy is seen to be a stable economy moving in the direction of achieving a single currency. This implies a single macroeconomic framework within which all discussions concerning industrial (and other types of) policy should be located. In this respect, a gradual reduction of public deficits is considered to be of vital importance, together with a restructuring of public spending priorities in favour of investment and job creation. Stable monetary policies are required in order to cut interest rates and encourage investment. Incomes policies should initially serve the goal of containing inflation, while at the second phase they will allow wages to increase in order to provide incentives for more investment.

The objective of creating an open European economy is based on an analysis concerning the unavoidable globalization trends characterizing the world economy. The assumption behind the analysis is that every major burst of growth in the past has started with a qualitative leap in international trade. In the present era, this leap forward in international trade is marked by the very fast integration of developing and former communist countries. The European Union favours strongly all negotiations (Uruguay Round, GATT) for a global agreement between industrialized and developing countries 'containing balanced concessions aimed at fair access to all markets' (p. 13). Although the problem is one of achieving some sort of a coherent world management of the problems posed by development inequalities and the concentration of poverty in certain regions, the Com-mission's emphasis lies with Europe's eastern and southern neighbours.

The decentralization objective remains rather more obscure, as it is described to encompass a number of distinct processes including the new forms of organization in the advanced societies, alongside the growing importance of the local level, together with the descaling movements of the business and corporate structures. Special reference is made to the flexibility and cooperation potential of small and medium-sized enterprises and the declining importance of hierarchical and linear empires in favour of interactive organizations often labelled as 'networks'. The decentralizing tendency is seen to stem from the workings of the free market, while the process becomes further accelerated by the diffusion of the new technologies, leading eventually to the emergence of the 'information society'.[16] Indeed, special emphasis is placed on information-sharing and communications. As has been argued earlier in this chapter, a partnership between public and private sectors is deemed necessary in order to accelerate the pace of the establishment of information networks and information highways (broadband networks) and the development of the corresponding services and applications.

The development of information networks constitutes one of the strategic priorities within the overall policy framework. The rationale is clear: throughout the world, production systems, methods for organizing work and consumption patterns are undergoing changes that will have long term effects comparable with the first industrial revolution. Changes are affecting in a variety of different ways consumption patterns, definitions of citizenship and employment. The aim must not be to slow down change but instead to control it in order to avoid its negative implications. It is in Europe's interests to meet this challenge since the first economies capable of accommodating fast change will inevitably hold competitive advantages. Europe's main handicaps are the fragmentation of the various markets and the lack of major inoperable links. To overcome them, it is necessary to mobilize resources and to channel efforts in a partnership between the public and the private sectors. The estimated funding needed over the next 10 years is of the order of ECU 150 billion.

In order to achieve the objective of a more competitive economy Europe has to address the twin goals of (a) drawing maximum benefit from the single market, and (b) stepping up the effort in the areas of research and cooperation. To make the best out of the single market, three basic conditions should be met. The first condition is the simplification and consistency of the various rules (laws, regulations, standards, certification processes) issued for the smooth functioning of the market across Europe. Linked to the above is the second condition which focuses on small and medium enterprises and the need to incorporate them into the dynamics of the single market by means of simplifying and integrating the regulatory framework and by putting more effort on information. The third condition is the accelerated establishment of trans-European infrastructure networks. The rationale for building these trans-European infrastructure networks is to promote better and safer travel at lower cost, to provide the mould for effective planning in Europe,[17] as well as to accelerate 'bridge-building' towards Eastern Europe. In order to act as a catalyst for the establishment of these networks, for the development of new environmental improvement projects and for the promotion of the information society, the Commission will (a) accelerate the administrative procedures required, and (b) will supplement the existing financial instruments through recourse to saving.

The development of the trans-European transport and energy networks constitutes the second strategic theme of the overall approach. The creation of networks is a complement to the single market, as they increase physical links, they save time and they contribute to increased competitiveness by minimizing costs to business and individuals as well as by optimizing existing capacities (via improving their compatibility). Europe's investment in infrastructure has been slowing down over the last decade and this partly accounts for the deterioration in the quality of life (waste of time, environmental damage and underutilization of the new telecommunications media). The necessary investment in infrastructure (ECU 250 billion by the end of the century) will at the same time act: (a) as an accelerator of economic growth; (b) as a factor improving the quality of life in Europe; as well as (c) as a passport of competitive edge with the rest of the world.

The other strategically interventionist aspect of the Commission's strategy is the need to step up the research effort and cooperation. As is explicitly stated 'without eschewing competition, the ability to co-operate and share risks is increasingly becoming a sign of creativity' (White Paper, p. 14). Hence, Community competition policy has to make broad allowances for the desirable new forms of intercompany cooperation. And last, but not least, in the terrain of research, the Commission identifies the urgent need to focus resources on a limited number of joint projects geared to: (a) new information technologies and their applications; (b) biotechnology, encouraging synergies between chemical companies and big users (in the health and agricultural sectors); and (c) ecotechnologies 'meaning radical innovations targeting the causes of pollution and aiming at environmental efficiency throughout the production cycle' (White Paper, p. 15).

In a nutshell, the strategy for enhanced competitiveness and growth for Europe is defined by six main axes. The first is making the most out of the single market. The second is supporting the development and adaptation of small and medium-sized enterprises. The third is pursuing the social dialogue by means of strengthening cooperation and joint decision-making by the main social partners in industry (business and labour). The fourth is creating the major European infrastructure networks. The fifth is preparing and laying the foundations for the information society. And the sixth is that, in pursuing the above, the consistence and compatibility with the overall macroeconomic policy should be maintained.

The need to build a European economy based on solidarity is dictated by the experience showing that 'the market is not without its failings' (White Paper, p. 15), as it tends to underestimate what is at stake in the long run, as it affects the different social categories unequally and as it promotes concentration spontaneously, thus creating inequalities between the regions.

Therefore, the European economy needs collective mechanisms ensuring solidarity between those who have jobs and those who do not; men and women; generations; the more prosperous and the more disadvantaged regions (the objective of economic and social cohesion);[18] and lastly, solidarity in the fight against social exclusion.

The objective of economic and social cohesion in particular is often seen as the process of transfer of funds to the needy member states in order to 'buy off' their concession for the further moves towards integration that the rich member states wish to pursue. This involves a process of redistribution, which is seen as the corollary of integration, and at the same time the expression of the Union's deepening process. The most important explicit instruments to cope with the need for redistribution are the Structural Funds, although other aspects of the European policy have an indirect (but not necessarily less important) effect on the less developed regions of the community (Mitsos, this volume).

The objective of the Structural Funds is to produce a real economic impact on the specific priority objectives that the Community has set for itself.[19] This has been expressed in financial terms by the well-known 'Delors Package' (1988) that led to the doubling by 1992 of the funds made available. The European Union Treaty (otherwise the Maastricht Treaty) gave a new push towards economic and social cohesion through the Community Support Framework including a further doubling of the funds made available to the less developed regions for a period of five to seven years, while the prospects of the Community Support Framework III are equally promising. Two additions were made to the European institutional set-up, namely the Committee of Regions and the Cohesion Fund. Although the former lacks decision-making powers, nevertheless it is important as it is being recognized for the first time that other levels of government (besides the national governments, the interest groups and the European Parliament) have a role to play.[20] The Cohesion Fund is making financial contributions only to those member-states where per capita GDP is below 90 per cent of the European average (thus the list of beneficiaries is limited to Greece, Ireland, Portugal and Spain). The most important distinguishing characteristic of this fund is its direct link to the overall macroeconomic policy of the country in question. According to the new principle of conditionality (introduced with respect to the Cohesion Fund), the beneficiaries have to pursue a programme of economic convergence approved by ECOFIN (the Committee of EU Finance Ministers). Thus the link with Economic Monetary Union (EMU) has been directly established.

The function of regional redistribution as an expression of solidarity has been reinforced over the past ten years. The structural policies for reducing national and regional disparities gradually abolished their marginal status and came to be seen as an EU obligation.

European policies in favour of small and medium enterprises[21]

Europe-wide policy initiatives in favour of small and medium-sized enterprises (SMEs) are taken in view of the completion of the Single European Market project. They reflect a growing interest in and concern for this category of firms which characterized both European policy-making centres and academic circles throughout the 1980s (Boissevain, 1981; Burns and Dewhurst, 1986; Levicki, 1984). Major points of interest, in this respect, have been: the problem of defining SMEs, using the appropriate maximum number of employees threshold; the statistical studies showing an astonishing reversal of previous trends and a remarkable survival capacity of small firms, linked to substantial job creation;[22] SMEs' contribution to innovation and their being considered the seedbed of entrepreneurial skill – as opposed to large bureaucratic organizations; their unfair competitive disadvantage *vis-à-vis* large firms; finally, the need for a policy in favour of SMEs designed with an eye towards employment and implemented on a regional or local level (Geroski and Schwalbach, 1986). This last point is indicative of the pro-decentralization mentality gaining momentum.

The academic ambience of the 1980s and (mainly) the 1990s was conducive to the consolidation of policies favouring small and medium-sized enterprises. Indeed, small firms are drawn at the centre of theoretical and empirical investigation via two complementary and to a large extent overlapping approaches: flexible specialization and the industrial districts literature. Both approaches share the view that the traditional emphasis on the firm's size as a measure of performance potential was justified by the conditions prevailing up to 15 years previously: mass production, standardization of products and unquestionable advantages of large firms over the smaller ones in the terrain of research and development capabilities. The situation in the late-1980s and 1990s, however, transformed this balance of advantages and disadvantages between large and small firms. The trends favouring diversification (even personalization) of demand eroded the advantages of long-run, mass production. More significantly, the character of technological progress changed radically. Computer-based equipment is characterized by divisibility, which means that it tends to be more friendly to smaller scale batch production. Furthermore, the dynamic sources of technological innovation are no longer in-house R&D but large scale scientific research taking place outside the firms, in the universities and other (mainly public) research institutions. In this respect, every firm, large or small, is small if compared with the new tasks (Becattini, 1990, p. 167).

Within this context, flexible specialization theorization is associated with the notion that craft principles can provide a dynamic, viable, efficient and innovative alternative mode of organization to the crisis-ridden system of mass production (Piore and Sabel, 1984). Although this new approach is primarily based on the experience of a number of developed industrial economies, it represents a challenge to peripheral economies as well, and small firms in particular. The model of flexible specialization is based on three defining characteristics. First, clusters of small firms produce a wide range of products for highly differentiated markets. The vertical disintegration of their productive system allows for constant re-adjustments in response to changing market requirements. The second defining characteristic is the use of flexible and widely applicable technologies in production: versatile and general purpose machines and equipment, instead of large and dedicated machine systems. Product innovation is not inhibited by massive capital investment in rigid technologies; the 'minimum change' strategy characteristic of mass production is replaced by a generalized drive to constant innovation. The third defining characteristic of flexible specialization is its system of micro-regulation aiming to balance competition and cooperation. The ideal combination of competition cum cooperation is the trigger for perpetual innovation, skills transmission and learning-by-doing practices, ensuring that productivity does not stagnate and that competition remains 'fair' (no sweating of labour).[23] Micro-regulation is accomplished through learned social practices, ethical values as well as more formal rules and institutions. These sets of ideological/ethical practices and institutions tend to be regional in nature, due to the spatial agglomeration of flexible firms and their reliance on dense inter-firm transactional relations.[24]

The industrial districts problematic rests on the observation that in the midst of recession and economic stagnation, a few exceptional localities exhibited a remarkable resilience and even growth. These exemplars of prosperity[25] were engaged in a variety of industries (comprising advanced and traditional sectors) and were highlighted as being localized economic constellations that 'were beating the recession' (Murray, 1991; Pyke and Sengenberger, 1990). Industrial districts, then, are geographically defined productive systems, characterized by a large number of firms that are involved at various stages (and in a variety of ways) in the production of a homogeneous product. These local industrial constellations combine both economic efficiency and superior standards of employment. A significant characteristic is that a very high proportion of the firms comprising the districts are small or even very small. These firms are adaptive and innovative, capable of rapidly responding to changing product demands; they rely heavily on a multi-skilled and flexible labour force, and build up flexible production networks of inter-firm cooperation (Capecchi, 1990; Piore, 1990; Sabel, 1989). The most widely quoted successful industrial districts are those of north-central and north-eastern Italy (Goodman *et al.*, 1989; Putnam, 1993; Pyke *et al.*, 1990).

Probably the most important aspect of the industrial district definition is the notion that the districts should be conceived as social and economic wholes, wherein close and complex inter-relationships develop between the different social, political and economic spheres. The functioning of each distinct sphere shapes and is being shaped by the functioning and organization of the others. Therefore, the success (as well as the failure) of industrial districts lies not just in the realm of the 'economic'; broader social and institutional aspects are just as important (Pyke and Sengenberger, 1990, p. 2). In this sense, industrial districts are historically rooted and socially embedded. Furthermore, the industrial district model contributes in a change of emphasis in the academic discourse on small and medium-sized firms. By switching attention away from the individual small firm in the direction of the nature, depth and quality of interfirm relations, it unravels crucial aspects of small scale industry performance which cannot be captured at the level of individual firm analysis (in particular the incidence of 'collective efficiency'). What is more important, the industrial districts model 'provides a critical advance in that it ties the relationship between firms to the social, cultural and political environment in which they reside' (Nadvi and Schmitz, 1994, p. 1).[26]

Industrial districts are not identical with flexible specialization. Rather they constitute *one possible organisational framework within which this form of production may flourish* (Zeitlin, 1992, p. 285). This is so because the industrial districts themselves were not deliberately and purposefully organized round the principles of flexible specialization. Instead they grew out of particular circumstances. As Murray (1992) aptly put it, the industrial districts 'were not driven by a theory: Each case…had its own specific history. Flexible Specialisation as a concept emerged as a way of recognising the significance of these cases, and suggesting their potential as an alternative to mass production' (Murray, 1992, p. 256).

Against this theoretical background, the official definition of SMEs up till 1996 (500 employees or less) was very broad, so as to comprise the quasi-totality of European enterprises. In 1996, the Commission adopted a new definition of small and medium-sized enterprises which is more appropriate because it narrows down the range of firms described as SMEs (250 employees and less).[27] The basic philosophy behind EU actions in favour of SMEs is to reduce their handicaps due to their small size and thus facilitate their incorporation in the large Single European market. In view of the creation of the internal market, small firms face a greater challenge than large, already well-established firms which have been operating for many years on a wide European level. The SMEs' obstacles are considered to be the following:

1. Financing, especially in view of the modernization needs entailed by the Single Market project. Both their self-financing possibilities and their access to risk capital are limited, particularly in the EU's less developed areas.

2. The new EU-wide reglementation and harmonization process is often a source of difficulties, especially when it involves the implementation of stricter legislation in such areas as health standards and workplace security.
3. SMEs also have, in comparison to large firms, a serious handicap due to lack of sufficient information as regards such issues as public procurements, EU programmes and other policies linked to the Single Market project.
4. Finally, again because of their limited size, SMEs often employ personnel who are inadequately trained and cannot keep up with new technologies and/or the EU decision-making process.

To these problems, one should also add the intensification of competition, the networking difficulties which are more acute for small firms, as well as the problems of innovation and take-up of new technologies.

These problems are dealt with by EU member states themselves, both at the national as well as the regional and local levels – for example, various government initiatives such as to help financing SMEs, or to inform them about '1992'. But, especially since the late 1980s, SMEs have also constituted an explicit goal which is supposed to complement, where necessary, national governments' efforts.[28] EU actions in favour of SMEs can be classified as follows.

Information: the assistance to SMEs as regards their information on the Single Market has been implemented since 1986 and has led, since 1990, to the creation of the Euro-Info-Centres; these 187 centres function on a decentralized and non-discriminatory basis and inform SMEs across the EU on legislative matters of interest to them (1992 project), on the EU's social and regional funds' aid, on participation in research programmes and other similar issues. These centres are supposed, eventually, to become financially independent of Community funding, by charging a certain fee for their services.

Cooperation: through the computerized Business Cooperation Network (BC-NET) founded in 1988, the EU aims to enhance the SMEs' access to information. But this time the information provided relates directly to the market, that is, to possibilities of cooperation of SMEs between themselves either by simply selling/buying, or through joint ventures and other forms of 'marriages'. By processing, since 1988, thousands of confidential 'cooperation profiles' provided by the interested SMEs, the BC-NET has been functioning as a *sui generis* 'market substitute': it brings together small firms which, under other circumstances, would have had great difficulty in finding each other and cooperating. Another similar policy, initiated in 1988, is the 'Europartenariat' programme.[29]

Financial support: Assisting SMEs through various forms of financial engineering has been implemented on a European-wide level since 1986. In particular, the European Venture Capital Association offers risk capital to innovative projects transcending national boundaries (total subsidy in 1988: 5.5 million ECUs). At the same time, a pilot plan for start-up capital has been operating for the period 1989 to 1994 with EU Commission funding of 11.6 million ECUs. A Eurotech-capital fund finances, since 1989, high-technology ventures, especially of SMEs, while, in the period 1982 to 1989, through the successive 'New Community Instrument' (NCI I, II, III, IV) and with the participation of the European Investment Bank (EIB), SMEs have benefited from the possibility of low-interest financing.

Other forms of support: These cover a variety of measures, such as: training SME management and employees; elaborating a more appropriate and flexible legal framework for the cooperation of SMEs on a European scale (European Grouping of Economic Interests – GEIE, European Company Law, etc); facilitating SMEs' access to the increasingly liberalized public procurement procedures; and encouraging the diffusion of new technologies among small and medium-sized enterprises with the CRAFT Programme (Co-operative Research Action For Technology) especially designed to assist relatively small companies (linking up their research interests with universities and institutes).

The most recent policy initiative *vis-à-vis* European SMEs was adopted in 1997 with the establishment of the task force BEST (Business Environment Simplification Task Force).[30] The objective set for BEST was to prepare an independent report that would make proposals for concrete measures to be taken by the Commission and the member states to improve the quality of legislation and eliminate the unnecessary burdens that restrain the development of European SMEs. This task also included a look at the issues of finance for SMEs, management and employee training, innovation and technology transfer and all aspects of administration. The task force adopted the view that it was necessary to take a broad view of the problems faced by enterprises beyond those directly concerned with administrative burdens and at the same time to concentrate on those aspects that were of greatest importance to SMEs and were more susceptible to policy remedy. A central theme has been the *promotion of entrepreneurship* along with the related concerns for *enhancing competitiveness and creating sustainable employ-ment*. A number of policy proposals were formulated in key areas such as education and training, taking on employees, access to finance and access to research and technology.[31]

It is clear from the above that until very recently there has been no single, easily defined EU policy *vis-à-vis* small and medium-sized business. Probably with the exception of the BEST Report which has put forward a coherent perspective *vis-à-vis* the SMEs (seeing them not exclusively in terms of their employment generation potential, but also as important contributors to growth, flexibility, competitiveness and entrepreneurial culture), the earlier policy initiatives were fragmented and lacked a coherent strategic framework. Therefore, the concrete measures towards SMEs can be methodologically divided along the following lines: they either consist in altering market conditions (for example, Single Market legislation, common commercial policy) or they amount to a form of financial assistance (regional fund subsidies, EIB low interest loans, training or research funding, etc). These two basic policy forms constituted the bulk of EU interventions in the economic sphere until the late-1990s. The only exception in this respect is the aforementioned EU information and cooperation policies (Info-Centres, BC-NET), which effectively aim, in a very original manner, to some form of 'market substitution'.

Assessment and conclusions

The discussion of the changing competitive profile in our times and of the variety of restructuring responses has suggested that the market forces should be disciplined within the confines of a broad strategic framework of priorities, a framework allowing the flexible accommodation of the variety and change characterizing contemporary economies. It has also stressed the importance of decentralization, the networking potential of smaller firms if adequately supported, and the developmental dynamism following the transcendence of hierarchies at the corporate and regional levels. Against this backdrop, the analysis of the strategic document of the European Union (the White Paper) has attempted to situate the European priorities in the wider context.

In particular, the preceding review of EU policies and actions in support of SMEs has revealed, alongside more conventional policy instruments, a new awareness with the issues of technology diffusion and cooperation (both at the level of individual firms and on a regional basis) that has produced innovative policies. The latter aim at 'market substitution' by means of strengthening information and technology flows, networking and cooperation. These innovative policy initiatives, however, (although they have gained some fresh momentum with the independent report produced by BEST) remain marginal as yet, largely incapable of filling the gap of lacking pre-existing (or parallel) local, regional and national initiatives, stemming from governments, government-sponsored institutions as well as from the civil society.

The redistributive intentions of the European regional policy notwithstanding, it seems that assessing the impact of the policies themselves at the regional (European) level is far from straightforward. Part of the problem lies in the absence of clear-cut objectives and priorities on the part of the donor agencies of the EU. As Mitsos argues later in this volume, the interventions made by the Structural Funds over the 1989 to 1993 period were far from homogeneous, as they reflected the different priorities of each member state as well as the varying degrees of regionalization (itself being a function of domestic political pressures). The Commission services kept a low profile in the process (the criticisms for 'passive role' levelled against them were frequent and justified for the most part). The variety and heterogeneity of the various Community Support Frameworks[32] is well illustrated in the diverging priorities concerning, for instance the share of basic infrastructure in the total funding.[33]

The capacity of the poorer regions to absorb the funds to which they were entitled constitutes a controversial issue, subject to considerable definitional confusion. On the basis of the financial execution data (which give a clear indication of the degree of actual realization of the initial decisions) it appears that the absorption of the poorer (objective one) regions is higher than the average. The good average rates of absorption, however, conceal significant discrepancies at the level of individual projects, where, as expected, the more innovative (and therefore, the more ambitious) the programme, the slowest its realization rate. The difficulty in implementing demanding projects (such as Business Innovation Centres, Information Networks and Applied Research Centres) implies that the peripheral structures which are in more urgent need of such instruments are in fact more resistant to them, and it will take probably longer than initially expected to produce a positive impact (Lyberaki, 1996).

A general remark concerning the gradual transformation of the EU's redistributive policies aiming at the acceleration of restructuring and growth in the less-favoured regions relates to the emergence of regionalism as a new prospect for Europe's future. Indeed, the reforms of structural policy have triggered a two-sided process involving on the one hand the decentralization of decision-making to sub-national levels of government and on the other the centralization of new powers at the supranational level.[34] The 'Europe of the Regions' refers to a system of governance in which decision-making is spun away from member-states in two directions: up to supranational institutions and down to diverse units of subnational governments. Major components of such a system are the principles of subsidiarity and partnership.[35]

The emergence of regionalism is seen as a means to promote democracy and administrative efficiency, but it is much more than this. In a sense, it corresponds to, as well as reflects, the pervasive changes occurring in the spheres of production, distribution and consumption under the combined impact of the economic upheaval starting from the mid-1970s and the diffusion of new technological options. The economic malaise associated with the 'trouble with fordism' and the system based on mass production is necessitating a shift of emphasis away from large-scale and centrally managed institutions in favour of coordinated, flexible, responsive, innovative and high-quality batch production with high territoriality content. Flexible specialization (Piore and Sabel, 1984) promises to liberate the economic system from its endemic rigidities without compromising its efficiency by means of realizing economies of scope instead of economies of scale. The combination of lean production (Wommack *et al.*, 1990) and just-in-time sourcing (Kaplinsky, 1994) rests on a continuum of related activities and at the same time transcends the notion of a 'fortress firm'. Networking (Putnam, 1993; Pyke, 1994) offers a new array of competitive advantages to spatially integrated production ensembles, while at the same time building on the strengths of intangible factors such as ethics and practices developed on the basis of an inherited common (place-specific) history. The moral of the story is clear: if the organization of standardized mass production was historically linked to the centralization of public control, the trend towards post-fordism and flexibility requires decentralized government and scope for self-administration.

The link between decentralization and economic growth can be established on the basis of the experience of the European economies. At the national level of analysis, Germany, France, Italy and Spain have extensive regional or federal intermediate government bodies, while Greece, Portugal (together with the Italian South) are lacking such an institutional tradition. It is hardly surprising, thus, that these same economies are characterized by a lack of adequate public infrastructure, the lack of a culture of social solidarity and associationalism, combined with an 'ephemeral' and short-sighted private industrial sector. From the point of view of regional performance, it is clear that the strongest regions are equipped with the most developed regional institutions while the weakest regions (most of them in Southern Europe) are poor from the point of view of regional institutions. Furthermore, the most dynamic regions (found in the area often called 'the third Italy') have had regional governments growing in institutional capability over the past two decades and demonstrating a higher level of governmental performance (Putnam, 1993). Finally, the strongest regions in Spain (the fastest growing among the SEEs) have the greatest degree of autonomous powers in the Spanish context (Leonardi and Garmise, 1993). It follows that centralized states have been less successful in mobilizing resources for the promotion of economic restructuring than their more decentralized counterparts in Europe. Thus, keeping all other factors constant (capital, labour skills, infrastructure, entrepreneurship), the existence of decentralized forms of policy making and administrative structures helps countries to accelerate their rate of development *vis-à-vis* centralized states (Leonardi and Garmise, 1993, p. 266).

By way of concluding the discussion, it can be argued that Europe's industrial policy, although far from constituting a clear and fixed instrument for intervention, nevertheless incorporates a number of elements of strategic thinking at least as far as two broad sectors are concerned: information technology and infrastructure networks. While designing an overall macroeconomic framework within which all other policies necessarily have to fit, the stabilization objective does not jeopardize the pursuance of structural interventions. The emphasis on 'soft measures', networking and dialogue for consensus building is quite near the problematique on the indispensable role of institutions as well as on the mechanisms for conflict resolution and reconciliation in shaping economic performance. The emphasis attributed to small and medium-sized firms assistance (although somehow dated in a number of respects), nevertheless echoes the experience with successful industrial districts and clearly distances itself from the older 'large-scale industry bias'. Finally, from the point of view of the beneficiaries of the structural funds, it can be argued that the generous increases of the past decade have upgraded structural policy from its marginal role and have reinstated the need for courageous redistribution.

Having said that, however, it should also be stressed that Europe's industrial policy leaves a lot to be desired, and indeed a lot to be done at lower levels (national, regional and local). Indeed, as has been extensively argued, there is a strong case for designing and implementing policies at the lowest possible level (transparency, in accordance with local needs, ease the process of consensus building, to mention but a few) (Geroski, 1989; Helm and Smith, 1989). Furthermore, the experience of SEEs shows that economic convergence with their more affluent and prosperous partners is not a spontaneous process simply deriving from the process of economic integration. Policies designed and implemented at the domestic level (or the lack of them) play a major part in determining economic performance and the capacity of individual economies to adapt to changing circumstances.

The comparative performance of Greece, Spain and Portugal over the 1980s is very revealing in this respect. Greece has sought to slow down the process of adjustment (by favouring the prolongation of the *status quo*) and has ended up with a stagnating economy and a relative decline of per capita GDP as a percentage of the European average. By contrast, Spain and Portugal experienced faster income growth than in other European countries, as a result of which they have started to catch-up with them (Larre and Torres, 1991; Lyberaki, 1993). In Spain and Portugal, structural reforms have stimulated investment. The dismantling of customs barriers was accompanied in Spain and Portugal by the restructuring of the productive sector. This did not happen in Greece. Furthermore, as export performance shows, changes in supply conditions are very closely related to structural reforms. Spain and Portugal managed to gain market shares because they adjusted their production structures in such a way as to sell products for which world demand was growing faster, while the competitiveness, quality and marketing of their exports improved. The opposite trend has characterized Greece, where protectionist measures were kept longer without any parallel attempt to induce any structural change in the economy (Larre and Torres, 1991, p. 89; Lyberaki, 1993).

So, while Greece had experienced convergence during the 1960 to 1980 period (more vigorous up to 1975, at a lower pace during the second half of the 1970s), it witnessed a reversal of this trend over the 1980s and the beginning of the 1990s. Despite the positive economic effects of the Community Support Frameworks and other EU funded programmes (such as the Integrated Mediterranean Programmmes for instance) GDP scores in Greece failed to improve both nationally and regionally, while investment patterns hardly changed at all, the increases in productivity had been clearly inadequate and there was a loss in competitive advantage, as reflected in trade figures (Caloghirou *et al.*, 1996).

The opposite is true as far as Spain and Portugal are concerned. Spain went through a difficult period in the late 1970s up till the mid 1980s, but there has been a significant improvement in growth performance in the post-1985 period. Indeed, the pace and depth of change in Spain led some observers to predict that by the end of the 1990s, Spain would be transformed into one of Europe's most dynamic economic entities (Leonardi, 1995). The pattern of investment behaviour in Spain shifted radically between the 1970s and the late 1980s in favour of activities with higher technology content, while at the same time the economy managed to raise its share in total OECD manufacturing exports (Caloghirou *et al.*, 1996, p. 23).

The same picture of early problems and later improvement characterizes Portugal as well, with marked changes in the investment pattern and significant progress in manufacturing productivity (Caloghirou *et al.*, 1996). The Portuguese economy managed to raise labour productivity and to almost double its share of OECD manufacturing exports. Overall, it raised its competitiveness in low technology industries and maintained its competitiveness in medium technology industries.[36] So though starting from a fairly similar manufacturing base, the differences in investment patterns among SEEs imply that these countries may be developing comparative advantages in different areas in the future (Caloghirou *et al.*, 1996).

It is interesting to note that the period stretching from 1980 to 1991 was a time of convergence for Europe taken as a whole. Leonardi (1995) has calculated the degree of economic convergence in Europe over the 1980s. His findings suggest that the European convergence dynamic becomes stronger with the addition of the South European new entrants, as the ratios between the top and bottom five regions drop from a level of 6.7/1 in 1981 to 5.1/1 in 1991 (Leonardi, 1995, p. 126).

Moving to the lower levels of administrative and policy implementation, though, the picture concerning the future prospects of the less developed parts of Europe becomes gradually more ambivalent. The Spanish regions have at their disposal a series of potential levers for development, that are not readily available in Greece and Portugal.[37] In contradistinction, Greece's ability to take advantage and make full use of European policies designed to stimulate restructuring and industrial growth has been less than adequate due to institutional shortcomings both at the national and the subnational levels. Greece's national administrative structure is centralized but 'weak' from an organizational and professional perspective,[38] while subnational institutions, to the extent that they exist, are too fragile and too overburdened with a number of 'infantile diseases' to outgrow the mould of clientelistic populist politics (Lyberaki, 1996; Papageorgiou and Verney, 1993).

In the face of the clear link between rich institutional endowment and successful economic performance, Leonardi and Garmise (1993, p. 254) have argued that 'there is a general feeling that the single market will stimulate institutional renewal and modernise the regional administration especially in the two countries [Greece and Portugal] lacking a long tradition of local government autonomy'. Institutional 'backwardness' is not solely confined in the terrain of regional/local institutions. Networking between producers, between producers and suppliers of 'real services', between state agencies and firms, etc is relatively less important in the regions of the European south (Cooke, 1993). Furthermore, institutional and administrative weaknesses by no means refer solely to the sub-national levels of administration. On the contrary, they tend to characterize national systems of administration as well.

The hegemonic policy ambience in Europe tends to favour the adoption of horizontal measures (with the exception of information-technologies and the provision of infrastructure) that encourage a 'market-led' restructuring process. As has been repeatedly argued so far, in order to be effective, this type of restructuring process requires the existence and benign interaction of certain structural aspects (linkages between financial and industrial firms ensuring a strategically oriented 'internal restructuring' process) and institutions. In cases where the 'appropriate' and necessary structural and institutional set up is missing, market-led restructuring tends to reinforce the existing *status quo* rather than altering it. Southern Europe lacks the structural and institutional heritage allowing endogenous restructuring (and the apparent failure of large numbers of business groups testifies to this). At the same time, supportive mechanisms (such as Business Innovation Centres, Infrastructure for the provision of 'real services' and business consulting) are weak and in most cases they have been only recently introduced from 'above', that is, from EU actions and initiatives linked to particular financial commitments. Successful restructuring enabling long-term competitiveness in Southern Europe thus involves more than financial flows. To the extent that the European Union moves inthe direction of allowing more space for local and regional initiatives while encouraging institutional build-up, it is possible that the economies of Southern Europe will benefit in the process. The end result, however, will necessarily depend on the ability of domestic and local actors to pursue policies tailored to their own needs, according to their own place-, time-, race-, and gender-specific attitudes and perceptions of industrial development.

Notes

1. Involving poor remuneration, lack of differentiation and low quality production.
2. The characteristics of industrial development and employment in southern European countries has been extensively discussed by Mingione in this volume. Here we concentrate on policies that attempt to support and improve Southern European countries' industrial structure.
3. Hayek's argument is that state intervention interferes with individual liberty, while others emphasized that there is no such thing as an autonomous state acting in the public interest. Irrespective of intentions, however, an increasing number of economists have been pointing out that government failure was as widespread as market failure and certainly no antedote to it.
4. Failures of commission include exceptionally high-cost public sector enterprises such as state marketing boards, state operation of mines and manufacturing activities, state firms enjoying monopoly rights for importing a variety of commodities, nationalized banking and insurance operations, pervasive and costly government controls over the private sector, high expenditures due to grand investment programmes. Failures of omission refer to the deterioration of transport and communication facilities (indirectly rising the costs for many economic activities), the maintenance of fixed nominal exchange rates, exchange controls and import licensing (Krueger, 1990, p. 10).
5. The theory of contestable markets emphasized the scope for effective competition, while the Austrian case against intervention stresses the formidable difficulties facing central planners due to the dispersed and incomplete nature of information and knowledge, as well as the fact that planning frustrates the operation of spontaneous market forces without allowing individuals to learn from their errors and modify their economic behaviour accordingly.
6. The importance of long-term, firm-specific investment (and the lack of such investment) has been stressed by Porter (1990) in the case of the US economy and by Franks and Mayer (1990) in the case of the UK.
7. The use of machinery has been the starting point of the realization that economies of scale and the sunk costs associated with the accumulation of physical and human capital, may inhibit the mobility of resources which is a precondition for the realization of competitive prices and the setting in motion of the process leading to beneficial progress.
8. A similar line has been adopted by others in the development literature; see in particular Datta-Chaudhuri (1990) for a discussion of the problems involved in the learning process and the crucial role for policy intervention deriving from the incapacity of the free market to deliver the necessary 'signals'.
9. Grindle (1997) argues that organizations of outstanding economic performance are characterized by cultures that emphasize commitment to organizational goals, a strong sense of professionalism, efficiency, elitism and hard work. 'A strong sense of mission, effective managerial practice and high expectations about employee performance were factors that led organisations to perform well, while some autonomy in personnel matters allowed a mission to be identified and enabled skilled managers to have some room to manoeuvre in setting standards for their organisations' (Grindle, 1997, p. 491).
10. This 'Marxism Today'-inspired catchword serves as a good summary term including processes referred to as postfordism, postindustrialism, postmodernism,

flexible specialization, industrial districts, new competition, lean production, just-in-time production, new techno-economic paradigm etc (Hall and Jacques (eds) 1989).

11. The idea of combining private and public actors to pool knowledge and authority in a cooperative behaviour for the sharing of information through networks is not new (Williamson, 1975).

12. For figures on the share of SMEs in Europe see European Observatory of SMEs (various years). Also, Liargovas, 1997; Lyberaki, 1998; Lyberaki and Pesmazoglou, 1994.

13. Dualist approaches to development in the past have emphasized the exclusivity of the peripheral areas in terms of their hosting small manufacturing establishments. In line with the prevailing mood of the 1970s, these were invariably seen to be 'traditional and backward'. This type of 'centre–periphery' divide is not accurate, since there exists plenty of evidence showing that smaller firms persisted even in the apogee of 'high fordism' and even in the industrialized core of Europe (the prime example being the area of Baden-Württenberg in Germany). Furthermore, the identification of 'peripheral small firms communities' as stubborn remnants doomed to disappear has proved to be equally false. Indeed, the postmodern renaissance of interest in small firms has revealed their dynamic potential in an number of European regions. For a discussion of these policy related issues see among others: Becattini, 1989; Belussi, 1996; Hirst and Zeitlin, 1991; Humphrey and Schmitz, 1996; Pyke and Sengenberger, 1992; Schmitz and Muzyck, 1993; Storper, 1995.

14. There are four fundamental reasons for disciplining the market forces by superimposing a coherent strategic framework in their operation: First, transnationalism: the asymmetry of power between a giant transnational corporation on the one hand (enjoying an international perspective and flexibility) and the locational rigidity of a specific local, regional or even national community (Cowling and Sugden, 1990). Second, short-termism: Although incremental change can be handled quite well by market institutions, more fundamental changes involving quantum leaps in products, processes or structures will not be handled as well (ibid). Third, centripetalism: is the tendency for higher level activities and occupations to gravitate to the centre, and thus to be lost to the periphery. Via a process of cumulative causation, regions and communities end up trapped in a vicious circle of decline which cannot be easily reversed by means of supply-side measures (investment in training and education) as long as the demand side remains outside their control (ibid). Fourth, while markets are capable of allocating resources between producers, and goods between consumers in very simple and very static settings, they fare less well in more demanding situations (monopolies, externalities, high risk and uncertainty, quality as opposed to quantity of goods, economies of scale in supply, inappropriabilities in sale) (Geroski, 1989, p. 21).

15. Institutions defined as formal and informal arrangements, regulations and voluntary restrictions on behaviour (Henley and Tsakalotos, 1993, p. 22).

16. The emergence of the multimedia world (sound, text and image) can provide an answer to old and new needs of the European societies: communication networks within companies; widespread teleworking; widespread access to scientific and leisure databases; development of preventive health care and home medicine for the elderly (White Paper, p. 13).

17. Interestingly enough the term 'planning' appears only with respect to infrastructure networks and the building of the information society, implying that

strategically oriented intervention is not alien to the European Commission problematique.

18. The term 'economic and social cohesion' is a new addition to the Euro-jargon, and represents a more elegant way of expressing the need for 'convergence'. The latter had acquired a prominent position in the EC's documents since the 1980s, but because it has tended to be taken to imply a number of different definitions it has been recently replaced by the term 'cohesion' (see Mitsos, 1993). Indeed, the term 'convergence' has been used with at least six different interpretations: nominal convergence (harmonization of inflation rates and other macroeconomic indicators; policy convergence (coordination of budgetary and other policies); structural convergence (structural adaptation to produce more closely related structures, and, thereby eliminating the vulnerability to external shocks); behavioural convergence (increasing similarity in various behavioural phenomena such as savings ratios); and finally real convergence (narrowing the gap in disposable incomes) (National Institute of Economic and Social Research (1991), *A New Strategy for Social and Economic Cohesion after 1992*, European Parliament, London, p. 13).

19. The development of lagging regions (objective one); the conversion of areas affected by industrial decline (objective two); combating long-term unemployment (objective three); the occupational integration of young people (objective four); the adjustment of agricultural structures (objective five-a); and the development of rural areas (objective five-b).

20. The exact role however remains open to debate. The strengthening of the role of the European Parliament on the final approval of the new funds' reglementation as well as the consultative role of the new Committee of Regions are seen by some analysts to constitute gestures increasing popularity rather than important institutional modifications (Mitsos, 1993, p. 32).

21. This section draws on Lyberaki and Pesmazoglou, 1994, pp. 510–15.

22. Although empirical evidence supports the employment generation potential of small firms (Birch and McCracken, 1982; Evans, 1987; Loveman and Sengenberger, 1990; Storey and Johnson, 1987), a number of factors warn against wholesale optimism. First, the international picture suggests that the vast majority of small new firms either remain small indefinitely or fail. Therefore, their contribution to employment creation remains modest. Much of the total increase in employment among small firms is attributable to the performance of few remarkably successful new small firms (Loveman and Sengenberger, 1990, p. 32). Second, some studies suggest that employment growth rates for new large firms are roughly equal to those of small firms (United States Small Business Administration, 1985). And third, the notion of net job creation should be treated with caution in the case of new firms, because it may simply reflect a redistribution of production from existing firms (via subcontracting), therefore hardly contributing in raising aggregate welfare (Sengenberger *et al.*, 1990).

23. From the point of view of workers involved in flexible production, the proponents of flexible specialization suggest that multi-skilling and broader skill-base tend to offer workers greater control over the work process. As work becomes more skilled, wages move upwards and employers are obliged to abandon authoritarian methods of control. Furthermore, job security is enhanced, as trained workers are more difficult to replace. Finally, preoccupation with quality rather than price/cost, weakens the drive of employers to engage in wage-cutting practices (Best, 1990; Piore and Sabel, 1984; Zeitlin, 1987). The above optimistic views have been challenged by a number of economists, on the grounds

that formidable problems arise from the point of view of labour solidarity and collective organization. Such critiques stress the enormous unevenness of conditions of work and the disproportionate bargaining strength derived from skill: a small group of workers exploit differentiation within the labour market and pursue an active strategy of protecting and reinforcing such differences. Finally, access to skilled jobs tends to rely on existing social inequalities regulated by gender, race/nationality and family connections (Cockburn, 1983; Gough, 1986; Hadjimichalis and Vaiou, 1990; Murray, 1987; Solinas, 1982). Thus, 'the exploitation of skill as a major bargaining weapon ... tends both to rely on and exacerbate reactionary divisions among workers' (Gough, 1986, p. 69). A further point of criticism to the overoptimistic generalizations focuses on the dynamics of the labour market, and more specifically on the supply of labour: in cases where there exist considerable labour reserves, employers tend to resort to sweating rather than innovation (Schmitz, 1989). For a discussion of these issues including counter arguments, see Lyberaki and Pesmazoglou, 1994.

24. The idea of a cluster of small firms reaping collectively the benefits of densely populated industrial communities is neither new in economic theory, nor exclusive to the flexible specialization model. A host of issues emphasized by the latter approach can be found in the literature on the 'economies of agglomeration' (Murray, 1975). They are based on the principle that 'distance is the enemy of time' and they refer to economies which are external to the individual firms but internal to the industrial community.

25. Such places of economic dynamism include Oyonnax in France, Jutland in Denmark, Baden-Württemberg in Germany, Smaland in Sweden, Barcelona in Spain, Silicon Valley in the United States, Cambridge in Britain and areas of Central and north-east Italy (see Benton, 1992; Schmitz, 1992; Kristensen, 1992).

26. The future prospects of successful industrial districts have been seriously questioned. It might be the case that the districts took advantage of the specific conditions associated with the world recession, and their future is uncertain as soon as economic activity and demand pick up. At the pessimistic end of the spectrum, some writers see the activities of large firms and in particular multinational corporations as a major threat (Amin and Robins, 1990a,b; Brutti and Calistri, 1990). Others, who are more optimistic, see no necessary incompatibility between large firms and industrial districts, as two distinct ways of organizing production which can co-exist (Storper, 1993; Zeitlin, 1987).

27. Small and medium-sized enterprises are defined on the basis of three criteria: they have fewer than 250 employees; they have either an annual turnover not exceeding ECU 40 million, or an annual balance sheet total not exceeding ECU 27 million; they are independent (they are not owned as to 25 per cent or more and no control can be exercised either individually or jointly. A small enterprise is defined as employing fewer than 50 employees, having an annual turnover not exceeding ECU 7 million or an annual balance sheet total not exceeding ECU 5 million and being independent. Finally, a micro-enterprise is an enterprise employing fewer than 10 people (Official Journal of the European Communities, L.107/8, 30.4.96).

28. Administratively, this increased interest initially led to the formation, in 1986, of a specific European Commission 'SME Task Force' which was to be replaced, in 1989, by a whole Directorate General (DGXXIII) dealing with enterprises, commerce, tourism and 'social economy'. This coincided with a new and more ambitious plan, approved in 1989, aiming at the improvement of the SMEs'

environment and at the overall promotion of their activities. This plan covered the period 1989–93 and was initially granted the amount of 110 million ECU – as opposed to the 135 demanded by the less developed EU regions (Official Journal of the EC, no. L239, 16/8/1989).

29. A region (or country) of the EU selects a series of local firms able and willing to offer cooperation proposals to other firms in the EU; these proposals then circulate and trigger responses and proposals from other areas of the Community; at the third and final stage, the interested parties meet in the region in question for two days to formalize an agreement. This has taken place in Ireland (1988), Andalucia (1989), Wales (1990), Portugal (1991) and Greece (1992).

30. The Amsterdam European Council in June 1997 confirmed a 'strong commitment to the simplification of existing and new legal and administrative regulations in order to improve the quality of Community legislation and reduce its administrative burden on European business, particularly small and medium sized business'. To this end, the Amsterdam Council invited the European Commission to establish a task force for this purpose, while the member states were asked to pursue comparable simplification measures at national level. The task force, consisting of entrepreneurs, public administrators and academic experts, worked intensively for 8 months and produced an independent report in June 1998.

31. Report of the Business Environment Simplification Task Force, BEST, Volumes 1 and 2.

32. The only exception here is the important share of rural development schemes which characterized largely all the countries/regions involved.

33. Spain got 51.9 per cent for basic infrastructure, while Ireland only 15.6 per cent, the latter attributing a far greater importance to direct industry aid schemes. This diverging allocation of resources echoes to a large extent the debate on the effectiveness of various policy instruments for raising productivity and enhancing competitiveness.

34. It can be argued that structural policy is moving in the direction of a system of 'multilevel governance' (Marks, 1993, p. 392) and 'co-operative regionalism' (Scott *et al.*, 1994, pp. 58–9) in which supranational, national, regional and local governments are enmeshed in territorially overarching policy networks (Paraskevopoulos, 1994, p. 24).

35. While partnership is a principle of cooperation between the supranational, national and subnational elites, subsidiarity ensures the allocation of decisions to the appropriate level of governance.

36. As Caloghirou *et al.* (1996, p. 26) aptly phrased it, 'compared to Spain, Greece has seemed hesitant to undergo the necessary structural change in order to upgrade its manufacturing. Compared to Portugal, Greece has seemed to lose ground in sustaining/enhancing competitiveness'.

37. 'Regions in Spain have institutional infrastructure that permits them to undertake their own "self-help projects", or to experiment in alternative forms of economic development. Administrative and political autonomy gives the regions the power to experiment with policies rather than to wait for the national government to come up with appropriate solutions. Greek and Portuguese regions do not have access to these alternative instruments and might therefore have to rely on state generated development schemes. These usually *take longer to have an impact at the regional level and cannot be customised to the exigencies of regional economies and societies*' (emphasis added) (Leonardi, 1995, pp. 131–3).

38. The main inadequacies of Greece's administrative structure can be summarized in the following points:

   1. inadequate linkages with the local population and institutions;
   2. inadequately qualified bureaucratic personnel in view of the increased activities allocated to national administrations;
   3. administrative job retention and promotion are heavily influenced by political connections;
   4. alternative institutions do not exist;
   5. national bureaucracy is overburdened with responsibilities (Leonardi and Garmise, 1993, p. 268).

Bibliography

Abramovitz, M. (1986) 'Catching-up, forging ahead and falling behind', *Journal of Economic History*, no. 46, June, pp. 385–406.

Amin, A. and Robins, K. (1990a) 'Industrial districts and Regional development: Limits and Possibilities', in Pyke, F., Becattini, G. and Sengenberger, W., *Industrial Districts and Inter-Firm Cooperation in Italy*, International Institute for Labour Studies: Geneva, pp. 185–219.

Amin, A. and Robins, K. (1990b) 'The re-emergence of Regional Economics? The Mythical Geography of Flexible Accumulation', *Environment and Planning D: Society and Space*, vol. 8.

Amsden, A. (1997) 'Editorial: bringing production back in – understanding government's economic role in late industrialization', *World Development*, vol. 25, no. 4, pp. 469–80.

Andreasen, L., Coriat B., den Hertog F. and Kaplinsky, R. (eds) (1995) *Europe's Next Step: Organisational Innovation, Competition and Employment*, Frank Cass, Il ford.

Bardhan, P. (1990) 'Symposium on the state and economic development', *Journal of Economic Perspectives*, vol. 4, no. 3, pp. 3–7.

Baumol, W. J. (1986) 'Productivity growth, convergence and welfare: what the long run data show', *American Economic Review*, no. 76, December, pp. 1072–83.

Becattini G. (1989) 'Sectors and/or Districts: Some Remarks on the Conceptual Foundations of Industrial Economics', in Goodman, E. and Bamford, J. (eds) *Small Firms and Industrial Districts in Italy*, London: Routledge, pp. 123–35.

Becattini, G. (1990) 'Italy', in Sengenberger, W., Loveman, G. and Piore, M. (eds).

Belussi, F. (1996) 'Local Systems, Industrial Districts and Institutional Networks: Towards a New Evolutionary Paradigm of Industrial Economics?', *European Planning Studies*, vol. 4, no. 1.

Benton, L. (1992) 'The Emergence of industrial districts in Spain: Industrial Restructuring and diverging regional responses', in Pyke, F. and Sengenberger, W., *Industrial Districts and Local Economic Regeneration*, International Institute for Labour Studies, Geneva.

Best, M. (1990) *The New Competition*, Polity Press, Cambridge.

Biehl, D. (1990) 'Deficiencies and reform possibilities of the EC fiscal condition', *Political Quarterly*, Special Number, pp. 85–95.

Birch, D. L. and McCracken, S. (1982) *The Small Business Share of Job Creation – Lessons Learned from the use of a longitudinal file*, Small Business Administration: United States.

Block, F. (1990) *Postindustrial Possibilities: A Critique of Economic Discourse*, University of California Press, Berkeley.

Boissevain, J. (1981) *Small Entrepreneurs in Changing Europe: A Research Agenda*, Centre for Work and Society, Maastricht.

Brutti, P. and Calistri, F. (1990) 'Industrial Districts and the Unions', in Pyke, F., Becattini, G. and Sengenberger, W., *Industrial Districts and Inter-Firm Cooperation in Italy*, International Institute for Labour Studies, Geneva, pp. 134–41.

Burns, P. and Dewhurst, J. (1986) *Small Business in Europe*, Macmillan, London.

Caloghirou, Y., Mourtzikou, A. Papayannakis L. and Vonortas, N. (1996) 'Structural change and competitiveness: recent trends in Spain, Portugal and Greece', Centre for International Science and Technology Policy, *Discussion Paper*, The George Washington University.

Capecchi, V. (1990) 'A History of flexible specialisation and industrial districts in Emilia-Romagna', in Pyke, F., Becattini, G. and Segenberger, W., *Industrial Districts and Inter-Firm Cooperation in Italy*, International Institute for Labour Studies, Geneva, pp. 52–74.

Chang, Ha-Joon (1994) *The Political Economy of Industrial Policy*, Macmillan, London.

Cockburn, C. (1983) *Brothers*, Pluto Press, London.

Commission of the EC (CEC) (1992) *Third Survey on State Aids in the European Community in the Manufacturing and Certain Other Sectors*, Office of the Official Publications of the European Communities, Luxembourg.

Commission of the EU (1996) Definition of Small and medium-sized enterprises, The Official Journal of the European Communities, L.107/8, 30.4.96.

Cooke, P. (1993) 'Regional innovation systems: an evaluation of six European cases', in Getimis, P. and Kafkalas, G.(eds), *Urban and Regional Development in the New Europe*, Topos Special Series, Athens.

Coriat, B. (1995) 'Organisational innovation: the missing link in European competitiveness', in Andreasen *et al.* (eds).

Cowling, K. and Sugden, R. (eds) (1990) *A New Economic Policy for Britain: Essays on the Development of Industry*, Manchester University Press, Manchester.

Datta-Chaudhuri, M. (1990) 'Market failure and government failure', *Journal of Economic Perspectives*, vol. 4, no. 3, pp. 25–39.

Diamandouros, N. (1991) 'PASOK and state-society relations in post-authoritarian Greece (1974–1988)', in S. Vryonis, Jr (ed.) *Greece on the Road to Democracy: From the Junta to PASOK 1974-1986*, Caratzas New Rochelle, New York.

Dowrick, S. and Nguyen, D. T. (1989) 'OECD comparative economic growth 1950–1985: catch-Up and convergence', *American Economic Review*, vol. 79, no. 5, December, pp. 1010–30.

European Commission (1994) Growth, Competitiveness, Employment: The Challenges and Ways Forward Into the 21st Century, White Paper.

Evans, D. S. (1987) 'Tests of Alternative theories of firm growth' *Journal of Political Economy*, vol. 95, no. 4, pp. 657–74.

Farrands, C. and Totterdill, P. (1993) 'A rationale for an appropriate level of regulation in the European Community', in Sugden, R. (ed.), *Industrial Economic Regulation: A Framework and Exploration*, Routledge London,

Franks, J. and Mayer, C. (1990) 'Capital markets and corporate control: a study of France, Germany and the UK', *Economic Policy*, No. 10, pp. 189–23.

Geroski, P. A. (1989) 'European industrial policy and industrial policy in Europe', *Oxford Review of Economic Policy*, vol. 5, no. 2, pp. 20–36.

Geroski, P. and Schwalbach, J. (1986) *Entrepreneurship and Small Firms*, Centre for European Policy Studies Brussels.

Goodman, E., Bamford, J. and Saynor, P. (1989) *Small Firms and Industrial Districts in Italy*, Routledge, London.

Grindle, M. (1997) 'Divergent cultures? When public organizations perform well in developing countries', *World Development*, vol. 25, no. 4, pp. 481–95.

Gough, J. (1986) 'Industrial Policy and Socialist Strategy', *Capital and Class*, no. 29.

Hall, S. and Jacques, M. (eds) (1989) *New Times: The Changing Face of Politics in the 1990s*, Lawrence & Wishart in association with Marxism Today, London.

Helm, D. and Smith, S. (1989) 'The assessment: economic integration and the role of the European Community', *Oxford Review of Economic Policy*, vol. 5, no. 2, pp. 1–19.

Henley, A. and Tsakalotos, E. (1993) *Corporatism and Economic Performance: A Comparative Analysis of Market Economies*, Edward Elgar, London.

Hirst, R. and Zeitlin, J. (1991) 'Flexible Specialisation versus Post-Fordism: Theory, Evidence and Policy Implication', *Economy and Society*, vol. 20, no. 1.

Humphrey, J. and Schmitz, H. (1996) *Trust and Economic Development*, IDS Discussion Paper, no. 355(August),Falmer, Brighton.

Kaplinsky, R. (1994) *Easternisation: The Spread of Japanese Management Techniques to Developing Countries*, Frank Cass, I1ford.

Kristensen, P. H. (1992) 'Industrial districts in West Jutland, Denmark', in Pyke, F. and Sengenberger W. (eds).

Krueger, A. (1990) 'Government failures in development', *Journal of Economic Perspectives*, vol. 4, no. 3, pp. 9–23.

Krugman, P. (1991) *Geography and Trade*, Leuven University Press and the MIT Press, Baltimore.

Lall, S. (1998) 'Exports of manufactures by developing countries: emerging patterns of trade and location', *Oxford Review of Economic Policy*, vol. 14, no. 2, pp. 54–73.

Larre, B. and Torres, R. (1991) 'Is Convergence a spontaneous process? The experience of Spain, Portugal and Greece', *OECD Economic Studies*, No. 16, Spring.

Lehner, S. and Meklejohn, R. (1991) 'Fair competition in the internal market: Community state aid policy', *European Economy*, no. 48, September, pp. 7–114.

Leonardi, R. (1995), *Convergence, Cohesion and Integration in the European Union*, St. Martin's Press, New York.

Leonardi, R. and Garmise S. (1993) 'Conclusions: sub-national elites and the European Community', in Leonardi, R. (ed.) *The Regions and the European Community: the Regional Response to the Single Market in the Underdeveloped Areas*, Frank Cass, Ilford.

Levicki, G. (1984) *Small Business: Theory and Practice*, Croom Helm, London.

Liargovas, P. (1997) *The White Paper on Growth Competitiveness and Employment and Greek Small and Medium Sized Enterprises*, paper presented at the International Conference on Industrial Policy for Europe, Royal Institute of International Affairs, London, (June).

Lyberaki, A. (1993) 'Greece-EC comparative economic performance: convergence or divergence?' in Psomiades, H. and Thomadakis, S. (eds) *Greece, the New Europe and the Changing International Order*, Pella, New York.

Lyberaki, A. (1996) 'Greece-EU comparative economic performance at the national and regional levels: why divergence?', *European Planning Studies*, vol. 4, no. 3.

Lyberaki, A. and Pesmazoglou, V. (1994) 'Mirages and miracles of European small and medium enterprise development', *European Planning Studies*, vol. 2, no. 4.

Lyberaki, A. (1998) 'Networking Flexible Specialisation and Small Firms', in Pitelis, C. and Antonakis, N. (eds) *International Competitiveness and Industrial Strategy*, Typothito, Athens, (in Greek).

Marks, G. (1993) 'Structural policy and multilevel governance in the EC', in Carfuny and Rosenthal (eds), *The State of the European Community: The Maastricht Debates and Beyond*, vol. 2, Longman.

Michie, J. and Prendergast, R. (1998) 'Government intervention in a dynamic economy', *New Political Economy*, vol. 3, no. 3, pp. 391–406.

Mitsos, A. (1993) 'The Community's redistributive and development role in the post-Maastricht era', SSRC Conference, Venice, April

Murray, R. (1975) 'The Internationalisation of Capital and the Nation State', in Radice, H. (ed.), *International Firms and Modern Imperialism*, Penguin Harmondsworth.

Murray, F., (1987) 'Flexible Specialisation in the 'Third Italy' Capital and Class, no. 33.

Murray, R. (1991) *Local Space: Europe and the New Regionalism*, CLES and SEEDS' Falmer: Brighton.

Murray, R. (1992) 'Flexible specialisation in small island economies: the case of Cyprus', in Pyke, F. and Sengenberger, W. (eds).

Nadvi, K. and Schmitz, H. (1994) 'Industrial clusters in less developed countries: review of experiences and research agenda', *IDS Discussion Paper*, no. 339.

Nelson, R. (1988) 'Institutions supporting political change in the United States', in Dosi, G., Freeman, Ch. Nelson, R., Silverberg, G., and Soete, L. (eds), *Technical Change and Economic Theory*, Pinter, London.

Papageorgiou, F. and Verney, S. (1993) 'Regional planning and the integrated mediterranean programmes in Greece', in Leonardi, R. (ed.), *The Regions and the European Community: the Regional Response to the Single Market in the Underdeveloped Areas*, Frank Cass, Ilford.

Paraskevopoulos, C. (1994) 'The principle of subsidiarity and the new european regional policy', unpublished thesis for the Msc in European Studies, London School of Economics and Political Science.

Piore, M. and Sabel, C. (1984) *The Second Industrial Divide*, Basic Books, New York.

Piore, M. J. (1990) 'Work, Labour and action: Work experience in a system of flexible production' in Pyke, F., Becattini, G. and Sengenberger, W., *Industrial Districts and Inter-Firm Cooperation in Italy*, International Institute for Labour Studies, Geneva, pp. 52–74.

Plaskovitis, E. (1993) 'On-going evaluation of the integrated Mediterranean programmes: the Greek experience, in Getimis, P. and Kafkalas G. (eds) *Urban and Regional Development in the New Europe*, Topos Special Series, Athens.

Porter, M. (1990) *The Competitive Advantage of Nations*, Macmillan, London.

Porter, M. (1992) 'Capital disadvantage: America's failing capital investment system', *Harvard Business Review*, vol. 70, no. 5, Sept–Oct, pp. 65–82.

Putnam, R. (1993) *Making Democracy Work*, Princeton University Press, Princeton: New Jersey.

Pyke, F. (1994) *Small Firms, Technical Services and Inter-Firm Co-operation*, International Institute for Labour Studies, Research Series no. 99, Geneva.

Pyke, F. and Sengenberger, W. (1990) 'Economic and social reorganisation in the small and medium enterprise sector', in Sengenberger *et al.* (eds).

Pyke, F. and Sengenberger, W. (eds) (1992) *Industrial Districts and Local Economic Regeneration*, ILO Geneva.

Pyke, F., Becattini, G. and Sengenberger, W. (eds) (1990) *Industrial Districts and Inter-Firm Cooperation in Italy*, International Institute for Labour Studies Geneva.

Rosenberg, N. (1992) 'Economic experiments', *Industrial and Corporate Change*, vol. 1.

Sabel, C. (1989) Flexible Specialisation and the Re-emergence of Regional Economies in Hirst, P. and Zeitlin, J. (eds), Reversing Industrial Decline? Industrial Structure and Policy in Britain and her Competitors, Oxford and Hamburg, Berg, pp. 17–70.

Schmitz, H. (1989) 'Flexible specialisation–A new paradigm of small-scale industrialisation?', *IDS Discussion Paper*, no. 261.

Schmitz, H. (1992) 'Industrial districts: model and reality in Baden-Württemberg, Germany', in Pyke, F. and Sengenberger W. (eds).

Schmitz, H. and Muzyck, B. (1993) *Industrial Districts in Europe: Policy Lessons for Developing Countries?*, IDS Discussion Paper, no. 324 (April), Falmer, Brighton.

Scott, A., Peterson J. and Millar, D. (1994) 'Subsidiarity: a "Europe of the regions' versus the British constitution?", *Journal of Common Market Studies*, vol. 32, no. 1, March, pp. 47–67.

Sengenberger, W. and Pyke, F. (1992) 'Industrial districts and local economic regeneration: research and policy issues', in Pyke, F. and Sengenberger W. (eds).

Sengenberger, W., Loveman, G. and Piore, M. (eds) (1990), *The Re-Emergence of Small Enterprises: Industrial Restructuring in Industrialised Countries*, ILO Geneva.

Shapiro, H. and Taylor, L. (1992) 'The state and industrial strategy', in Wilber, C. K. and Jameson, K. P. *The Political Economy of Development and Underdevelopment*, 5th edn McGraw-Hill New York, London and Toronto.

Solinas, G. (1982) 'Labour Market Segmentation and Worker's Careers: the case of the Italian knitwear industry', *Cambridge Journal of Economics*, vol. 6, no. 4, pp. 331–52.

Storper, M. (1993) 'Regional Worlds of Production: Learning and Innovation in the Technology Districts in France, Italy and the USA', *Regional Studies*, vol. 27, no. 5, pp. 433–55.

Storper, M. (1995) 'The Resurgence of Regional Economies, Ten Years Later: The Region as a Nexus of Untraded Interdependencies', *European Urban and Regional Studies*, vol. 2, no. 3.

Sugden, R. (ed.) (1993) *Industrial Economic Regulation: A Framework and Exploration*, Routledge London.

United States Small Business Administraation (1985) *Your Business and the SBA*, Issued by Public Communications Division, OPC-2, February.

Wade, R. (1990) *Governing the Market*, Princeton University Press, Princeton NJ.

Westphal, L. (1990) 'Industrial policy in an export-propelled economy: lessons from South Korea's Experience', *Journal of Economic Perspectives*, vol. 4, no. 3, pp. 41–59.

Williamson, O. (1975) *Markets and Hierarchies*, Free Press, New York.

Wommack, J., Jones D. and Roos, D. (1990) *The Machine that Changed the World*, Rawson Associates: New York, Collier Macmillan Canada: Toronto, Maxwell Macmillan International: New York.

Zeitlin, J. (1987) 'The third Italy: inter-firm co-operation and technological innovation', SEEDS Conference, Brighton, March.

Zeitlin, J. (1992) 'Industrial districts and local economic regeneration: overview and comment', in Pyke, F. and Sengenberger, W. (eds).

7
The Comparative Politics of Industrial Privatization: Spain, Portugal and Greece in a European Perspective

Vincent Wright and George Pagoulatos[1]

Privatization has been on the policy agenda of almost every country in the world, whatever the nature of its regime or its political hue.[2] The purpose of this chapter is to place the industrial privatization programmes of Spain, Portugal and Greece in a European context in order to underline and explain their common as well as their distinctive characteristics.[3] What ties these programmes together is that they have been geared towards a common objective of 'catching up' with the ongoing economic transformation inside the EC/EU. This transformation is driven by convergent pressures exercised more or less upon all West European economies over the 1980s and 1990s. Evidently, the differentiating factor of Southern European economies (SEEs) from the rest of EC/EU economies, and their own shared predicament, is that the distance to be covered is larger. 'Catch-up' in their case encompasses a double challenge: modernize to the point of being able to compete from an equal ground with the rest of Western Europe, and then successfully persevere the competition.

The main question then to be addressed is why, given similar convergent pressures throughout Western Europe, have the scale, nature, timing and pace of the three countries' privatization programmes differed if not diverged? The argument to be developed is that convergent pressures have been felt at different times and with different degrees of intensity, have been translated into different policy ambitions, and have been mediated by different constitutional, political and institutional milieux, each of which had been shaped by different historical experiences.

The chapter will first examine the convergent pressures throughout Western Europe and illustrate how they have been felt in Spain, Portugal and Greece. After a brief description of the industrial public sectors of the three countries it will then look at their privatization ambitions, before turning to an explanation for the distinctive features of their respective programmes.[4]

Convergent pressures

The pressures that have squeezed governments everywhere in Western Europe into privatization programmes have been multiple, cumulative, and generally convergent in impact. They are, of course, interconnected, each feeding the other in a process in which cause-and-effect often become difficult to unravel.

The first such pressure has been the general macro-economic paradigm shift, rooted in the perceived failure of Keynesianism, industrial policy and *dirigisme*. Scepticism about the efficacy of state interventionism has clearly grown everywhere in Europe. This has been shared not only by many right-wingers in Spain, Portugal and Greece, but also be reformist circles of the respective socialist parties. All three countries have been pressured into greater financial orthodoxy as the result of reactions against high taxation, worrying levels of inflation, ballooning public deficits and public indebtedness. This has certainly been the case in Portugal and Greece since at least the mid-1980s and, to a lesser extent, in Spain. Such reactions have been all the more pressing in the light of the Maastricht criteria on public debt (where an upper limit of 60 per cent for the debt/GDP ratio was set) and public deficits (which should not exceed 3 per cent of GDP).

As a percentage of GDP, accumulated public debt in Portugal rose from 18 per cent in 1973 to 41 per cent in 1976, to 62 per cent in 1984, peaking at 80 per cent in 1986. By 1989 it was still at the uncomfortable level of 74 per cent. The public deficit also remained high despite the efforts of the Soares and Cavaco Silva governments. The attempt to drive it down to 3 per cent of GDP was clearly proving immensely difficult: originally set at 4.8 per cent of GDP in the 1992 budget it had risen to 8 per cent by mid-1993, forcing the government into the introduction of a supplementary budget (*The Economist*, 30 October 1993). Similarly, Spain's total budget deficit amounted to 5.6 per cent of GDP in 1982 and 7 per cent in 1985. By 1991, as a result of fiscal tightening and a first wave of privatizations, it was reduced to, a still unsatisfactory, 4.9 per cent of GDP (OECD, 1993a), with public debt in the area of 60 per cent.

In Greece, the problem was especially acute (Stournaras, 1990). In 1980, after six years of New Democracy government led by Karamanlis, public debt stood at 39.3 per cent of GDP. By 1985 this figure had risen to an alarming 85.2 per cent, and by April 1990, when New Democracy returned to office under Mitsotakis, it had reached 110 per cent. The figure peaked at 116.2 per cent in 1992. Public debt was still 'breathtakingly high' in 1994, and many experts also believed that official figures underestimated the real extent of the problem, with *The Economist* (18 March 1995) suggesting the true figure to be nearer 160 per cent of GDP. The total public sector deficit in that year was no less than 9.6 per cent of GDP, although the Greek government was promising an implausible figure of 1.9 per cent by 1996 (which indeed was not realized). The public sector borrowing requirement expanded rapidly in the period 1979 to 1985 (from less than 6 per cent to 17.5 per cent of GDP) to stabilize at a damagingly high level (it was still 19.6 per cent of GDP in 1989 and 21 per cent in 1990) – the highest in the Community. In spite of a new stabilization plan, introduced after the election of the PASOK government in 1993, the situation remained worrying. It was only towards 1998–9 that the fiscal front was finally able to emit well-founded optimism regarding Greece's entry into the EMU.

Governments in all three countries have been forced to question the bases of previous policies and weaken, dismantle or restructure the 'distributional coalitions' which sustained them. Nowhere were those budget-expanding coalitions more entrenched than in the public sector. The financial squeeze on governments has also meant that they no longer have the resources to feed an ailing public sector with a panoply of state aids – disguised or otherwise. In fact, the industrial public sectors in all three countries were in dire straits at some point in the 1980s (often as the result of their politicized expansion). Thus, in 1985 the total losses of the Portuguese public sector were put at $317 million, and the government was continuing to pump in subsidies to doomed industries such as steel, chemicals and shipbuilding. Between 1978 and 1992, the state poured $2.6 billion of subsidies into state-owned non-financial companies – the equivalent of 25 per cent of the country's GDP in 1991. In Greece, the experience was similar. Total debt of public enterprises had climbed from $4.2 billion in 1980 to over $7.2 billion in 1985, to reach $10.1 billion by 1990, an equivalent of approximately 15 per cent of GDP. The majority of public enterprises carried heavy deficits throughout the 1980s and in the first half of the 1990s (Georgakopoulos, 1987; Lioukas, 1993; Provopoulos, 1985); only a few sectors had profits, notably banking, petroleum and the Greek Telecommunications (OTE) which, to a certain extent, could still benefit from its monopoly position in a highly protected environment. Moreover, the entire Greek industrial sector had suffered serious decline from the mid-1970s and particularly after 1979. By 1983 the number of loss-making private industrial firms had reached a record high and a whole group of such private firms were taken over by a state holding company, the Industrial Reconstruction Organization (IRO) which was created for the purpose of restructuring them. As a result, by 1985 the Greek public sector was further burdened with an additional $780 million of cumulative losses of those ailing firms, which reached $1.35 billion in 1990 (Commission of the European Communities, 1992).

In Spain, the situation was somewhat better, but still unhealthy. The Instituto Nacional de Industria (INI), the major state holding group, saw its losses rocket from $338 million to $1.3 billion ten years later. From 1983 to 1993 the state poured $40 billion into the public sector. The Socialist authorities throughout the 1980s attempted to address the issue of public sector losses by restructuring, rationalizing and privatizing. However, although many public firms became profitable, INI continued to make losses, especially after the beginning of the recession in 1990–1: $705 million in 1992, $981 million in 1993. Revenues raised by privatization have sometimes been earmarked to pay for expensive restructuring programmes of the loss-making companies in the group (in the case of Iberia and of Inespal the aluminum company). This was one of the reasons for the restructuring of the public industrial sector in 1992 when INI was split into two groups. The first, renamed Teneo, comprised the profit-making and viable firms which in 1994 accounted for 80 per cent of the total sales of INI, 57 per cent of employment and 70 per cent of foreign sales. All links between firms and the state budget were to cease, so Teneo was obliged to operate as a private holding company with the right to issue shares or accept outsider participation. For the remainder – the loss-making firms grouped under Grupo INI – some were to be sold to the private sector, others liquidated and yet others restructured. Indicative of the difficulties faced, in 1995 INI was restructured for a second time, its two holdings renamed, debts accumulated by the loss making companies being transferred to the profitable ones (OECD, 1996a).

In all three countries, therefore, as in the rest of Western Europe, governments have been obliged to demand that nationalized industries cut losses by acting more like private industries. This has often required massive restructuring and redundancies, with the result that nationalized industries, once the haven of overmanning, have shed labour – often more mercilessly than the private sector. That has helped to delegitimize the public sector in the eyes of many of their erstwhile supporters (notably the workers in the public sector).

The second major pressure for privatization has been the changing character of many public-sector industries (Heath, 1990). Part of the argument in favour of nationalization had always been rooted in the need for the state to control natural monopolies in strategic areas or producing public goods – airlines, railways, gas, electricity, telecommunications, postal services – or to provide aid for high-risk industries requiring heavy capital outlay and promising low returns. Yet new technology has been dramatically undermining the extent of natural monopoly in several industries (by driving down unit costs and lowering barriers to existing markets, notably in electricity distribution and telecommunications), and has been transforming single-product monoliths into complex multi-product enterprises. Technology is also breaking down national frontiers: Britain now imports electricity supply from France; one of the reasons why the managements of state-owned monopolies such as Deutsche Telekom and France Télécom were pressing for privatization was that international competitors (for example, the British privatized BT and US Sprint) could now transmit data across frontiers and were offering cost-cutting deals to French and German industrial customers.

Advocacy of nationalization in terms of the need to control 'the commanding heights' of the economy has also been weakened as result of the changing nature of strategic industries: shipbuilding, steel and coal – the traditional pillars of industrial *dirigisme* are everywhere in decline and in financial crisis. This has been particularly true in all three SEEs. It should be noted that these traditional industries had always proved problematic as effective public policy instruments. Endowed with multiple and conflicting objectives and flawed by opaque command structures, they became the source of neo-liberal hostility and general government anxiety. There has been a growing perception of the critical disjunction between the conventional structures of economic activity in a competitive capitalist society and the conditions of effective state control of a business corporation: doctrines of profit maximization and managerial autonomy do not sit well with state control (Feigenbaum, 1992). This perception may have been misplaced – the link between ownership and efficiency is far from clear – but it has been widespread and nourished by the unappealing general image of public industries. Spain, Greece and Portugal had no TGV or Airbus as flagships of the public sector, but sleepy and generally inefficient giants.

It is also worth emphasizing that the new strategic industries in high-tech areas are even less susceptible to effective state control, since they are often fragmented, function in highly competitive markets and are subject to rapid product innovation. They also require massive capital injections – which states are increasingly unwilling or unable to supply. Even profit-making concerns – such as OTE, the Greek dozy telecommunications monopoly – need hefty capital for modernization. They are, therefore, obliged to go to the international financial markets for recapitalization. This point leads us to the third major pressure on the traditional public sector: the liberalization and globalization of both product markets and financial circuits – twin processes facilitated and pushed by technological innovation.

Many industries have to resort to international cooperation because of problems of compatibility and cost. Economies of scale are no longer national in character. At both the international and European level, the period since the early 1980s has been marked by surges of takeovers, mergers, research agreements, joint ventures, equity swaps (Cool *et al.*, 1993). In some industries, international strategies for enterprises, whether public or private, have become imperative. Thus, national airlines in Spain, Portugal and Greece – which are all financial disasters – simply cannot survive without effective international partnerships, since, like many other enterprises, they are now clearly boxed into an international marketplace (Alonso, 1991). Telefónica, the Spanish telecommunications firm, had to restructure in 1986 as part of its international expansion which has subsequently taken the form of, for example, an agreement with General Motors and a joint venture with AT&T. It is significant that the company is listed not only on the London and Tokyo stock exchanges, but has become the first

Spanish company to achieve full listing on the New York Stock Exchange. The restructuring of major firms such as Tabacalera (grocery) and Campsa were both dictated by international strategy considerations. Public ownership is often perceived as an impediment to these essential international strategies.

The process of industrial globalization is, of course, greatly eased by the liberalization of European and international financial flows. Under pressure from both European Community and domestic financial interests, the regulatory frameworks on both inflows and outflows have been eased. These processes of internationalization are blurring the identities of many major enterprises – public and private – and are rendering them problematic as 'national champions' (Dunning *et al.*, 1990; Hayward, 1995). Throughout Western Europe, including Spain, Portugal and Greece, governments are tolerating or even encouraging their major public firms to pursue internationalized strategies, often by buying private companies. However, privatizing governments or governments with an extensive private sector are demanding reciprocity. The right to take over and to purchase equity, it is argued, should be reciprocal: public ownership should not be used as a barrier to shield an enterprise against a takeover. This principle of reciprocity is also firmly embedded in the logic of the European Union integrated market – the fourth major pressure on the traditional public sector.

In principle, the existence of an extensive public sector is perfectly compatible with the stipulations of the Treaty of Rome. However, whatever derogations the Southern Europeans have negotiated, there are clearly aspects of market integration which will progressively undermine part of the rationale for a public sector. Thus, monetary convergence, despite the turbulence of 1993, together with the application of the principles of the free movement of capital, and sectoral and banking liberalization, with competition policy (state aids, public procurement policy) and transparency, financially disciplines member state governments into meeting the Maastricht criteria. Brussels has made clear, in its interpretation of Articles 85, 86 and 90 of the Treaty, that state authorities in their investment policies towards public enterprises must treat them as a private investor would deal with a private enterprise. Although the Commission has not always been consistent in applying its principles (which is not surprising, given the political bargaining which accompanies all major state aid occasions), the general thrust of its policy is clear, and several governments have been severely called to order. The increasingly tight control over aid to state-controlled industries has occasionally infuriated both governments and public-sector managers. Many of the latter add this factor to the list of reasons why they wish to escape into the private sector. However, Brussels has also furnished some of them with the pretext to carry out programmes they did not dare initiate on their account but which were deemed necessary: in that sense, the

European Commission becomes a convenient scapegoat. Thus, for instance, the restructuring plans for the coal mining industry and of Iberia in Spain in 1994 and of Olympic Airways in 1995 in Greece were imposed on willing governments.

A final major pressure for privatization has been the emergence and diffusion of an ideologically powerful pro-privatization model, based largely on the experience of the UK. The alleged success of the British programmes has fed the ideological aspirations of neo-liberals and brushed aside the traditional ideological inhibitions of market socialists in other West European countries, has provided ammunition for the growing number of pro-privatizers in the UN, the European Commission, the World Bank, the IMF, and the GATT as well as among public-sector managers, and has sharpened the financial appetites of revenue-starved governments of all political colours.

There have, therefore, been several broad and interlocked pressures at work in Western Europe, which, combined, have seriously undermined many of the arguments in favour of the public industrial sector. However, it should be emphasized that these pressures have been felt with varying degrees of intensity and at different times in Spain, Portugal and Greece. One of the obvious reasons for this is that the SEEs had very different industrial sectors – a point which warrants a brief analysis.

The public sector

The first key to an understanding of the different privatization programmes in Spain, Portugal and Greece is less the total size than the scope of their respective public sectors. Comparisons in this area are somewhat hazardous because different criteria are employed over time in the same country, and across the three countries. But however crude, the lessons to be drawn are clear.

At the beginning of the 1980s, and in spite of the state-sector expansion of the post-1945 period, Spain had, in relative terms, the smallest public industrial sector of the three countries – indeed, by most criteria, one of the smallest in Europe. It has been organized in three major groups.

First, there is the Instituto Nacional de Industria (INI, Table 7.1), founded under Franco in 1941 and inspired, in part, by the Italian model of public enterprises (Martín Aceña and Comín, 1991). Initially very small, the group expanded into steel, shipbuilding and transportation in the immediate postwar years. By 1954, the state owned over a dozen firms, a controlling interest in 37 and a minority interest in a further 12. All these firms were in basic industries (steel, hydro-electric power, shipbuilding, chemicals, textiles, automobiles and fertilizers). It expanded further from the early 1970s, being obliged, like IRI, its Italian counterpart, to bale out bankrupt firms, at a politically-sensitive time in politically-sensitive regions (including the Altos Hornos Steelworks in 1978). It acquired in the process

Table 7.1   Major companies under the Instituto Nacional de Industria (INI) (1987)

Name	Activity	Turnover $million	Employment	% of Nat. Prod	
Endesa	Electricity	3,715	15,850	Coal	48
Ensidesa	Steel	1,136	17,610	Electricity	32
Enasa	Automobiles	839	6,960	Steel	31
Inespal	Aluminium	730	6,130	Aluminium	100
Endiasa	Food	509	2,430	Potassium	27
Casa	Air transport	423	10,550	Cellulose	32
Bazán	Defence equipment	418	11,400	Shipbuilding	35
Enusa	Electricity	337	830		
Ence	Chemicals, paper	330	1,220		
Hunosa	Coal	268	19,670		
Sidmed	Steel	264	1,680		

nearly 200,000 workers and huge debts. At the time of Franco's death in November 1975, INI controlled a total of 61 firms. Five years into the transition this figure had risen to 175. After a period of intense rationalization in the early 1980s (notably in July 1984), INI had come to employ 164,000 people, accounted for 10 per cent of domestic industrial production, and had an annual turnover of $9.7 billion. Its companies ranged from those in rustbelt industries such as shipbuilding, mining and steel, to high-tech aerospace and electronics.

Second, Instituto Nacional de Hidrocarburos (INH), an oil and natural gas group, was formed in 1981. In 1987, it was converted into a new group, Repsol. Finally, Dirección General de Patrimonio del Estado (DGPE) has been an administrative department, linked to the Finance Ministry. In charge of state assets, it has had a controlling interest in several fields including banking, transport and telecommunications.

In all, by 1986 the Spanish state held a direct majority share-holding in 180 companies (with 300 subsidiaries) and a minority stake in over 500 companies. Yet Table 7.2 reveals the relatively modest dimensions of the state sector.

The Greek industrial public sector was traditionally small. With the restoration of democracy in 1974, and under the nationalistic centre-right government of Karamanlis, the sector modestly increased its size to encompass Olympic Airways, as well as a newly created petroleum corporation and the Commercial Bank of Greece (thereby gaining indirect control of several companies). A number of ailing firms were also taken over by state banks or other public institutions. However, it was not until the advent of the PASOK government in October 1981 that the public sector really extended its tentacles, mainly by collecting a host of unloved and unwanted bankrupt firms. The 1983 law codified takeover procedures of

Table 7.2 The importance of the state-owned company in Spain and Europe (1985)

Size	Spain (%)	Average EU (%)
– Employment by state-owned firms/total employment	5	10
– Investment state-owned firms/ total investment	10	20
– Value added by state-owned firms/GNP (excluding agriculture)	8	12
– % value added by state-owned firms by sectors:		
Energy	29	70
Transport & Communications	45	70
Banks	10	30

Source: European Centre for the State-Owned Company: *Yearly Statistics, 1987.*

these firms, and the euphemistically named Industrial Reconstruction Organization (IRO), as mentioned earlier, with a capital of $60 million, became the principal instrument. Any firm was entitled to apply to the IRO to be protected. If the application was accepted it became an 'ailing' firm, entitled to suspend debt repayments and interest payments for up to 36 months. A new management was installed to restructure and recapitalize (with state help) the firm and the state became its biggest shareholder.

After 1983, the sector continued to grow. Thus, in March 1984, the state purchased the ESSO chemical plant, refinery and oil product distribution network, and in August 1985, Hellenic Shipyards fell into the hands of the state-owned Hellenic Industrial Development Bank. State expansion continued throughout the latter part of the 1980s in textiles, mining, cement, fertilizers and sawmills. Whole sectors of the Greek economy came to be dominated by the state-controlled banks, energy, transports, telecommunications. In 1985, manufacturing firms in which the state controlled at least 20 per cent of the equity accounted for 3 per cent of total number of firms, 20 per cent of total employment, and 50 per cent of total fixed assets in manufacturing. Many firms became the target of clientelistic politics, flooded, like the rest of public sector, with patronage appointees at a steady rate which nonetheless would increase sharply with every election year.[5] Public sector firms were unproductive, lacking in strategic vision, tightly but inefficiently controlled, politically vulnerable, often union-dominated and badly managed. By 1990, when the Greek privatization programme was initiated, the public enterprise sector comprised 52 public enterprises directly controlled by ministries, of which 13 were utilities; and 152 enterprises directly owned or controlled by state-controlled banks and the IRO. In addition, state controlled banks and the IRO held minority equity stakes

Table 7.3   Public enterprises in Greece in the beginning of the 1990s

	Public enterprises*	Total of business sectors	%
Number of enterprises	204	10,431	2.0
Total assets ($billion**)	108	146	73.3
Total employment ('000 of people)	265.7	654.7	40.6 (7.2)***

Notes: *Public enterprises defined here as all organizations of state majority control and 'commercial' orientation.
**Data on 173 public enterprises were available.
***As percentage of total employment.
Source: Lioukas, 1993, p. 31.

in another 293 enterprises, in many of which equity participations added up to majority state control (Lioukas, 1993; Table 7.3).

In Portugal, the expansion of the public industrial sector dates essentially from the heady days of the 1974 revolution. Until then only a small number of enterprises (postal services, defence industries, ports) were fully state controlled, although the government had holdings in transport, electricity, oil refining and telecommunications. On the whole, state enterprises were 'conspicuous by their absence' (Baklanoff, 1986). The April 1976 Constitution, of Marxian inspiration, explicitly provided protection for a rapidly extended public sector. For General Vasco Gonçalves, nationalization was a method of weakening the ruling dynasties. As early as June 1974 the Lisbon Water Company was taken into public ownership, and the major banks quickly followed. As foreseen in Article 85 of the Constitution, Law 46/77 of July 1977 listed those industries in which private enterprise was not allowed: they included banking, insurance, air, rail and urban transport, iron and steel, cement manufacture, postal services and telecommunications, electricity generation and distribution, petroleum refining and basic petrochemicals and the arms industry. The Law made clear that all nationalizations carried out after the 25 April 1974 were 'considered to be the irreversible victory of the working class'. The impact of *Gonçalvismo* was rapid and radical: some 244 enterprises (with a total of some 2,000 subsidiaries) in key sectors were taken over (Martins and Rosa, 1979). By 1976, the state was the dominant actor in the sectors of electricity, banks and insurance, petroleum, shipbuilding, railways, tobacco, pulp and paper, glass, mining, chemicals, beer, air transport, radio and television and newspapers. Public enterprises accounted for 22 per cent of the economy's value added (63.2 per cent in banking, insurance and real estate, 75 per cent in transport and communications, 100 per cent in electricity, gas and water), 34 per cent of all fixed capital investment, 76 per cent of fixed investment in manufacturing, and 9 per cent of all employment. It was not quite

Eastern Europe, as the critics contended, but it was remarkable in terms of the West European norm.

By the mid-1980s, the structure of this vast public sector was as follows (OECD, 1988a, p. 60):

- a core of 50 non-financial enterprises, entirely state-owned, making up the public non-financial enterprises group (EPNF);
- a national corporation (Investimentos e Participaçoes do Estado) controlling 70 subsidiary enterprises in which it held between 2 and 100 per cent of the equity;
- a number of government agencies manufacturing or selling goods and services, which were grouped with nationalized enterprises for national accounts purposes (their sphere of activity being arms, agriculture, public infrastructures, ports, etc); and
- a large number of EPNF subsidiaries operating under private law. The non-financial enterprises group (EPNF, public agencies and over 50 per cent EPNF-owned subsidiaries) accounted for around 25 per cent of value added, 52 per cent of investment and 12 per cent of total employment at the end of the 1970s.

OECD data suggest that the weight of public enterprises increased sharply between 1977 and 1985, in terms of value added, but that their share in investment and employment fell slightly (Table 7.4).

There was an early policy of exploiting the public enterprises as engines of investment and employment growth – a policy which would reach alarming proportions. The workforce of Setenave (the shipbuilding and

Table 7.4 Non-financial public enterprises in the Portuguese economy, 1977–86

	Percentages				
	1977	*1980*	*1982*	*1984*	*1986*
Total					
Gross value added/					
national value added	10.0	13.0	14.8	17.7	15.1
Gross fixed investment/					
gross fixed investment	20.0	18.3	17.1	19.4	14.7
Employment/national					
employment	4.5	5.2	5.2	4.9	4.6
Borrowing requirement/GDP		−9.25	−11.50	−8.0	−2.0
Industrial public enterprises					
Value added/value added					
in industry	11.6	15.8	17.1	16.1	10.0
Employees/employees in					
industry	4.9	5.0	5.4	5.0	4.7

Source: OECD 1988a.

Table 7.5   Public enterprises in Southern Europe

	Spain 1980 %	Spain 1985 %	Greece 1980 %	Greece 1985 %	Portugal 1980 %	Portugal 1985 %
Size of the public enterprises sector[1]						
Share in value added	9.0*	14.0	–	–	13.0	17.6
Share in investment	22.0*	21.0	12.7	19.0	18.3	17.0
Share in employment	5.0*	6.0	3.5	4.5	5.2	4.7
Borrowing requirement/GDP[2]	–0.7	–1.2	–1.9	–2.7	–9.3	–6.2
State subsidies to public enterprises (per cent of GDP)	2.1	2.4	2.4	3.0	4.8	4.3

Productivity (1985)[3]	Spain	Greece	Portugal	4 major European countries
Telecommunications	35.2	15.8	12.6	22 to 30
Railways	11.7	4.2	4.6	22 to 25
Electricity supply	180.1	48.0	43.5	96 to 198

* 1982

[1] For Spain, the size of the public enterprise sector is measured with respect to the non-agricultural sector. For Portugal, data refer to non-financial enterprises.

[2] For Spain, refers to the operating deficit of the main non-financial public-sector groups.

[3] Productivity is measured as the ratio of total sales (in dollar terms) to employment.

Source: Larre and Torres, 1991, p. 80.

repairs group) rose from 14,000 in 1973 to 62,000 in 1977, while the nationalized banks were told to provide an additional 7,000 jobs for people coming from the former colonies. The consequences for these bloated enterprises were swift, and had to be addressed once the revolutionary phase petered out.

Even a cursory glance at Table 7.5 suggests that, on the whole (and aggregate data can be misleading), the public productive sector was faring far better in Spain than in Portugal and Greece. Its productivity was higher, its borrowing requirement lower, and it received a smaller proportion of GDP by way of subsidies. And as noted above, many of its enterprises had been made profitable by the mid-1980s. However, the recession of the early 1990s was to change this comfortable picture.

The privatization environment: the determining factors

Any analysis of the factors that have shaped the various privatization programmes must distinguish between those that have affected the extent and those that have determined the timing and the pace of programme implementation. We have already noted two major factors: the size of the sector to be privatized, and the ambitions of the privatizers. We may now turn to the other factors. It is worth examining them in the light of the Franco-British privatization programmes, for in both those countries conditions have greatly facilitated radical policy-making (Wright, 1995).

In the first place, certain industrial and financial conditions were highly propitious in Britain and France. Thus, almost all the major public firms were eminently privatizable: they were either profitable or they held solid (sometimes monopolistic) or strategically attractive market positions, and they were well managed by state-appointed managers who were generally imbued with a private-sector ethos. This situation was not always apparent in Southern Europe. Many public-sector enterprises were hopelessly unattractive and had to be liquidated or sold off to foreigners looking for an entrance into the domestic market. Others have required prolonged organizational, financial and managerial restructuring to prepare them for privatization. For instance, the Portuguese state has had to write off the very considerable debts of CNP, the petro-chemical group, Quimigal and Setenave before adding them to the privatization list. The relative failures of the privatization of Transinsular, the shipping company, and of Centralcer, the brewery, suggested that investors could be discriminating in their choice of privatized stock. In Spain, the losses of enterprises such as Renfe (railways), Aesa and Astano (shipbuilding), Ensidesa (steel) and Iberia rendered them unenticing investments. The latter alone was counting losses estimated at $235 million in 1994. In Greece, a plan to sell off Olympic Airways, an enterprise of legendary inefficiency and, in 1993, a $1.3 billion debt (*Financial Times*, 21 May 1993) was withdrawn as an early privatization prospect because no one expressed any interest (OECD, 1992, p. 67). There was the same problem with the shipyards as well as with many of the ailing firms under IRO, while the attempted flotation of 25 per cent of OTE in 1994 was met with indifference from investors in a world financial market already saturated with far more lucrative offers. Thus, one of the major pressures to privatize – the need to rid the state of costly loss-making enterprises – has also sometimes been a constraint on its capacity to do so.

Of equal importance to the success of the Franco-British programmes has been the availability of internationalized, liberalized and expanding financial markets capable of coping with major privatization issues. Here we touch upon one of the factors which has greatly contributed to the nature of the Southern European privatization programmes. In spite of almost revolutionary changes all three countries – until well into the mid- or later-1990s – had inadequate financial markets. In January 1986, for instance, after a rapid boom, the capitalization of the Spanish stock exchange amounted to only $17 billion, compared with $320 billion for the UK, $151 billion for West Germany, $72 billion for Switzerland and $52 billion for Italy, $45 billion for the Netherlands, $24 billion for Sweden and $19 billion for Belgium; as a proportion of GDP, it amounted to only 10.6 per cent (*Actualité*, 13 January 1986). Only 312 firms were quoted on the Madrid stock exchange (which represents more than 70 per cent of the country's transactions), and two-thirds of all transactions involved banks, electricity companies and Telefónica (OECD, 1988b, p. 53). However, it should be emphasized that there has been an expansion, reorganization and modernization of the stock exchange as the result of *El Big Bang Español* of the late 1980s, (notably Law 34/88), that there has been a greater inclination by industry to use equity markets for fund-raising rather than expensive direct loans from the banks, and that foreign dealings on the Madrid *Bolsa* have increased rapidly and massively (Fraser, 1988). By mid-1993, the market capitalization of the Madrid equity market stood at $121 billion, which represented 5.4 per cent of the EU's total, and 401 firms were quoted (*Financial Times*, 4 March 1994).

On the Lisbon and Oporto stock exchanges in 1986 only 30 shares were quoted. By 1995, the situation had changed as the result of several bouts of liberalization (in December 1992 – well before the EU deadline – Portugal authorized free capital movements), modernization (culminating in the Sapateira Law) and rationalization (from 1 June 1994 all cash transactions have been centered in the Lisbon Stock Exchange, following an agreement on market specialization between the Lisbon and Oporto Stock Exchange Associations). These reforms were designed to ensure greater operational efficiency, transparency, continuous trading in a national market, accessibility and closer supervision. In 1994 the *Bolsa* of Lisbon moved from its eighteenth-century building where it had operated since 1769 into a new state-of-the-art complex in a new financial centre taking shape in the city. By 1995, however, and even after a period of unparalleled, if disjointed growth, the two Portuguese exchanges had a capitalization of only $12 billion (compared with $32 billion for Turkey), and most major companies were not quoted. The financial market still suffered from the absence of institutional investors or well-capitalized, dynamic domestic groups, the lack of domestic capital to absorb major issues, high taxes on profits, dividends and dealings, over-bureaucratized regulations, and no tradition of popular investment (the Portuguese were given to saving – they have been among the biggest savers in Europe, hoarding between 17 and 18 per cent of income – rather than investing). It also failed to attract international investors: thus, a study by Carnegie International, a stockbroker, found that Portuguese shares represented less than one per cent of the continental European investments of large British funds. Matters were not helped by the October 1987 international stock market crisis which hurt many Portuguese investors, and by the damaging events surrounding the purchase of a controlling stake in the recently privatized Banco Totta e Açores (BTA). When, in February 1994, Champalimaud, a financier who had been a prop of the Salazar regime, bought 50 per cent of the equity of the bank, the government waived the elaborate takeover rules which would have obliged him to bid for the remainder of the shares. Five members of the body that regulates Portugal's capital markets resigned in protest, and international investment confidence was shaken (*The Economist*, 13 May 1995).

The financial market situation was even worse in Greece where issues of securities accounted for less than 0.25 per cent of total identified finance to the public sector during the period 1976 to 1986. In 1987 only 116 companies were listed on the Athens stock exchange – and many of these were moribund. Only 25 of the 100 largest Greek industrial companies were quoted: many of the most important Greek companies remained owned and managed by families persuaded of the disadvantages of the higher profile for tax authorities and of the accountability to shareholders that stock market quotation would involve. Institutional investors were non-existent, pension funds rarely traded on the Athens market and international investors were generally wary. Other stock exchange related services have been thin, a large part of the private sector has been highly dependent on state-controlled banks, industry has been skewed towards shipping and tourism and characterized by a mosaic of small firms, and the public is reluctant to invest (OECD, 1986). Rapid changes designed to widen and deepen share holdings have taken place since 1990: total capital raised in the Greek *Bourse* amounted to $86 million in 1989 but had risen to $1.2 billion in 1990 and was $1.1 billion by 1994 (Niarchos, 1995). Still, total market capitalization of the Greek stock exchange which, at the end of the first quarter of 1994, stood at $14 billion, barely exceeded 17 per cent of GDP (*Financial Times*, 20 May 1994) a clear indication of the development potential that lay ahead. Thus, although the situation had changed, the changes were insufficient, and too recent to have provided a good investment environment for the major privatization projects of the first half of the 1990s. It was only after the complete liberalization of capital movements in 1994, and especially after the drachma's entry to the European Monetary System (EMS) in March 1998, that the financial market – bolstered by Greece's high interest rate differentials – really took off.

Of course, by the early 1990s equity issues throughout Europe were becoming liberalized and internationalized. It was, therefore, possible to escape the confines of the domestic capital market. And, indeed, the Spanish and Portuguese have been increasingly prepared to issue privatized equity on several markets simultaneously. But such flotations raised delicate political questions (see below) in Greece and Portugal, and could do so in Spain if the control of a major privatized company was in question. Moreover, the internationalization and liberalization of equity issues is a double-edged sword: it facilitates the raising and the consolidating of capital but also its withdrawal, and this may penalize the weaker emerging markets of Southern Europe.

Finally, in terms of the propitious industrial and financial environment in Britain and France, mention must be made of the highly favourable general environment: a modern, competitive, internationalized and efficient banking system; liberalized foreign trade flows, capital movements, exchange rate controls, labour markets; a pool of managerial expertise and an entrepreneurial class allegedly ready to take risks. In spite of considerable progress on all these fronts in all three countries, the overall record remained patchy with a wide scope of government control over the banking systems, especially of Portugal and Greece (Dermine, 1990; Ferri, 1990; Gibson and Tsakalotos, 1992; OECD, 1990). The Greek position in particular until 1997–8, when a series of bank privatizations began, left something to be desired for the investment community.

In short, privatization, in order to be pursued in a radical fashion, requires a highly favourable industrial and financial environment. This has increasingly been the case in Spain and to some extent in Portugal, but it is less evident in Greece. Of no less importance to the success of the Franco-British programmes was the highly favourable political and institutional environment.

An analysis of the Franco-British programme reveals a number of points. First, *privatizers in Britain and France were able to create small, ideologically-like-minded, politically cohesive and relatively closed policy units, which were not bogged down in 'the quagmire of corporatism', were served by an efficient administrative apparatus, were unhindered by the querulous reluctance of sponsoring ministries or state holding companies, and were able, when necessary, to restructure the traditional, and potentially disruptive policy communities.* In Spain, Portugal and Greece most, but not all of these conditions appear to have prevailed, although it is an area which merits further research. Again, Spain appears to have been best placed. For instance, the socialist government seems not to have had any problems with the public-sector managers of the major holding companies, with whom they shared somewhat similar views, and the Spanish administration, although inefficient at the base, is served by a highly competent corps of higher civil servants. In Greece, on the other hand, privatization from 1990 to 1993 was guided basically by an inter-departmental committee (comprising the Ministers of National Economy, of Industry, and of Finance as well as the Minister heading the department in whose jurisdiction belonged the organization to be denationalized) together with a Secretariat for Denationalization. Yet this apparently streamlined arrangement proved surprisingly unwieldy when it came to curbing the reaction of ministers who felt their public-sector domains threatened, as well as of party scepticists seriously concerned with the political cost (Pagoulatos, 1996). At the end of the day privatization became personally identified first with the Industry Minister and finally with the National Economy Minister who was given *carte blanche* from Premier Mitsotakis to ignore resistance and move ahead. After the election of the PASOK government in 1993, and as privatization had acquired a negative political significance and although the same legal framework remained, the process was decentralized and pushed down to the lower echelons of the governmental hierarchy, leaving them to deal with the strong internal opposition. Moreover, as in Portugal, bureaucratic inefficiency has been apparent throughout the implementation of the privatization programmes (OECD, 1992; *The Economist*, 23 May 1993).

Second, *British and French privatizers were able to rely on the backing of a strong and united government.* This was not always the case in Spain, Portugal and Greece. In Portugal, between 1985 and 1987, the Socialist members of the government were able to restrain their Social Democratic partners, and even after July 1987 heated discussions in the Cavaco Silva government probably prevented the politically-delicate restructuring of certain enterprises, thus making their privatization more difficult (Corkhill, 1994). In Spain, only the partial privatization of Telefónica in 1995 caused real division. In Greece, between 1990 and 1993, the centre-right wing New Democracy government had a very narrow parliamentary majority, faced fierce internal nationalistic opposition and was finally overthrown by a small group of its own MPs over the twin issues of OTE privatization and Macedonia (see below).

Third, *French and British decision makers could count on the blessing of their respective party or party majorities in Parliament.* This was certainly true in Portugal where governmental party leaders – often liberal technocrats – have been able to still the occasional grumblings about foreign takeovers and the rationalization plans (involving labour shedding) of enterprises to be privatized. In Spain, early privatizations encountered few party obstacles. However, as the programme became more radical clear divisions arose between the market-minded right-wing of PSOE and an important pro-public sector group. Moreover, matters were complicated for Felipe Gonzales after the formation of his minority government, since his Catalan nationalist allies were keen privatizers. In Greece, the reform-minded technocrats in the second half of the 1980s were easily marginalized in the leader-dominated PASOK which harboured, for ideological and clientelistic reasons, a strong public-sector group and which faced competition from the pro-public-sector Left. For the party, extensive privatization was never a real option. In the short parenthesis of coalition governments (1989–90) that followed, the only emerging pro-privatization consensus seemed to involve the IRO ailing firms, but essential political commitment was lacking. Then in April 1990 the New Democracy government came to power with a united party backing and a strong 47 per cent popular mandate to implement its privatization programme; both, however, were gradually to dissipate, as discomfort spread about its most radical privatization projects. Opposition culminated in the summer of 1993 as the highly controversial privatization of OTE was being hurried through Parliament. The proposed sale of a substantial minority holding-cum-management to foreign investors touched a raw nerve in a body politic already sensitized by the 'sell-out' over Macedonia. The two issues were fused to provide the opponents of privatization with a potent nationalistic weapon, and some wavering New Democracy MPs with a pretext to bring down the government.[6]

Fourth, *in Britain and France the right-wing governments were able to mobilize some powerful group support, notably from private-sector financial and industrial interests and from public-sector managers who were keen to acquire autonomy for themselves and their companies.* The same situation prevailed in Spain with a powerful and autonomous banking community organized in the Spanish Banking Association (AEB) which is influential in the CEOE – the employers' federation (Lancaster, 1985). The latter had gained a respected status as the result of its role in the 'pacted' process of democratic transition. Moreover, in Spain, INI management, once stabilized (there were no fewer than five different chairmen between 1975 and 1980), became wedded to pragmatic and partial privatization. The same may be said of the bosses of individual public-sector enterprises such as Iberia (*ABC*, 26 June 1989). Once again, the situation in Greece has been somewhat different. The Federation of Greek Industries is dominated by the biggest enterprises but many of these are dependent on the state, and the Federation has never become a major pro-privatization lobby. Similarly, Greece lacked the type of powerful and organized financial interests that have spearheaded privatization in several European countries. Moreover, until the early 1990s state-controlled banks, which still held more than 80 per cent of all Greek commercial bank deposits (Gortsos, 1992), were under partisan control (thus, the governors of the four major state-owned banking groups were changed when PASOK returned to office in 1993) and the tight regulatory regime imposed on the credit and financial system was relaxed all too recently to allow for strong organized pro-privatization interest coalitions to emerge.

Fifth, *the opposition to privatization in Britain and France was weak, demoralized or divided.* The picture was more varied in Spain, Portugal and Greece. In Spain, opposition rarely took the form of organized protests against privatization *per se* but against those restructuring plans of public companies which involved massive lay-offs. Hence, the proposed $1 billion restructuring plan of the loss-making and debt-laden Iberia, announced in October 1994 and involving the loss of 2,200 of the company's 23,000 workforce, provoked immediate threats of strike action. If the industrial protest assumed a regional dimension (as it did in the Basque Country and in Asturias for the shipbuilding, mining and steel sectors) it could slow down the implementation of the plans. In Portugal, opposition has been muted for a variety of reasons. The principle of privatization was negotiated with the opposition Socialists who, under a Soares government (notably with the decree-law 422/76 of April 1976), had previously committed themselves to a mixed economy and the need to stimulate the private sector. The Communist-dominated CGTP was hostile to privatization, but its opposition was ineffective, while the Socialist-dominated UGT, which was well entrenched in the public banking and insurance sectors had no objection, in principle, to privatization, but expressed disquiet about foreign control, and stressed the need for worker participation in privatized industries. Given the highly politicized nature of the Greek public sector, opposition was surprisingly ineffective, at least until the 'radicalization' of the government's privatization programme in 1992. Then, with a minimal organizational effort and given the divisions of the Left, PASOK gradually managed to exploit growing popular discontent against New Democracy, and successfully relaunch itself as a reliable alternative. In government since 1993, its more modest privatization programme has met with scattered and low-key opposition, not the least important of which came from PASOK's own party apparatus and trade unions entrenched in public sector enterprises.

Sixth, *British and French governments built into their major programmes a set of incentives for the public, as well as for the customers and the employees of the privatized industries*, by reserving for them a proportion of the equity at politically fixed discount prices. No real attempt was made in Southern Europe to emulate this practice, although the Portuguese government made early sporadic attempts, and since the government reshuffle of December 1993 has declared its intention of systematically adopting it through extending incentives to small investors (OECD, 1996b, p. 65). In Greece, the proposed sale of 49 per cent of OTE under the ND government involved the retention of 4 per cent of the stock for workers and pensioners. The Spanish government, with some notable exceptions (Repsol, Argentaria and Endesa) has preferred selling public firms directly to private groups. However, in the 1995–7 part privatizations through stock exchange of their Telecom monopolies, all three countries attracted massive public interest, which could even lay claim to a Southern European version of popular capitalism. More than 81,000 small Portuguese investors applied for shares in the June 1996 offering of 22 per cent of Portugal Telecom, and a record high of 240,000 private investors (including some 700 international institutional investors) enlisted their interest in the June 1997 flotation of a 10 per cent stake of the Greek OTE, which raised expectations that its privatization could finally exceed the 25 per cent total upper limit set by the PASOK government (*Kathimerini*, 15 June 1997). Of similar success were the public offers of Telefónica in the Spanish stock exchange.

Seventh, *privatizers in Britain and France were able to construct a legitimizing discourse for their programmes*. In Spain, to the extent that such a discourse was required, privatization was linked with modernization, and was presented as part of a wider package to dismantle the protectionist heritage of Francoism and dictatorship. In Portugal and Greece, the ideological message has been occasionally spiced with pro-market sentiments, but in general it has been more directed against the inefficient and 'politically corrupt' public sector. However, in both countries, the anti-privatizers have been armed with a potent message: privatization may involve foreign control.

Eighth, *in both Britain and France there was a sustained political commitment to back the programmes.* This has been obvious in Spain, although it has not always been needed. However, in Portugal and in Greece, this has not always been the case. Before Cavaco Silva, former Bank of Portugal economist and Finance Minister, took over in October 1985, only half-hearted attempts at liquidating inefficient public enterprises were made by unstable, short-lived and weak administrations. Cavaco Silva's long reign (party leader and Prime Minister for ten years) was an undoubted factor in the success of the Portuguese programme. Greece has gone through all phases. After an extended period of no privatization commitment (the entire pre-1990 period under PASOK and coalition governments), the New Democracy's zeal for an extensive privatization programme wavered until 1992, only to reach its rather suicidal apex by 1993. Since 1993 PASOK has been quietly devoted to its own modest privatization targets with a relative expansion of ambition after its 1996 re-election, and especially after the privatization commitments undertaken *vis-à-vis* the EU following Greece's March 1998 entry to the EMS. At times, programmes have been disrupted by exogenous factors such as political instability (in the short period between June 1989 and April 1990 there were no fewer than three general elections) or an outright political barrier (with the electoral defeat of New Democracy in October 1993).

In exploring the *differences* in the privatization programmes of France and the United Kingdom, four major factors emerge. They also explain some of the differences in Southern Europe. They were:

Constitutional. The French Constitution appears to rule out the privatization of the public service monopolies (as well as public services, such as defence, prisons, health and education) whereas the British are unhindered by constitutional considerations: there is a sovereign Parliament, unhampered by judicial review. In France, too, the Constitutional Council imposed certain conditions on the privatization process. Constitutional factors have had no impact in Spain (Article 38 of the Constitution guarantees the country's mixed economy) or in Greece, but they clearly impinged upon the Portuguese privatization programme. The text of the 1976 Constitution referred to 'the irreversible nature of the nationalizations' decreed by General Vasco Gonçalves. Several attempts by the Democratic Alliance centre-right government to open commercial banking and insurance to private interests were rejected by the military-dominated Revolutionary Council on constitutional grounds. An amendment to reverse the irreversible required a two-thirds majority in Parliament, and, therefore, the agreement of the Social Democrats and Socialists. Successfully negotiating the necessary support demanded over two years of often fraught negotiations.[7]

Legal. Unlike in Britain, the legal status of certain firms or certain groups of employees in France required time-consuming and bartered modification before privatization could proceed. Legal factors that have affected the privatization programmes in Southern Europe, but especially Portugal and Greece, have included the need to change the status of certain enterprises. In Greece, too, there have been complex legal obstacles deriving from the claims by previous private owners for compensation, relating to the takeovers of the 1970s and 1980s.

Political. The electoral defeat of the French Right in 1988, and the highly effective trade union mobilization against at least one privatization (Air France) are good examples of political constraints. We have already explored most of the political factors that have shaped the Southern European privatization programmes. There have, however, been other such factors which certainly have not eased the path to privatization in the three countries. Thus, in Portugal, the spectre has loomed large over the programme of the 40 great family business dynasties which, often allied with the land-owning aristocracy, had dominated the private sector before the Revolution. Two privatizations in 1990 led to criticisms that the purpose of the programme was to permit the reinstatement of these dynasties: the first involved the acquisition by the de Mello family (in collaboration with a Scandinavian consortium) of Lisnave, the shipbuilding and repair company; in the second case, that of Tranquilidade, the insurance company, the Espiritu Santo family banking group regained a control it had enjoyed before the Revolution. In Spain, the location of several major public enterprises in the politically-sensitive Basque Country, Asturias (with chronically loss-making mines) and in Catalonia made the Socialist governments wary about restructuring and privatizing with alacrity. In Greece, on the other hand, problems of a local nature have entered the political calculus mainly when it came to privatizing firms located in electorally sensitive districts. Finally, on a top central level, there was critical opposition by powerful economic interests who had 'captured' particular public enterprise sectors, such as telecommunications, or were benefiting from favourable contracts with the state.

Cultural. Compared with the situation in Britain, in France there has been a more deeply-seated set of pro-state norms, prejudices and instincts, sometimes rooted in constitutional doctrine, but generally unwritten, which have set the parameters of public policy making and have restrained policy makers. This has taken the form of erecting a barrage of instruments to retain some state influence and to protect privatized industries against foreign predators. The British have been more half-hearted in this respect though caps of foreign stakes have been established for some privatized industries. Similar protective devices may be seen in the Southern European countries. Vestiges of the much commented-upon cultural aversion towards the market have been apparent in a number of ways. First, many traditional public sector industries, including the public service monopolies, are destined to remain in state hands, even if the Portuguese and the Spanish have been seriously toying with the idea of some disposals, and all three governments have experimented with the sale of minority stakes in these monopolies. Thus, in Spain, Gesa (electricity) and Endesa (electricity) have become public-private hybrids, even if the government retained full control. Second, even in Spain there has been a clear reluctance to lose some form of control over largely privatized firms: in the public sectors of transport, minerals, finance and telecommunications, minority stakes will carry veto powers. In Portugal and Greece it was hoped to exercise continued influence through the state-controlled financial sector. That most zealous of privatizers, Cavaco Silva, made clear that urban rail and other transport services, the Post Office and TAP, the state airline, would remain in state hands. This was not the case in Greece until 1993, when the New Democracy government failed to delineate clearly the areas in which state jurisdiction was not negotiable (Kazakos, 1993). Third, in several privatized companies in Portugal the government retained a golden share which conferred veto power over certain decisions: this was the case, for example, with Petrogal and with Siderurgia Nacional.

Reluctance to withdraw the state completely is linked to another powerful cultural factor: nationalism. The Spanish government did not hesitate to sell some public enterprises to foreigners: Seat to the Germans in 1986; the SKF Española ball-bearing plant to SKF Sweden (already a minority share-holder) in 1985; Purolator (a filter manufacturer) to the West German company AG in early 1986; Secoinsa (electronics) to Fujitsu; MTM to Alsthoum-France; Enfersa to the Kuwaiti Investment Office; and Ensa (the truck-maker) to Fiat. It should also be pointed out that the part privatization of Repsol in 1987 involved the issuing of 11 million of the total of 65 million shares in the USA and 3 million in Tokyo. This operation was a further indication of the easing of rules and regulations introduced by the PSOE government itself in 1982. However, it should be emphasized that – possibly with the exception of Repsol – the Spanish have yet to cede control of a major strategic company to foreigners (Rodríguez-Arana, 1991). Rather, they have either rid themselves of loss-making firms and those which are marginal to the core interests of the public-sector groups, or they have accentuated the traditional public–private hybridization of the country's industry.

The Portuguese government has also organized several off-market sales to foreigners, and the original ceilings on foreign stakes (which ranged from 2 to 35 per cent) have either been eased, abolished or ignored. Foreign ownership was limited until November 1992 when it was announced that foreigners could take control of a privatized firm 'on a case-by-case basis' (*The Economist*, 7 November 1992). At the end of 1993 the decision was taken slowly to lift many restrictions on foreign holdings and to abandon the policy of keeping certain (but not all) strategic companies in Portuguese hands (OECD, 1996b, p. 65). Hence, when the Banco Pinto e Sotto Mayor (BPSM) and Soponata (the country's oil shipping company) were sold it was agreed to place foreign investors on the same footing as those in Portugal. In truth, the restrictive policy had already been seriously weakened in practice. For instance, a French insurance group had taken over the privatized Aliança Seguradora (Portugal's sixth biggest insurer), despite a 30 per cent cap on foreign ownership, by side-stepping the restriction: the French bought a Portuguese company which also held a stake in the privatized insurance company. Similarly, a 10 per cent limit on foreign ownership did not inhibit the Spanish Banesto group from acquiring directly or indirectly more than a 40 per cent stake in Banco Totta e Açores (BTA) before the limit was officially changed in June 1993 to 20 per cent and then later to 35 per cent (still lower than the stake acquired). Nevertheless, the fear of foreign penetration has inspired opposition to privatization in the country. This emerged sharply when BTA was sold in 1989: the role of Banesto, a dangerously expanding Spanish bank, in the battle for control raised uncomfortable questions about the predatory activities of Portugal's immediate neighbour. The events following the privatization of Aliança Seguradora in September 1989 heightened the fears of foreign takeovers, since the Paris-based UAP not only rapidly purchased 20 per cent of the stock but was reported to have secured control through its subsidiaries in Portugal. When Total, the French oil company, acquired 25 per cent of Petrogal, the partially privatized oil company, voices were raised in protest. 'Portugal for sale!' became the rallying cry of the opponents of privatization and led to demands for tighter control (*The Economist*, 21 January 1994) on foreign buying. It is revealing that one of the reasons given by the government in December 1993 for trying to create a domestic mass shareholding was that it would contribute to keeping privatized industries in Portuguese hands. It is no less revealing that the government is not expected to relinquish total control of Portucel, given the importance of this vertically integrated group to the country's economy.

It has been in Greece that nationalism has been the most potent force. Several small 'ailing firms' have been sold to foreigners, and mobile telephone licenses have been sold by auction to STET, the Italian telephone operator, and to a British consortium. None of these operations ruffled nationalistic feathers, not least because major Greek media owners were partners in the consortia. The same could not be said of repeated efforts to sell three shipyards to foreign investors, whose representatives in some cases were nearly harassed away from the premises by angry trade unionists. Most of all it could not be said of the sale, in March 1992, of a controlling interest in the previously nationalized enterprise AGET-Heracles (one of Europe's biggest cement exporters) to Calcestruzzi, the cement subsidiary of the Italian Ferruzzi group. The collapse of the latter group's ownership amid corruption allegations which spilled over to the Greek side merely enflamed further nationalistic opposition. This opposition was to be given a further boost over the proposed sale of 49 per cent cum-management of OTE, the country's telecommunications monopoly (as seen earlier). It came as no surprise, therefore, that among the very first measures announced by the new Papandreou government of 1993 was the withdrawal of its predecessor's privatization plan. Nationalistic sentiment against PASOK's privatization policies has been virtually non-existent, following the programme's low political importance, the only possible target being the attempted sale of the Hellenic Shipyards, one of the largest in the Mediterranean. There, the Socialist government, in line with the past policy of New Democracy, has sought to appease reactions by making reference to its inescapable obligations to the EU.

This short survey of the factors that have shaped the three Southern European privatization programmes tends to show that the Spanish context for privatization has been, in several respects, the most propitious, even though certain elements in the general economic and financial environment could still be seen to be unsatisfactory by investors. Portugal has made considerable strides in creating conducive circumstances for privatization but was initially hampered by constitutional factors and continues to be constrained by administrative and cultural factors as well as by the parlous state of certain public-sector industries and the vestiges of an inflexible and bureaucratized financial environment. It is, however, in Greece where the constraints on privatization have been most apparent in almost every respect.

We are thus confronted with the paradox that a relatively modest Spanish programme has emerged in the most propitious environment, while the relatively radical privatization ambitions of the Portuguese were forged in less propitious ones. But the paradox may be more apparent than real. The Spanish 'technopols' have had less to privatize, have been less pressured to do so, and have not been galvanized into action by ideological zeal. In Portugal and Greece, on the other hand, privatization has been seen by right-wing elites or reform-minded socialists as a key ingredient in reshaping unfavourable domestic environments. It is not merely a mechanism of adjustment or a money-raiser: it is an integral part of a wider programme destined to transform the economy of the country.

Ambitions, programmes and outcomes

Privatization programmes are defined not only by need (the scale and intensity of pressures), scope (what there is to privatize), and constraints, but also by ambition (what governments would like to privatize). Having examined the first three points we may now turn to the fourth. The briefest of explorations of the ambitions of the three countries immediately reveals the initial differences between Spain and the other two countries.

In Spain, privatization has never become an ideological crusade. The Socialist leadership always treated the public industrial sector in pragmatic fashion (Silvestre, 1988), and the managers and technocrats close to, and often belonging to the Gonzales government (technopols, to use the current jargon), always viewed privatization in non-ideological terms. For the *solucionadores* – problem-solvers – who run the public holding companies privatization is but one part of the overall strategy of restructuring and modernizing Spanish industry: they do not wish to lose overall control of their empires, but they are prepared to rid themselves of loss-making enterprises such as Seat or firms involved in non-core activities. If privatization is deemed unnecessary on grounds of efficiency it need not be pursued. And although public ownership may have been a factor in slowing down the modernization or closure of some enterprises (see below), it has not prevented, for instance, the INI management from an aggressive international strategy based on joint-ventures, technological collaboration and the acquisition of subsidiaries. Nor has that management been stymied in its ambition radically to restructure the group in a way that minimizes the impact of the politically and socially sensitive loss-makers on the overall performance of the group. It was not until the full impact of the recession was felt in the 1990s that financial imperatives pushed more radical privatization onto the policy agenda. At no stage, however, has dogma dictated the scope and pace of the programme. This largely remained the case after the 1996 rise to power of the Popular Party.

The Greek privatization programme has clearly been driven by budgetary considerations, both under New Democracy and PASOK. The difference between them was that New Democracy promoted privatization as part of a distinctly ideological anti-statist agenda, thus leaning closer to the Thatcherite end of the spectrum. The Socialist programme, on the other hand, clearly more modest in its ambition, was put forth by the reformers and technocrats within PASOK, thus resembling more the 'pragmatic' Spanish paradigm described above. A first such effort by PASOK took place in 1986-7, with the attempt to sell off a batch of ailing firms, but the reformers led by the then minister Simitis were quickly discouraged, as the populist wing of PASOK prevailed. Thus, the first effective attempt to privatize was made by New Democracy; the financial needs of the state (often pressurized by its European Union partners) and of the firms merely convinced the Mitsotakis government that privatization was not only desirable but also urgent. The bold initiation of state retreat by New Democracy enabled PASOK's reform-minded economic policy makers under both the 1993 Papandreou and particularly the 1996 Simitis governments to follow up in largely the same direction facing far less political reaction.

The Portuguese government had similar ambitions of reducing the level of public debt (80 per cent of the proceeds of privatization were earmarked for this purpose) and of improving the balance sheets of public-sector firms (often to improve the chances of privatization). But other considerations also entered into the privatization campaign. These were made explicit in the Privatization Law of April 1990, and in subsequent ministerial declarations (notably after the December 1993 reshuffle) and included the need to strengthen the capacity of national enterprises, to vitalize the financial markets through major flotations, to rationalize certain sectors, to create a *capitalismo popular a la portuguesa*, as well as ensuring a stake in the privatized firms for their workforce. The programme was also underwritten by an ideological commitment: *Menos Estado, Melhor Estado* (less state, better state) – which, although lacking the stridency of the Thatcherite message, was persistently stressed.

What programmes emerged from these policy ambitions? Not surprisingly, the Spanish programme was, at least initially, the least far-reaching. The PSOE government elected in 1982 did not rush into privatization. And like the British, but unlike the French, Portuguese and Greek governments, it has never promulgated a general framework law indicating the companies to be privatized. It was not until 1986 that the policy was pursued in any serious way. Previously, between 1984 and 1986, it had sold off or liquidated some 30 smaller enterprises (often to foreigners) in an attempt to cut the public sector's losses or to rationalize the sector. Several of these enterprises had been absorbed into the public sector during the troubled early days of transition to democratic government. The programme started in earnest in October 1986 when INI placed 38 per cent of Gesa (an electricity company) on the Madrid stock exchange, thus reducing the state holding from 94 to 56 per cent. A flurry of sales of minority holdings followed, including Empresa Nacional de Celulosas (Ence) and Empresa Nacional de Electricidad (Endesa). Between 1988 and 1990 the Spanish sold $490 million worth of companies to shrink the state sector (*The Economist*, 17 November 1992).

After a brief lull, the pace of Spanish privatization picked up in 1993. The need to reduce the public deficit (which had reached 7 per cent of GDP in 1992) in a period of recession weighed heavily in the decision. The partial (24.9 per cent) privatization of Repsol, the oil group, in March, raised $1.1 billion, in the biggest operation ever undertaken on the Spanish capital markets. A similar chunk of Argentaria (created in 1991, with the merger of all the public-sector banks) was successfully sold in April and May 1993. The success led the government to commission a report by Argentaria on the prospects for further privatization in Spain. It was this report which was to serve as the basis for the later programme which included the sale of another 25 per cent of the stock of Argentaria, in November 1993, the sale of another 10 per cent stake in Endesa in 1994, 12 per cent of the 34 per cent held by the state in Telefónica (telephone monopoly), and a further 15 per cent tranche of Repsol in 1995. The privatization momentum continued after the election in government of José Maria Aznar's Popular Party (PP). The conservative PP had committed itself, before the May 1996 electoral victory, to privatize 'all privatizable enterprises' (including, notably, profit-making concerns), estimated then to be worth $16–24 billion (*El Mundo*, 20 March 1995). A sign of the radicalization of the programme: the Aznar government was even considering, as part of a longer-term strategy, the part or full privatization of public-service industries such as Renfe and Feve (railways), postal services and Aena (the company which manages Spanish airports), and indicated that it would reduce its holding in Telefónica to a token level before 1998. The privatization process in Spain has not been an entirely smooth one, and has been punctuated with mishaps such as the suspension of the sale of the third tranche of Argentaria in 1994 because of unfavourable market conditions and the postponement of the partial privatization of Telefónica in 1995 because of internal government disputes. However, this fitful implementation has produced significant results, affecting notably the oil, energy and banking sectors favourably.

In Portugal, political and constitutional factors effectively prevented the implementation of the privatization ambitions of centre-right dominated governments in the 1980s, although from 1983, with the formation of the PS-PSD coalition, legislation was introduced to liberalize and open up the Portuguese industry. It was not until the elections of 1987 that privatization could proceed. The privatization ambitions of the Cavaco Silva single-party government elected in that year embraced almost the entire productive sector. Only a few major public utilities were to be spared. Three days after the election, the Prime Minister announced his intention of restructuring the capital of the public enterprises. He distinguished between (1) essential service companies (urban transport, railways and the national flag carrier TAP) which had to remain state-controlled; (2) companies which, because of heavy indebtedness or inappropriate corporate structures, could not be privatized; he quoted, as examples, Quimigal (fertilizers and chemicals), Electricidade do Portugal, Siderurgia Nacional (steel) and Setenave (shipbuilding); and (3) those which were in good enough shape to be sold. The first stage in the programme was the March 1988 Law, which enabled the transformation of public enterprises into corporations in which the state would retain a majority stake.[8]

The passage of the Law was quickly followed by the partial privatization of Unicer (brewery), Banco Totta e Açores (BTA), Aliança Seguradora, and Tranquilidade (two big insurance companies). The share issues were vastly oversubscribed, which augured well for the rest of the programme. The constitutional amendment of June 1989, providing for full privatization, paved the way for the April 1990 Law. Sixty major companies were targeted for privatization: the total value of the 15 biggest represented one-third of the country's GDP. Within two years, many remaining stakes in Unicer, Tranquilidade, Aliança Seguradora, Banco Totta e Açores had been sold, and the state had also disposed of the whole or parts of Centralcer (brewery), Banco Português do Atlantico (BPA), Banco Espíritu Santo e Comercial de Lisboa, (the country's biggest commercial bank), Sociedade Financeira Portuguesa, Transinsular (shipping), Petrogal (Portugal's biggest commercial enterprise, oil), Mundial Confiança (insurance), Rodocargo (Road transport), Diário de Notícias, and the nucleus of the Grupo BPA which comprised some 70 companies. In all, between April 1989 and March 1992 the government wholly or partly privatized 17 major companies, raising $2.7 billion. Almost all major sectors of the Portuguese economy were affected: banking, insurance, steel, chemicals, breweries. Some 212,000 investors bought the 100 million shares offered in vastly over-subscribed issues. Four-fifths of the proceeds were used to amortize the public debt, with the remainder channelled into improving the balance sheets of the remaining public firms.

From mid-1992 there was a marked slow-down in the programme because of adverse market conditions. In 1993, the government failed to sell a bank, a cement producer and a steel company, either because bids were too low or there was no bid at all, and privatization receipts reached only $435 million instead of the predicted $1.4 billion. In December 1993 in order to facilitate the promised acceleration of the programme it was decided that all the proceeds of privatization could be used to recapitalize debt-laden public enterprises such as Portucel, Siderurgia Nacional and TAP. This change, together with the easing of restrictions on foreign ownership, the internationalization of share issues, and the decision to encourage popular participation, indicated that the plan to rid the state of all but a few public utilities was to be stepped up.

An ambitious timetable was drawn up in early 1994. It was hoped that by the end of 1994 privatized stock would represent 50 per cent of the country's stock market capitalization. After some initial disappointments (the placement of 20 per cent of Cimpor, the dominant cement group, in summer 1994, was 'less than a great success') the programme picked up, notably from early 1995. Privatization operations taking the form of public offers on the Lisbon stock exchange raised a total of $72 million in the first quarter of that year. They involved the sale of stakes in the Banco Pinto e Sotto Mayor and in Rodoviária Sul do Tejo, a major bus company. By the

Summer of 1995 the government had disposed of 26.3 per cent of Portugal Telecom in a 'resoundingly successful' flotation (the demand for shares was four times higher than the number on offer and $867 million were raised, and the company acquired 56,000 shareholders, including 276 foreign investors). The remaining 22 per cent of the 49 per cent total privatized stock was sold in June 1996 by the Guterres Socialist government and was heavily oversubscribed, raising $943 million in what was branded 'Portugal's most successful privatization to date'. The Cavaco Silva government had also sold Rodoviária de Lisboa, another major bus company, and had reduced its holding in Banco Totta e Açores. The government had extended the privatization list to include Portucel, the paper, pulp and packaging group: in February 1995, it was announced that 40 per cent of Portucel-Industrial, its main pulp production division, which accounted for 60 per cent of the group's sales, would be sold through a global offer, and that Gescartão, its brown paper and packaging division, would be disposed of entirely to a single buyer. Both operations were successfully concluded.

Thus, by the second half of the 1990s, the Portuguese government had not only profited financially but had radically begun to shift the public–private boundary in many sectors, and especially in the key financial sector. In all, between 1985 and 1995, the weight of state companies in Portugal's GDP was halved from 20 to 10 per cent, and privatizations brought in revenues worth over $6.7 billion.

The Greek 1990 to 1993 government of New Democracy had equally radical privatization ambitions (Table 7.6).

According to the programme presented by Premier Mitsotakis Parliament in April 1990, the government's privatization plans involved: the disposal

Table 7.6 Greek privatization programme, 1991

	Enterprises available for privatization by holder (number)
Agricultural Bank	36
Commercial Bank	9
Industrial Development Bank (ETBA)	18
National Bank	12
Industrial Reconstruction Organization (IRO)	54
Ministry of Defence	1
Ministry of Finance	2
Ministry of Industry	10
Ministry of Tourism	21
Ministry of Transport and Communications	7
Total	170

Source: Commission of the European Communities (1992, p. 17).

of all ailing firms under IRO; the transfer of all enterprises controlled by state banks to the private sector, or the liquidation of those that were not viable; the dissolution of all state trade firms which intervened in the market and disrupted competition; the construction of important public projects by private firms by means of self-financing; and the activation of the private sector in specific fields where public utilities (that is, electricity, telecommunications, transport), traditionally operated (for example, mobile telephone licences to private companies, permission for private airline companies to operate).

Additional references were made to market liberalization and deregulation measures such as liberalization of the banking system and of capital markets, and the need to allow public enterprises to function under private-economy criteria. Quite notably, there was no mention at that point of privatizing any public utility; on the contrary, it was explicitly stated that utilities would remain under state control.

In the implementation process however the programme became more ambitious, as attempts were made, at various stages, partially to privatize public utilities by selling minority stakes of OTE and Olympic Airways or by contracting the construction of electric power plants for the Public Power Corporation (DEH). None of these projects was achieved. Olympic Airways found no interested purchaser or anyone to undertake its management without drastic cuts in its personnel. And the construction of electric power plants for DEH was halted by Premier Mitsotakis for political reasons. OTE was far more adventurous. The privatization bill, which envisaged the sale of 35 per cent of its shares to a strategic partner who would also undertake the management, and an additional 14 per cent to the public, made it through the Parliament, but the New Democracy government fell a few weeks before signing the contract, as mentioned earlier. The Socialist government that followed, hard-pressed for revenue, made a second attempt in November 1994 to sell 18 per cent of OTE on the international stock markets and 7 per cent to domestic investors, a total 25 per cent of the company. The flotation was postponed however at the last moment, as the government estimated it would fail to raise the anticipated $1.3 billion and feared political repercussions by domestic opposition (*Financial Times*, 9 November 1994). In the end, to play it safe, a modest 8 per cent of total equity share was floated in March 1996 and was many times oversubscribed; a further 10 per cent followed successfully in June 1997.

Thus, the only public utility that was effectively privatized, in 1992, was the Athens Urban Transport Company (EAS). The company was, however, taken back into the public sector as soon as PASOK returned to power. The 1993 Papandreou government also halted the process for the sale of two major refineries (ELDA and EKO), but went forward with the implementation of some tourism projects, the sale of the remaining two of a total of four state-owned shipyards (Neorion and Hellenic Shipyards)[9] as well as with plans for selling a minority stake of the Public Petrol Enterprise (DEP). Other successful privatization projects have included bank subsidiaries, Olympic Catering, the Hellenic Sugar Industry, the first company sold through the Stock Exchange, and most of the IRO ailing firms. In total, by the end of 1995, and in a time span of five years, some 100 firms had been privatized and $1 billion had been raised, far less than the amount that had been anticipated. Half the receipts came from the controversial sale of the cement industry AGET. The 1996 PASOK government under Costas Simitis, who took over as prime minister after Andreas Papandreou's death, was more decisive than its direct 1993 predecessor in following up a number of privatization projects initially placed on the agenda under the 1990 New Democracy administration. Thus, control over the Bank of Attica, a small Commercial Bank subsidiary, was transferred in early 1997 to the independent engineers fund, and two additional small banks (Bank of Crete and Bank of Central Greece) were also privatized. The sale of Ionian Bank, the largest state bank to enter the privatization programme, initially failed to attract the desired combination of acceptable price and credible buyers, and was declared fruitless. That did not prevent its final privatization despite fierce reaction from its trade union. A share offering of about 10 per cent of DEP was also envisaged until end of 1997, and so was the privatization of the airport duty free shops as well as up to 45 per cent of the Athens Stock Exchange. The Simitis administration hoped to be totally rid of IRO and its ailing subsidiaries by the end of 1998 (but then so were its predecessors, with IRO initially scheduled by the New Democracy government to close down from as early as 1994), and was anticipating a total $1.6 billion privatization revenue for 1997, half of which would go to the central government.

While then recognizing that the political identity of the party in power does make a difference in shaping the agenda, it would not be ill-founded to observe a deepening and widening of the privatization ambitions and programmes in all three countries. This could well include the new Socialist governments of 1993 in Greece and 1996 in Portugal if one considers their new policies against the background of their previous terms in office. The Cavaco Silva governments clearly appear as the most far-reaching with privatization. The relatively radical and ideological nature of the Portuguese programme may be seen not only in the ambitions and the speed of implementation, but also in the means employed: share issues on the stock exchange have been increasingly preferred to off-market sales and have been internationalized; a proportion of the sales are generally reserved for employees and small investors; a more market-oriented (although there were still restrictions) approach has been adopted towards foreign investors, in spite of protests in opposition ranks. The Spanish and Greek governments have also sold enterprises to foreigners, but much more prudently (generally small non-strategic firms – with the exception of

AGET – some of which were even losing money). Moreover, until 1994 only three issues of Spanish privatized stock had taken place on the stock exchange, and at no stage had the price been politically fixed to attract a mass shareholding.

Concluding remarks

The governments of Spain, Portugal and Greece have been squeezed by a number of cumulatively convergent pressures into adopting privatization programmes: these pressures may be seen at the domestic, European Union and international level, and they are ideological, budgetary, managerial and technological in nature. Our analysis of the response of the three governments shows distinct variations in the scope and pace of their response to these pressures. We have attempted to explain the variations by exploring four major factors: the intensity and the timing of the impact of the pressures; the size and nature of the public sector to be privatized; the degree of ideological commitment or programmatic ambition; and the facilitating or inhibiting effects of a general policy environment that comprises industrial, financial constitutional, political, institutional, legal and cultural factors. A study of the interplay of these four levels of analysis provides us with some explanation for the specificity of each country's programme.

However, the distinctiveness of each experience should not disguise the fact that broadly convergent pressures have led to increasingly convergent ambitions (if not programmes or outcomes). Even the Greek Socialists under Papandreou came to recognize that they can no longer afford an undifferentiated and uncritical approach to the public sector, that greater sensitivity to market forces may be required and that privatization can be a lucrative affair for the state (interview of Papandreou before the 1993 election, *To Vima*, 10 September 1993). With the PASOK Minister of National Economy, Papantoniou, championing the need for structural adjustment and a faster pace in privatization (*To Vima*, 19 January 1997), Greek socialists have indeed come a long way. Similarly, the 1996 elect Portuguese Socialist government asserted its commitment to a mixed economy based on a 'partnership between the public sector and private initiative' as the competitive strategy for 'meeting the challenge of increasingly global markets' (interview of Economy minister Mateus, *Economic Barometer, Portugal*, May 1996). We have also seen a Spanish Socialist government abandoning its early rather cautious and limited approach and, under budgetary pressure, embracing a somewhat more radical stance.

Perhaps we are witnessing an accelerated adjustment of SEEs to the vast processes of globalization, European integration, rationalization and liberalization which are pushing towards, and are fed by privatization. Clearly, we cannot dissociate privatization from the wider macroeconomic and industrial policies being pursued in all three countries. Of course, there are limits. In all three countries, as we have seen, nationalism and protectionism are still evident, expressed in the golden share, the retention of majority stakes by the state, and the ceilings imposed on foreign holdings. They are also expressed in the desire to retain key industries in the public sector. The conflicting pressures of these twin factors – the market and nationalism – suggests some redrawing of the public–private boundary, but nothing close to an eradication of the public domain. Furthermore, a study of other economic and industrial policies suggests that the state remains a key economic actor. The result is, therefore, an extension of the mixed public–private sector where borderlines are unstable and intrinsically difficult to trace. Managing this internationalized, Europeanized and mixed industrial tissue must surely represent one of the greatest challenges to Southern European governance.

What political lessons may be drawn from the privatization experiences of the three countries? In the first place, political institutional factors matter, but perhaps decreasingly so. They may shape timing and pace but less and less the substance of a programme such as privatization. In any case they are more closely associated with the contextual constraints upon rather than the content *per se* of reform. More important in shaping privatization programmes are the shape and state of the public sector and of the domestic stock market. Secondly, the three experiences appear to reveal the relative ease with which hard-pressed or determined governments can dismantle apparently powerful coalitions – in this case, those which protected the public sector. While this is much more the case for Portugal and Spain than it is for Greece, there is certainly a steadily decreasing role to be played by anti-privatization interest coalitions in all three SEEs. This raises some interesting questions about the preconditions for the durability of stable and influential policy communities. And this, in turn, links to the third political lesson of the privatization programme: that all three countries may no longer be so tightly hemmed in by the 'confining conditions' of transitional politics, to borrow Maravall's phrase (Maravall, 1991a) – that the 'primacy of politics' or redistributionalist accommodation which characterized the democratic transition may have given way to more sober attention to economic considerations. This suggests that if the transitional phase engendered a number of 'confining conditions' it may also have contained a number of elements which were to enable modernizing elites to escape them.

More intriguing is the question of what has been the role of democracy in promoting economic reform in Southern Europe. On the one hand, in all three countries, the transition to democracy was accompanied by a reinvigoration of state control over the economy. That was politically motivated in a triple sense: it identified democratization with some allegedly efficiency-maximizing state-grip over the economic process; it viewed nationalization as a means for seizing power from the hands of capitalists who had been tolerant towards the dictators; and it relied on an extensive public sector for boosting the democratic regime's political legitimacy through a symbolic transfer of power to the people and the increased capacity for redistributionist policies. In all these ways, the transition to democracy in Southern Europe led SEEs to the exactly opposite direction from the privatizing zeal of the later 1980s and 1990s. As the pro-market ideological forces were identified with the *anciens régimes* (less in Spain than in Portugal or Greece), the transitional phase gave a strong push to socialist and social-democratic ideas, even in the sense of forcing conservative politicians and parties into adopting programmatic projects of mixed economy of higher state control. At the same time, and on a less short-term manner, democratization in its phase of consolidation unleashed the winds of politicization and confrontational dynamics, exposing more than ever before economic policy making to political criticism. Given an environment of unprecedented political pluralism and press freedom, market-oriented economic reform, and privatization even more strongly so, were deemed to invite vigorous and widespread controversy concerning not only the 'objective' effectiveness of the adopted policies but also the alleged 'subjective' motives behind them. It could also be claimed that democratic party competition intensified the pressures and prerequisites of re-election or at least rolled them down from the level of oligarchic elite accommodation to that of mass politics. Thus political cost became a primary consideration, electoral cycles salient as ever, clientelistic exchange and the wooing of powerful interest groups crucial re-election preconditions. But economic change as structural reform means undertaking to confront a lot of the above. In that sense, the political dynamics of the democratic game in SEEs provided some of the heaviest constraints upon economic reform policy making.

On the other hand, the forces of democratization opened SEEs not only to the institutional and economic interdependence identified with the EU project, but to that same logic of economic rationalization and reform gaining ground in the more advanced EU states. By presenting domestic economic modernization as an inextricable part of a broader European agenda, national reform-oriented elites were able to add compelling persuasiveness and legitimacy to their programmes. In all three Southern European countries the forces of international competition were systematically invoked by governments as the external threat the national economy should be prepared to confront or, more positively, as the challenge to which it should strive to rise. Paradoxically then, the popular feeling of national pride and similar traditional ethnocentric themes would be invoked by modernizing Europeanizing governments to advance the cause of higher involvement in the European integration process and a dynamic response to adjustment pressures. So Southern European democratization worked both ways with regard to economic reform: it obstructed it, and it engendered it. Though far from a clear-cut distinction, the stage of transition to democracy in all three SEEs seemed to be strongly associated with policies of public sector strengthening and expansion; democratic consolidation, on the other hand, paved the way for a higher involvement of all three SEEs in the European integration process, increased their openness to international economic and institutional pressures, and thus enhanced their readiness to adjust by converging towards the broader privatization policy paradigm (cf. de la Dehesa, 1994, p. 134; Torres, 1994).

Finally, and perhaps more profoundly, the privatization programmes represent yet another sign of the partial break not only with the politicized politics of transition but also with more entrenched historical reflexes: there can be no return to the closed, highly regulated and anti-capitalist system of *Salazarismo* in Portugal (Maravall, 1991b) (as Cavaco Silva made clear in his speech of 17 August 1987), and there is a clear attempt to accelerate the movement away from the 'assisted capitalism of Francoism' in Spain (Maravall, 1991b). Greece, with its industrial culture imbued with deep-seated suspicion of private entrepreneurship (Diamandouros, 1994; Kazakos, 1993) appears slowly and sometimes reluctantly to be moving in the same direction. Southern European exceptionalism, which has always disguised significant disparities across its constituent states, may be tenacious, but there are clear signs of erosion.

The growing primacy of policy over politics, demonstrable in the redrawing of the public–private boundary in SEEs, may then be of such seminal importance as to warrant reference to a *New* Southern Europe. This would not refer so much to the actual achievement of economic change or 'catch-up', which still remains contestable and varies across the three countries, but to the political prerequisites of such change. More recognizable are the signs of a new Southern Europe in the expanding public consensus over the necessity of somehow rolling back the state, in the growing convergence of Southern European centre-left and centre-right wing parties towards the same principal programmatic blueprints of market-oriented, EU-driven reform, overall in the advancing depoliticization and the growing adherence to the apparent axiom of the desirability of privatization and market liberalization. The striking resemblance of electoral programmes and government policies of social-democratic and conservative/liberal parties in Spain, Portugal and Greece through the 1990s over the reduced role of public sector bears witness to those effects. Even an aggressive ideological redefinition and an embracing of privatization by new socialist governments as a strategy for promoting a socialist agenda of social justice, equality and economic integration is demonstrable as 'the true difference', rather than the size of the public sector, between left and right (Portuguese prime minister, António Guterres, quoted in *Economic Barometer Portugal*,

266 Gibson: Economic Transformation

July 1996). Regardless then of whether these newly acquired political preconditions will in effect lead to the aspired economic catch-up, it remains more important that they finally do carry the solid *potential* of bringing about this *new*, economically transformed Southern Europe. Change is with us, for change is on its way.

Appendix: Major privatizations

Table 7.7 Major privatizations in Spain (1985–97)

Year	Enterprise and holder	Sector	Percentage sold
1985	Textil Tarazona (INI)	Textiles	69.6
1985	Secoinsa (INI)	Electronics	69.1
1985	SKF Española (INI)	Ball-bearing	98.8
1985	Marsans (INI)	Tourism	100
1986	Entursa (INI)	Tourism	100
1986 (in two tranches: 75% in 1986 25% in 1990)	Seat (INI)	Automobile	100
1986	Gesa (INI/Endesa)	Gas/Electricity	39
1988 (in two tranches: 20.4% in 1988 8.7% in 1994)	Endesa (INI)	Electricity	29.2
1988 (in two tranches: 39.3% in 1988 14.5% in 1995)	Ence (INI)	Paper	53.8
1989/96 (in five tranches: 1989/92/93/95/96)	Repsol (INH)	Gas/Oil	79
1989	Astican (INI)	Naval Constructions	90.72
1989 (in two tranches: 85% in 1989 15% in 1992)	Aleinsa (INI)	Equipment	100
1989 (in two tranches: 80% in 1989 20% in 1991)	Enfersa (INI)	Fertilizers	100

Table 7.7 (contd)

Year	Enterprise and holder	Sector	Percentage sold
1989	Oesa (INI)	Grocery	100
1989	Pesa (INI)	Electronics	97.4
1991 (in two tranches: 60% in 1991 40% in 1993)	Enasa (INI)	Automobile	100
1991 (in two tranches: 90% in 1991 10% in 1992)	Gr.Empr. Alvaarez(INI)	Handicrafts	100
1992	Icuatro(INI)	Hospital equipment	90
1993 (in two tranches: 24.99% in 1993 25% in 1996)	Argentaria (Patrimonio del Estado)	Banking	49.99
1993	Automoción 2000 (INI/Teneo)	Automobile	100
1993	Fabrica S. Carlos (INI/Teneo)	Equipment	100
1994	Enagas (INH)	Gas	91
1994	C. Trasatlántica E. (INI/Teneo)	Maritime trans.	100
1994	Artespaña (INI/Teneo)	Handicrafts	100
1994	Sodiga (INI)	Industrial Development	51.2
1995	Telefónica (Patrimonio del Estado) (first tranche)	Telecommunications	10.7
1995	Lesa (Patrimonio del Estado/Tabacalera)	Grocery	100
1997	Telefónica (Patrimonio del Estado) (second tranche)	Telecommunications	21
1997	Repsol (INH)	Gas/Oil	10
1997	Endesa (INI)	Electricity	25
1997	Telefonica International (TISA)	Telecommunications	24

Source: Cuadernos de Información Económica, 119, February 1997; OECD, 1998a.

Table 7.8 Major privatizations in Portugal (1989–97)

Year	Enterprise	Sector	Percentage sold
1989	Banco Totta e Açores (first tranche)	Banking	49
1989	Tranquilidade	Insurance	49
1990	Banco Totta e Açores (second tranche)	Banking	31
1990	Centralcer	Food/beverages	100
1990	Banco Português Atlantico (first tranche)	Banking	33
1991	Banco Espiritu Santo (first tranche)	Banking	40
1991	Banco Fonsecu Burnay	Banking	80
1992	Banco Espiritu Santo (second tranche)	Banking	60
1992	Banco Português Atlantico (second tranche)	Banking	17.6
1992	Petrogal (first tranche)	Oil	25
1992	Imperio	Insurance	100
1992	CPP	Banking	100
1993	União Bancos Português	Banking	61.1
1993	Banco Português Atlantico (third tranche)	Banking	17.5
1994	Banco Português Atlantico (fourth tranche)	Banking	7.5
1994	SECIL (first tranche)	Cement	51
1994	CMP (first tranche)	Cement	80
1994	CIMPOR	Cement	20
1994	BPSM (first tranche)	Banking	80
1994–96	Banco de Fomento e Exterior	Banking	85
1995	Rodoviária Sul do Tejo	Transport	100
1995	Banco Português Atlantico (fifth tranche)	Banking	24.4
1995	BPSM (second tranche)	Banking	20
1995	Rodoviária de Lisboa	Transport	100
1995	SECIL (second tranche)	Cement	7.9
1995	CMP (second tranche)	Cement	20
1995	Portugal Telecom (first tranche)	Telecommunications	27.3
1995	Portucel	Pulp and paper	44.3
1995	Petrogal (second tranche)	Oil	20
1995	SN-Longos	Steel	90
1996	CIMPOR	Cement	45
1996	Portugal Telecom (second tranche)	Telecommunications	22
1996	Banco Totta e Açores (third tranche)	Banking	13
1997	Portugal Telecom (third tranche)	Telecommunications	25.7
1997	EDP	Electricity	30

Source: OECD 1995 and 1998b; Finance Ministry of Portugal.

Table 7.9 Major privatizations in Greece (1990–98)

Year	Enterprise and holder	Sector	Percentage sold
1991	Bank of Piraeus (Commercial Bank)	Banking	66.67
1992	AGET-Heracles (IRO)	Cement	69.8
1992	Athens Bus Company (Government)*	Transport	100
1992/ 1997	Eleusis Shipyards (Commercial Bank)	Shipyard	100
1993	Bank of Athens (National Bank)	Banking	66.67
1993	Hellenic Sugar Industry (Agricultural Bank)	Agro-industry	49
1994	Neorion Shipyards (National Bank and Industrial Development Bank)	Shipyard	100
1995	Hellenic Shipyards (Industrial Development Bank)	Shipyard	49
1996	OTE (Government) (first tranche)	Telecommunications	8
1997	Bank of Attica (Commercial Bank)	Banking	49.5
1997	OTE (Government) (second tranche)	Telecommunications	10
1998	Hellenic Petroleum (Government)	Energy	23
1998	Bank of Crete (Government)	Banking	97
1998	Bank of Central Greece (Agricultural Bank)	Banking	51
1998	Duty Free Shops (Government)	Commercial	20
1998	Athens Stock Exchange	Financial	10
1998	OTE (Government) (third tranche)	Telecommunications	10

* The company was renationalized in 1994.
Source: National Economy Ministry of Greece; IRO and bank sources; OECD, 1998c.

Notes

1. We would like to thank Euclid Tsakalotos of the Athens School of Economics and Business, and Maria Asensio of the Instituto Juan March for comments on an earlier draft.
2. The literature on privatization is very extensive. For comparative analyses of the phenomenon see Glade, 1986; Goodrich, 1990; Gormley, 1991; Kernaghan, 1990; Macavoy, 1989; Ramamurti and Vernon, 1991; Richardson, 1990; Suleiman and Waterbury, 1990; Targetti, 1992; Vickers and Wright, 1989.
3. For basic data the following sources have been used: OECD country surveys for the three countries; *The Economist* and *Financial Times*; particularly useful have been Bermeo, 1990; Maravall, 1991. On Spain, see Fernández, 1989; Cuervo and Fernandez, 1986; de Moral, 1989; de la Dehesa, 1992; Las privatizaciónes en España, 1992, 1993. On Portugal, see Baklanoff, 1986; Corkhill, 1994. On Greece, see Bermeo, 1990; Teitgen-Colly, 1985.
4. All figures in pesetas, escudos or drachmas have been converted into US dollars, based on the mean annual exchange rate as listed on Eurostat/Eurostatistics, various issues.
5. See, Trends in Public Employment, in Commission of the European Communities, 1992, p. 16.
6. The sale of the largest profitable Greek public utility and the predicted compromise on the Macedonia isse were presented as 'a double sell-out' by the New Democracy government to 'foreigners'. See Pagoulatos, 1994.
7. On the constitutional and legal aspects of privatization see Daintith, 1994.
8. The main provisions of the 1988 Law were as follows:

   - a quota of at least 20 per cent of the shares was reserved to be sold to small shareholders and to the workers of the company;
   - no non-public entity could buy more than 10 per cent of the shares to be sold;
   - the amount of shares being acquired by groups of foreign entities could not exceed 10 per cent of the stock to be sold;
   - the receipts of the State from the operation would be allocated to the financial assistance of loss-making public companies and to the repayment of public debt; and
   - buyers of this first sale of shares would have preferential rights on subsequent sales of the remaining equity, to be honoured after the constitutional amendment enabling full privatization.

9. When in opposition PASOK had vigorously campaigned against the New Democracy government's efforts to privatize these two shipyards. Hellenic Shipyards, by far the largest in Greece and one of the largest in the Mediterranean, found no interested investors due to around $300 million in accumulated losses, and was finally rescued in 1995 by an employee buy-out scheme with the participation of state-controlled banks.

Bibliography

Alonso, J. A. (1991) 'La empresa española y los mercados internacionales', *Economía*, vol. 11.

Baklanoff, E. N. (1986) 'The state and economy in Portugal: perspectives on corporatism, revolution, and incipient privatization', in Glade W.P., pp. 257–81.

Bermeo, N. (1990a) 'Public enterprise: some historical and comparative perspectives', *Modern Greek Studies Yearbook*, Vol.6, 1990, University of Minnesota Press.

Bermeo, N. (1990b) 'The politics of public enterprise in Portugal, Spain and Greece', *The Political Economy of Public Sector Reform and Privatization*, in Suleiman, E. and Waterbury, J. (eds), pp. 137–62.

Bresser Pereira, L. C. (1993) 'Economic reforms and economic growth: efficiency and politics in Latin America', in Bresser Pereira, L. C., Maravall, J.-M. and Przeworski, A. (eds), *Economic Reforms in New Democracies: A Social-Democratic Approach*, Cambridge University Press, Cambridge.

Clarke, T. (ed.) (1994) *International Privatisation: Strategies and Practices*, de Gruyter, Berlin.

Commission of the European Communities, Directorate-General for Economic and Financial Affairs (1992) *Country Studies: Greece*.

Cool, K., Neven, D. J. and Walter, I. (eds) (1993) *'European Industrial Restructuring in the 1990s*, Macmillan, London.

Corkhill, D. (1994) 'Privatization in Portugal', in Wright, V. (ed.), *Industrial Privatization in Western Europe*, Pinter Publishers, London.

Cuervo, A. and Fernández, Z. (1986) 'Una nueva estrategia para el sector público empresarial: privatización', *Privatización de la Empresa Pública*, Colegio de Economistas, Madrid, pp. 17–22.

Daintith, T. (1994) 'The legal techniques of privatisation', in Clarke, T. (ed.).

de la Dehesa, G. (1992) 'Privatización Europea: el caso de España', *Información Comercial Española*, no. 707, pp. 55–71.

de la Dehesa, G. (1994) 'Spain', in Williamson, J. (ed.), *The Political Economy of Policy Reform*, Institute for International Economics, Washington, DC.

de Moral, J. (1989) 'El proceso de Reprivatización del Grupo Rumasa', *Papeles de Economía Española*, 38.

Dermine, J. (1990) *European Banking in the 1990s*, Basil Blackwell, Oxford.

Diamandouros, P. N. (1994) 'Cultural dualism and political change in postauthoritarian Greece', Centro de Estudios Avanzados en Ciencias Sociales of the Instituto Juan March de Estudios e Investigaciones, Madrid, Working Paper 1994/50.

Dunning, J. H., Kogut, B. and Blomström, M. (1990) *Globalization of Firms and the competitiveness of Nations*, Lund University Press, Lund.

Feigenbaum, H. (1992) 'Public enterprise in comparative perspective', *Comparative Politics*, 15, pp. 101–22.

Fernández, Z. (1989) 'Alcance del proceso privatizador en España', *Papeles de Economía Española*, 38.

Ferri, P. (ed.) (1990) *Prospects for the European Monetary System*, Macmillan, London.

Fraser, R. (ed.) (1988) *Privatization: the UK Experience and International Trends*, Longman, London.

Georgakopoulos, T., Prodromidis, K. and Loizides, J. L. (1987) 'Public Enterprises in Greece', *Annales de l'Economie Publique, Sociale et Cooperative*, vol. 75, no. 4, pp. 351–67.

Gibson, H. and Tsakalotos, E. (eds) (1992) *Economic Integration and Financial Liberalization: Prospects for Southern Europe*, Macmillan, London.

Glade, W. P. (ed.) (1986) *State Shrinking: A Comparative Inquiry into Privatization*, Institute of Latin American Studies, Austin, TX.

Goodrich, J. N. (1990) *Privatization and Deregulation in Global Perspective*, Pinter Publishers, London.

Gormley, W. T. (1991) *Privatization and its Alternatives*, University of Wisconsin Press, Madison.

Gortsos, C. (1992) *The Greek Banking System*, Hellenic Banks Association, Athens.

Hayward, J. (1995) *Industrial Enterprise and European Integration: From National to International Champions in Western Europe*, Oxford University Press, Oxford.

Heath, J. (1990) *Public Enterprise at the Crossroads*, Routledge, London.

Kazakos, P. (1993) 'O rythmistikos rolos tou kratous stin economia: Provlimata kai prooptikes tis politikis apokratikopoieseon stin Ellada' [The regulatory role of the state in the economy: problems and perspectives of the privatization policy in Greece], in Tsoukalis, L. (ed.), *I Ellada stin Evropaiki Koinotita: I Proklisi tis prosarmogis* [Greece in the EC: The Challenge of Adjustment], Papazissis, Athens.

Kernaghan, K. (ed.) (1990) 'Symposium on the progress, benefits and costs of privatization', *International Review of Administrative Sciences*, vol. 56, no. 1, pp. 5–147.

Lancaster, T. (1985) 'Spanish public policy and financial power', in Lancaster, T. and Prevost, G. (eds), *Politics and Change in Spain*, Praeger, New York.

Larre, B. and Torres, R. (1991) 'Is convergence a spontaneous process? The experience of Spain, Portugal and Greece', *OECD Economic Studies*, no. 16.

Las privatizaciónes en España (1992) in *Información Comercial Española*, 707, pp. 55–71.

Las privatizaciónes en España (1993) *Informe Mensual*, Madrid, La Caixa, Servicio de Estudios, pp. 56–62.

Lioukas, S. (1993) 'Privatisation in Greece' in Ramanadham V. V. (ed.), *Privatisation: A Global Perspective*, Routledge, London.

Macavoy P. W. *et al.* (1989) *Privatization and State-Owned Enterprises*, Kluwer Academic Publishers, London.

Maravall, J.-M. (1991a) 'Economic reforms in new democracies: the Southern European experience', Juan March Institute, Working Paper no. 22.

Maravall, J.-M. (1991b) 'The politics of economic reforms: the Southern European experience', *Occasional papers*, University of Chicago, Department of Political Science, No. 2, November.

Martín Aceña, P. and Comín, G. (1991) *50 años de industrialización en España*, Ed. Espasa Calpe, Madrid.

Martins, M. B. and Rosa, J. C. (1979) *O Grupo Estado*, Edições do Jornal Expresso, Lisboa.

Niarchos, N. (1995) 'O rolos tou Chrimatistiriou' [The role of the Stock Exchange]', *Epilogi*, Special Annual Issue.

OECD (1986) Economic Surveys, *Greece*, 1985–86, OECD, Paris.

OECD (1988a) Economic Surveys, *Portugal*, 1987–88, OECD, Paris.

OECD (1988b) Economic Surveys, *Spain*, 1987–88, OECD, Paris.

OECD (1990) Economic Surveys, *Greece*, 1989–90, OECD, Paris.

OECD (1992) Economic Surveys, *Greece*, 1991–92, OECD, Paris.

OECD (1993a) Economic Surveys, *Spain*, OECD, Paris.

OECD (1993b) Economic Surveys, *Greece*, OECD, Paris.

OECD (1995) Economic Surveys, *Portugal*, OECD, Paris.

OECD (1996a) Economic Surveys, *Spain*, 1996, OECD, Paris.

OECD (1996b) *Privatisation in Asia, Europe and Latin America*, OECD, Paris.

OECD (1998a) Economic Surveys, *Spain*, OECD, Paris.

OECD (1998b) Economic Surveys, *Portugal*, OECD, Paris.

OECD (1998c) Economic Surveys, *Greece*, OECD, Paris.

Pagoulatos, G. (1994) 'The press and politics of denationalization in greece: from knee-jerk reaction to agenda-setting opposition', paper to the London School of Economics conference *Greece: Prospects for Modernisation*, London, 17–19 November 1994.

Pagoulatos G. (1996) 'Governing in a constrained environment: policy making in the Greek banking deregulation and privatisation reform', *West European Politics*, vol. 19, no. 4, pp. 744–69.

Provopoulos, G. (1985) *O Dimosios Tomeas stin Elliniki Oikonomia* [Public sector in the Greek Economy], IOBE, Athens.

Ramamurti, R. and Vernon, R. (eds) (1991) *Privatization and Control of State-Owned Enterprises*, World Bank, Washington.

Richardson, J. J. (ed.) (1990) *Privatization and Deregulation in Canada and Britain*, Dartmouth Publishing Company, Aldershot.

Rodríguez-Arana, J. (1991) *La Privatización de la Empresa Publica*, Ed. Espasa Calpe, Madrid.

Sachwald, F. (ed.) (1993) *L'Europe et la Globalisation: Asquisitions et accords dans l'industrie*, Masson, Paris.

Silvestre, J. (1988) 'Notes on the Spanish public firms under the Socialist administration, 1982–87', unpublished paper.

Stournaras, Y. (1990) 'Public sector debt and deficits in Greece: the experience of the 1980s and future prospects', *Rivista di Politica Economica*, vol. 80, no. (7–8), July–August, pp. 405–40.

Suleiman, E. N. and Waterbury, J. (eds) (1990) *The Political Economy of Public Sector Reform and Privatization*, Westview Press, Boulder, Co.

Targetti, F. (1992) *Privatization in Europe: West and East Experiences*, Dartmouth, Aldershot.

Teitgen-Colly, C. (1985) 'Grèce', in Timsit, G. (ed.), *Les entreprises du secteur public dans les pays de la Communauté Européenne*, Bruylant, Bruxelles, pp. 179–235.

Torres, F. (1994) 'Portugal', in Williamson, J. (ed.) *The Political Economy of Policy Reform*, Institute for International Economics, Washington, DC.

Vickers, J. and Wright, V. (eds) (1989) *The Politics of Privatization*, Frank Cass, London.

Wright, V. (1995) 'The industrial privatization programmes of Britain and France: the impact of political and institutional factors', in Jones, P. (ed.), *Party, Parliament and Personality*, Routledge, London.

8
The Changing Role of Finance in Southern European Economies: Will There be an Improvement in Economic Performance?

Heather D. Gibson, Yiannis Stournaras and Euclid Tsakalotos[1]

The financial sector in any economy is crucial to the health of the whole economy. Financial intermediaries and markets act to bring together those who wish to save with those who wish to invest. Savers usually want immediate access to their funds, they often require some certainty about the return and they may wish to save in small amounts. Investors, by contrast, require long-term loans, often in large amounts for projects which may have uncertain returns. The raison d'être of financial intermediaries is that they act to satisfy both savers and investors. As such, changes that take place in the financial sector are important not only in and of themselves but also because they affect the potential performance of the economy as a whole and the real economy in particular.

The four Southern European economies experienced rapid change within their financial systems in the 1980s and this continued throughout the 1990s. For these economies, being as they are relatively less developed and with lower standards of living than the core EU economies, such changes play a crucial role in determining their economic performance and in particular the likelihood of their catching up their more developed EU partners. In this chapter we analyse the prospects for these economies in the light of the rapid change experienced and we ask whether the changes warrant the countries being known as the 'New Southern Europe'. The main thrust of the argument is as follows. It is clearly the case that reform of the financial sectors of these countries was well overdue and the direction of the reforms undertaken is likely to increase the operational efficiency of the financial sectors as well as giving consumers more choice. Indeed, there is already evidence that this is the case. However, we argue that the specific reforms introduced might not be without their own set of problems. In particular, we argue that the reforms should in the future focus more on the creation of financial institutions to aid development rather than on the development of financial markets.

The chapter is organized into three main sections. In the first section we examine the changes that have been taking place in all four Southern European economies. We note in particular that the general trend has been towards less government intervention in finance. In the second section, we discuss the rationale for these changes. In particular, we note that many of the changes can be seen as part of the political strategy for greater integration within the EU. We also point to the economic arguments put forward by the proponents of the changes. Finally, in the third section, we discuss the prospects for the future. We address some potential consequences of these changes and discuss whether they may bring about some problems for these economies in the future.

The financial sectors in Southern European economies

Until the beginning of the 1980s, a major characteristic of all four countries was the high degree of control exercised by the government over the

Table 8.1   Characteristics of Southern European financial systems (pre-liberalization)

Characteristic	Southern Europe	UK
Degree of concentration in banking	high except Italy	high, but banks have many competitors because of free access to offshore markets
Existence of non-bank financial markets	limited	well-developed stock markets/futures markets/ government debt markets, etc
Interest rates (real) – levels	largely negative	positive (except mid-1970s)
– degree of government control	high (wide range of interest rates for different deposits/loans)	none, except general level for monetary control
Forced financing of government deficits through reserve holdings	yes	no
Role of government in credit allocation	large via specialized credit institutions and controls on bank loans	none (except ceilings on total volume of lending until 1981)
Controls on capital movements	yes	removed in Oct. 1979

financial sectors. This was true both in the domestic role played by banks and other financial intermediaries and in their external relationships. Table 8.1 provides a summary of some of the characteristics of the financial sectors of Southern European countries relative to the UK, the latter having been chosen as an example of a country with a highly developed financial sector. Regulations in Southern European countries covered areas such as interest rates, reserve requirements, the allocation of credit and capital movements. The changes that occurred during the 1980s can be characterized as a move towards more liberalized and market-determined financial systems, both domestically and externally.

Domestic financial liberalization[2]

Domestic liberalization began first in Spain in the mid-1970s. It was halted somewhat in the period 1979 to 1983 as a result of a severe banking crisis, which reduced the number of banks by one-half. In Italy, liberalization began at the beginning of the 1980s when a number of reforms to the operation of monetary policy occurred, such as the granting of some limited independence to the central bank from the Treasury.[3] Changes to the financial system here were encouraged by growing financial integration with the rest of the EU via membership of the Exchange Rate Mechanism (ERM) of the European Monetary System (EMS). It is important to note that Italy was the only Southern European country in the ERM throughout the 1980s. However, it did maintain controls on capital movements until the late 1980s thus largely insulating it from financial changes elsewhere in the EU. In Portugal and Greece, liberalization did not get under way until the mid-1980s. In Portugal the financial sector remained largely nationalized up until 1984. In Greece, although some tentative reforms occurred in the early 1980s (for example, the number of interest rates was reduced from 14 to 5), liberalization did not begin systematically until after 1985. The liberalization process in each country involved a number of areas including: entry regulations; interest rate levels; reserve requirements and the development of markets in government debt; and credit allocation programmes. We address each in turn in the following paragraphs.

In all the countries except Italy, there is a high degree of concentration in the banking system as Table 8.2 shows. These figures provide only a snap-shot picture of concentration in Southern European banking and as such do not offer any information about changes that may have been occurring in the 1980s and 1990s. However, while some liberalization with respect to entry laws has been undertaken in all countries, the level of concentration has not changed dramatically.[4] Indeed, changes to entry structure usually only operate slowly on existing levels of concentration.

Liberalization of entry regulations took the form of allowing foreign banks to enter the markets in all four countries. In addition, private banks were encouraged to set up particularly in Portugal and Greece. These banks

Table 8.2 Concentration levels in Southern European banking

Country	Date	Level of concentration
Spain	end-1986	7 largest banking groups had more than 80% of total assets (OECD, *Economic Survey*, 1988, p. 50).
Italy	1980	14 largest banks had 40% of total banking activity (OECD, *Economic Survey*, 1987, p. 45).
Greece	1989	2 largest banks had 74.5% of bank credits (Katseli, 1990, p. 39).
Portugal	pre-1984	8 largest banks dominated bank ing activity (Braga de Macedo, 1990c, p. 328).

play a small, but increasing, role in the means of payments systems and the allocation of credit and are important in providing a competitive fringe even if banking systems remain dominated by a few large banks. We discuss the likely future changes in structure in the four countries in the third section of this chapter.

An important part of the liberalization process involved an attempt to raise the *level* of real interest rates. During the 1960s and 1970s, low nominal interest rates to encourage investment meant that real deposit interest rates were on the whole negative or only slightly positive. This situation was reinforced in the 1970s when inflation was also high. The attempt to raise real interest rates during the 1980s was largely successful – real rates turned positive in Italy, Spain and Portugal in the early 1980s and in Greece in 1986.

The requirement that commercial banks hold a certain proportion of their assets with the central bank (that is, reserve requirements) is a common feature of most EU countries. In Southern European countries reserve requirements were, and in the case of Greece still are, much larger than elsewhere in the EU. The importance of these reserves lay not only in the conduct of monetary policy (and the control of credit creation), but also in their role in financing large government budget deficits. Reserve requirements operate as an implicit tax on the banking system and are particularly important in countries where tax systems are underdeveloped or where there is only a thin Treasury bill market. Reductions in reserve requirements in the 1980s were limited in all countries. Instead, liberalization measures focused on attempts to develop markets for government securities. In Italy, the market for government debt started to grow rapidly from as early as 1975. This resulted in part from the favourable tax treatment given to Treasury bills (the interest was tax exempt) and in part from the ceilings on bank lending to the private sector.[5] In Spain, the market for Treasury bills has grown rapidly since 1984 when the government began to pay market interest rates on its debt. As a result, in March 1990, Spain was able to abolish the 17 per cent compulsory reserve requirement and replace it with a 5 per cent cash reserve ratio (a figure more in line with the EU average). In Greece and Portugal, by contrast, markets in government debt were still rather young at the beginning of the 1990s with the consequence that markets were thin and the range of maturities limited. Given the public deficit problems that these countries had, a major programme in the 1990s was the continued development of markets for various kinds of government debt, something that has been successfully achieved. These developments along with the adoption of more market-oriented monetary policies facilitated the phasing out of reserve requirements. With the introduction of the Euro and the formation of the Euro area, Italy, Spain and Portugal (all among the first wave of participants) reduced reserve requirements to levels consistent with other EU countries.[6] Greece still maintains reserve requirements at 12 per cent, for reasons of monetary control (seeking to reduce the structural surplus in the domestic money market, which has arisen from large capital inflows).

The final area of government intervention in banking in Southern European countries was through credit allocation programmes. In general, the requirement that banks hold government debt or reserve requirements is only one part of the control that can be exercised by the authorities over the allocation of credit. Government control over credit allocation can take a number of forms (World Bank, 1989, p. 56): control over the quantity of credit allocated to different sectors; control over the price of that credit; government guarantees; and the establishment of special credit institutions designed to serve the financing needs of certain sectors that are seen as critical to the country's development. In Southern European countries, controls of these type were very common and hence much of the liberalization programme was directed at reducing government control in this area.

In Spain, credit was allocated to specific sectors, often at subsidized interest rates, via official credit institutions and government intermediaries. These loans were financed largely through compulsory holdings of government securities by commercial banks. Commercial banks, themselves, also faced controls on their allocation of credit. These had all been phased out by the end of the 1980s (Caminal *et al.*, 1990, p. 267).

In Italy, there are two main types of banks – commercial banks and the Specialized Credit Institutions (SCIs) and, at least in the past, the distinction between them was strong. The former took in deposits and specialize in short-term lending. The latter were the main channel through which subsidized credit to selected sectors was allocated. The SCIs specialized in the provision of medium to long-term credit to agriculture, industry, and construction projects and, in addition, they were responsible for the allocation of large amounts of credit to the poorer regions of southern Italy. Their source of funds came mainly from the issuing of long-term bonds which commercial banks were required to hold. Between 1973 and 1978, often as much as 40 per cent of the increase in deposits held by banks were used to purchase long-term bonds issued by SCIs. In 1978 the amount was lowered to around 6 to 8 per cent and in 1983 to 4 per cent and thus the role of the SCIs as providers of finance fell. Further measures taken in 1987 freed lending by banks for periods of 18 months or more and reduced significantly the degree of bank specialization. This trend continued into the 1990s.[7]

Before 1975, in Portugal banks had traditionally been tied to the large (family owned) industrial conglomerates which characterized the country. In 1975, when the banks were nationalized, it was relatively simple to continue close links with industry (especially as these large industries were also nationalized). Credit allocation policies thus were organized through the nationalized commercial banking sector (Braga de Macedo, 1990c, p. 329). Throughout the 1980s the importance of selected credit allocation to the private sector declined. This, however, was a result of the growing public sector deficit and the need for the banking sector to finance it, rather than a conscious effort to allow banks greater freedom in their allocation of credit (Borges, 1990, pp. 213–14). The development of a deep government bond market was thus a priority of the reform process.

Finally, credit allocation in Greece followed a similar pattern. Government control over credit occurred both through SCIs (which offer loans both to agriculture and construction projects) and through commercial banks. Around 75 per cent of banks' portfolios were constrained, directed towards the public sector, long-term investment for industry and handicrafts and also support for ailing firms (OECD, *Economic Survey*, 1986, p. 52). Liberalization throughout the second half of the 1980s reduced the controls on interest rates and on portfolio allocation.[8] In particular, the role of SCIs declined (with a fall in the subsidies and the special status they enjoyed) and the obligatory investment ratio through which bank loans were directed to certain sectors was phased out in mid-1993 (OECD, *Economic Survey*, 1991; 1992).

To sum up, the pattern in all Southern European countries appears to be rather similar. Prior to the 1980s, all four financial sectors were subject to much government control, particularly over the allocation of credit and its price. Attempts were made in the 1980s to liberalize and indeed liberalization did proceed in all countries. The process proceeded more quickly in Spain and Italy than in Greece and Portugal. Nonetheless, in all countries, financial institutions were largely free of government controls of the type discussed above by the mid 1990s.

The development of financial markets[9]

If the 1980s saw much of the deregulation of domestic financial *institutions* and their activities, then the 1990s were characterized by the liberalization

of financial *markets*. We have already discussed above the process undertaken to develop markets in government debt. In addition, Southern European countries have been keen to develop stock markets and markets in
marketable debt instruments such as commercial paper and certificates of
deposit. The motives for this development are numerous and complex. For
instance, the development of stock markets has been a necessary accompa-
niment to the privatization programmes that became more common in the
late 1980s and 1990s.[10] More generally, the emergence of financial markets
reflects attempts by Southern European governments to promote greater
competition, thereby improving and increasing the choice of finance available to industry. To this end, Greece, Italy, Portugal and Spain have been
introducing substantial reforms to their stock markets. By and large, pre-
reform, financial markets in these countries had a number of common
characteristics. Where they existed, they were narrow and trading was thin.
The number of companies listed on the stock exchange, for example, was
small and overall capitalization low compared to other OECD countries.
Legislation protecting small investors was poor and trading often occurred
off-market at individually negotiated prices with the result that few individuals were encouraged to invest. At the same time, there was little incentive for firms to seek quotations on the stock market and many small/
medium-sized firms were reluctant to give up control.

Reforms have focused on increasing the efficiency and transparency of
stock markets (and capital markets more generally). Computer trading and
quoting, better methods of settlement and stricter controls on insider trading were all introduced. The creation of new financial institutions such as
investment funds and mutual funds, which operate in these markets, were
encouraged.[11] More specifically, in Spain, a Law passed in 1988 involved
the linking of quotations in the three major exchanges in Madrid,
Barcelona and Bilbao (from April 1989) and allowed a greater number of
institutions and individuals to operate within the market. Both these
changes aimed at increasing the number of transactions within the market
thereby improving its efficiency.

In Greece, too, the goal has been to increase the volume of transactions.
A greater role for the stock market has been sought by widening access
to the market. Thus mutual funds and insurance companies were given
permission to invest in existing shares without Bank of Greece approval
(previously they had only been allowed to invest in new issues); and commercial banks were allowed to undertake new share issues/bond issues
without Bank of Greece approval. Additionally, the efficiency and transparency of the market was enhanced by the introduction of screen-based
trading (1992), dematerialization of shares (1997) and various measures to
improve the stability of brokers operating on the exchange (1997).

Similar moves were undertaken in Portugal in the early 1990s: in 1991, for
example, the exchanges in Lisbon and Oporto were unified, and continuous

trading was introduced; and in 1992 a centralized delivery and settlement system came into operation. These reforms have helped the recovery of the Portuguese stock market for the first time since 1976 when the various regional markets were closed.

Finally, in Italy, legislation concerning the stock market in 1991 and 1992 completely reformed the legal framework in which the stock market operates. Firms explicitly designed for securities investment (SIMs) were introduced and, along with banks, have the right to trade in organized security markets. Regulations protecting small investors were laid down (for example, all trading now has to occur in the regulated market) along with controls on insider trading and procedures for takeover bids. The establishment of new investment funds was permitted in 1992 and closed-end funds in 1993. Reforms continued into the later 1990s.

Clearly at this stage in these reforms, it is difficult to draw any concrete conclusions with respect to the impact of these changes on company borrowing. Traditionally, as we indicated above, banks played a significant role in the provision of investment finance through their administration of government credit allocation programmes. The reforms, with their emphasis on the development of financial markets, may indicate that the importance of banks will decline slightly. Indeed, there are already indications in this direction. In Spain where the development of markets has proceeded quite rapidly, a growing commercial paper market which began in the 1980s has been providing companies with a new source of funds. Banks, in turn, have been becoming more involved in off-balance sheet finance.[12] Similar changes are evident in Portugal in the mid-to-late 1980s (OECD, *Economic Survey*, 1989, p. 72). Finally, for Greece, such trends have become more evident in the late 1990s (OECD, *Economic Survey*, 1998, p. 85). The changes are also being affected by developments at the EU level and it is to these that we now turn.

External liberalization and developments within the EU

Alongside the domestically induced changes taking place in the financial systems of Southern European countries, there has been pressure for change stemming from the moves towards greater financial integration at the European level. For our purposes here, there are two specific EU policies that can be mentioned. The first involves the removal of controls on capital movements. Capital movements can take a number of forms. Long-term capital flows (that is, flows of greater than one year) comprise, among others, foreign direct investment (FDI) and portfolio investment (that is, investment in overseas securities). The former have been liberalized in Southern Europe for some time. The latter were liberalized during the 1980s and early 1990s. Short-term capital flows involve investment in assets with less than one year to maturity (for example, short-term Treasury bills, short-term bank deposits). These flows are usually the last to be liberalized.[13]

It was agreed at an EU Council Meeting in 1988 that all controls on capital flows be removed by July 1990. Of the Southern European countries, this deadline applied only to Italy, which had been a member of the Exchange Rate Mechanism (of the EMS) from its inception in 1979, although it subsequently left in 1992 along with the UK. Italy largely liberalized capital movements at the beginning of 1987. By 1988, the other three countries were still outside of the ERM and thus were given extensions to the deadline.[14] Spain was given until the end of 1992 and Greece and Portugal until end-1995. Spain had removed all controls by mid-1992 but reimposed them briefly during the turmoil within the ERM in September 1992. Greece and Portugal both continued loosening their controls – for example in 1991, Greece liberalized outward investment in securities and real estate and in 1994 the remaining controls on short-term capital flows were phased out.

The second EU initiative is the Second Banking Directive which came into force at the end of 1992. It was concerned with bank access to foreign markets and enshrines two main principles. The first is *mutual recognition*: if an EU bank gains a licence in one EU country, then it has the right to operate in all EU countries and to undertake activities in those countries which are allowable under the rules of the licensing authority. The second principle is *home country control*, which states that the licensing authority will be responsible for supervision of banks to whom it has granted licences. Thus, in essence, the Directive allows a bank, once it has a licence from its home country, to undertake activities in any EU country, irrespective of the regulations in the host country.[15]

The Second Banking Directive has implications for two main areas of banking activity – retail banking and investment banking.[16] We discuss the implications for retail banking in some detail below. With respect to investment banking, Walter and Smith (1990, p. 106) believe that the 1992 initiatives will 'eventually lead to a substantial reordering of the investment banking business in Europe'. In particular, they argue that greater competition between banks for corporate customers will lead to an increased use of securities markets (both debt and equity securities) by European companies; an increased role for mergers and acquisitions and in particular hostile takeovers; and growing connections between securities markets, which will increase their depth and attractiveness as a means of raising external finance. They base their arguments on changes in corporate finance that were occurring in the boom years of the mid to late 1980s. Here we can note a few examples. First, companies in Germany, Italy, France and Spain made increasing use of debt securities to finance investment – traditional bank loans became less important and, as noted above, this trend can also be found in Portugal and Greece. Secondly, mergers and acquisitions in Continental Europe have increased (see Walter and Smith, 1990, Table 4.7, p. 121) partly in response to the restructuring of EU industry in the run up to 1992 and the Single Economic Market. Finally, they note that there was an emergence of opposed takeovers bids (that is, hostile bids) within Continental European countries. The significance of this is that traditionally hostile takeovers as a means of promoting corporate efficiency are a feature of Anglo-Saxon financial systems rather than continental systems.

Indeed, in general, the reforms of financial markets, discussed above, were aimed at increasing the choice of funding opportunities available to firms thus helping to promote a move away from financing via internal funds and banks. Thus, stock market reforms, for example, sought to make it more attractive for firms to raise funds on the stock exchange and for investors to demand shares either directly or via new financial institutions (investment funds, mutual funds, etc).

Evidence that the EU is perhaps moving towards a more market-oriented approach to corporate finance is also evident in Commission activity. Franks and Mayer (1990) point to regulatory changes, which seem to be aimed at extending the UK type system of takeovers to the rest of the EU. In particular, regulations concerning disclosure of share interests, equal treatment of shareholders, requirements to make full bids once certain shareholdings have been exceeded and timetables for bids have all been introduced. The implications of these changes and the potential dangers of moving towards a more Anglo-Saxon style of corporate finance are taken up in the third section.

The rationale for domestic and external liberalization

We have argued above that Southern European economies have been going through numerous changes to their financial systems, within a relatively short space of time. It is certainly true to say that the financial systems of all four countries bear little resemblance today to their pre-liberalization state. In this sense, we can certainly speak of a 'New Southern Europe' in the financial sector. However, it is also important to examine the rationale for these changes, not least to enable us to assess the future prospects (more broadly defined) for these countries in the final section of the chapter. Thus in this section, we do not offer a critique of the stated rationales – that assessment will come later.

At a rather general level, an important political economy rationale for the changes comes both from growing interdependence within the world economy and the moves toward greater EU integration. Increased interdependence within the world economy has in part come about due to the growth of offshore banking markets and the associated increase in capital mobility.[17] These developments have made it increasingly difficult for countries to undertake independent policies. Growing pressures for EU integration have partly been a response to this increased interdependence: one of the aims of integration has been to make the EU a much larger and hence more effective economic force within the world economy. Part of the EU programme of integration has involved greater financial integration. Hence changes to the financial systems of Southern European countries can be seen as a response to their desire to participate fully in the wider process of European economic and political integration.

At the level of economic theory, we can be more specific on the perceived advantages of these changes. We focus first on the rationale for the changes taking place domestically, before examining the EU changes and their impact.

The rationale for the removal of constraints on the domestic financial sector was put forward by McKinnon (1973), Shaw (1973) and, more recently, by the World Bank (1989).[18] They argue that controls on interest rates (for example, interest rate ceilings imposed by the government), the allocation of credit and other aspects of financial repression all operate to reduce the operational and allocational efficiency of the financial sector and hence the growth of the economy. In a financially repressed economy, savings are kept artificially low (as a result of low interest rates on deposits). Low loan rates encourage a large amount of investment demand. However, with low savings, not all that investment demand can be met and hence credit rationing is common. That is, investment is quantitatively constrained by the low level of savings.[19] Liberalization, in the form of a loosening of the interest rate ceiling, raises real deposit interest rates. This causes more savings to be forthcoming thus allowing investment to increase, which in turn improves the economy's growth performance.

In addition to this quantitative effect of liberalization on investment, McKinnon and Shaw both argue that liberalization will also lead to investment of a better quality being undertaken. When the economy is characterized by credit rationing (that is, when low savings constrain investment), those investment projects that are financed tend to have rates of return which are just above the government imposed interest rate ceiling. The justification for this in the literature appears to be that banks prefer to give the available funds to less risky projects. Projects with greater expected returns have higher risks and the ceiling prevents banks from charging a risk premium to compensate them for the extra risk. Thus in the preliberalization period, a large part of the unsatisfied investment demand is likely to include projects which are potentially more profitable, but did not receive funding because of their larger risk. Removing the ceiling on interest rates thus not only increases the quantity of investment, but also allows some of these more profitable investments to be undertaken. Growth in thus further boosted.

Thus the rapid change in the degree of government intervention in financial markets that we outlined in the first section of this chapter should, if we accept the McKinnon–Shaw theory, lead to improved growth prospects for Southern European economies. But additionally, there is also a number of arguments that suggest that EU pressures for external liberalization of financial markets should reinforce this conclusion. In particular, the EU Commission argued that the creation of a European financial area, through both the liberalization of capital movements and the Second Banking Directive, should lead to significant welfare gains – both the allocative and technical (or operational) efficiency of the financial sector should improve.

With respect to allocative efficiency, there are the traditional gains from trade arguments associated with EU integration. Krugman (1987) argues that the gains in financial markets can be seen to arise from both inter-industry type and intra-industry type gains. The inter-industry gains arising from free capital movements take the form of allowing countries to decide whether to consume now (in which case a capital inflow is required) or later (leading to a capital outflow). The intra-industry gains, which Krugman argues are likely to be more important, are the result of two-way flows of capital – enabling countries to specialize in the type of financial services they provide and allowing individuals to diversify their portfolios. Free capital movements thus allow an optimal allocation of resources.

The gains from increased operational efficiency were investigated by a study conducted by Price Waterhouse (1988). This indicated that the welfare gains from 1992 in the financial sector may be as large as 1.5 per cent of EU GDP. The gains, which are shown in Table 8.3, arise from the increase in competition that Price Waterhouse argued would occur as a result of the Directive. They calculated the prices of financial services in a number of EU countries. The large price dispersion they found was then attributed to a lack of competition with the result that increased competition post-1992, would ensure that price in each EU country would converge on the average of the four cheapest.[20] Expected average price reductions are quite large, particularly in Spain and to a lesser extent in Italy. Greece and Portugal were not included in the study, but there is little reason to doubt that, using the same methodology, there would be similar gains for these countries.

Allocative and operational efficiency should also be encouraged if the developments envisaged by Walter and Smith (1990, see above discussion), particularly in the area of mergers and acquisitions, are encouraged. The market for corporate control operates, via mergers and acquisitions, to ensure that management of companies make the best possible use of the resources that they control. Managements which are believed to be underperforming or investing in areas where the returns are not as high as they could be will experience falling share prices. This makes them vulnerable to a takeover (see Jensen, 1984). Thus the more market-oriented approach which, as we argued in the first section, may be evident in the Commission's activity aims at improving company performance by 'keeping management on their toes'.

Table 8.3   Price Waterhouse: gains from 1992 in the financial sector
(a) *Proposed price reductions*

	Belg	Ger	Spa	Fra	Ita	Neth	UK
Banking	8.0	13.0	20.0	13.0	9.0	5.0	9.0
Insurance	16.0	5.0	19.0	12.0	26.0	0.5	2.0
Securities	26.0	6.0	26.0	12.0	17.0	9.0	6.0
Financial Services (Average)	11.0	10.0	21.0	12.0	14.0	4.0	7.0

Belg = Belgium; Ger = Germany; Spa = Spain; Fra = France; Ita = Italy; Neth = Netherlands.

(b) *Estimated gain in consumer surplus**
(millions of ECUs)

Belgium	685
Denmark	4619
Spain	3189
France	3683
Italy	3996
Netherlands	347
UK	5051
Average gain (% of GDP)	1.5%

*This gain results from price falls in the three areas of banking, insurance and securities and are calculated on the basis of the weighted averages in part (a).
Source: Price Waterhouse (1988).

To sum up, the EU Commission has tended to treat financial markets much as it sees the markets for goods and other services. Since the 1992 changes were aimed at increasing competitive pressures within the EU, it was concluded that this would generate large welfare gains for consumers. Similar argument are also being voiced following the creation of the Euro area. These gains, in combination with the gains resulting from domestic liberalization of interest rates and credit allocation, lead to the conclusion that Southern Europe should be doing very well out of European integration. Whether such optimism is warranted is the issue we take up next.

Prospects for the future

The prospects for Southern European countries into the twenty-first century clearly depend on the appropriateness of the above reforms and the economic arguments put forward in their favour. For if we are able to talk of a 'New Southern Europe' not just in the financial sector, but also more generally in terms of the economic performance of these countries, then the financial reforms must have a successful impact on the real economy.

Thus, in this section, we discuss the likely success of the programmes of reform and also indicate potential problems that may arise. In particular, we focus on a number of criticisms that can be made of the rationale for the type of change undertaken in Southern European countries. Additionally, we examine the related aspect of whether the interests of the real economies of Southern European countries are best served merely by the promotion of financial *markets* or whether the focus of reform should not also be on the building of appropriate *institutions* for economic convergence.

The reforms to the financial sector in Greece, Italy, Portugal and Spain have all been successful in aiding the path of economic reform within these economies and also in furthering their integration into the EU – this is particularly the case for Greece, Portugal and Spain who joined the EU only in the 1980s. Additionally, greater competition within the financial sectors has been making financial institutions more responsive to the needs of their customers: there is now greater technical or operational efficiency, although the actual size of the gains is often difficult to estimate. However, there appear to be several issues that are raised by the form of the reforms. First, there is the question of the extent to which the Second Banking Directive and preparations for the formation of the Euro area led to structural change within the banking sector. In particular, is there any evidence that Southern European economies have been facing a major period of restructuring in the provision of banking services? If so, then this restructuring needs careful management in order to avoid financial instability. The second issue is the impact of liberalization on the real economies. In particular, we question whether a liberalized banking system can meet the needs of the real economy – there are good reasons in economic theory for thinking that certain sectors may not get access to funds, that is, credit rationing persists even in liberalized banking markets. Finally, we address the tendency towards the development of financial markets in Southern European countries, and we ask whether such moves are indeed conducive to economic growth.

Structural changes in European banking

The Commission's view that increased European financial integration is leading to large gains in welfare presumably rests on the assumption that entry or, at least, the threat of entry stemming from the changes implied by the Second Banking Directive and the formation of the Euro area are inducing banks to greater efficiency. The implications for structural changes within European banking are ambiguous – whether structural changes occur presumably depends on the capacity of existing banks to respond to greater competition.

There are a number of authors[21] who are highly critical of the Commission's view. They argue that retail banking is inherently imperfectly competitive and that as a result EU reforms are not resulting in any great increase in competition. This, in turn, suggests that there are few efficiency gains and hence little rationale for any structural changes. Their argument rests on two main points. First, banking is characterized by important entry barriers.[22] Second, there are large switching costs of moving from one bank to another. These lower the incentives for customers to switch to banks that are offering a more efficient service. Consequently, banks have little incentive to improve their efficiency and hence EU liberalization has not had much impact.

These authors clearly offer more insights into the specificities of banking than do either the EU Commission or the Price Waterhouse report, which tend to treat banking like any other industry. However, it is unclear whether their prediction that 1992 would have little impact on banking has turned out to be correct. This is particularly true with regard to Southern European countries. There are several points that can be made here about the characteristics of Southern European banks at the end of the 1980s, and the changes that occurred in the 1990s.

First, evidence on Southern European banks at the end of the 1980s suggests that they were particularly inefficient relative to other EU countries. The existence of such inefficiency is perhaps not surprising given the degree to which these economies were financially repressed. While liberalization proceeded rather rapidly in the 1980s, there was still evidence that Southern European banks were inefficient relative to their northern European counterparts.[23] Evidence from Spain suggested that, relative to the EU, operating costs were high, staff costs were high (particularly due to overbranching) and the spread between deposit and lending rates was also high (Caminal *et al.*, 1990, Table 8.5). This latter observation indicates that Spanish banks could pass on their inefficiency to their customers and this accounted for the fact that Spanish banks were highly profitable. In Italy, controls on bank branching had led to the development of numerous local banks, which, although highly profitable (because they often have considerable local monopoly power), tended to be rather inefficient (Bruni, 1990, especially Table 9.2). Similar inefficiencies were found in Greece and Portugal.[24] Moreover, the lessons from Greece suggested that such inefficiency cannot necessarily be eliminated merely through domestic liberalization. In Greece, the spread between deposit and loan rates widened substantially after liberalization (in 1985 it was 5.5 per cent; by 1992 it had increased to 10.8 per cent). Such a widening was probably the result of the dominance of the two major commercial banks: domestic liberalization merely led to monopoly profits (see Stournaras, 1993). Moreover, by comparison with Spain and Italy, Greek and Portuguese banks still had a large amount of non-performing loans. For example, non-performing loans were three times the equity of the Portuguese banking sector in 1986 (Braga de Macedo, 1990b). These non-performing loans largely reflected the problem of poorly performing public enterprises (known in Greece as the 'ailing' firms). Banks were encouraged in the 1970s and 1980s to lend to these companies and subsequently found themselves substantially overextended. This problem made restructuring in Greece and Portugal more difficult if instability and bank failures were to be avoided.

A second argument supporting the view that structural change in Southern European banking was likely arises from the observation that size is important. In other words, structural change need not arise only from efficiency motives. The analysis of those who are critical of the Price Waterhouse report may be good normative economics (that is, there are no efficiency gains and hence there *should be* no structural changes). However, it is probably not good positive economics since structural change may occur even without an efficiency rationale. Of particular relevance here is the fact that banks in Southern Europe tended to be small relative to their Northern European rivals. This results in part from their enforced absence from the international wholesale markets until recently.[25] Table 8.4 indicates that banks in Portugal and Greece were small relative to the rest of the EU. This was less true of Italy and, to some extent, Spain. It may be thought that bank size is largely irrelevant, particularly given that evidence in favour of the existence of economies of scale and scope in banking is

Table 8.4   Top European banks by capital base
Top 500 European banks by capital base (end December 1990 or March 1991)

	Total	*Top 100*	*101–200*	*201–300*	*301–400*	*401–500*
Greece	9	1	2	3	2	1
Portugal	13	1	2	4	3	3
Spain	50	10	9	11	13	7
Italy	103	20	18	21	22	22
France	26	12	4	3	4	3
Germany	89	17	23	11	17	21
UK	35	10	4	11	5	5

The top 1000 banks by capital base (end December 1991 or March 1992)

	0–100	*101–500*	*501–1000*	*Total*
Greece	0	4	4	8
Portugal	0	2	8	10
Spain	5	14	26	45
Italy	10	29	56	95
France	9	10	8	27
Germany	9	32	46	87
UK	7	9	18	34

Source: *The Banker*, September 1991 and July 1992.

difficult to come by.[26] However, size may be important to allow banks to serve the needs of their large corporate customers and yet still gain from diversification. Furthermore, size can be seen as a protection against takeover (Revell, 1987, 1988). Thus cooperative mergers/takeovers may have occurred in Southern Europe because banks found it necessary to protect themselves against hostile takeovers and, moreover, banks may have been keen to grow larger even if it was at the expense of some efficiency. Similar arguments continue to hold today following the creation of the Euro area.

The final point we can make in relation to the potential for structural change in Southern European banking arises from the evidence of the 1990s. On the one hand, governments in some of the Southern European economies have been promoting change arguing that it is necessary if domestic banks are to compete at a European level. On the other hand, there have been some cross-border deals between banks in different EU countries.[27]

Looking first at the intra-country changes, both Italy and Spain undertook strong initiatives to promote and facilitate structural changes in their banking systems. In Italy, the Amato Law (1990) sought to enable restructuring of public banks through the injection of private capital. Mergers have been taking place between small regional banks in an attempt to reduce overbanking. Table 8.5 presents evidence for the early 1990s. In the later 1990s, structural change has continued both through privatizations and mergers (Table 8.6) and through a growing presence of foreign banks in Italy. In Spain, an independent study commissioned by the government (see Revell, 1987) suggested that the authorities encourage structural change to enable Spanish banks to compete after 1992. Table 8.5 shows the mergers that occurred in the wake of this report. Indeed, the Spanish government itself actually took the lead in this respect. In April 1991, following the failure of a proposed merger between Banesto and Banco

Table 8.5   Merger activity between banks in the same country

Italy	1989	Cassa di Risparmio di Roma acquired Banco di Spirito Santo
	1990	Banca Commerciale Italiana (BCI) merged with Credito Italiano
	1990	Banca Commerciale Italiana (BCI) acquired 51% of Banca Sicula
	1990	Banco Ambrosiano Veneto acquired 92% of Citibank Italia
	1990	Cassa di Risparmio di Roma acquired 65% of Banco di Roma
	1991	Banco di Spirito Santo and Banco di (Roma both owned by Cassa di Risparmio di Roma) merge to form Banco di Roma
	1991	Institute Bancario San Paola di Torino acquired Crediop
Spain	1987	Banco de Bilbao merged with Banco de Vizcaya
	1991	Banco Hispano Americano merged with Banco Central
	1991	Merger of all state-owned banks into Corporacion Bancaria de Espana (or Argentaria)

Source: *Financial Times*, individual reports over the period 1988–93.

Table 8.6   Privatizations and recent mergers in Italy

Privatizations	Date
Credito Italiano	1993
Banca Commericale Italiano	1994
Istituto Mobiliare Italiano (IMI)	1994–96 (3 parts)
Banco di Napoli	1996
Cassa di Risparmio delle Province Lombarde (CARIPLO)	1997
Istituto Bancario San Paolo di Torino	1997
Banca Nazionale del Lavoro (BNL)	1998–99
Mergers	
Ambrosiano Veneto	1997
CARIPLO	
Istituto Bancario San Paolo di Torino	1997
IMI	

Source: OECD, *Economic Surveys: Italy*, 1999.

Table 8.7   Portugal: privatizations (1989–97)

Bank	Proportion privatized (%)	Date
Banco Português do Allântico	100	1990–95
Banco de Fomento e Exterior	85	1994–96
Banco Espírito Santo e Comercial de Lisboa	100	1991–92
Banco Totta & Açores	93	1989–96
Banco Fonsecas & Burney	100	1991–92
Banco Pinto & Sotto Mayor	100	1994–95
Crédiro Predial Português	100	1992
União de Bancos Portuguêses	100	1993–96
Sociedade Financeira Portuguêsa	100	1991

Source: OECD, *Economic Surveys: Portugal*, 1998.

Central, the government merged all state-owned banks and credit institutions into one financial institution – the Corporacion Bancaria de Espana (or Argentaria). This institution was subsequently privatized with 75 per cent being sold off between 1993 and 1996 (OECD, *Economic Survey*, 1998).

In Portugal, structural change has been promoted through privatization (Table 8.7) and also through foreign entry. Initially, foreign banks were allowed either to set up in Portugal or to buy privatized banks provided they made some payment which was designed to go to the existing, established banks, which, as we noted above, were suffering from a large amount of non-performing loans. In this way, the Portuguese authorities restructured and strengthened their banking system.[28]

Table 8.8   Privatizations and mergers in Greece (1998–9)

Bank	Proportion sold (%)	Buyer	Date
Privatizations			
Bank of Macedonia-Thrace (owned by consortium of state banks)	37	Pireaus Bank	1998
General Bank (owned by Greek Army's Pension Fund)	100	Interamerican Insurance Group	1998
Bank of Crete (state-owned)	70	Eurobank (privately owned)	1998
Bank of Central Greece (owned by Agricultural Bank of Greece)	51	Egnatia Bank (privately owned)	1998
Ionian Bank	51	Alpha Credit Bank (privately owned)	1999
Mergers			
National Bank of Greece and National Mortgage Bank of Greece	–	–	1998

Source: OECD, *Economic Surveys: Greece*, 1998 and Bank of Greece.

Finally, in Greece, privatizations and mergers have been taking place recently (Table 8.8) after a period where smaller private banks were encouraged to compete with the larger, more-established, state-owned banks.

In addition to intra-country restructuring, there was also some activity of a cross-border type in the early 1990s and, as Table 8.9 shows, this has frequently involved banks in Southern European countries. To some extent, the forms that cross-border activity have taken can be seen as seeking to avoid the large set-up costs involved in establishing a banking network in another country from scratch. Thus cross-border activity has partly involved the takeover of smaller banks by larger EU banks and partly the development of cooperative agreements through minority shareholdings or mutual shareholdings.

In conclusion, some structural change within Southern European banking has been taking place, although activity slowed with the recession of the early- to mid-1990s only to pick up again in the late-1990s. While such changes may well have resulted from domestic financial liberalization alone, the form of the changes suggests that a large part of the impetus has come from growing EU integration in general and, in particular, the Second Banking Directive and the removal of capital controls and, latterly, the formation of the Euro area. However, such changes have required careful management by the supervisory authorities. The experience in Scandinavia

Table 8.9 Cross-border activity between EU banks

Acquisitions		
Banco Bilbao Vizcaya (Spa)	Lloyds (Port)	1991
Barclays Bank (UK)	L'Europeene de Credit (Fra)	1990
	Merck Finck (Ger)	1990
Credit Lyonnaise (Fra)	Banco Commercial Espanol (Spa)	1990
	Banco Jover (Spa)	1991
	BfG Bank (Ger)	1992
Deutsche Bank (Ger)	Banca D'America D'Italia (Ita)	–
	Banco Commercial Transatlantico (Spa)	1991
	Morgan Grenfell (UK)	1989
	Sociedade de Investmentos (Port)	–
	Banco de Madrid	1993
Instituto Bancario San Paolo di Torino (Ita)	Banca Catala de Credit (Spa)	1991
National Westminster (UK)	Banco March (mainland operations, Spa)	1991
	F van Lanshot Bankiers (Neth)	1990
Rabo Bank and Hanwha First Investment (Neth)	Bank of Athens (Gr)	1993
Credit Commercial de France (Fra) and Berliner Handels-und Frankfurter Bank (Ger)	Charterhouse (UK merchant bank)	1993
Minority shareholdongs		
Banco de Santander (Spa) and Royal Bank of Scotland (UK)	Banco Commercio e Industria (Port)	1990
Banesto (Spa)	Banco Totta & Açores (Port)	1991
Berlin Handels-und- Frankfurter Bank (Ger)	Halder Holdings (Dutch)	1991
	Pastorino and Partners (Ita, Stockbroker)	1991
Bank of Scotland (UK)	45% of Finanziaria Italiana Mutui (Ita)	1992
Banque Nationale de Paris (Fra)	5% of Kleinwort Bensen	1991
Banco Central Hispano- americano (Spa)	Commerzbank (Ger)	10% 1991
	Banco Commercial Português (Port)	10% and 2% 1993
Banco Hispano Americano) (Spa)	Banco di Roma (Ita)	5% 1991
Bayerische Vereinsbank (Ger)	Banco de Sabadell (Spa)	1990

Table 8.9   contd.

Dresdner Bank (Ger)	Banque National de Paris (Fra)	1991/92
Generale Bank (Belg)	Amsterdam Rotterdam Bank (Neth)	25%
		1988
Royal Bank of Scotland (UK)	Banco de Santander (Spa)	2.5% and
		10%
		1989

Source: Financial Times, individual reports over the period 1988–93.
Belg = Belgium; Fra = France; Ger = Germany; Gr = Greece; Ita = Italy; Port = Portugal; Spa = Spain.

in the early 1990s with the promotion of a more competitive banking system showed that increased competitive pressures in a more liberalized environment can often lead to increased financial fragility. Increased competitive pressures often lead banks to take on increasing risk without a commensurate increase in their expected return – increased competition leads to declining risk premia, a loosening of credit limits and an increase in speculative activities such as taking a view on currency or interest rate movements.[29] As a result, banks become increasingly fragile and if one bank gets into difficulties, problems can easily spread throughout the system. The supervisory authorities in Southern European countries have thus had an important balancing act to undertake: on the one hand, they sought to promote greater efficiency within domestic banks; on the other, they had to maintain an orderly and stable financial system. Such concerns continue to be an issue for bank supervision in these countries.

Financial liberalization and sectoral borrowing constraints

The second issue that needs to be addressed when assessing the changes occurring in Southern European financial sectors is whether a liberalized system will ensure credit is available to all sectors of the economy. One of the major disadvantages of a repressed financial system is that, as we argued above, it leads to credit rationing. That is, there are a number of profitable projects which could be carried out, but which cannot get access to funds because savings are so low. One of the advantages of liberalization is that such credit rationing is supposed to be eliminated as the rise in interest rates raises the amount saved in the economy thus allowing more investment to be financed. The problem with such a simple conception of the way in which credit markets operate is that it ignores the problems of information asymmetries. Information asymmetries lead to credit rationing and sectoral borrowing constraints even within fully liberalized financial systems.

Stiglitz and Weiss (1981) examine the implications of asymmetric information within a perfectly competitive credit market. Asymmetric information occurs because the borrower always knows more about the prospective project than the lender. The lender knows that the quality of borrowers differs and has to find some screening device to control the amount of risk that it assumes as the lender. If banks use the interest rate as a screening device (the rationale being that a higher interest rate will generate a higher expected return and hence compensate the bank for extra risks), then instead of controlling risk, it will merely exacerbate it. This occurs because of two effects. First, there is the adverse selection effect. This states that as the bank raises the interest rate it attracts borrowers who are unworried about whether or not they will repay the loan. In other words, as the interest rate rises, the probability of default also increases: at some point, the overall expected return to the bank, which depends both on the interest rate and the probability of payment, begins to fall. The second effect is the incentive effect and this arises because as the interest rate rises, so the net present value of all investment projects falls. Those projects which were of low risk and low return thus become unprofitable, leaving only riskier projects which the bank can finance. As a result of these two effects, Stiglitz and Weiss argue that banks should practise credit rationing as a risk-controlling strategy.

However, their argument does not stop here. In addition to borrowers generally facing limits on the amount that they can borrow, specific sectors may be excluded from borrowing altogether. If a bank can identify a group of borrowers (for example, a sector or industry) which, on average, is considered to be high-risk, then it may decide to exclude all members of that sector from borrowing. This occurs even if it is the case that some members of the groups are perfectly acceptable risks or have projects that are acceptable, because the bank cannot distinguish between members of the groups as a result of asymmetric information.

Cho (1986) examines this argument within the context of financial liberalization and it leads him to argue that countries seeking to liberalize their financial markets should also develop stock markets. He argues that they can better handle risky investments because the investor derives the benefits of a risk project, should it pay off (unlike the bank which only receives a fixed return irrespective of how successful the project is).

Cho's analysis thus provides support for the strategy being adopted by Southern European countries – namely the development of a range of financial *markets* alongside the removal of the controls that have largely determined the kind of loans that banks have made. To determine whether such a strategy will be successful, or whether other policies may be required to deal with these sectoral borrowing constraints, we turn now to a consideration of the problems that might arise from allowing financial markets a greater role in financing industry.[30]

Financial markets and short-termism

In this section we assess the extent to which the move towards greater reliance on financial *markets* will be beneficial to Southern European economies. In particular, we focus on the question of whether financial *markets* will help in the development of the real economies of Southern European countries and hence aid the convergence of their economic performance on that of the other EU member states.

The question of what kind of financial system can best help the needs and development of the real economy is one that has received much attention recently in British and American debates. The Anglo-Saxon financial system, with its reliance on financial markets and the discipline that they are seen to impose on companies, has been much criticized. This is particularly true if it is compared to the systems of Japan and Germany where banks have a much larger and more active role in industry.

The essential criticism levelled at the Anglo-Saxon style of financial system is that it tends to promote short-termism and that this has contributed to the poor performance of these economies since the end of the 1960s. In essence, the short-termist argument is that companies cut expenditure on R&D, training, capital expenditure and other factors which might improve the longer-term economic performance in order to maximize current profits and hence dividends. Clearly, the implication is that the real economy suffers with respect to long-term growth prospects.[31]

We can identify three specific criticisms in the literature that have been levelled at the Anglo-Saxon style of financial system.[32] First, it is argued that the Anglo-Saxon system does not operate to foster long-term relationships between companies, suppliers and banks. It tends to underproduce efficiency-improving implicit contracts. The issue of implicit contracts has been discussed by Schleifer and Summers (1988). They argue that efficiency is often improved by a company having a large number of implicit contracts between itself and its workers/suppliers, etc. These contracts are implicit because complete contracting is too costly. What they promote is investment by employees in firm-specific skills. In return, the employee can expect to receive certain returns in the form of, say, job security, internal promotion, etc. Within Anglo-Saxon financial systems, takeovers play an important role in ensuring that companies are run as efficiently as they can be. However, Summers and Schleifer argue that when a company is taken over, particularly if it is a hostile takeover, such contracts are broken. This results in a redistribution of wealth from those with whom the firm had an implicit contract (workers/suppliers, etc) to the shareholders. This redistribution occurs through the rise in the share price which accompanies the announcement that a takeover is likely. The result however is that the takeover need not be welfare improving for society. Indeed Schleifer and Summers argue that it could involve a net loss to society since the potential for takeover results in employees underinvesting in firm specific skills. Thus within Anglo-Saxon systems the fear of takeover is not conducive to a long-term cooperation between management and workers which can operate to the benefit of the firm.

The second criticism which has been levelled at Anglo-Saxon style financial systems is the tendency to promote a culture of 'deal-making'. Tobin (1984), for example, has argued that 'we are throwing more and more of our resources, including the cream of our youth, into financial services remote from the production of goods and services, into activities that generate high private rewards disproportionate to their social productivity' (p. 294). This argument is based on an important information failure.[33] If, for example, there is a company which I know is worth £1 billion but the market values it at only £800 million, then I can buy it and make a profit of almost £200 million instantaneously. However, the private benefits of such 'deal-making' are much larger than the social benefits. There is therefore an incentive for overinvestment in working out the true value of companies because the potential private gains are much larger than the social gains.

The final point that can be made against the Anglo-Saxon financial system is that it tends to neglect long-run issues related to investment and the 'real' side of the economy. This argument has three potential aspects to it. First, Mayer (1993, pp. 12–13) argues that one major problem in Anglo-Saxon systems is that because companies have numerous shareholders, there is a free-rider problem in commitment. In a situation where ownership is very dispersed, each individual shareholder has a negligible impact on the company's policy-making. If an alternative investment prospect arises then each individual shareholder may sell his/her shares without affecting any other individual shareholder. But if enough shareholders sell out, then ownership changes hands and the policy of the company towards a long-term investment project can change. Each individual shareholder considers only the private net benefits from selling out – he/she does not consider the wider consequences of a possible change in ownership.[34] Mayer compares this with a situation where there are one or more major shareholders and a number of smaller shareholders (this is more like the German system of ownership). In this case the smaller shareholders can buy and sell as much as they want without ownership changing hands and hence without the long-term investment strategy of the company being disrupted. Mayer argues that in this case concentration of ownership helps to internalize the externality that results from free-riding. The implication of shareholder behaviour in the Anglo-Saxon system is that it becomes difficult for firms to make long-term commitments to R&D, investment, etc. because of the potential for change of ownership and hence company policy. As with the Summer and Schleifer story, long-term commitments are not encouraged in such a system.

A second argument states that an active market for corporate control may cause firms to try to deter takeover by raising dividends to the detriment of investment. Dickerson *et al.* (1998) develop a model where the existence of credit constraints leads to a trade-off between dividends payments and investment in profitable opportunities. It is shown that, in any economy where takeovers are prevalent, companies have an incentive to pay out higher dividends even if this is to the detriment of their long-run performance. Empirical support for this proposition is given in that Dickerson *et al.* find that, for a large sample of UK companies, an increase in dividends can reduce significantly the probability of a company being taken over. Thus, if a firm wishes to avoid takeover, then it would be better to distribute the marginal £1 of earnings as dividends rather than investing. Under such circumstances, corporate investment may well be suboptimal.

The third, and final, aspect of the tendency of Anglo-Saxon systems to neglect long-run issues arises from a possible mispricing of a company on the stock exchange. In particular, companies which take a long-term view may suffer from a depressed share price, leaving them vulnerable to takeovers or making it more difficult for them to raise external funds for investment projects. Defenders of the UK/US system, such as Jensen (1984) and Marsh (1990) argue that financial markets operate in such a way as to price companies efficiently. That is, changes in the share price of a company reflect changes in the net present value of the expected returns the company will generate. So, for example, a company which chooses to cut its dividend in order to invest the retained profits in a project whose returns are expected to continue for a long time into the future should not experience a fall in share price. If it does, then it would be possible for investors to identify companies which are undervalued and hence make an abnormal profit on their investment. There is clearly not enough space here to enter into the large debate on whether or not financial markets are efficient. Suffice it to say that view has been questioned by a number of economists.[35] What we can say here is that the concept of efficiency employed by authors such as Marsh and Jensen seems particularly narrow. They do not consider the efficiency of a market-based system relative to more institution-based systems (such as those found in Japan and Germany). What the efficient market view seems to say is that with a given financial system (with its given institutions and *modus operandi*), an individual investor cannot beat the market and make excess returns. However, the argument of those who support the idea that market-based systems lead to short-termism is that if the nature of the institutional structure is changed, then it will be possible for large improvements in economic performance to be made. In other words, the case for and against short-termism must be settled through a comparison of all the possible systems available. It cannot be settled by arguing that the present system does as well as it could.[36]

In conclusion, therefore, the attempt to cultivate financial markets in Southern European economies as well as the possible pressures from the EU to move towards a more Anglo-Saxon type system may have its drawbacks. Anglo-Saxon systems are certainly one way in which corporate or managerial efficiency can be encouraged. However, the potential for short-termism and its impact on investment is hardly conducive to economic growth. As Franks and Mayer (1990, p. 215) conclude there is likely to be a trade-off between 'correcting managerial failure [static efficiency] and promoting investment [dynamic efficiency]' and economies which are seeking to grow quickly 'will probably opt for arrangements that promote dynamic over static efficiency'. It is important therefore that the changes occurring in the financial system of Southern European countries be tailored to the interests of the real economy.

Conclusions

There is little doubt that the economies of Southern Europe still face a major challenge in future years. This would have been the case even without the process of European integration as the result of such forces as the growing interdependence of the world economy, rapid technological change and so on. But European integration, even if it provides major opportunities, is also in itself a shock for these economies (see Gibson and Tsakalotos, 1992). What are the prospects for these economies in view of this challenge?

In the 1980s and 1990s the emphasis was very much on liberalization, increasing competition and 'getting markets right'. We have seen this with respect to financial liberalization but a similar process was under way in many other areas of the economy as well. For many authors this liberalization will itself improve the economic performance of Southern European economies, promote the consolidation of the 'New Southern Europe' and speed up the process by which these weaker economies undergo a process of 'catch-up' to their more developed Northern European partners.[37]

However, other authors take a less sanguine view. They point to the fact that the potential for catch-up is dependent on what Abramovitz (1986) has termed 'social capability', which he defines in terms of 'political, commercial, industrial and financial institutions' (p. 388). This has also been the emphasis of this chapter. This is not to say that liberalization is not important and indeed we have argued with respect to finance that the measures taken in Southern Europe have led to improvements in operational efficiency and the service provided by financial institutions. It is certainly the case that we can talk about a 'New Southern Europe' if the focus of our attention is confined only to their financial systems *per se*. On the other hand, we have also argued that the financial system that these economies may end up with may not best serve their real economies. We have pointed to three possible areas of concern: the increase in the potential for financial instability; the likelihood that certain sectors of the economy, especially those with high risk, R&D expenditure and long-term pay-back horizons, may be starved of funds; and finally that the Southern European economies may begin to develop the kind of short-termism that is characteristic of Anglo-Saxon financial systems. There is no need to repeat the arguments here. Thus, in our view, the future development and prosperity of southern European economies may in the future rely as much on 'getting institutions right' as on 'getting markets right'.

Appendix

In this appendix we illustrate the McKinnon–Shaw hypothesis diagrammatically. Under financial repression, savings are kept artificially low because of ceilings on deposit rates. Low loan rates encourage a large amount of investment demand. However, with low savings, not all investment demand can be met: realized investment is thus along the savings function. Figure 8.1 illustrates this situation, along with the effects of loosening the controls. The interest rate on deposits and loans is assumed initially to be constrained at r_1. At this interest rate, OA savings are forthcoming, whereas OB funds are demanded for investment projects. Credit is thus rationed to an amount equivalent to AB.

Assume now that the government undertakes some loosening of the interest rate ceiling and deposit interest rates are allowed to rise to r_2. McKinnon and Shaw argue that this allows for greater savings, which in turn induce greater income growth (through the higher investment), leading to a rightward shift in the savings function (from S to S_1). In the new equilibrium greater savings (OC) allow more investment demand to be

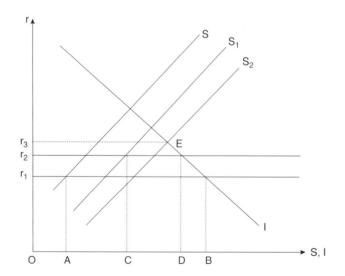

Figure 8.1 The effect of financial liberalization

satisfied – credit rationing thus falls to CD. If interest rates were liberalized completely, then the economy would end up at E, where all investment projects which are profitable at the new interest rate r_3 would be undertaken. Thus financial repression essentially acts to promote current consumption rather than savings and it is the rise in savings that accompanies liberalization, which in turn allows a larger volume of investment to be financed, that brings forth the increased growth within the economy.

Notes

1. We would like to thank Allan Williams and Massimo Roccas for their helpful comments on this chapter.
2. OECD Economic Surveys for all countries in the 1980s and 1990s provide a useful source of information on regulatory changes that have occurred in financial markets. In addition, papers by Katseli (1990), Borges (1990), Braga de Macedo (1990b,c), Caminal *et al.* (1990), Bruni (1990) provide useful analyses of the changes that have been taking place in Southern Europe since the beginning of the 1980s.
3. This was mainly with respect to the compulsory purchase of Treasury bills: the Bank of Italy is now no longer obliged to finance the government deficit.
4. For example, in Portugal, the liberalization of entry laws led to a reduction in the share of the eight nationalized banks in total credit from 98 per cent in 1979 to 91 per cent in 1987. While this is indicative of what we might expect to happen in the future, Portuguese banking is still dominated by the 8 nationalized banks and will continue to be so for some time.
5. The ceilings on bank lending encouraged banks to invest deposits, in excess of what they could lend to the private sector, in Treasury bills.
6. By 1998, Spain and Portugal had already reduced reserve requirement to 2 per cent; in August 1998, Italian reserve requirements stood at 6 per cent and were being further reduced towards the Euro area.
7. In 1993, for example, the Banking Law enlarged the permitted range of operations for both ordinary banks and SCIs. Banks can now extend medium and long-term credit and issue bonds while SCIs can extend short-term credit.
8. Note that since mid-1993 banks have no longer been obliged to invest new deposits in Treasury Bills. Additionally they have been given the option to transform their past holdings of Treasury Bills into long-term marketable debt.
9. See OECD *Economic Surveys* especially those of the 1990s.
10. See chapter 7 in this volume.
11. See, for example, OECD (1987) Survey on Italy (p. 50) on the development of investment funds in the mid-1980s in Italy.
12. Off-balance sheet finance refers to banks' growing involvement in business which does not increase their assets or liabilities, that is the business does not appear on their balance sheet. An example is underwriting services where a bank performs an intermediary service by placing bonds, shares or whatever with investors. The bank receives a fee for the provision of such a service, but the assets sold do not appear on the bank's balance sheet.
13. Control over short-term capital flows is particularly important for preventing speculative attacks on currencies. Frequently controls of this nature have been used to maintain a covered interest differential between domestic and foreign

assets (see Gibson and Tsakalotos, 1991, 1993a for a discussion of the use of capital controls within the ERM).

14. Clearly it is not necessary that a country liberalize its capital controls *after* joining the ERM. However, it could be argued that the currencies of weaker countries within the EU are more likely to suffer from speculative attacks within the ERM. Thus it is probably better for weaker countries to join the ERM *before* they remove controls on capital movements. We can note that Italy and France in the early 1980s benefited a lot from capital controls during speculative crises (see, for example, Gibson and Tsakalotos, 1991).

15. This is undoubtedly the spirit of the Directive. However, there is some lack of clarity with respect to regulations which are imposed for monetary control purposes. Host authorities have some right to apply regulations to *all* banks operating within their jurisdiction to enable successful monetary control. Quite how this will be interpreted in practice remains to be seen. See Davis and Smales (1989) and Gibson and Tsakalotos (1993b) for further discussion of this issue.

16. Investment banking includes the underwriting of new issues, mergers and acquisitions, and secondary market trading and brokerage activities.

17. Clearly the growth of world trade has also been a factor in increasing interdependence.

18. We present here only the basic rationale for domestic financial liberalization. The McKinnon–Shaw model has been extended in numerous directions since it first appeared. See Gibson and Tsakalotos (1994) for a detailed and critical survey of this literature.

19. For a more formal statement of the McKinnon–Shaw argument, see the Appendix.

20. In fact, they calculate two possible price reductions. The price reduction implied by the average of the 4 cheapest EU countries they call the theoretically potential price reduction. The existence of a large amount of cross-subsidization within banking leads them to conclude that the actual (or 'proposed') price reductions will not be so great. The figures presented in Table 8.3 are the proposed price reductions and on average are 40–60 per cent of the theoretically potential price reductions.

21. See, for example, Neven (1990), Grilli (1989a,b), Vives (1990) and Branson (1990). A more detailed discussion of their views is undertaken in Gibson and Tsakalotos (1993b).

22. These entry barriers include, among others: monetary authority control over takeovers of domestic banks by foreign banks (Neven, 1990); large set-up costs since retail banking often involves the setting up of a branch network (Neven, 1990; Vives, 1990); and information barriers – often a local bank knows much more about local customers than does an incoming entrant (Branson, 1990).

23. It should be noted that information on bank efficiency is notoriously difficult to come by. Usual measure of productivity or unit labour costs are difficult to calculate because of problems of measuring bank output and because of the large amount of cross-subsidization of services which banks undertake.

24. See the evidence presented in Borges (1990) and Braga de Macedo (1990b,c) for Portugal and Katseli (1990) for Greece.

25. A major source of growth for banks in the 1970s and 1980s was participation in international banking – in particular the Eurocurrency markets (see Gibson, 1989).

26. This results mainly from the difficulty of measuring bank output. See Gibson (1989) for a review of the evidence.

27. Cross-border activity tends to be pro-cyclical. Hence in the mid-1990s, activity slowed as a result of the recession which affected most European countries. But it picked up again in the late 1990s in anticipation of the creation of the Euro area.
28. It is interesting to note that in many cases privatization has returned banks to the old family owned industrial conglomerates that characterized the economy pre-1975.
29. See Gibson and Tsakalotos (1993b) for a discussion of the implications of 1992 for stability in Southern European countries. See also Gibson and Oppenheimer (1992) on the role of competition in financial fragility.
30. An alternative approach to the problem of sectoral borrowing constraints is for the government to take an active role in promoting investment in areas which are likely to suffer from a lack of funding, that is areas such as R & D, risky, long-term projects and so on. The means by which this could be achieved are discussed in Tsakalotos (1991) and Gibson *et al.* (1992).
31. Evidence that mergers and acquisitions are detrimental for firm performance as measured by profitability is given in Dickerson *et al.* (1997).
32. We discuss these issues in more depth in Gibson et al. (1992).
33. We are indebted to Evan Davis, formerly at the Institute for Fiscal Studies, now BBC Economics Correspondent, who raised this point in a conversation we had on the issue of short-termism.
34. For a model which takes the form of a dynamic game between shareholders and managers and which generates the result of underinvestment because of a lack of commitment, see Dickerson *et al.* (1995).
35. See Gibson *et al.*, 1992, pp. 1–7 for a survey of some of the literature.
36. Indeed, Marsh (1990, p. 48) appears to concede this point when he argues that the radically different financial systems of Japan and Germany may indeed explain the relative success of their real economies.
37. See Larre and Torres (1991) for a very up-beat account along these lines.

Bibliography

Abramovitz, M. (1986) 'Catching up, forging ahead and falling behind', *Journal of Economic History*, vol. XLVI, no. 2, pp. 385–406.
Borges, A. M. (1990) 'Portuguese banking in the single European market', in Dermine, J. (ed.).
Braga de Macedo, J. (1990a) 'Financial liberalisation and exchange rate policy in the newly integrating countries of the European Community', in Ferri, P. *Prospects for the European Monetary System*, Macmillan, London.
Braga de Macedo, J. (1990b) *'External liberalization with ambiguous public response: the experience of Portugal'*, CEPR Discussion Paper, no. 378, February.
Braga de Macedo, J. (1990c) '"Comment" on Borges', in Dermine, J. (ed.).
Branson, W. H. (1990) 'Financial market integration, macroeconomic policy and the EMS', in Bliss, C. and Braga de Macedo, J. (eds), *Union with Diversity in the European Economy*, CUP, Cambridge.
Bruni, F. (1990) 'Banking and financial reregulation towards 1992: the Italian case', in Dermine, J. (ed.).
Caminal, R., Gual, J. and Vives, X. (1990) 'Competition in Spanish banking', in Dermine, J. (ed.).

Cho, Yoon Je (1986) 'Inefficiencies from financial liberalisation in the absence of well-functioning equity markets', *Journal of Money, Credit and Banking*, vol. 18, no. 2, pp. 191–9.

Davis, E. and Smales, C. (1989) 'The integration of European financial services', Chapter 5 in CBS/LBS *1992 Myths and Realities*, London Business school, London.

Dermine, J. (ed.) (1990) *European Banking in the 1990s*, Basil Blackwell, Oxford.

Dickerson, A. P., Gibson, H. D. and Tsakalotos, E. (1995) 'Shortermism and underinvestment: the influence of financial systems', *The Manchester School*, vol. XLIII, no. 4, pp. 351–567, December.

Dickerson, A. P., Gibson, H. D. and Tsakalotos, E. (1997) 'The impact of acquisition on company performance: evidence from a large panel of UK firms', *Oxford Economic Papers*, vol. 49, pp. 344–61, July.

Dickerson, A. P., Gibson, H. D. and Tsakalotos, E. (1998) 'Takeover risk and dividend strategy: a study of UK firms', *Journal of Industrial Economics*, vol. XLVI, no. 3, pp. 281–300.

Franks, J. and Mayer, C. (1990) 'Capital markets and corporate control: a study of France, Germany and the UK', *Economic Policy*, April, pp. 191–231.

Gibson, H. D. (1989) *The Eurocurrency Markets, Domestic Financial Policy and International Instability*, Macmillan, London.

Gibson, H. D. and Tsakalotos, E. (1991) 'European monetary union, the removal of capital controls and macroeconomic policy in Southern Europe: the case for positive integration', *Journal of Public Policy*, vol. 11, no. 3, pp. 249–73.

Gibson, H. D. and Tsakalotos, E. (1992) *Economic Integration and Financial Liberalization: Prospects for Southern Europe*, Macmillan, St. Antony's series, London.

Gibson, H. D. and Tsakalotos, E. (1993a) 'Testing a flow model of capital flight in 5 European countries', *The Manchester School*, vol. LXI, no. 2, June, pp. 144–66.

Gibson, H. D. and Tsakalotos, E. (1993b) 'European integration and the banking sector in Southern Europe: competition, efficiency and structure', *Banca Nazionale del Lavoro Quarterly Review*, no. 186, pp. 299–325.

Gibson, H. D. and Tsakalotos, E. (1994) 'The scope and limits of financial liberalisation in developing countries: a critical survey', *Journal of Development Studies*, vol. 30, no. 3, April, pp. 578–628.

Gibson, H. D. and Oppenheimer, P. M. (1992) 'Financial crises and the international debt problem', Oxford Institute of Economics and Statistics, Applied Economics Discussion Paper Series, no. 135, April.

Gibson, H. D., Stournaras, Y. and Tsakalotos, E. (1992) 'The real and financial sectors in Southern Europe: catch-up, convergence and financial institutions', University of Kent, *Studies in Economics*, 92/10, August.

Grilli, V. (1989a) 'Financial Markets and 1992', *Brookings Papers on Economic Activity*, no. 2.

Grilli, V. (1989b) 'Europe 1992: issues and prospects for the financial markets', *Economic Policy*, no. 9, October.

Jensen, M. C. (1984) 'Takeovers: folklore and science', *Harvard Business Review*, November–December, pp. 109–21.

Katseli, L. (1990) 'Structural adjustment of the Greek economy', CEPR Discussion Paper, no. 374, February.

Krugman, P. (1987) 'Economic integration in Europe: some conceptual issues', in Padoa-Schioppa, T. (ed.), *Efficiency, Stability, Equity*, Oxford University Press, Oxford.

Larre, B. and Torres, R. (1991) 'Is convergence a spontaneous process? The experience of Spain, Portugal and Greece', *OECD Economic Studies*, no. 16, Spring, pp. 169–98.

McKinnon, R. I. (1973) *Money and Capital in Economic Development*, Brookings Institution, Washington, DC.

Marsh, P. (1990) *Short-termism on Trial*, Institutional Fund Managers' Association, London.

Mayer, C. (1990) 'Financial systems, corporate finance and economic development', in Hubbard, R. G. (ed.), *Asymmetric information, Corporate Finance, and Investment*, NBER, University of Chicago Press, Chicago.

Mayer, C. (1993) 'Ownership', inaugural lecture to the University of Warwick, 1 February.

Neven, D. J. (1990) 'Structural adjustment in European retail banking: some views from industrial organisation', in Dermine, J. (ed.).

OECD (various) *Economic Surveys: Greece*, OECD, Paris.

OECD (various) *Economic Surveys: Italy*, OECD, Paris.

OECD (various) *Economic Surveys: Portugal*, OECD, Paris.

OECD (various) *Economic Surveys: Spain*, OECD, Paris.

Price Waterhouse (1988) 'The cost of non-Europe in financial services', prepared for the Commission of the European Communities, March.

Revell, J. (1987) *Mergers and the Role of Large Banks*, Institute of European Finance, Bangor.

Revell, J. (1988) *Bank Preparations for 1992: Some Clues and Some Queries*, IEF Research Paper, Bangor, RP88/17.

Shaw, E. S. (1973) *Financial Deepening in Economic Activity*, Oxford University Press, New York.

Schleifer, A. and Summers, L. H. (1988) 'Breach of trust in hostile takeovers', in Auerbach, A. J. (ed.), *Corporate Takeovers: Causes and Consequences*, NBER, Chicago University Press, Chicago.

Stiglitz, J. E. and Weiss, A. (1981) 'Credit Rationing in market with imperfect information', *American Economic Review*, vol. 71, no. 3, pp. 393–410.

Stournaras, Y. (1993) 'The evolution of the Greek financial system and its role in economic development: prospects and problems', Speech (in Greek) given to the Federation of Greek Bank Unions and the Economic Chamber.

Tobin, J. (1984) 'On the efficiency of the financial system', *Lloyds Bank Review*, no. 153, July, pp. 1–15.

Tsakalotos, E. (1991) *Alternative Economic Strategies*, Gower, Avebury.

Vives, X. (1990) 'Banking competition and European integration', CEPR Discussion Paper, no. 373, April.

Walter, I. and Smith, R. C. (1990) 'European investment banking: structure, transactions flow and regulation', in Dermine, J. (ed.).

World Bank (1989) *World Development Report*, World Bank, Washington, DC.

9
The Community's Redistributive and Development Role and the Southern European Countries

Achilleas Mitsos[1]

> Like 'motherhood and apple pie', cohesion is something that few oppose, but it is difficult to judge the depth of support for it.
>
> (Begg and Mayes, 1989)

For most people economic and social cohesion is another elegant expression (of French origin, of course), invented to hide and embellish the transfer of Community funds to the needy member-states, synonymous, to put it bluntly, with 'buying off' the poor countries' concession for the further moves towards integration that the rich member-states decide to pursue.

Although it is true that the Community's structural funds are (by far) the most important means to achieve cohesion, and, moreover, that a further substantial increase of the funds directed towards the poorer countries is a *conditio sine qua non* for those countries' approval of certain restrictions on their economic policies, economic and social cohesion is not just that. Economic and social cohesion is the corollary of integration and, at the same time, the expression in concrete terms of the Community's deepening.

If one had to identify the single most important Community policy from the Southern European countries' point of view, the 'cohesion policy' would be the most obvious candidate. Since the early days of the 1955 Messina Conference, Italy, the only 'Southern Country' at the time, was advocating the creation of an 'investment fund'.[2] Greece's accession in 1981 was directly associated with the introduction of the integrated development approach in the Community jargon, and Spain's and Portugal's accession in 1986, and the corresponding dramatic change in the inter-Community balance of power, led to the establishment of a redistribution policy as an integral part of the Community's overall policies.

The most obvious reason for the importance Southern European countries pay to the 'cohesion policy' lies with the macroeconomic significance of the amounts involved. Southern European countries (and Ireland) are not the sole but, by far, the main beneficiaries of 'cohesion policy', capturing almost 80 per cent of the total amount of the structural funds.[3] For the period 1994 to 1999 the annual, *direct* impact (that is, without taking into account any multiplier effects) of the Community structural funds to the GNP of Southern European countries is 3.4 per cent in the case of Greece and 3.2 per cent in the case of Portugal,[4] and their contribution to gross fixed capital formation goes up to 11.9 per cent in the case of Greece and 8.3 per cent in the case of Portugal. (As regards the two other Southern European countries, the overall incidence of the structural funds is somewhat smaller and more difficult to establish, due to the partial coverage of their regions by the priority objective of Community action.)[5]

'Cohesion policy', is the only redistributive mechanism in the otherwise rather regressive Community budget, and, at the same time, it aims at fulfilling other, equally important, objectives: it compensates those regions that suffer from the implementation of concrete measures of the Community policy in other domains, and, moreover, it represents the only policy that aims at reversing or, at least, reducing the negative impact of the functioning of the internal market for the less prosperous Southern regions.[6]

Furthermore, 'cohesion policy' contributes to the modernization of the Southern European economies with the aim of not 'leaving them behind' in the process of European integration, in view in particular of the imminent major steps in this direction. The development effort in Southern European countries has been (partly, or even wholly – in the case of Greece) transferred to the Community level. Very few public investments are being financed outside the so-called 'community support framework', and the direct or indirect aid to private investment is also channelled mainly through the Community funds.

Finally, and maybe most importantly, 'cohesion policy' represents the Southern European countries' dimension in Community life in general. Cohesion is not defined in the Maastricht Treaty, but, what is explicitly specified is that 'in particular, the Community shall aim at reducing disparities between the levels of development of the various regions and the backwardness of the least favoured regions ... ' (article 130a of the Treaty). Moreover, according to article 130b 'the formulation and implementation of the Community's policies and actions and the implementation of the internal market shall take into account' these same objectives.

The concept of economic cohesion was introduced into Community jargon only recently. It has been substituted for the word 'convergence', that was used until 1985–6, with three important advantages. First, it creates somewhat less confusion, because the term 'convergence' has been used with at least eight different interpretations: nominal convergence (harmonization of inflation rates and other macroeconomic indicators); policy convergence (coordination of budgetary and other policies); structural convergence (structural adaptation to produce more closely related structures and thereby diminishing vulnerability to external stocks); behavioural convergence (increasing similarity in various behavioural phenomena such as savings ratios); inputs convergence (convergence in terms of availability of factors of production, that is, with respect to the competitiveness potential); output convergence (narrowing the gap in incomes); welfare convergence (convergence in not just nominal incomes but in total welfare, that is, taking into account also the provision of public goods and local services); and finally real convergence (narrowing the gap in disposable incomes).[7] Second, the ambiguity created by the term 'convergence' was not ideologically neutral, since it sometimes implied that the coordination of, for example, monetary policies (policy convergence) and the reduction of the gap in, for example, inflation rates (nominal convergence) would necessarily lead to the reduction of real income disparities. Finally, cohesion is easily linked to 'political cohesion' – an obvious prerequisite for further integration.

After a brief survey of the theoretical foundations of positive Community action for strengthening economic and social cohesion, we present and critically assess the steps already taken in this direction, during the 1986 to 1991 period ('the Single Act era'), and those measures that were rendered necessary by the new Treaty of European Union.

Theoretical foundations for strengthening economic and social cohesion

Fostering economic and social cohesion at the Community level can be theoretically founded on a number of arguments that can be grouped in three distinct 'families' of theories. The first argument for direct Community involvement to diminish regional disparities lies on pure equity considerations, that can be analysed either on the basis of the classical Musgravian attribution of the redistribution function to the more central level of government,[8] or following modern public choice approaches, according to which total welfare would increase if regional inequalities were removed, because important groups of the population feel that regional inequality is socially unacceptable and unfair. In that sense, regional redistribution is not a zero-sum game because it is valued also in the donor region, and the transfer provides some benefit to them also.

This rationale was beautifully explored in the famous MacDougall Report,[9] which has had the privilege of being very influential among academics who deal with European affairs, and is extensively quoted in documents and theses arguing for fiscal federalism and substantial increases of the Community budget. However it has not had any real impact on the actual process of European integration. Not surprisingly, the prospects of economic and monetary union have led to the revival of interest in the subject.[10]

But equity and regional redistribution on what grounds? What constitutes the 'regional problem'? Quoting from the 'Bible' of 'One Market, One Money':[11]

> the following goals … might be considered in alternative or complementary ways:
>
> - a spatially balanced distribution of population and economic activities in order to avoid externalities and long-run social and environmental problems;
> - an adequate level of provision and accessibility of public goods and local services to all populations;
> - equalisation of levels of GDP per capita; and
> - equalisation of levels of personal disposable, or per capita consumption, or welfare.

These goals are not equivalent and the policies required to reduce disparities in the one or the other sense are not necessarily the same. What is certain though, is that regional disparities within the European Community, according to each of these criteria, are huge ('twice as wide as those in the USA'),[12] and reducing them is a long-term challenge.

Presenting these disparities in terms of GDP per head and rates of unemployment remain the most common way of illustrating the range of regional inequalities. In the Appendix, Tables 9.11 and 9.12, we calculate the percentages of each member-state's population belonging to different levels of these two criteria. The enormous income differential between the Greek, Portuguese and Irish regions on the one hand, and the more advanced regions of Germany, France or the UK, the dualism of the Italian economy with over 30 per cent of her regions' population belonging to the lowest ranges of GDP per capita and over 60 per cent to the highest ones, the relatively normal distribution of for example, Germany's or Denmark's regional population according to both criteria, and the acute unemployment problem of a major part of Ireland's and Spain's regions, that is added to the income gap that separates these regions from the Community average, are illustrated in these tables.

More complex, but at the same time containing greater explanatory and operational value, are the indicators that deal with the 'economic potential' of the region, representing the availability of inputs and the proximity of markets to the region.[13] The related concept of 'peripherality',[14] a notion of distance (in the geographical as well as the economic sense of the word), is another widely used criterion for regional classification.

Meaningful indices of welfare disparities should include a much wider range of economic and social characteristics, like the number of households with certain durable goods, number of hospitals, doctors and teachers, and so on, but the non-availability of such data at the sub-national level (especially in less advanced countries) reduces the usefulness of these exercises.

The equity approach outlined above is built upon the socially and politically unacceptable situation in terms of 'outcome' disparities and asks the 'central' authorities to deal with this problem. An alternative approach would start from the source of these disparities asking questions about the causes of unequal development and try to deal directly with these.

A central element of this 'development approach' lies in the inadequacy of 'invisible hand' ideas to deal with real world regional economics,[15] and in that sense the New Trade Theory, with the explicit acknowledgement of the role of imperfect competition, economies of scale and transport costs can give much more convincing predictions of regional outcomes.[16]

This is of course not a new issue and the literature on regional development, the determinants of regional competitiveness and the factors that shape regional growth is very substantial.[17] What needs to be underlined for the purposes of this chapter is that different theories lead to different policy strategies.[18]

The neoclassical theory, emphasizing the factor mobility element would lead to capital incentives and measures to counterbalance labour market imperfections. The neo-Keynesian recipe would include direct investment by state-owned firms and public income transfers to households. Infrastructure provision and intersectoral linkages planning will be central in the 'stages of development' approach. Endogenous growth theory would stress decentralization of regional policy management and education and vocational training measures. Innovation-led development theories advocate subsidizing innovation, and technology parks. Finally modern 'milieux innovateurs' approaches favour integrated packages with emphasis on local participation and interregional cooperation and networking.

An alternative justification for positive Community action in the regional sphere, is founded on purely compensatory grounds. The argument in its brute form treats cohesion as a mere side-payment to those Community Member-States who would not otherwise be willing to accept some steps to further integration.[19] This *do ut des* reality of Community negotiations could be theorized however by trying to identify gainers and losers from the different Community policies and stressing the need to compensate the latter on the basis of the principle of 'fair burden sharing', or, following Gretschmann, 'to avoid undue appropriation of Community savings by one country or region'.[20]

The argument in its theoretical formulation goes as follows: free trade gains are not equally distributed. Producers in the more developed regions profit from the 'open market' situation. As a consequence, the higher income and tax capacity of the more developed regions are, to a certain extent, the result of these 'gains from trade', that are not due to 'private' but to 'public' competitiveness. Under these conditions the richer regions should transfer to the poorer ones that part of their higher tax returns that is derived from the latter keeping their markets open and accepting the decline of their less competitive producers.[21]

We do not attempt to even touch upon the extended literature on gainers and losers from Community policy. The subject is a very controversial one and the reader is referred to the classical sources.[22]

The main arguments outlined above (equity, development and compensation) constitute complementary bases for positive Community action. The ambiguity of the ultimate objective however undermines any evaluation of the impact of Community action, because the specific recommendations on the exact type of action may differ substantially. A lump-sum transfer or a fiscal equalization scheme could satisfy much more directly the need for equity. A direct contribution to reduce the gap in infrastructure or R&D endowment or human capital or a direct grant to private investors correspond to the different theories of development. Finally the compensation approach would most probably require an intervention directly linked to the cost incurred by the Community policy in question (financed by the region or country that has acquired the additional gain).

The Single Act and the reform of the Community's structural policy

In terms of the actual implementation of the theoretical principles outlined in the previous section, the historic turning point has undoubtedly been the *Single Act* of 1986 – the legal and institutional expression of the new balance that had to result from the extremely ambitious '1992 project'. It is in this new Treaty that, for the first time, income redistribution from the richer to the poorer regions of the Community is acknowledged among the objectives of the Community. The use of the rather ambiguous term 'economic and social cohesion' instead of a more direct reference to 'redistribution' does not create a real problem, because, as already mentioned, the notion of 'cohesion' is clarified with the sentence on the need to 'reduce disparities between the various regions and the backwardness of the less-favoured regions'.

It is equally important not only that the new objective is acknowledged, but also, that the need to provide the Community with the appropriate means to cope with this objective is explicitly made. These means were to be both financial and non-financial, as article 130b explicitly asked for cohesion to be taken into account in 'the implementation of the common policies and of the internal market'. In other words, the actual implementation of Community policies, such as the common agricultural policy or the research policy, as well as the Community's position in commercial negotiations with, for example, the USA, should also include the cohesion dimension.

Concentrating first on the financial expression of the objective of economic and social cohesion, through the structural funds of the Community, one can raise the objection: 'Why is the Single Act considered as the "historical turning point" when funds already existed long before the Single Act?' The Single Act can be considered the turning point for two reasons. First, because from the moment that the reduction of the development gap between, say, the Greek islands and the central European regions becomes the objective of the Community, this Community becomes a partner of the Greek authorities, at national as well as at regional or local level, having a similar objective. As in all cases of partnership, each partner should contribute with whatever resources he has to the achievement of the common objective. Second, the explicit introduction of this new objective has direct implications for the *size* and the *design* of the structural funds. Their 'philosophy' changes, and henceforth their functioning must guarantee the maximization of their economic impact.

These may sound like purely theoretical considerations, but they are not. In the pre-Single Act period, the main guiding principle of the Structural Funds was the need to 'raise the Community's flag' in as many actions as possible. What was important was to show that the construction of road A or training seminar B was realized with a contribution of the Community budget. The *ex ante* decisions that had to be taken concerned (a) the total amount of each Fund, (b) the quota for the member-states (explicitly or implicitly) and (c) some basic rules of eligibility.[23]

The 'partnership' principle on the contrary leads to the substitution of the 'approach by fund' by the 'approach by objectives'. The three existing Funds should become nothing but instruments to achieve the specific priority objectives that the Community has set for itself[24] – the development of lagging regions (objective 1), the conversion of areas affected by industrial decline (objective 2), combating long-term unemployment (objective 3), the occupational integration of young people (objective 4), the adjustment of agricultural structures (objective 5a), and the development of rural areas (objective 5b).[25]

The pursuit of 'real economic impact' has had a number of extremely important implications, both of a quantitative as well as of a qualitative nature. The Community cannot hope to fulfil even partially the ambitious objectives it set itself, unless (a) the amounts involved become really important, and (b) the functioning of the Funds becomes much more impact-oriented.

The financial expression of this need for a real economic impact was the well-known 'Delors package' of 1988, that lead to the doubling by 1992 of the funds for the less developed regions[26] and, by 1993, for the other regions and objectives. As a result of this unequal increase, two-thirds of the total amounts are concentrated in the four Southern European countries, 23.3 per cent in Spain, 17.4 per cent in Italy, 13.3 per cent in Portugal and 12.8 per cent in Greece (Tables 9.1 and 9.2).

The annual rate of growth for the period 1986 to 1992 for the Structural Funds was 18.9 per cent, second only to the rate of growth for the 'R&D, energy, education, environment' part of the Community budget (25.2 per cent).[27] As a result of this important increase, the share of the three funds in the Community budget reached 20.2 per cent in 1990, compared to

Table 9.1 Structural funds 1989–93, breakdown by objective (1989 prices, share of total)

	Billion ECUs	Share (%)
Regional objectives		
Obj.1(lagging regions)[a]	38.3	63.4
Obj.2 (industrial decline)	7.2	11.9
Obj.5b (rural areas)	2.8	4.6
Horizontal objectives		
Objs.3,4 (labour market)[b]	7.5	12.4
Obj.5a (agric. structures)	3.4	5.6
Other action[c]	1.1	1.8
Total	*60.4*	

[a] Including objectives 3, 4 and 5a in these regions.
[b] Excluding regions of objective 1.
[c] 'Community initiatives', transitional measures, innovative actions.
Source: Commission EC (1992a).

Table 9.2 Structural funds 1989–93: breakdown by objective and country (%)

	Obj.1	Obj.2	Objs.3,4	Obj.5a	Obj.5b	Other	Total
Belgium	–	4.3	2.1	0.5	1.2	1.0	1.0
Denmark	–	0.6	1.3	0.8	0.9	0.2	0.4
France	2.4	18.4	13.1	5.2	36.8	8.0	8.4
Germany	–	9.3	7.5	1.9	20.1	3.9	3.8
Greece	18.1	–	6.7	22.4	–	10.3	12.8
Ireland	9.7	–	4.3	13.1	–	5.4	7.0
Italy	21.0	6.3	17.7	13.6	14.8	13.0	17.4
Luxembourg	–	0.4	0.1	–	0.1	0.1	0.1
Netherlands	–	2.5	3.2	0.7	1.7	0.5	1.0
Portugal	19.8	–	5.1	20.2	–	10.7	13.3
Spain	27.2	20.3	21.2	17.3	10.9	17.0	23.3
UK	1.7	38.0	17.9	4.3	13.4	7.1	10.0
non alloc.	–	–	–	–	–	22.9	1.6

Note: The objective 1 column does not include the funds' contribution to the horizontal objectives (objs.3,4,5a) in the obj.1 regions.
Source: Commission EC (1992c) and Commission services, Community Support Frameworks.

17.2 per cent in 1980, 6.3 per cent in 1975 and 1.2 per cent in 1970 (when neither the Regional nor the structural part of the Agricultural Fund were established).[28]

For the recipient countries the amounts are, for the first time, really important, even from the macroeconomic point of view. The annual commitments of the three funds represent 2 to 4 per cent of the GDP of each of the three countries entirely covered by the objective 1 (Greece, Portugal, Ireland).[29] Furthermore, they correspond to 43 per cent (for Ireland), 67 per cent (for Portugal) and 170 per cent (for Greece) of the 1989 foreign direct investment in these countries.[30]

For illustration purposes we present in Table 9.3 a comparison between the five-year-period funds and some macroeconomic variables for each member-state. The amount for the five-year-period corresponds to 14.5 to 18 per cent of the 1989 GDP of the two less prosperous Southern European countries, to around 40 per cent of their total annual imports, to between 48 and 62 per cent of their total annual exports, and to an amount equivalent to, or greater than, the yearly receipts from all taxes on production and imports. For Italy and Spain the corresponding percentages are far smaller, due to the partial coverage of these two countries by 'objective 1'.

From the 'rich' countries point of view though, these same amounts are almost marginal, since the yearly amount for the development of lagging regions represents only 0.12 per cent of the 'rich' countries annual GDP.

Table 9.3   Total funds 1989–93 as a percentage of macroeconomic variables 1989

Country	GDP[1]	Imp[2]	Exp[3]	Cons[4]	Cap[5]	Taxes[6]
Belgium	0.42	0.57	0.53	0.55	1.91	3.87
Denmark	0.23	0.75	0.68	0.30	1.27	1.35
France	0.54	2.34	2.33	0.69	2.45	3.78
Germany	0.20	0.76	0.63	0.27	0.92	1.7
Greece	14.47	45.19	62.90	15.91	70.68	96.61
Ireland	12.47	22.15	18.96	17.38	66.42	74.64
Italy	1.23	6.10	6.04	1.56	5.76	6.04
Luxembourg	0.63	0.63	0.62	0.88	2.37	3.83
Netherlands	0.28	0.51	0.48	0.37	1.30	2.45
Portugal	18.01	39.00	48.08	22.63	61.82	116.27
Spain	3.75	17.54	20.70	4.80	14.85	36.23
UK	0.73	2.62	3.03	0.88	3.56	5.01
Total	1.24	4.48	4.36	1.60	5.76	9.95

[1] GDP at market prices, 1989.
[2] Total imports of goods and services, 1989.
[3] Total exports of goods and services, 1989.
[4] Final national consumption, 1989.
[5] Gross capital formation, 1989.
[6] Taxes on production and imports, 1989.
Source: Community Support Frameworks and Eurostat (1993).

An interesting comparison of the significance of the overall amounts would be with the Marshall Plan. As regards the recipient countries, the annual average rate of expenditure for the four years 1948 to 1951 as a percentage of GDP was 1.5 per cent for W. Germany, 1.9 per cent for the UK, 2.4 per cent for Italy, 2.9 per cent for France, and 5.7 per cent for the Netherlands, shares that compare to the structural funds' shares for the period 1989 to 1993. By contrast, there is no similarity from the donor's point of view, with the US contributing 2 per cent of its GDP per annum, compared with only 0.12 per cent from the European Union 'rich' countries.[31]

The need for maximizing the real economic impact resulted not only in this substantial increase of the available funds, but also, as already mentioned, in the modification of the functioning and the administration of the Funds, with the generalization of an impact-oriented approach based mainly on a programming and management method in three stages.

The first phase concerns the preparation of the development (or reconstruction) plan, and obviously, the prime if not the sole responsibility lies in the hands of the member-states, usually at central government level. By contrast, in the second phase, that of the establishment of the Community Support Framework, the role of the Commission becomes important. The Community Support Frameworks should be based upon the priorities as expressed in the national multiannual plans, with the Commission adding the 'Community dimension' to them, either positively where priorities established at the Community level (for example, improving the communications network between the regions) require so, or, much more often, negatively, in the cases where the national priorities contradict community legislation, for example, in the competition area or that of environmental protection. The final document is negotiated with the relevant national and regional authorities and it is officially approved by the member-state in question. Finally, during the implementation (third) phase, the monitoring arrangements established give the regional and local authorities considerable responsibilities, even in those member-states where regionalization is less developed.

It should be noted though, that this three-stage programming system did not function equally well in all cases. The 'development plan' has often been a non-substantive document, while the 'Community Support Framework' preparation and negotiation has proven to be a very unequal exercise, with the Commission officials, in certain cases, playing only a passive role, while in others deciding on issues lying clearly in the domestic domain. Finally, and most importantly, the implementation phase has not always been left 'to the authority closer to the citizen', but has been directed by Commission officials, who have neither the concrete knowledge nor the democratic legitimacy for that.[32]

A parenthesis may be useful at this stage to say a word about the so-called community initiatives, specific programmes that is, that stem from the Commission's initiative and are added to the part of the Community Support Framework that is based upon national plans, that is national initiatives.[33] The point that should be emphasized here is that the distinction between these two types of measures lies merely in which side takes the initiative, and not in the prevailing of national or Community interest. This is an important point because it summarizes the fundamental change in the role of the structural funds, introduced by the Single Act. The notion of 'Community interest' is present equally in the Community and the national initiatives. From the moment the development, or the reconstruction, of a region has become a Community objective, the Community interest is served by the pursuit of this.

Assessment of the first period

In an attempt to evaluate the functioning of the structural funds of the first post-Single Act generation, we concentrate on issues of effectiveness ('doing the right thing') as well as efficiency ('doing the thing right'), constrained, obviously, by the fact that it is far too early to judge the full extent of the *ex post* impact of the actions taken.[34]

The *ex post* analysis of the Structural Funds' interventions during the period 1989 to 1993 by sector or major category of investment confirms that the different priorities of each member-state, the varying degrees of regionalization (due mainly to domestic political reasons), coupled with a rather passive role of the Commission services in most (but not all) cases, led to different structures of the Community Support Frameworks.

As shown in Table 9.4[35] for the Southern European countries covered by 'objective 1', the share of basic infrastructure in the total funding varies

Table 9.4 Major categories of structural funds interventions (as a percentage of total) objective 1 countries, 1989–93

	Greece	Ireland	Portugal	Italy	Spain
Infrastructure	37.4	15.6	21.6	45.4	51.9
Transport	14.0	15.0	9.9	6.4	31.0
Industry, Services	12.8	26.4	23.9	27.8	9.4
Tourism	1.9	4.1	–	10.4	1.9
Rural Dev., Agric.	23.3	26.5	18.8	9.8	15.3
Obj.5a	15.5	8.6	9.8	4.7	5.1
Human Resources	26.0	31.0	35.4	16.5	23.0
Obj.1	11.5	22.2	27.7	5.2	9.5
Objs.3,4	14.4	8.7	7.7	11.3	13.5
Techn. Assist. etc.	0.6	0.5	0.4	0.5	0.5

The percentages refer to the multiregional part of the Community Support Framework for each country.
Source: Commission services; Community Support Framework for each country.

from 21.6 per cent in Portugal to 51.9 per cent in Spain, while that of industry varies from 9.4 per cent in Spain to 27.8 per cent in Italy.[36] This reflects radically different positions regarding the well-known debate on direct *vs* indirect aid to capital formation. Direct subsidies artificially lower the costs of private investment leading to greater investment at the possible risk of implementing sub-optimal investment projects, while investment in physical and human capital is expected to lead to the increase of private investment by an improvement in the marginal productivity of capital.[37]

Rural development (agricultural structures share) is important in all regions (reflecting *inter alia* the relative bargaining power of the Ministries of Agriculture as well as the agricultural services of the Commission). Finally, it is interesting to note that the human resources element is present in all countries, but within this category the shares of objective 1 funding (the funding of training activities directly linked to the development of the regions and countries concerned), and of objectives 3 and 4 funding (training to combat long-term unemployment and the insertion of young people in the productive sectors) vary considerably from country to country.

Turning now to the question of 'absorption' of the funds (that seems to remain the central one in internal debates within each member-state as well as within the Commission services), we must first define the term because different people give it different interpretations, with not always innocent intentions. Since there are many stages for the execution of the initial decision, one ends up with entirely different results depending on what is compared to what. There is first the *ex ante* decision – the amount for the specific action as decided during the programming phase. There is, second, the budgetary commitment that the Community decides with an extremely complicated system of annual decisions, taken separately for each fund and linked to the actual execution of a predetermined part of the previous commitment. There is, third, the actual budgetary payment decision of the Community, either as an advance or as a final payment of the annual *tranche*, that also depends on the actual execution of the programme in question. There is, finally, the actual execution phase (the building of the road, or the payment to the final beneficiary of the public aid, or the completion of the training seminar, etc).[38]

One of the central pillars of the 1988 reform of the structural funds – and a rather obvious one given the need to pursue concrete objectives with (increased and important *per se*, but still) scarce resources – was the need to concentrate the Community action where it was most needed. A first indication of whether this concentration has been achieved or not would come from the comparison of the share of member-states' population covered by each fund before and after the reform. In reality, however, this share cannot be calculated. What can be calculated instead is the share of population that is *eligible* for the funds' intervention before and after the reform.

But being 'eligible' and being 'covered' are not necessarily equivalent. Regarding this 'geographical eligibility' the only notable changes between the two periods are: (a) The extension of objective 1 coverage to include also the relatively more advanced regions within the less advanced countries. This shift represents a shift of emphasis from the Community assistance to the regional policies of the member-states towards a Community regional policy.[39] (b) The extension of Regional Fund eligibility to the new objective of rural development. (c) A slight reduction in the coverage of objective 2 regions, especially in Germany where the population eligible to Regional Fund interventions dropped from 37.5 per cent before the reform to 18.3 per cent after the reform (with 7.4 per cent of it being eligible under the obj.5b and excluding the eligibility of the new eastern Länder).[40]

An indirect, but very clear, illustration of concentration of total effort (or, better, the lack of it) is based on the rates of Community intervention within each country, in other words, the share of the total cost (or the total public expenditure) of each action covered by the Structural Funds. Although, with the 1988 reform, the *maximum* rate of Community intervention has been increased up to 75 per cent of total cost and 100 per cent of public expenditure, the *actual* rate of this intervention has not changed significantly, reflecting a preference of the authorities for a dispersion of the total amount to a greater number of projects.[41]

A better indication of the degree of success of the concentration effort, as well as some first indications of the redistribution impact of the structural funds, stems from an analysis of the per capita contribution of these funds in the different regions and countries.[42] The results of this analysis, completed by the Commission services, are presented in Table 9.5. As expected, the average per capita contribution of the Community funds to objective 1 regions is much higher than the average contribution to the other objectives' regions. It is important to note the large discrepancies observed within each objective. Portugal and Greece receive on a per capita basis 136 per cent and 127 per cent of the Community average, Spain receives only 85 per cent of the average per capita for objective 1 regions, but 138 per cent and 175 per cent for her regions covered by the two other regional objectives, while Italian regions receive considerably smaller per capita funds irrespectively of the objective involved. What is really striking though is that in Ireland the per capita contribution is 50 per cent higher than that in Greece, although Irish per capita GDP was 18 per cent *higher* than Greece![43]

In order to explore the central question of the redistributive effects of structural interventions even further we attempt a number of cross-regional regressions with dependent variable structural funds' total intervention per region 1989–93 and independent variables various characteristics of these regions (GDP per capita, rate of unemployment, shares of industry and agriculture in total employment). The results are presented in the Appendix

Table 9.5   Structural funds 1989–93 per head,
by country and objective (ecu, 1989 prices)

Country	Obj.1[a]	Obj.2	Obj.5b
Belgium	–	108.0	129.0
Denmark	–	99.0	215.0
France	455.4	104.0	165.0
Germany	182.0[b]	67.0	124.0
Greece	536.5	–	–
Ireland	810.6	–	–
Italy	298.3	95.0	133.0
Luxembourg	–	109.0	735.0
Netherlands	–	110.0	99.0
Portugal	572.7	–	–
Spain	357.4	153.0	278.0
UK	322.5	117.0	215.0
Average	421.0[c]	111.0	159.0

[a] Excluding Objs.3,4.5a in these regions.
[b] New East German Länder. 1991 prices. Highest per capita contribution: Mecklembourg 204.6, lowest: Berlin-Est 126.3, Saxe: 149.5 ecu per capita.
[c] The average does not cover the East German regions.
[d] Highest per capita contributions: Aubagne (Belgium) 2211, Vestlolland (Denmark) 212, North Wales (United Kingdom) 184, Pais vasco (Spain) 178 ecu per capita. Lowest per capita contributions: Berlin 56, Saarland (Germany) 63 ecu per capita.
[e] Highest per capita contributions: Rioja (Spain) 1235.4, Euskadi (Spain) 1140.1, Champagne-Ardennes (France) 1058.2, Haute Sure (Luxembourg) 735.3, Cantabria (Spain) 580.0, Madrid 379.5, Highlands-Islands (UK) 371.1, Schleswig-Holstein (Germany) 340.6, Lanquedoc-Rousillon (France) 334.7 ecu per capita. Lowest per capita contributions: Alsace (France) 77.3, Hageland (Belgium) 83.5 ecu per capita.
Source: Commission services.

(Table 9.13) and they confirm the hypothesis that Community structural intervention is negatively related to the level of regional income per capita and positively related to the rate of unemployment. The statistical significance of the results for objective 2 regions is much higher, especially regarding the rate of unemployment, while the inclusion among the independent variables of the GDP per capita of the member-state (and not just the region concerned) adds significantly to the explanation of the dependent variable.

An underlying, hidden, assumption of the analysis so far is that the additionality principle has been respected. In simple terms, according to this principle, Community funding should be added to the national one, and therefore, the increase of structural funds should result in at least an equal increase of total aid (national plus Community). This hypothesis of additionality (or better, of non-substitution) is necessary because otherwise an increase of Community intervention in area A (in absolute or relative to the other areas of the same country terms) could be offset by an opposite movement of national public intervention.

The additionality principle has caused tremendous difficulties at the negotiations in the Council of Ministers, as well as at the practical verification level, and has led to great confusion in both the internal political discussion in certain member-states and some academic analyses of the functioning of structural funds.[44] Generally speaking, after a thorough examination, the Commission services have concluded that the additionality principle has been fully respected in the countries entirely covered by the funds' action, while problems persist only with respect to some particular areas in certain relatively advanced member-states, because of the lack of transparent data at regional level.

It is important to note however, that respect for the additionality principle imposes a constraint on the management of national and regional budgets, and this constraint may be of significant proportions for the countries for which the relative magnitude of transfers from Community funds is greater.[45]

It is obviously far too early to assess the real impact of the structural action of the Community in this first post-Single Act period, but the Commission has devoted considerable resources to the evaluation of the potential (and thus, *ex ante*)[46] economic impact of these actions. The only quantifiable part of this exercise concerned the short-run effect of the structural funds to the generation of extra domestic demand. The larger share of Community grants, however, is targeted on physical as well as human capital investment, whose main impact is on the supply side of the economy. Because of the lack of any standardized model that could provide answers to the different macroeconomic or sectoral questions, the Commission services used both classical input–output models, as well as dynamic general equilibrium models, where the availability of data made this possible.[47]

According to these studies the immediate demand stimulus that the grants create results to an additional annual growth for the objective 1 countries from 0.3 per cent for Spain and Italy to 0.7 per cent for Portugal. This result obviously underestimates the true impact because of the structural nature of the Community Support Framework. To illustrate this under-estimation, the study for Portugal showed that, even under the assumption that there is no further increase in the Community grants, the *permanent* acceleration of the growth rate of the economy is of the order of 0.5 per cent per annum.

Finally, a note must be made on the positive impact of the extra activity created by the structural funds on the 'donor countries', because of the import content of investment expenditure. As shown in Table 9.6, the

Table 9.6   Impact of structural funds objective 1 on imports from other member-states (Return flows*) (%)

Greece	35
Portugal	46
Ireland	16
Spain	26
Italy	18[a]

* Return Flow (RF) definition: RF = DM/DF, with: DM: Increase in intra-EC imports, DF: Increase in structural funds' payments. Decomposition: RF = DY/DF * DM/DY * Y/M * M/Y
given that: DY/DF: Multiplier, DM/DY * Y/M: Elasticity of intra-EC imports, M/Y: Share of intra-EC imports in GDP.
[a] Return flow to the Italian Centre-North regions: 22%.
Source: Commission services.

'return flow' – the (intra-EU) import content – of structural funds in objective 1 regions is between 16 per cent for Ireland and 46 per cent for Portugal.[48]

The Maastricht era

If the turning point concerning the role of cohesion in the process of integration has been the Single Act, the European Union Treaty should be the point of consolidation of this role. The Treaty of Maastricht, being the result of the need to abolish the last major obstacle to complete market integration (the existence of different moneys in different parts of the integrated market), should lead to a new push towards economic and social cohesion of the Community.

But has it? In order to attempt to answer this question one should examine first the relevant modifications of the Treaty itself, second the decisions on the quantitative means for the post-Maastricht period, and third, the modifications in the actual working of the system that resulted from these decisions.

The first, and by far the most important, concrete new element in the Maastricht Treaty is the establishment of a new fund, the Cohesion Fund.[49] The creation of this new fund has been presented as a negotiating victory of the four 'cohesion countries' (Spain, Ireland, Portugal and Greece), but this initial triumphalism should be mitigated to some extent for a number of important reasons:

(a) As already mentioned, the impact-oriented approach of the Community's structural action is already seriously undermined by the persistence of different funds with separate budgets, various administrative and budgetary procedures and distinct 'clients'. A truly integrated approach would lead to a unique fund by objective. Instead of doing precisely that the Maastricht Treaty adds to the confusion by creating yet another fund (and with a title that *a contrario* suggests that the other funds are not cohesion oriented).

(b) The Cohesion Fund is geared not towards regions but towards member-states (the four 'cohesion countries'). This, of course, suits Spain – the only 'cohesion country' not fully covered by objective 1 – but it diminishes the, already weak, regional income redistribution impact of the funds in total, because the poorest regions of Greece or Portugal will get an even smaller share of the total. Furthermore, one of the essential positive elements of the pre-Maastricht structural funds is that they lead, if not institutionally, at least effectively,[50] to a decentralization of the decision-making process within some countries, at least. Instead of promoting this trend further, the Maastricht Treaty returns to the traditional partnership between the two classical 'partners' – the Commission and the representatives of the central authorities of each member-state.

(c) Contrary to the other structural funds, the Cohesion Fund is not aimed at financing total programmes but concrete, non-integrated into overall planning scheme projects. Leaving aside the question of defining what a 'project' is (should the construction of 20 km of a national road be defined as a project of its own?), this constitutes another backward move and it provides arguments for all those who regard 'programming' as a futile exercise *in vitro*, and nothing more.

(d) The projects to be financed by the Cohesion Fund must be in two major areas where externalities are present – transport and environmental infrastructure. It would be difficult to argue against the need to invest in these specific areas, but what should be noted is that this restriction of eligibility subordinates in a sense the objective of cohesion *per se* to that of coping with certain externalities. Cohesion, that is, 'reducing the disparities between the levels of development of the various regions' (art. 130a of the Treaty) is *not* the objective of the Cohesion Fund (contrary to that of the 'structural funds').

(e) The final and most controversial point concerns the direct link of the financing of the Cohesion Fund to the overall macroeconomic policy of the country in question. According to the Protocol on Economic and Social Cohesion, annexed to the Treaty on European Union, 'the Cohesion Fund ... will provide Community financial contributions ... in Member States ... which have a programme leading to the fulfilment of the conditions of economic convergence as set out in Article 104c' (on excessive government deficits).

This conditionality, in other words, the direct link between Community financing of a specific project and the way macroeconomic objectives are pursued by the recipient member-state, did not (and does not) apply to the structural funds. What is questionable though is not the – obvious – need for a member-state to follow coherent macroeconomic policies, but the implication that the Community has an increased, and quite special, role in implementing this coherence, simply because a special Community effort has been decided on purely cohesion terms.

A second important institutional development is the establishment by the Treaty (art. 198a) of the Committee of the Regions. A direct involvement of regions and local authorities in the process of European integration with the right to express an opinion on all policies directly or indirectly concerning them may prove to constitute a fundamental constitutional development, but it may also prove to be just another bureaucratic reason for decision-making delays.

Coming now to the second phase of the decisions linked to the Treaty on Union, the budgetary decisions, one should start by saying that the Commission has proposed a far reaching plan, 'the means to match our ambitions' (the 'Delors II package'), that includes a further doubling of the available funds for the least developed regions and countries within the next five to seven years. This doubling would be partly covered by the three existing structural funds, and partly by the establishment of the Cohesion Fund.

The long and very intensive negotiations that followed in the Council of Ministers resulted in a formal decision at the European Council of December 1992 at Edinburgh. A decision, full of quantitative as well as qualitative clauses and provisions that may sometimes lead to conflicting interpretations, but also a decision that is undoubtedly (and surprisingly for most observers) highly beneficial for the recipients of the Community's structural assistance.

Some of the sources of the complications stem from the fact that the commitments taken concern not only the total amounts, but also the allocation by objective and the allocation by group of countries, that do not necessarily coincide. There are commitments, for example, on the total amount for the 'cohesion countries' (Greece, Portugal, Ireland and Spain), but, part of this amount will be financed by the objective 1 allocation for which only certain Spanish regions are eligible, and another part will be financed by the newly created Cohesion Fund (and the 'Cohesion instrument' that will be functioning in the place of the Cohesion Fund as long as the Maastricht Treaty, that provides its legal basis, has not been implemented), for which the whole of Spanish population is eligible.

The multiannual decisions cover the period 1993 to 1999, which makes any comparison with the previous period difficult, since 1993 was also the final year of the previous period. Nevertheless, the basic quantitative elements of this decision are reproduced in the Table 9.7. There we also provide two sets of comparisons: (a) with respect to the previous multiannual decision (and with the disadvantage that we are comparing a 6-year period with a 4-year one); (b) comparing the 1994–9 period to the 1988–93 one.

Table 9.7   The December 1992 decision on the Delors II package

	1993–99		1994–99	
	billions of ecus	*% 1989–93*	*billions of ecus*	*% 1988–93*
Structural actions	176.4	253	155.1	194
Structural funds	161.3	231	141.5	177
Cohesion fund	15.2	–	13.7	–
Obj.1 regions	108.7	245	96.4	184
Other objectives	38.4	218	34.1	195
Cohesion Fund				
countries	85.4	274	75.9	217

On the basis of this last comparison, and some logical assumptions on the distribution within each group of countries (confirmed by the decisions that the Commission took in October 1993 on the indicative range of total structural interventions for each country), the total amounts for all member-states (those of objective 1 as well as the others) will double,[51] with two notable exceptions: the objective 1 regions of the countries not covered by the Cohesion Fund (mainly the Italian Mezzogiorno), where the increase will fall short of doubling, and Spain, who is clearly the big winner, getting an increase of more than 260 per cent.

The third phase of the Maastricht era arrangements concerns the qualitative modifications to the existing regulations. The aim was not to change but to consolidate the basic principles that govern the functioning of the structural funds, to rationalize some of the administrative elements and to strengthen the monitoring and evaluation procedures.

Two considerable modifications demand a special mention though. The first concerns the redefinition of the 'social objectives', by adding the need to facilitate the integration into working life of the 'persons exposed to exclusion from the labour market' and the new objective 4 – 'facilitating the adaptability of workers of either sex to industrial changes and to changes in production systems'.

The second major change that goes clearly in the wrong direction as regards the principle of concentration of resources is the map of objective 1 regions, widened to cover not only the new German Länder (and East Berlin), but also Cantabria (Spain), Hainaut (Belgium), arrondissements of Avesnes, Douai and Valenciennes (France), Flevoland (Netherlands), Highlands and Islands Enterprise area and Merseyside (UK). The only member-states with no objective 1 regions were Denmark and Luxembourg!

The cohesion dimension of overall Community policy

If the structural funds' action is the only Community action with redistribution explicitly as its objective, it is clearly not the only Community policy with a redistributional impact. Many, if not all, other Community policies affect regional redistribution, some directly through the Community budget and some indirectly through their regulatory effects.

As already mentioned, the Single Act of 1986 introduced not only economic and social cohesion as a new objective for the Community as a whole, but asked for cohesion to be taken into account in 'the implementation of all community policies'. In this respect, the Maastricht Treaty went an important step further and widened the scope of Article 130b to cover not only the implementation but also the formulation of Community policies.

Without minimizing the importance of this new Treaty wording, we must however admit that its practical implementation has not been very successful up to now, partly because of the – expected – resistance of the 'northern countries', and partly because even the 'southern countries' did not wish to press hard in this area, fearing that this would harm their negotiating power in the direct budgetary transfer discussion.

A lengthy discussion of the existing possibilities for fostering economic and social cohesion through Community action in areas other than the structural funds would exceed the scope of this chapter. It would be useful, however, to incorporate some brief remarks, and in order to do so we present three tables. Table 9.8 gives an overview of the structure of the

Table 9.8   Revenue, expenditure Community budget

	mn.ecu	Growth rate (1982 = 100)	Share (%)
Expenditure			
Total	72874.8	326	100
Administration	3644.7	343	5.0
FEOGA-guarantee	36297.0	293	49.8
Structural funds	18912.1	463	26.0
Social operations	587.0	327	0.8
Research and technol. development	3015.9	681	4.1
International cooperation	4521.7	503	6.2
Other	5896.4	180	8.1
Revenue			
Total	69492.2	308	100
Agricultural levies	922.5	61	1.3
Sugar levies	1382.1	196	2.0
Tariffs	12420.0	182	17.9
VAT-based revenue	36313.5	303	52.2
GDP-based revenue	18454.6	–	26.6

Total does not add to 100% because of 'other revenue', etc.
Source: Court of Auditors, 'Annual Report', *Official Journal EC*, various issues.

Community budget and its evolution, and, in an attempt to examine the 'cohesion friendliness' of the different elements of both the revenue and the expenditure side of the budget, Table 9.9 shows the respective shares of Southern European countries in each of these elements, as compared to their shares in the total Gross Domestic Product of the European Union, as well as the correlation coefficients between GDP and the main budgetary elements.

'Net soldes'[52] tables have never been published officially because the Commission has always argued that this net budgetary solde does not constitute even an approximation of the net benefit or net loss of one country from the working of the Community in general, since the most important Community action has no budgetary impact *per se*. It is worth noting though, that, based on the *ex post* budgetary analysis published every year by the Court of Auditors,[53] among the greater 'budgetary beneficiaries' are not only Greece and Ireland but also Luxembourg and Belgium and that the net solde per capita for Denmark is higher than that for Spain.[54]

On the budget revenue side the least that one could say is that the Community budget does not reflect even the more basic concerns of fairness. About half of Community revenue comes from the so-called VAT resource, in reality from a direct national contribution following an accounting definition of the VAT base, that tends to be relatively larger in countries with a high consumption rate, which tend to be the poorer States.

On the expenditure side, structural funds are a growing but still relatively small part of the total expenditures of the Community budget. They represented 26 per cent of total expenditure in 1996, compared to 17 per cent in 1981, a growth rate that, taking into account the overall growth rate of the Community budget, leads to a five times increase of their volume since 1981. As expected the very important shares of Southern European countries in the structural funds render the correlation coefficient between this expenditure and the GDP significantly negative, especially after the 1989 reform. The improvement of the funds' relative position in the budget as a whole, together with the improved relative position of the less developed countries' shares in the funds themselves, have led to an overall negative correlation coefficient between GDP and total expenditures, although still at rather low levels.

The major, although decreasing, part of the Community budget continues to be directed to the 'guarantee' part of the Agricultural Fund (almost 50 per cent today, compared to 55 per cent in 1991, 60 per cent in 1988 and 65 per cent in 1980), rendering the old discussion on the redistributive impact of the Common Agricultural Policy extremely relevant. The literature in this area is already huge and need not be surveyed here.[55] It should be noted though that: (a) some of the most important benefits from the Common Agricultural Policy (the import restrictions and the export

Table 9.9 Share of Southern European countries in Community GDP and Community budget (%), correlation coefficients between GDP and revenues, expenditures Community budget

	Greece	Spain	Italy	Portugal	SEE	Correlation coefficient
GDP, market prices (PPS) (1991–93)	1.82	8.80	17.38	1.89	29.89	
Total budget revenue (1991–94)	1.81	10.39	18.95	1.84	32.99	0.161
VAT-based revenue (1992–94)	1.63	9.20	15.46	1.75	28.03	0.150
GDP-based revenue (1992–94)	1.34	7.85	16.15	1.35	26.68	0.161
Tariffs revenue (1992–94)	1.28	4.41	8.35	1.07	15.11	0.161
Sugar etc levies (1992–94)	1.56	4.38	10.70	0.02	16.65	0.232
Agricultural levies (1992–94)	0.76	12.33	16.57	8.53	38.18	−0.062
Total budget expenditure (1991–94)	9.61	16.50	16.09	5.64	47.84	−0.214
FEOGA-guarantee, total (1991–94)	9.48	13.83	18.35	1.68	43.34	−0.025
Cereals, rice (1991–94)	2.63	8.82	11.27	1.27	23.99	0.279
Sugar (1991–94)	0.50	4.88	6.40	0.50	12.27	0.220
Fats (1991–94)	8.02	25.26	22.56	1.61	57.45	0.163
Fruit, vegetables (1991–94)	27.38	22.01	29.55	2.74	81.68	−0.095
Wine (1991–94)	3.24	33.07	39.49	3.88	79.68	−0.112
Tobacco (1991–94)	41.56	9.25	37.92	1.02	89.74	−0.135
Milk products (1991–94)	0.20	2.36	5.25	0.85	8.67	−0.344
Meat, eggs (1991–94)	3.40	8.93	8.13	1.53	21.99	−0.369
Structural funds (1991–94)	14.29	28.19	18.96	16.27	77.70	−0.566
FEOGA-guidance (1991–94)	15.02	22.62	16.42	15.42	69.49	−0.430
Social fund (1991–94)	10.39	24.57	17.50	11.10	63.56	−0.599
Regional fund (1991–94)	16.70	32.85	21.20	19.98	90.73	−0.438

Correlation coefficients various years:
Total revenue: 1981: 0.043, 1985: 0.049, 1988: 0.197, 1993: 0.157, 1994: 0.162.
Total expenditure: 1981: −0.037, 1985: −0.161, 1988: −0.02, 1993: −0.231, 1994: −0.226.
FEOGA-guarantee: 1981: 0.056, 1985: −0.104, 1988: 0.120, 1993: −0.033, 1994: −0.064.
Structural funds: 1981: −225, 1985: −319, 1988: −392, 1993: −449, 1994: −570.
Source: GDP: Eurostat, *National Accounts ESA, Aggregates 1970–1993*.
Budget: Court Auditors, Annual Report, *Official Journal EC*, various issues.

promotion measures) do not have direct budgetary consequences, but may very well include an even larger anti-cohesion bias; and (b) that the present tendency to shift emphasis from price support to income support constitutes an important step in the right direction, not only from the point of view of agricultural support but also from the cohesion point of view.

Fourth, among the policies that, although their immediate budgetary effect is rather minimal, can contribute to assuring the longer-term competitiveness and an increasingly autonomous catching-up process by the less-developed regions, is the Research and Technological Development Policy of the Community. At present there are very considerable disparities in R&D expenditure between the member-states, with a very high and increasing concentration of R&D and innovation activities in the old industrial core of Europe. As an illustration, and although the share of R&D expenditures in GDP has increased in the Southern European countries more than in the European Union as a whole (in Greece the growth rate between 1981 and 1993 of the percentage of GDP going to R&D has been the highest in Europe),[56] per capita expenditure on R&D in the four less advanced countries is in the range of 13 to 28 per cent of the Community average, while the respective business enterprise expenditure lies between 4 and 26 per cent of the Community average.

In this context emphasis should be placed on training actions for enhancing the number of highly qualified people. Furthermore, there may be scope for increasing the participation of poorer regions by reinforcing backup activity such as publicity and promotion of transregional networking. Within the framework of the R&D programme of the Community, cohesion can be promoted by assuring that the Community effort adequately promotes research relevant to the lagging regions. Finally, there could be a strengthening of mechanisms that foster the transfer of technical know-how and the promotion of innovation in these regions.[57]

Another policy area where cohesion considerations could run counter to the general aims governing the policy is the commercial policy, and more generally, the external economic relations policy of the Community. This is a highly controversial issue, but no-one seriously doubts that, for example, the agreements with some of the Central and Eastern Europe countries imply greater openness of the Community market in certain sectors that are especially sensitive for less developed member-states.[58] This anti-cohesion bias of this policy was recognized implicitly many years ago, with the use of parts of the structural funds to compensate for these losses, and more recently with the special measures for the Portuguese textile industry that had to be taken in order for the new GATT agreement to be ratified.

Finally, among Community policies, competition policy is the one that should have a natural role in supporting cohesion. In theory, since the establishment of this policy, measures to deal with regional problems of underdevelopment or industrial decline have been one of the major exceptions to a generally reserved attitude to state aids. The maximum limit on aid for lagging regions is a net grant equivalent to 75 per cent of investment cost, whereas for all other eligible regions the limit is 30 per cent. These are largely theoretical differentials however, as the lagging regions in most instances cannot avail themselves of the full scope of the higher limit. In practice, more often than not, state aid policy does not run parallel to structural policy, but on the contrary, it offsets some of the redistribution effects of structural policy, or, to be more precise, does not succeed in obliging the member-states not to offset the effects of structural policies. As shown in the Table 9.10,[59] the state aid per head in some of the more advanced member-states is three times as high as state aid in Portugal or Greece. Even more strikingly, the actual per capita state aid to the manufacturing sector of the former East German Länder was, during 1990–92 thirteen times bigger than to the Greek manufacturing sector! And this without taking into account the direct transfer of resources to the budgets of the new Länder through the 'Finanzausgleich' system.[60]

Table 9.10 Comparison between GDP per capita and state aid (to industry and total) per employee

	GDP per capita (1990–92)		State aid to industry per employee (1990–92)		Total state aid per employee (1990–93)	
	(mn ecu)	*(EU = 100)*	*(mn ecu)*	*(EU = 100)*	*(mn ecu)*	*(EU = 100)*
B	16230.4	107	1527	118	966	137
DK	16155.1	107	638	49	399	57
D	16732.2	110	1099	85	1090	155
EL	9029.8	60	1579	122	335	48
ES	11696.6	77	493	38	420	60
F	17039.5	112	1138	88	801	114
IRL	11312.8	75	1411	109	502	71
I	15762.0	104	2611	202	1165	165
L	23152.4	153	1573	122	1513	215
NL	15464.1	102	978	76	338	48
P	9598.1	63	625	48	178	25
UK	14917.7	98	525	41	189	27
EU	15151.2	100	1293	100	704	100

mn = million.
For Germany, the state aids to industry figure data are published separately.
West Germany (979 ecu per employee) and the new Länder (4385 ecu per employee).
The 1099 ecu figure corresponds to the period 1988–90.
Sources: GDP: Eurostat, *National Accounts ESA, Aggregates 1970–1993*, pp. 60–1.
State Aids: European Commission, *Fourth Survey on State Aids in the Manufacturing and Certain Other Sectors*, 1995.

Concluding remarks

The recent and radical change in the Community's attitude towards the issues of equity, redistribution and regional development has transformed the structural policies of the Community from a rather marginal issue to a central and highly political question. A key factor in understanding this large shift of interest is the 'communitization' of the goal of development of less developed regions, the acceptance by the Community that reducing the disparities is not only a national goal but also a Community obligation.

This very happy outcome (from the Southern European countries' point of view) of the inter-Community negotiations since the Single Act represents, at the same time, these same countries' contribution to the European integration cause. Their direct and very quantifiable national interest has led to the establishment of economic and social cohesion as a new dimension of Community policy, a dimension synonymous to the deepening of the integration process itself. The strengthening of the geographical redistribution function, and, moreover, the commitment of the central authorities to the solution of the fundamental problems of the periphery, are characteristics of an advanced level 'federation'.

A policy objective, however, that has been only partially pursued is often the cause of complications and confusion. The logical paths for the Community structural policy would be either to assist openly member-states' policies, or to trace an independent Community policy. The first path would imply direct redistribution from richer to poorer countries and regions; the second path would imply the setting of clear Community priorities. The Community has chosen a middle road, sometimes subsidizing national action, sometimes intervening, without always clear and objectively set intentions and procedures. The direct transfer procedure could be justified if generalized, and so would a much more interventionist policy if objectively defined. But, as long as the first is not generalized it can easily be criticized as a 'buying off blank cheque', and the second, as long as it is not objectively defined, leads to criticisms of the Commission's behaviour as a kind of neocolonial power with respect to sovereign member-states.[61]

A pure communitarian approach would require the setting of specific targets with respect to the level of physical and human infrastructure in all regions, a quantification of these requirements and a long-term decision on their financing. After all, the Maastricht Treaty innovated in setting extremely precise and quantitative objectives for the nominal convergence of the member-states, why should we not have similar objectives in the real convergence sphere?

Similarly, for example, in the state aid area, where the present system of national aid to industry can hardly be justified, one would expect that moving towards higher levels of integration would lead to the replacement of this system with a Community-wide industrial policy, whereby there would be only one chart of 'compatible' public aid (financed by Community and/or national budgets) – the ones corresponding to Community objectives.

But, obviously we are not there. It is this author's belief that the present phase is a transitory one and, sooner or later, the European Union will have to clarify its goals. One could envisage a system with a combination of the two paths, but in clear and predetermined ways. Specific, quantified targets on the minimum provision of certain public goods, plus income redistributing transfers. Meanwhile, and as long as the domestic administrative structures in Southern Europe remain the biggest constraint for development, the Community's greater contribution to the development of these regions comes from the activation of their idle endogenous development potential, generated by Community funds and the consultation, programming, monitoring, and evaluation procedures linked to the functioning of the overall economic and social cohesion policy of the European Union.

Appendix: statistical tables

Table 9.11 GDP per head disparities (percentage of each member-state's population per different levels of GDP per head – index EEC:100)

	up to 60	60 to 75	75 to 90	90 to 100	100 to 110	110 to 125	125 to 140	over 140
Belgium	–	–	19.4	41.8	–	38.8	–	–
Denmark	–	–	–	11.8	54.9	–	33.3	–
France	2.3	–	28.9	24.5	20.4	5.8	–	18.1
Germany	–	–	3.1	24.3	21.2	27.2	14.8	9.3
Greece	94.1	5.9	–	–	–	–	–	–
Ireland	–	100.0	–	–	–	–	–	–
Italy	3.8	27.9	2.9	1.4	2.5	38.5	23.2	–
Luxembourg	–	–	–	–	–	100.0	–	–
Netherlands	–	1.4	16.3	28.6	34.0	15.6	–	4.1
Portugal	64.3	35.7	–	–	–	–	–	–
Spain	20.9	26.1	51.2	–	1.8	–	–	–
UK	–	–	23.3	17.9	31.4	15.4	–	11.9
Total	8.4	10.3	17.7	15.1	16.3	17.6	7.4	7.3

Source: Commission EC (1991c).

Table 9.12 Unemployment disparities (percentage of each member- state's population per different levels of rate of unemployment – index EEC:100)

	over 150	120 to 150	100 to120	80 to100	50 to 80	up to 50
Belgium	13.3	10.2	11.2	40.8	24.5	–
Denmark	–	–	–	66.7	33.3	–
France	–	23.1	19.8	54.2	2.9	–
Germany	–	–	1.1	31.8	30.3	36.7
Greece	–	–	34.7	12.9	45.5	6.9
Ireland	100.0	–	–	–	–	–
Italy	33.4	9.4	3.7	9.4	26.7	17.3
Luxembourg	–	–	–	–	–	100.0
Netherlands	–	4.3	–	85.8	9.9	–
Portugal	–	6.1	–	35.7	–	58.2
Spain	85.8	11.6	2.6	–	–	–
UK	5.4	11.2	14.4	26.3	24.9	17.7
Total	18.7	9.7	8.6	29.2	18.5	15.3

Source: Commission EC (1991c).

Table 9.13 Regression results (*t*-statistics)

	dependent[1]	R^2[2]	d.f.[3]	GDP[4]	UNEM[5]	CGDP[6]	IND[7]	AGR[8]
1.1	Obj.1	52	5	−0.522				
1.2	Obj.1	72	4	−0.135	−0.293			
1.3	Obj.1	132	3	−0.095	−0.207	−0.455		
1.4	Obj.1	235	3	−0.527	0.199		0.801	
1.5	Obj.1	335	2	−0.384	0.149	−0.039	0.523	
2.1	Obj.2	100	57		2.521			
2.2	Obj.2	138	56	−1.565	1.904			
2.3	Obj.2	102	56		2.406		−0.295	
2.4	Obj.2	140	55	−1.556	1.804		−0.317	
2.5	Obj.2	149	54	−1.531	1.686	−0.785	−0.472	
5.1	Obj.5a	54	45					1.595
5.2	Obj.5a	58	44	−0.474				1.281
5.3	Obj.5a	63	43	−0.036	0.443			1.292
5.4	Obj.5a	60	43	−0.520		−0.302		1.127
R.1	Regions	180	82	−4.246				
R.2	Regions	184	81	−3.458	0.619			
R.3	Regions	184	80	−3.400	0.603		−0.004	
R.4	Regions	228	80	−3.124	0.469	−2.135		
R.5	Regions	228	79	−3.044	0.426	−2.128	−0.154	
T.1	Countries	146	10	−1.306				
T.2	Countries	190	9	−0.838	0.705		−0.258	
T.3	Countries	197	8	−0.771	0.637	−0.258		

[1] Dependent variable: Obj.1 or Obj.2 or Obj.5b or REG (all regions) or M-S (member-states);
[2] R squared; [3] degrees of freedom; [4] GDP per capita; [5] Rate of unemployment; [6] GDP per capita of the country; [7] Share of industry in total employment; [8] Share of agriculture in total employment.

Notes

1. The ideas and opinions expressed here remain entirely personal, although the paper draws heavily on the work accomplished within the Directorate-General for the Coordination of Structural Policies and, even more importantly, on the views exchanged with many colleagues in the Commission services.
2. See Comité ... (1956).
3. It should be noted that the inclusion of regions from richer countries among the beneficiaries of the structural funds has always been a controversial point, with the European Commission and, often, representatives of southern countries arguing in favour of this inclusion for negotiation purposes and in order not to strengthen the already existing 'ghetto' element of structural policies.
4. The corresponding percentages almost double if one adds the contribution of the national (or regional) budgets to the financing of the specific projects cofinanced by the structural funds. See Commission (1996), ch. 1.
5. The direct impact to the GNP of Spain of the funds' contribution to the Spanish less developed regions is estimated at 2.2 per cent, and the percentage of Gross Fixed Capital Formation at 6.4 per cent. The corresponding percentages for the Italian Mezzogiorno are 1.1 and 4.7. (Commission, 1996).
6. The literature on the 'divergence/convergence debate' is huge. See e.g. Abraham and Van Rompuy (1992), Begg (1989), Camagni (1992), Dunford and Perrons (1993), Keating and Hooghe (1994), Pacolet and Gos (1993), Perrons (1992), Prud'homme (1993), Leonardi (1993, 1995). On the definition, types etc of convergence see Bennett (1991).
7. See also: Begg and Mayes (1989), p. 13.
8. Biehl (1990).
9. MacDougall (1977).
10. See for example Wistricht (1989), Biehl (1990), Wildasin (1990), Casella and Frey (1992), Buiter and Kletzer (1992), Inman and Rubinfeld (1992), Bureau and Champsaur (1992), Prud'homme (1992), and the studies conducted for the European Commission: Van Rompuy *et al.* (1991), Reichenbach *et al.* (1993) [especially the contributions by Walsh (1993), Spahn (1993a, b), Costello (1993), Prud'homme (1993), Santos (1993)], TEPSA (1991), and Commission (1993). The 'classical' references on fiscal federalism include Pauly (1973), Oates (1977).
11. Commission EC (1990a), p. 213.
12. Commission EC (1990a), p. 213.
13. Clark *et al.* (1969).
14. Keeble *et al.* (1988), and Commission (1990a), ch. 9.
15. Padoa-Schioppa *et al.* (1987).
16. See for example Kierzkowski (1987), Krugman (1989), and the analysis in the 'MacDougall II Report', [Begg and Mayes (1989)], as well as the literature on the 'divergence/convergence debate' referred to in note 1.
17. For surveys on the theories of regional development, see e.g. Wadley (1986), O'Donell (1991), Cappelin (1993). On regional disparities the *Periodic Reports* published by the DG for Regional Policies of the Commission EC are very valuable, and so is the work by Leonardi (1993, 1995).
18. See also the useful classification produced by Camagni (1992a) in a research project for the Commission.
19. On this 'side-payments' approach see Marks (1992, 1993), Marks *et al.* (1995), Pereira (1992), Dehousse (1992), Hooghe (1993, 1995), Walsh (1993), Costello (1993), Courchenne (1993), Teutemann (1993).

20. Gretschmann (1991).
21. Biehl (1990).
22. For example, on the more recent steps towards higher levels of integration (the '1992' project and the process towards EMU) see Buigues *et al.* (1990), Bliss and Braga de Macedo (1990), and Commission EC (1991b).
23. The only exceptions to this 'quota cum eligibility' approach, and forerunners therefore of the Single Act reform, were the Regional Fund 'hors-quota programmes' and the (much more significant because of the amounts involved and their innovatory character) Integrated Mediterranean Programmes and the other integrated operations. For a very analytical overview of the legal framework for the operations of the Regional Fund before the 1988 reform see Curall (1988). See also Croxford *et al.* (1987) and Cheshire *et al.* (1991). On the history of the Integrated Mediterranean Programmes and their role in the shaping of the Community's regional policy see Mitsos (1989 – in Greek).
24. A far more rational and coherent decision would be to abolish the funds altogether and to create budgetary lines (and the relevant administrative structure within both the Commission and the member-states) that correspond directly to these objectives. This brave attempt failed because of the conservatism of bureaucratic inertia and the well-established 'clientelism' between each Fund and the respective national administration bodies as well as private lobbying.
25. It must be noted that the objectives themselves were not entirely new. Even before the Single Act the different Funds' missions included in one way or another these objectives. What is new though is the approach.
26. This doubling corresponds to the total contribution of the structural funds in the objective 1 *regions* (Greece, Portugal, Ireland, the Italian Mezzogiorno, a major part of Spain, Northern Ireland, Corsica, and the French 'Departements d'outre mer' – Guadeloupe, Martinique, Guyane and Reunion), i.e. including the horizontal objectives 3, 4 and 5a, and not just the funding of objective 1 strictly speaking.
27. The rate of growth for the budget as a whole was 10.1 per cent (*European Economy*, no. 50).
28. *European Economy*, no. 42, based on several issues of the Court of Auditors *Annual Report*.
29. Commission EC (1991a), p. 100.
30. Commission services.
31. Calculations made by Commission services based on Milward (1984).
32. The most extreme examples are, on the one hand, the programming of the Community's action in the new German Länder, where the Commission has simply 'rubber-stamped' the domestic decisions, and, on the other hand, the funds' contribution to the development of the Greek regions, where, almost everyone seemed to agree that, in order to overcome the inertia of the system, the decisions should be taken 'in Brussels' and 'imposed' on the Greek authorities.
33. The Community initiatives for the period 1989 to 1993 concerned coal areas (RECHAR), environmental protection (ENVIREG), r&d capacity improvement (STRIDE), transborder cooperation (INTERREG), ultraperipheral zones (REGIS), natural gas (REGEN), small and medium size enterprizes etc (PRISMA), telecommunications (TELEMATIQUE), rural development (LEADER), new transnational employment opportunities (EUROFORM), equal opportunities between men and women (NOW) and, handicapped people integration (HORIZON). See Commission EC (1990b) and Commission (1994a) for the post-1993 'Community initiatives'.

34. Some of the comments made in this section are, partly, based on the studies elaborated by the Commission services and external contractors under the leadership of the DG for the Coordination of Structural Policies, in which the author of this chapter works as the director. These studies are briefly presented in the Communication from the Commission EC (1992a).
35. This table is based on the national, multiregional part of each member-state's Community Support Framework, assuming i.e., that within each regional section of the CSFs the shares of each major category is the same as the shares in the national section. This hypothesis is not far from reality, with the notable exception of the direct aid schemes and the objectives 3 and 4 funding, that are normally financed at national level. The alternative procedure of treating the regional programmes separately leads often to major 'misunderstandings', giving the impression that the regional programmes are of a residual and 'clientelistic' nature that does not correspond to reality.
36. The programme for industry in Ireland was the largest single programme of the Funds in the period concerned (total cost: 3239 millions of ecus, total public expenditure: 1690 millions of ecus, total Community contribution: 1019 millions of ecus).
37. Pereira (1992).
38. A major 'technical' problem, linked to the issue of 'absorption', has to do with the delays that exist in the different stages of implementation; delays within the Commission, from the moment of the decision to the actual payment, as well as delays within the member-states.
39. The only member-state for which this change has had important effects was Greece, with the inclusion of Athens. In Ireland and Portugal the totality of the population was eligible even before the reform.
40. Commission EC (1991a), p. 55. It must be remembered that dealing with industrial declining areas was included in the ERDF mission from the establishment of this fund.
41. The actual share of Community grants in total public expenditure in objective 1 countries was 54 to 58 per cent, and in total cost between 40 and 52 per cent (calculations based on the Community Support Frameworks of the member-states).
42. Once again the calculation of this per capita contribution is based upon the eligible population and not the actual share of the population covered.
43. Within the other objectives, the differences between regions are much bigger, with the range going from 56 ecus per capita in Berlin and 63 ecus per capita in Saarland (Germany) to 2211 ecus per capita in Aubagne (Belgium) in objective 1, and, within objective 5b, from 77.3 ecus per capita in Alsace to 1235.4 ecus per capita in Rioja (Spain). A very elaborate exploration of the existing data on this subject can be found in the Final Report to the Commission of EC, DG for the Coordination of Structural Policies, by REMACO (1992).
44. An example, but not the only one, is Wildasin (1990), where the whole argument is based on the assumption that additionality is not respected ('total spending from all sources … in the region remains roughly constant').
45. Commission EC (1990a).
46. The author of these lines has been a witness and a 'victim' of unbelievably long and tough discussions at the Council of Ministers level concerning the various meanings of the word evaluation and/or assessment, *ex post*, *ex ante*, ongoing, macro, micro, meso, per country, per groups of countries, per region, per sector,

etc. For the purposes of this chapter however we can easily accept the distinction between evaluation of potential vs. evaluation of realized impact.

47. The first complete analysis of the expected impact of the structural funds will be published in the so-called 'cohesion report' (College of Europe *et al.*, 1996). See also, *inter alia*, the reports prepared by Beutel (1995), CEPI (1995), Gray (1995), ISMERI (1995), Pereira (1995), Price Waterhouse (1995), QUASAR (1995), Skouras (1995). Some of the initial results of the assessment studies are presented in the so-called Mid-Term Review (Commission EC, 1992a).

48. The return flow is defined as change in imports over change in grants, and is decomposed to become the product of the multiplier, the income elasticity of (intra-EC) imports and the share of (intra-EC) imports in GDP.

49. Article 130d and Protocol on Economic and Social Cohesion of the Treaty on European Union. Because of the delays in the implementation of the Treaty, the tasks of the Cohesion Fund in 1993 have been accomplished by a temporary 'Cohesion Instrument' (Regulation 792/93), similar (if not identical) in nature, but one that does not require the Maastricht Treaty as its legal base.

50. In Laffan's words 'the Gini was finally out of the bottle'. See also the papers presented at the conference on 'EC Cohesion Policy and National Networks', Centre for European Studies, Nuffield College, Oxford, December 1993.

51. Contrary to the pessimists, who based their gloomy predictions on the new interest of the Community in the relations with the Central and Eastern European countries, and the share that would be demanded by Germany because of the problems facing the new Länder.

52. For each member-state its total receipts from the Community budget minus its total contribution to it.

53. *Official Journal of the EC*, various issues.

54. On the equity element in the Community budget as a whole and the proposal for the introduction of an equity safeguard mechanism, see Padoa-Schioppa *et al.* (1987). See also Ardy (1988).

55. See Demekas *et al.* (1988). See also Strijker and de Veer (1988), Sarris (1994) and the old, but interesting from the methodological point of view RICAP ('Regional Impact of Common Agricultural Policy') studies Commission (1981a, b).

56. College of Europe *et al.* (1996), p. 54.

57. See College of Europe, *et al.* (1996), Kuhlman (1992), Commission (1992e), Grote (1993), Cappelin-Orsenigo (1993), Costello (1993d).

58. On the links between the commercial policy and cohesion see Commission (1983), Molle (1988), Brocker-Peschel (1988), as well as the rapidly growing literature on the 'eastern enlargement' repercussions (for example National Economic Research Association (1992), Commission (1992f), Commission (1994)).

59. See also the very interesting survey on the subject by Lehner and Meklejohn (1991).

60. On the German 'Finanzausgleich' system, see Kuhn and Hanusch (1992), Krupp (1992), Costello (1993c).

61. Begg and Mayes (1989), p. 123.

Bibliography

(Commission References: for simplicity, all the publications of the Commission of the EC or European Commission are referred to as Commission irrespective of the language used or the official title of the 'Commission' at the time of publication.)

Abraham, F. and Van Rompuy, P. (1992) 'Convergence-divergence and the implications for Community structural policies', *Cah. Econ. Brux.*, vol. 135, no. 3, pp. 279–378.

Ardy, B. (1988) 'The national incidence of the European Community budget', *Journal of Common Market Studies*, vol. XXVI, no. 4, June, pp. 401–29.

Begg, J. (1989) 'European integration and regional policy', *Oxford Rev. Econ. Policy*, vol. 5, no. 2, pp. 90–104.

Begg, I. and Mayes, D. (1989) (National Institute of Economic and Social Research, London), foreword by Sir D. MacDougall, 1991, *A New Strategy for Social and Economic Cohesion After 1992*, European Parliament, Regional Policy and Transport Series, no. 19.

Benko, G. and Dunford, M. (eds) (1991) *Industrial Change and Regional Development*, Belhaven Press, London.

Bennett, C. J. (1991) 'What is policy convergence and what causes it? Review Article', *British Journal of Political Science*, vol. 21, pp. 215–33.

Beutel, J. (1995) *The Economic Impact of the Community Support Frameworks for the Objective 1 Regions 1994–1999*, Report for the Commission.

Biehl, D. (1990) 'Deficiencies and reform possibilities of the EC fiscal constitution', in Crough, C. and Marquand, D., pp. 85–99.

Bliss, C. and Braga de Macedo, J. (1990) *Unity with Diversity within the European Economy; The Community's Southern Frontier*, Cambridge University Press, Cambridge, UK.

Brocker, J. and Peschel, K. (1988) 'Trade', in Molle, W. and Cappelin, R., pp. 127–51.

Buigues, P., Ilzkovitz, F. and Lebrun, J.-F. (1990) 'The Impact of the internal market by industrial sector: the challenge for the member states', *European Economy – Social Europe*, special edition.

Buiter, W. H. and Kletzer, K. M. (1992) 'Fiscal policy coordination as fiscal federalism', *European Economic Review*, vol. 36, pp. 647–53.

Bureau, D. and Champsaur, P. (1992) 'Fiscal federalism and European economic unification', *American Economic Review*, vol. 82, no. 2, May, pp. 88–92.

Cafruny, A. W. and Rosenthal, G. G. (eds) (1993) *The State of the European Community, The Maastricht Treaty and Beyond, vol. 2*, Longman, London.

Camagni, R. P. (1992a) *Development Prospects of the Community's Lagging Regions and the Socio-Economic Consequences of the Completion of the Internal Market, An Approach in Terms of Local 'Milieux' and Innovation Networks*, Research Project for the Commission of the EC, Final Report, June.

Camagni, R. P. (1992b) 'Development scenarios and policy guidelines for the lagging regions in the 1990s', *Regional Studies*, vol. 26, no. 4, pp. 361–74.

Cappelin, R. (1993) 'Patterns and policies of regional development and the cohesion among regions of the EC', part of Leonardi, R. (1993a).

Cappelin, R. and Orsenigo, L. (1993) 'The impact of EC R&D and competition policies on cohesion', part of Leonardi, R. (1993a).

Casella, A. and Frey, B. (1992) 'Federalism and clubs', *European Economic Review*, vol. 36, pp. 639–46.

CEPI (1995) *The Contribution of the Community Structural Policies to the Economic and Social Cohesion of the European Union: The Case of Portugal*, Report for the Commission.

Cheshire, P., Camagni, R. P., Gaudemar, J.-P. de and Cuadrado Roura, J. R. (1991) '1957 to 1992: moving toward a Europe of regions and regional policy', Rodwin, L. and Sazanami, H., pp. 268–300.

Clark, C., Wilson, F. and Bradley, J. (1969) 'Industrial location and economic potential in Western Europe', *Regional Studies*, vol. 3, pp. 197–212.

College of Europe, University of Sussex, Synthesis (1996) *The Impact of Community Policies, other than the Structural Policies, on Economic and Social Cohesion, Draft final Report*, vol. 1, Chapter 2.

Comité Intergouvernmental créé par la Conférence de Messine (1956) *Rapport des Chefs de Délégation aux Ministres des Affaires Etrangères*, Bruxelles, 21 Avril.

Commission (1981a) *Regional Impact of the EEC's Fisheries Policy, Economic and Social Situation and Outlook for the Fisheries Sector in Certain Regions of the Community*, Luxembourg: Office for Official Publications of the EC.

Commission (1981b) *Regional Impact of the Common Agricultural Policy*, Regional Policy Series, no. 21.

Commission (1983) *Etude de l'impact régional de la politique commerciale de la Communauté*, Etudes, Politique régionale, no. 22.

Commission (1990a) 'One market, one money, an evaluation of the potential benefits and costs of forming an economic and monetary union', *European Economy*, no. 44, October.

Commission (1990b) *Guide to Community Initiatives*, Office for Official Publications of the EC, Luxembourg.

Commission (1991a) *The Regions in the 1990s*, Office for Official Publications of the EC, Luxembourg.

Commission (1991b) 'The economics of EMU; background studies', *European Economy*, special edition no. 1.

Commission (1991c) (DG for Regional Policies) *The Regions in the 1990s, Fourth Periodic Report on the Social and Economic Situation and Development of the Regions of the Community*, Office for Official Publications of the EC, Luxembourg.

Commission (1992a) *Community Structural Policies; Assessment and Outlook*, COM(92)84, March.

Commission (1992b) (DG for the coordination of structural policies) 'The Community's structural interventions', *Statistical Bulletin*, no. 3, July.

Commission (1992c) (DG for the coordination of structural policies) 'The Community's structural interventions', *Statistical Bulletin*, no. 4, December.

Commission (1992d) *Third Survey on State Aids in the European Community in the Manufacturing and Certain Other Sectors*, Office of the Official Publications of the European Communities, Luxembourg.

Commission (1992e) *Evaluation of the Effects of the EC Framework Programme for Research and Technological Development on Economic and Social Cohesion in the Community*, Research eval. 48.

Commission (1992f) *Socio-economic Situation and Development of the Regions in the Neighbouring Countries in Central and Eastern Europe, Final Report*, Regional Dev. Studies.

Commission (1993) 'Stable money – sound finances, Community public finance in the perspective of EMU, report of an independent group of economists', *European Economy*, no. 53.

Commission (1994a) *The Future of Community Initiatives under the Structural Funds*, COM(94)46.

Commission (1994b) *Guide to the Community Initiatives 1994–1999*, Office for Official Publications of the EC, Luxembourg.

Commission (1996) *6ème Rapport Annuel sur les Fonds Structurels 1994*, COM(95)583 final, 11. 1. 1996.

Costello, D. (1993a) 'Intergovernmental grants: what role for the European Community?', *European Economy*, no. 5, pp. 101–20.

Costello, D. (1993b) 'Public finances in federations and unitary states', *European Economy*, no. 5, pp. 243–64.

Costello, D. (1993c) 'The redistributive effects of interregional transfers: a comparison of the European Community and Germany', *European Economy*, no. 5, pp. 269–78.

Costello, D. (1993d) 'Public interventions to promote economic efficiency: implications for the EC budget', *European Economy*, no. 5, pp. 369–94.

Courchene, T. J. (1993) 'Reflections on Canadian federalism: are there implications for European economic and monetary union?', *European Economy*, no. 5, pp. 123–66.

Crough, C. and Marquand, D. (eds) (1990) *The Politics of 1992, Beyond the Single European Market*, Basil Blackwell, Oxford.

Croxford, G. J., Wise, M. and Chalkley, B. S. (1987) 'The reform of the European regional development fund: a preliminary assessment', *Journal of Common Market Studies*, vol. XXVI, no. 1, September, pp. 25–38.

Currall, J. (1988) 'Le fonds Européen de developpement régional des origines jusqu'a l'Acte Unique Européen', *Cahiers de Droit Européen*, vol. 24, no. 1–2, pp. 39–102.

Dehousse, R. (1992) 'Integration v. regulation? On the dynamics of regulation in the European Community', *Journal of Common Market Studies*, vol. 30, no. 4, pp. 383–402.

Demekas, D. G. *et al.* (1988) 'The effects of Common Agricultural Policy of the European Community: a survey of the literature', *Journal of Common Market Studies*, vol. XXVII, no. 2, December, pp. 113–145.

Dunford, M. (1991) 'Endogenous development, developmental state and world markets' (in Greek), *Topos*, vol. 91, no. 2, pp. 33–62.

Dunford, M. and Kafkalas, G. (eds) (1993) *Cities and Regions in the New Europe: The Global-Local Interplay and Spatial Development Strategies*, Belhaven Press, London.

Dunford, M. and Perrons, D. (1993) 'Regional inequality as a cause and consequence of slower growth', in Getimis, P. and Kafkalas, G., pp. 9–35.

Eurostat (1993) *National Accounts ESA 1979–1990*, Office for Official Publications of the EC, Luxembourg.

Frangakis, N., Papayannides, A. D. and Apostolides, R. (eds) (1994) *The Third Greek Presidency of the Council of the European Union*, Hestia, Athens.

Getimis, P. and Kafkalas, G. (eds) (1993) *Urban and Regional Development in the New Europe*, Topos Special Series, Athens.

Gray, A. W. (1995) *European Union Structural Funds and Other Public Sector Investments, A Guide to Evaluation Methods*, Gill and Macmillan, London.

Gretschmann, K. (1991) *Fiscal Union*, part of the TEPSA Study for the Commission EC on 'Methods for Achieving Greater Economic and Social Cohesion in the EC'.

Grote, J. R. (1993) 'Diseconomies in space: traditional sectoral policies of the EC, the European technology community and their effects on regional disparities', in Leonardi, R. (1993a), pp. 14–46.

Hooghe, L. (1993) 'Political-administrative adaptation in the EC and regional mobilisation', in Wright, V. *et al.*

Hooghe, L. (1995) *Subnational Mobilisation in the European Union*, Eur. Univ. Inst., EUI Working Paper 95/6, Florence.

Inman, R. P. and Rubinfeld, D. L. (1992) 'Fiscal federalism in Europe, lessons from the United States experience', *European Econ. Review*, vol. 36, pp. 654–660.

ISMERI (1995) *Impact of the Structural Funds on Economic and Social Cohesion in Italy*, Report for the Commission.

Keating, M. and Hooghe, L. (1994) *The Politics of EC Regional Policy*, Chicago, Conference of Europeanists, March.

Keeble, D., Offord, J. and Walker, S. (1988) *Peripheral Regions in a Community of Twelve Member States*, Commission EC, Luxembourg.

Kierzkowski, H. (1987) 'Recent advances in international trade theory: a selective survey', *Oxford Review of Economic Policy*, vol. 3, no. 1, pp. 1–19.

Krugman, P. R. (1989) 'Increasing returns and economic geography', *NBER Working Paper*, Washington, DC.

Krupp, H.-J. (1992) 'Political change and intergovernmental fiscal relations: the case of German unification', in Prud'homme, R. (ed.), pp. 368–78.

Kuhlmann, S. (1992) *Thematic Evaluation of Community Support Frameworks for Research and Technology Development in Greece, Final Report*.

Kuhn, T. and Hanusch, H. (1992) 'Vertical and horizontal equity and the grants to communities in the Federal Republic of Germany', in Prud'homme, R., pp. 211–22.

Lehner, S. and Meklejohn, R. (1991) 'Fair competition in the internal market: Community state aid policy', *European Economy*, no. 48, September.

Leonardi, R. (1993a) *The State of Economic and Social Cohesion in the Community Prior to the Creation of the Single Market: The View from the Bottom-Up*, London School of Economics and Political Science, The European Institute, study for the Commission of the EC.

Leonardi, R. (1993b) 'Peripheral ascendancy in the European Community', in Leonardi, R. (1993a).

Leonardi, R. (1993c) 'Cohesion in the European Community: illusion or reality?', *West European Politics*, vol. 16, no. 4, pp. 492–517.

Leonardi, R. (1993d) *The Regions and the European Community*, Frank Cass, London.

Leonardi, R. (1995) *Convergence, Cohesion and Integration in the European Union*, St. Martin's Press, New York.

Leonardi, R. and Garmise, S. (1993) 'Conclusions: sub-national elites and the European Community', in Leonardi, R. (ed.), pp. 247–274.

MacDougall, Sir D. (1977) 'Report of the study group on the role of public finance in European integration', Commission EC, *Collection Studies*.

Marks, G. (1992) 'Structural policy in the European Community', in Sbragia, A. M., pp. 191–224.

Marks, G. (1993) 'Structural policy and multilevel government in the EC', in Cafruny, A. W. and Rosenthal, G. G., pp. 391–410.

Marks, G., Hooghe, L. and Blank, K. (1995) *European Integration and the State*, Eur. Univ. Inst., EUI Working Paper 95/7, Florence.

Marks, G., Nielsen, F. and Salk, J. (1993) 'Regional mobilization in the European Union', in Wright, V. *et al.*

Milward, A. S. (1984) *The Reconstruction of Western Europe 1945–1951*, Methuen, London, UK.

Mitsos, A. (1989) *The Greek Industry in the International Market*, (in Greek), Themelio, Athens.

Mitsos, A. (1991) 'La reforme des fonds structurels communautaires', *Europe Social*, vol. 2, no. 91, pp. 12–16.

Mitsos, A. (1992) 'A new role for the structural funds?', in Pijpers, A., pp. 119–26.

Mitsos, A. (1993) 'Post-Maastricht process towards European Union and the economic and social cohesion of the Community', in Getimis, P. and Kafkalas, G., pp. 1–6.

Mitsos, A. (1994) 'Convergence and cohesion', in Frangakis, N. *et al.*, pp. 96–105.

Molle, W. (1988) 'Industry and services', in Molle, W. and Cappelin, R., pp. 45–64.

Molle, W. and Cappelin, R. (1988) *Regional Impact of Community Policies in Europe*, Gower Avebury.

National Economic Research Association (1992) *The Changes in Foreign Investment and Trade Due to the Economic Reform in East and Central Europe and their Impact on the Regions of the Community in general and Its Lagging Regions in particular*, study for the European Commission.

O'Donell, R. (1991) *The Evolution of the Theory of Regional Development*, part of the study for the Commission of the EC by TEPSA.

Oates, W. E. (ed.) (1977) *The Political Economy of Fiscal Federalism*, Lexington, Lexington, MA.

Oates, W. E. (1992) 'Fiscal federalism: an overview', in Prud'homme, R., pp. 1–18.

Pacolet, J. and Gos, E. (1994) 'Regional imbalances and national or federal social protection', in Georgakopoulos, T., Paraskevopoulos, C. C. and Smithin, J. (eds), *Economic Integration between Unequal Partners*, Edward Elgar, Aldershot, pp. 122–33.

Padoa-Schioppa, T. with Emerson, M., King, M., Milleron, J.-C., Paelinck, J., Papademos, L., Pastor, A. and Scharpf, F. (1987) *Efficiency, Stability and Equity; A Strategy for the Evolution of the Economic System of the European Community*, Oxford University Press, Oxford.

Pauly, M. V. (1973) 'Income distribution as a local public good', *Journal of Public Economics*, vol. 2, pp. 35–58.

Pereira, A. M. (1992) *Contributions for the Debate on the Future of Structural Transfers in the EC*, study prepared for the DG for the Coordination of Structural Policies of the Commission of the EC, December.

Pereira, A. M. (1995) *Evaluation of the Community Support Framework for 1994–1999*, Report for the Commission.

Perrons, D. (1992) 'The regions and the single market', in Dunford, M. and Kafkalas, G., pp. 170–94.

Pijpers, A. (ed.) (1992) *The European Community at the Crossroads – Major Issues and Priorities for the EC Presidency*, Martinus Nijhoff Publishers, Dordrecht, The Netherlands.

Price Waterhouse (1995) *Evaluation of the Community Support Frameworks for the Objective 1 Regions in the Period 1989–1993*, Synthesis Report for the Commission.

Prud'homme, R. (ed.) (1992) 'Public finance with several levels of government', *Proceedings of the 46th Congress of the International Institute of Public Finance, (Brussels 1990)*, Foundation Journal Public Finance, Hague.

Prud'homme, R. (1993) 'The potential role of the EC budget in the reduction of spatial disparities in a European economic and monetary union', *European Economy*, no. 5, pp. 317–52.

QUASAR (1995) *Evaluation of the Structural Policies Impact on the Economic and Social Cohesion: The Spanish Case*, Report for the Commission.

Reichenbach, H. *et al.* (eds) (1993) 'The economics of Community public finance', *European Economy*, no. 53.

REMACO SA (1992) *The Concentration of Community Assistance as a Means towards Improving the Efficiency of its Structural Policy; Methods of Measurement and Empirical Results*, study for the Commission of the EC, October.

Rodwin, L. and Sazanami, H. (eds) (1991) *Industrial Change and Regional Economic Transformation, The Experience of Western Europe*, HarperCollins Academic, London.

Sandholtz, W. and Zysman, J. (1990) '1992: Recasting the European bargain', *World Politics*, pp. 95–128.

Santos, P. (1993) 'The spatial implications of economic and monetary union', *European Economy*, no. 5, pp. 353–68.

Sarris, A. H. (1994) 'Consequences of the proposed Common Agricultural Policy reform for the Southern part of the European Community', *European Economy*, no. 5, pp. 113–32.

Sbragia, A. M. (ed.) (1992) *Euro-Politics. Institutions and Policy-Making in the 'New' European Community*.

Skouras, T. (1995) *The Contribution of Community Structural Policies to the Economic and Social Cohesion of the Union – The Case of Greece*, Report for the Commission.

Spahn, P. B. (1993a) 'The design of federal fiscal constitutions in theory and practice', *European Economy*, no. 5, pp. 63–100.

Spahn, P. B. (1993b) 'The consequences of economic and monetary union for fiscal federal relations in the Community and the financing of the Community budget', *European Economy*, no. 5, pp. 541–84.

Strijker, D. and de Veer, J. (1988) 'Agriculture', in Molle, W. and Cappelin, R., pp. 23–44.

TEPSA (1991) *Methods for Achieving Greater Economic and Social Cohesion in the EC*, study for the Commission EC.

Teutemann, M. (1993) 'Interpersonal vs. interregional redistribution at the European level – as seen from the perspectives of fiscal federalism and public choice theory', *European Economy*, no. 5, pp. 395–414.

Van Rompuy, P. *et al.* (1991) 'Economic federalism and the EMU', *European Economy*, special edition no. 1.

Wadley, D. (1986) *Restructuring the Regions*, OECD, Paris.

Walsh, C. (1993) 'Fiscal federalism: an overview of issues and a discussion of their relevance to the European Community', *European Economy*, no. 5, pp. 25–62.

Wildasin, D. E. (1990) 'Budgetary pressures in the EEC: a fiscal federalism perspective', *American Economic Review, Papers and Proceedings*, May, pp. 69–74.

Wistricht, E. (1989) *After 1992: The United States of Europe*, Routledge, London.

Wright, V. *et al.* (1993) *EC Cohesion Policy and National Systems – The Role of EC Structural Funds in the Territorial Restructuring within Member States*, Conference Nuffield College, Oxford.

10
Concluding Remarks

Heather D. Gibson

We began this book by stating that its aim was to examine the evolution of a group of countries with a number of shared characteristics in their particular niche and to chart their progress of economic transformation during a period characterized by the consolidation of democratic government. In the first part of the book, the focus was on the characteristics of these economies and the changes that have occurred. To this end, the chapters examined the changing structure of trade and industry, the role of tourism and the nature of labour markets and labour–capital relations. The focus then shifted in the second part towards the implementation and design of policies in specific areas, which both have helped and could help to facilitate economic change – industrial policy, financial policy and regional policy. In these concluding remarks, the aim is to bring together the findings of the research by focusing on a number of the themes, which have permeated the book as a whole.

A major aim of the book was to assess the extent to which economic transformation has occurred to such an extent that we can talk of the new Southern Europe. We have seen that the SEEs, on the eve of democratization, were characterized by a number of common features. Their agricultural sectors were large, fragmented and inefficient relative to other European countries. (Spain was perhaps an exception to this, at least in terms of the size of the sector.) Infrastructural development was also poor, both with respect to transport links and education and training. Industrial development was based on semi-skilled cheap labour and concentrated in low value-added activities. This led to a concentration of exports in traditional areas where the growth of demand was weak, where price competition was paramount and products not sufficiently differentiated. Non-price factors such as the level of innovation, the use of quality control methods and sophisticated marketing techniques and the provision of after-sales service were largely absent. In this, Greece, Portugal and Spain shared many of the characteristics of Italy in the immediate postwar period.

This largely 'backward' or underdeveloped structure of the economy was accompanied by an emphasis on the use of traditional, what might now be termed 'old-fashioned', economic policies. The major characteristic of these policies was that they fostered inward-looking, closed economies. Indeed, of the three countries, Spain, the most developed, was also the most closed. Thus, tariffs and quantitative import controls protected almost all sectors of the economy. The state frequently subsidized ailing sectors or companies, with the aim of promoting restructuring never being fulfilled. Competition, already limited by tariffs and subsidies, was not actively encouraged between domestic firms and monopolies or near monopolies often dominated key sectors. State intervention was also heavy in the labour market with regulations covering all aspects of firms' employment policies (hiring, layoffs, redundancies, overtime, etc). The financial sectors of Greece and Spain were dominated by state-owned banks. In Portugal banks were owned by the large industrial groups that dominated the economy and had close links with the government. Following democratization, they were taken into state hands. In all three countries, banks had little autonomy in the granting of credit – credit was directed to various sectors prioritized by the government (and including the government itself) and interest rates were tightly controlled. This all-pervasive state intervention severely limited economic development, producing as it did, economies that lacked an inherent dynamism and capacity for modernization and change.

To what extent have the contributions to this book shown that transformation of these economies has occurred? By and large, transformation and modernization of the economy can be said to have been accomplished at the level of economic policies. The extent to which the effect of these changes in policy has been felt in the rest of the economy and has resulted in improved economic performance is, perhaps, more contentious.

Focusing initially on economic policies, we can identify a number of changes that have occurred within a relative short period of time (broadly, since the mid-1980s). All three SEEs have opened up their economies to international influences via the removal of import controls and tariffs and controls on capital movements, including foreign direct investment and portfolio investment in, mainly, financial instruments (see the chapters by Katseli and Gibson, Stournaras and Tsakalotos). As a consequence, these economies are affected to a greater extent by conditions in the world economy, in general, and in Europe, in particular. There has also been a significant reduction in the degree of state intervention in industry through a decrease in the use of state subsidies and the privatization of large parts of the public sector. Indeed, privatization (or, at least, the sale of part of state companies) has even been extended to the public utilities in an attempt to introduce a more dynamic and customer-oriented service (Pagoulatos and Wright). Domestic financial liberalization has also proceeded apace, as the chapter by Gibson, Stournaras and Tsakalotos shows. Financial institutions are now free to manage their own portfolios, interest rates have become market-determined and the development of financial markets, including the stock market, is being actively encouraged. Finally, more recently, attention has focused on reform of labour markets with the implementation of the OECD jobs strategy involving substantial deregulation and reduce state interference.[1] At the same time, an increased emphasis is being placed on the importance of education and training in promoting industrial restructuring towards production which uses higher levels of skill and technology.

What have been the implications of this rapid and compressed transformation of economic policies? It is useful to discuss this issue in the context of two broad areas of the economy: macroeconomic performance and the performance of the real economy. We deal with each in turn.

The adoption by all three countries of an orthodox macroeconomic stabilization programme, towards the end of the 1980s in the case of Portugal and Spain and in the 1990s in the case of Greece, has culminated in impressive progress with reducing the macroeconomic imbalances which appeared following democratization. As Figures 10.1 to 10.6 show,[2] significant progress towards convergence of nominal economic indicators has been made, particularly by Portugal and Spain, but, more recently, even by Greece. That Portugal and Spain are now part of the Euro area, having satisfied the Maastricht criteria for joining European economic and monetary union (EMU) is indeed testimony to the progress made by these

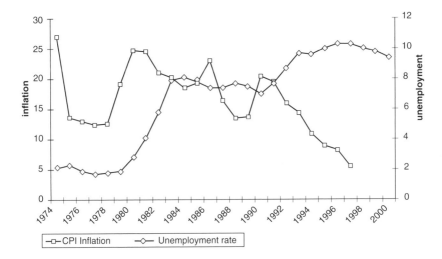

Figure 10.1 Inflation and unemployment in Greece
Source: OECD Economic Outlook, December 1998.

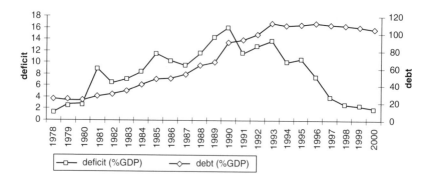

Figure 10.2 Government deficits and debt in Greece
Source: OECD Economic Outlook, December 1998.

Figure 10.3 Inflation and unemployment in Portugal
Source: OECD Economic Outlook, December 1998.

countries.[3] The Greek government aims to join from January 2001. Indeed, Portugal and Spain did better than Italy, whose integration into Europe occurred over a much longer period and who was a founding member of the European Monetary System (EMS).

The progress made with respect to *nominal* convergence of the SEEs on other EU countries in such a short period of time has thus been impressive. However, an examination of the progress made on *real* convergence suggests that a more sanguine conclusion about the extent of economic transformation in SEEs is in order. Overall, the performance and structure of the real economy is less supportive of the idea of a new Southern Europe. The chapters of this book have shown that, while transformation has occurred,

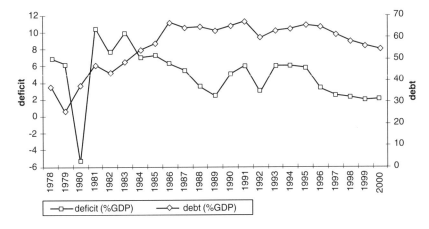

Figure 10.4 Government deficits and debt in Portugal
Source: OECD Economic Outlook, December 1998.

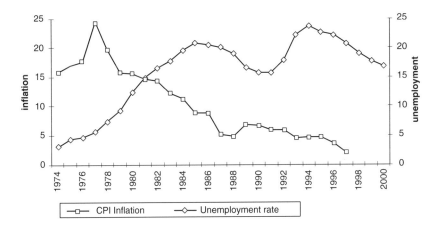

Figure 10.5 Inflation and unemployment in Spain
Source: OECD Economic Outlook, December 1998.

it has often been painful and slow. The most obvious outward manifestation of this conclusion is the fact that income per capita in Spain is around 75 per cent of the EU average and that in Greece and Portugal it is even lower at around 60 per cent. Moreover, these values have not altered much since the transition to democracy in the mid-1970s.[4] As Katseli shows, the pattern of specialization has not altered much since the opening of these economies with the consequence that the majority of exports are still in areas of weakly growing demand. At the same time, of course, the removal

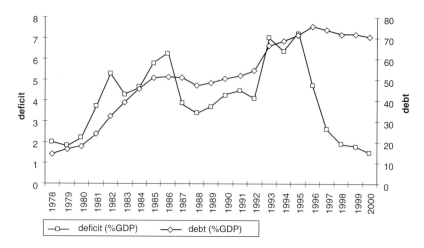

Figure 10.6   Government deficits and debt in Spain
Source: OECD Economic Outlook, December 1998.

of tariffs and other import controls has led to large increases in imports of consumer goods while a dependence on foreign capital goods continues. This poorer performance of the real economy is manifested in the figures for unemployment (Figures 10.1, 10.3 and 10.5), which show that the costs of macroeconomic stabilization in terms of increased unemployment, especially in Spain, have not been small.

To what can we attribute these experiences? It might well be argued that the modernization of these economies and the transformation of economic policies has laid the ground for real economic gains, but it is yet too early to see their effect. Indeed, the return to macroeconomic stability is to be welcomed in this respect. At the same time, it has to be remembered that transformation has taken place in a largely unfavourable international economic environment, and the fact that the transition to democracy and its subsequent consolidation occurred at a time when the 'golden age' of the postwar economic performance was coming to an end and the world economy was rocked by the two oil price shocks. In this respect, Greece, Portugal and Spain were much less fortunate than Italy where the consolidation of democracy and the transformation of the economy had been underway for some time before the end of the 'golden age'. However, while all small open economies and not just those of Southern Europe have faced a similar international economic environment, they exhibit differing degrees of economic success. Hence it is necessary to delve deeper into individual country experiences to explain the performance of Greece, Portugal and Spain.

A first consideration has to be the role of the consolidation of democracy. It has been argued, however, that the link between democracy and economic performance is a tenuous one (Roccas and Padoa-Schioppa). Recent research certainly points to a role for economic growth and good economic performance in general in consolidating democratic regimes once they have been established (Przeworski *et al.*, 1996). However, the evidence on whether the political regime affects economic growth is much less conclusive. Indeed, in a review of the literature on this question, Przeworski and Limongi (1993, p. 65) argue that 'politics does matter, but regimes do not capture the relevant differences... It does not seem to be democracy or authoritarianism *per se* that makes the difference'. This conclusion has been a theme of this book and fits well with the Southern European experience.

So, in what way does politics matter? We can draw out a few lessons from the analysis of this book. Perhaps the most important role for politics stems from the increasing integration of these countries into the 'European project'. Democratization paved the way for their entry into the EU and, in spite of the major economic context of the 'European project', the political aspects of European integration have proved to be just as important in determining the speed and timing of reform in the EU. For example, the state of French–German relations has more often than not been a major determining factor behind the success of many of the initiatives. And for SEEs in particular, entry into the EU can be seen as having helped to support democratization and, as in the case of Greece, to provide greater security from external threats. Moreover, political factors have proved to be critical in the major economic decisions which have been made (The Single Economic Market, The Maastricht Treaty and the potential establishment of economic and monetary union to name but a few).

The implications of the SEEs' participation in the European project have been explored in some depth in this book. Once the critical policy decision had been taken to join the EU, certain economic consequences followed. It is these consequences which have largely mapped out the transformation of Greece, Portugal and Spain since democratization, since economic policy was to a great extent directed towards entry even before it took place. The increasing integration of these countries into Europe was outlined by Katseli in her chapter, where the implications for Greece, Portugal and Spain of changing trade and economic relations were considered. EU considerations have also been critical in determining the course of change in economic policies which we mentioned above. Many of the policies in the area of trade, industry, finance and with respect to the regions have been shown to stem directly from EU Directives and initiatives in these areas. Moreover, since many of the EU policies adopted reflected the changes in the policy environment that had already occurred in northern European countries, the SEEs, in adopting the new policies, have become more similar to their northern partners. This is most obvious in the area of macroeconomic policies and the increased attention given in northern European economies to budget deficits and inflation in the aftermath of the second oil shock. But it also extends to other areas – as Pagoulatos and Wright have shown, even the policy of privatization as a means of restructuring weak industries was borrowed from the UK and France, two of the pioneers and most enthusiastic of 'privatizers' in Europe. Thus a very clear conclusion that emerges is that European integration has played a paramount role in much of the transformation that has occurred.

Indeed, European integration can probably also account for the speed of change – and here a contrast with the Italian experience is instructive. The pace of change in Italy began with an opening of her economy following entry, as a founding country, into the Common Market in the late 1950s. This facilitated the real economic integration, at least of northern Italy, into Europe. Monetary and financial integration followed much later, from 1979 onwards with the formation of the EMS. Controls on capital movements were still actively used in the early to mid-1980s, being removed finally only in 1987. Macroeconomic adjustment proceeded throughout the 1980s into the 1990s and was accompanied from the mid-1980s by domestic financial liberalization. By contrast, in the case of Greece, Portugal and Spain, all these policy changes (the removal of import controls, financial liberalization, macroeconomic adjustment etc) were compressed into a very short period from the mid-1980s onwards.[5]

Focusing more on events at the level of individual countries themselves, we can point to a role for politics in influencing economic outcomes in the clear interaction between the aspirations of parties in the position of newly elected governments and the economic policies followed. Both Portugal (in the immediate post-dictatorship period) and Greece (following the elections of the socialists in 1981) flirted with inward-looking economic policies and autarkic solutions. Furthermore, all three economies faced pent-up demands from the large sections of the population which had been excluded during the dictatorship if not for longer. The balance between using the available funds to meet these demands immediately and directing them towards restructuring and modernization was tricky and, as Roccas and Padoa-Schioppa argue, not always successfully negotiated. However, given the divisions in society which were the legacy of civil war or dictatorship, this lack of success is probably not surprising. But that aside, many of the more recent policies enacted by these countries can be seen as attempts to undo what are now perceived to be the 'excesses' of the post-dictatorship period. The analysis of the privatization process particularly in Portugal, but also in Greece and Spain, can be seen in this light.

The contributions in this book all make clear the idea that economic performance depends on the institutional environment in which economic agents operate, not just the political institutions, but also the social, commercial, industrial and financial. These institutions work alongside markets and support the latter by providing information and reducing uncertainty. Economic change is often a painful process. The ability of economies to respond to changing economic conditions around them, in ways that minimize the costs and maximize the benefits in terms of economic performance, depends as much on the quality of their institutions as it does on markets.

We have seen that the new economic policies of SEEs place much greater attention on reforming markets. However, a number of chapters indicate that consideration should also be given to reform of institutions and that improved real economic performance and the restoration of convergence may only be achieved through radical change to these institutions, while, in some cases, this requires their creation. This seems even more true if we consider that path dependence can as easily lock a country into a vicious circle as it can into a virtuous one.

Thus, to be more concrete, with respect to policy towards trade and industry, the removal of controls on imports and the opening of these economies to international competition (the introduction or extension of the role of the market) may not be sufficient to promote transformation. Nor may the changes of ownership implied by privatization release further forces for change if other problems are not dealt with. For example, Katseli pointed in her chapter to weaknesses in the existing private sector. Management skills are often poor and companies lack the support networks, be it in the areas of finance, marketing or research and development. The success of the northern Italian model (discussed by Mingione) also highlights the importance of informal networks and relationships between companies and their suppliers as well as the purchasers of their products.

Similarly, policies towards the financial sector cannot rely solely on liberalization and the fostering of markets. Market failures and particularly the absence or imperfect nature of information which pervades financial markets limit their capacity to service the real economy. Gibson, Stournaras and Tsakalotos pointed to other areas where reform of financial institutions could lead to closer and more productive links between the financial system and companies.

Finally, in labour markets, it is not enough to rely simply on a removal of rigidities and government regulations. Market-oriented labour markets can lead to increased uncertainty and hamper the ability of economic agents to take the risks necessary to provide dynamism in the economic system.[6] Moreover, labour market institutions are necessary which are better able to mediate disagreements between workers and employers if the consequence of economic change is not simply to be growing industrial unrest and unemployment.[7]

In this manner, a number of the contributions to this book have shed doubts on the likelihood that the changes to the economic environment in

SEEs have gone far enough to put them on a path that restores real convergence. Indeed, the termination of the rather promising performance of Portugal and Spain at the end of the 1980s further strengthens this point – it now appears that their superior performance was largely a consequence of the favorable international environment rather than evidence of a new beginning and a fundamental transformation of economic structures. Only Pagoulatos and Wright are optimistic that fundamental change will result from the privatization process now underway.

This emphasis on institutions is important if another lesson of this book is to be learnt, namely that we cannot assume that all countries will or indeed can successfully follow the same model of development. Throughout the book, comparisons and contrasts have been made with other countries, especially in Europe. The conclusion that can be drawn is that of Mingione who argues that one cannot talk of *one* model of development applicable across all time and space – in particular, we cannot assume that the successful model of Northern Italy can be glued on as it were to existing structures either in the south of Italy or in the other three countries. But if this is true, then neither can we simply assume that the institutions and policies that are necessary or suited to Northern European countries are those which are appropriate for Southern Europe. Rather, SEEs have to foster the development of institutions that can be tailored to their specific needs.

So what can we say in conclusion about the emergence of a new Southern Europe from an economic perspective? We have seen that Greece, Portugal and Spain have undergone a rapid transformation of their economies in the period since democratization. This change has been very much at the level of economic policies and we have seen how these countries have adopted, within a very short space of time, the policy framework of other EU countries. This transformation has proved successful especially in the area of macroeconomic performance and is manifested in the extent to which nominal convergence with their European partners has occurred. The success of these policies in transforming the real economy and restoring real convergence has been more limited. Industrial structures still remain weak, characterized (especially in Portugal and Greece) by fairly isolated small-scale enterprises which in many cases are ill-equipped to compete in today's global markets. The tourist industry, for example, an important source of foreign exchange earnings in the past, is entering a critical phase and, as Williams argues, its future success may well depend on the ability to move up-market and into areas where the growth of demand is higher than in the mass tourism market for which these countries cater at present. Regional inequalities abound, not helped by the structural decline in agriculture which has contributed to rural unemployment especially in Spain and Greece. Thus, the shocks brought about partly as a result of European integration had the consequence that SEEs have experienced, and are likely to continue to experience, a difficult period of transition.

The question which remains relates to the likely prospects for these countries. We have seen that, even if problems remain, significant changes have taken place and modernization has already occurred and continues to do so. Help is available from the EU, both in terms of funds and initiatives in both industrial and regional policy. As Mitsos shows, much of EU funding finds its way into infrastructural projects and a significant amount into human resource projects (including training and a variety of programmes to deal with the long-term unemployed). Both can significantly improve the environment in SEEs and can help to create conditions that could promote further transformation.[8] But, of course, many of these are only necessary conditions for change, not sufficient. Infrastructural projects in and of themselves, while useful in the short run as means of creating jobs, do not provide a long-term solution. Similarly training programmes will only be useful in the long run if there are jobs for the retrained workers in their new skill area. Furthermore, it cannot be assumed that the Northern European members of the EU will continue to support the weaker SEEs through large transfers. If EU enlargement, for instance, takes place and encompasses many of the Eastern European countries, then the strain on EU resources may significantly reduce the amounts available to SEEs. As we have seen, the authors in this volume differ in the extent to which they are optimistic about the future prospects for SEEs, something which is not surprising given the speculative nature of the question.

It should not be forgotten that the future for these economies involves further potential large shocks, the most immediate of which is the new framework of EMU for Portugal and Spain and the likely membership of Greece in 2001. As we have seen, EMU has already been making its presence felt for a number of years through the macroeconomic criteria that are a prerequisite for joining and macroeconomic adjustment in SEEs in the 1990s has taken the form of inflation convergence, interest rate adjustment, a reduction of budget deficits and public debt/GDP ratios and exchange rate stability. But such impressive convergence, especially with respect to public finances, has granted governments only limited room for manoeuvre in terms of the provision of public finance to support economic change.

With the creation of the Euro area from 1 January 1999, a number of new questions are being raised for SEEs. There is much support for monetary union in SEEs and even those who are less enthusiastic see little alternative for these peripheral countries. However, monetary union involves certain costs, not least the giving up of the exchange rate as a means of reacting to shocks which hit member countries asymmetrically. The ability to adapt through other means and to restructure in response to shocks in the least-cost way, will be crucial to determining their success in the monetary union. This makes it all the more important that the process of economic change is continued and that the resources made available to facilitate that change are used wisely to strengthen the institutional framework so as to ensure that the infrastructure is in place to meet the challenges which lie ahead.

Notes

1. See the OECD *Country Studies* for Greece, Portugal and Spain in 1996 for a review of the recommendations made by the OECD and for an account of the progress made to date in their implementation.
2. The figures for 1998 are estimates; where figures exist for 1999 and 2000, there are forecasts.
3. The Maastricht Treaty, signed in December 1991 by EU member countries, laid out the timetable for the move to EMU and the adoption of a single currency. The set of criteria which countries have to meet to be eligible for joining the single currency include both macroeconomic factors (i to v) and institutional factors (vi): (i) inflation must not exceed the average of inflation in the 3 lowest inflation countries by more than 1.5 per cent; (ii) the exchange rate must have been fixed within its ERM narrow bands without a realignment for at least 2 years; (iii) the interest rate on long-term government bonds must not exceed by 2 per cent average interest rates in the 3 countries with the lowest inflation rates; (iv) the government deficit must not be more than 3 per cent of GDP; (v) the government debt to GDP ratio must not exceed 60 per cent; and (vi) the statutes of the central bank must be compatible with those of the proposed ECB. This essentially implies that the central banks must be independent of their respective governments.
4. It is worth recalling that this picture is unchanged if we use the US as a benchmark.
5. Greece, of course, joined the EC in 1981, five years before Portugal and Spain. However, its rather ambivalent attitude to European integration in the early 1980s meant that transformation got underway around the same time as in Portugal and Spain, if not a little later (in the case of financial liberalization and macroeconomic stabilization, for example).
6. This is a point emphasized in the recent (1996) OECD *Country Study* for the UK, where labour market reforms in the 1980s involved the removal of a variety of rigidities and government regulations making it one of the most 'flexible' in Europe.
7. See Henley and Tsakalotos (1993).
8. A caveat was noted by Lyberaki in respect to the distribution of EU funds. She argues that the condition of public administrations in SEEs, the bodies responsible for distributing the funds, is worrying since funds sometimes do not reach their intended targets.

Bibliography

Henley, A. and Tsakalotos, E. (1993) *Corporatism and Economic Performance*, Edward Elgar, Aldershot.
Przeworski, A., Alvarez. M., Cheibub, J. A. and Limongi, F. (1996) 'What makes democracies endure?', *Journal of Democracy*, vol. 7, no. 1, January, pp. 39–55.
Przeworski, A. and Limongi, F. (1993) 'Political regimes and economic growth', *Journal of Economic Perspectives*, vol. 7, no. 3, Summer, pp. 51–69.

Index